自动控制专业英语

（修订版）

主　编　李东林
副主编　王　清　杨旭东

哈爾濱工業大學出版社

内 容 提 要

本书以培养学生的专业英语阅读能力为主要目标,内容共分为三部分:第一部分为古典控制理论;第二部分为现代控制理论;第三部分为科技文献阅读。读者通过对前两部分的学习,不但可以熟悉自动控制常用专业词汇,而且也可对现代控制理论较为活跃的理论分支有一定了解;后一部分旨在为读者最终阅读专业文献铺设最后的桥梁。

本书可作为高等院校自动控制专业学生的英语阅读教材,也可作为自动控制类专业技术人员的学习、参考用书。

图书在版编目(CIP)数据

自动控制专业英语/李东林主编. —2 版(修订本).
哈尔滨:哈尔滨工业大学出版社,2003.6(2024.1 重印)
ISBN 7-5603-1371-9

Ⅰ.自… Ⅱ.李… Ⅲ.自动控制-英语-阅读教学-高等学校-教材　Ⅳ.H319.4

中国版本图书馆 CIP 数据核字(2003)第 024686 号

责任编辑	王桂芝　黄菊英
封面设计	卞秉利
出版发行	哈尔滨工业大学出版社
社　　址	哈尔滨市南岗区复华四道街 10 号　150006
传　　真	0451-86414749
网　　址	http://hitpress.hit.edu.cn
印　　制	哈尔滨圣铂印刷有限公司
开　　本	880 mm×1 230 mm　1/32　印张 10.125　字数 280 千字
版　　次	2003 年 6 月第 2 版　2024 年 1 月第 10 次印刷
书　　号	ISBN 978-7-5603-1371-9
定　　价	32.00 元

(如因印装质量问题影响阅读,我社负责调换)

修订版前言

《自动控制专业英语》自1999年1月出版以来,由于专业知识覆盖面广,所选文献代表性强,教学操作余地大,在教学中收到了良好的使用效果,受到了相关专业广大师生的认同。目前已重印3次,总印数达14 000册。与此同时,在教学中也发现第1版中的某些不足,为使本书有更好的使用效果和更强的生命力,哈尔滨工业大学出版社建议我们在征求广大读者意见的基础上,结合作者的教学实践和体会,修订再版。

本次修订主要做了以下工作:

(1) 为使本书图文并茂,对书中的插图进行了重新绘制,使其更有助于相关内容的理解。

(2) 为提高本书的使用效果,对每篇文献和词汇进行了核准,纠正了第1版中的错误。

(3) 为满足广大作者的要求,对书中文献进行了补充和完善,提高了本书的教学可操作性。

虽然作者进行了多方面的修改和完善,但由于时间仓促,仍难免有某些不妥之处,恳请读者继续多提宝贵意见,以使本书更加完善。

作　者

2003年3月

前　　言

我们处在一个前所未有的信息时代，信息的互通与传递正深刻地改变着世界的面貌，而语言的互通作为信息交流的必要手段已为越来越多的人们所共识。为了更快、更准确地了解本专业的国际发展动向，借鉴外国的先进科技思想，专业外语的阅读能力已经成为每个高等院校学生所必备的素质之一。对于这方面的能力，国家教育部门高度重视，国家教育部颁布的《大学英语教学大纲》把专业英语阅读列为必修课而纳入英语教学计划，强调通过四年不断线的英语教学使学生能顺利阅读英文专业文献。为了满足高等院校自动控制专业英语教学的需要，我们编写了这本《自动控制专业英语阅读》。

专业英语阅读的困难来自两个方面：专业及语言。因此本书的内容除了自动控制专业人员必备的古典控制理论外，现代控制理论部分几乎涵盖了所有近期较为活跃的控制理论分支。这样，通过对本书的学习，学生一方面能了解专业动向，同时也就熟悉了这些内容所常用的专业用语及用法。为了使广大读者学到地道、正确的专业英语，本书素材均选自国外原版材料，同时为了节省版面，对部分图表作了必要删节。另外为了便于教学，编者对书中的生词和难句，均做了注释与翻译。

本书在编写过程中得到了哈尔滨工业大学自动控制专业许多老师和同学无私的帮助，作者在此表示衷心的感谢，同时对本书参考文献的作者表示感谢。

作为本书的编者，我们衷心地希望我们的努力能赢得读者的显著进步。受编者理论修养与实践经验所限，书中难免有疏漏之处，敬请读者斧正。

编　者

1998 年 12 月

CONTENTS

PART 1 **CHAPTER ONE**

1 Introduction and Linearized Dynamic Models

1.1 Introduction

In the first part of this chapter, after a general introduction, the concepts of open-loop and closed-loop control are discussed in the context of a water level control system. This example is then used to introduce fundamental considerations in control system analysis and design.

In the second part of the chapter, Laplace transforms are discussed and used to define the transfer function of a system. This is a linearized model of the dynamic behavior of the system that will serve as the basis for system analysis and design in most of this book. Block diagram reduction is used to obtain the transfer function of a system consisting of interconnected subsystems. This completes the framework necessary for Chapter 2, in which transfer functions are derived for a variety of physical (sub) systems.[注1]

1.2 Examples and Classifications of Control Systems

Control systems exist in a virtually infinite variety, both in type of application and level of sophistication.[注2] The heating system and the water heater in a house are systems in which only the sign of the difference between desired and actual temperatures is used for control. If the temperature drops below a set value, a constant heat source is switched on, to be switched off again when the temperature rises above a set maximum. Variations of such relay or on-off control systems, sometimes quite sophisticated, are very common in practice because of their relatively low cost.

In the nature of such control systems, the controlled variable will oscillate continuously between maximum and minimum limits. For many applications this control is not sufficiently smooth or accurate. In the power steering of a car, the controlled variable or system output is the angle of the front wheels. It must follow the system input, the angle of the steering wheel, as closely as possible but at a much higher power level. [注3]

In the process industries, including refineries and chemical plants, there are many temperatures and levels to be held to usually constant values in the presence of various disturbances. Of an electrical power generation plant, controlled values of voltage and frequency are outputs, but inside such a plant there are again many temperatures, levels, pressures, and other variables to be controlled.

In aerospace, the control of aircraft, missiles, and satellites is an area of often very advanced systems.

⋮

One classification of control systems is the following:

(1) Process control or regulator systems: The controlled variable, or output, must be held as close as possible to a usually constant desired value, or input, despite any disturbances. [注4]

(2) Servomechanisms: The input varies and the output must be made to follow it as closely as possible.

Power steering is one example of the second class, equivalent to systems for positioning control surfaces on aircraft. Automated manufacturing machinery, such as numerically controlled machine tools, uses servos extensively for the control of positions or speeds.

This last example brings to mind the distinction between continuous and discrete systems. The latter are inherent in the use of digital computers for control.

The classification into linear and nonlinear control systems should also be mentioned at this point. Analysis and design are in general much simpler for the former, to which most of this book is devoted. Yet most systems become nonlinear if the variables move over wide enough ranges. The importance in practice of linear techniques relies on linearization based on the assumption that the variables stay close enough to a given operating point.

1.3 Open-Loop Control and Closed-Loop Control

To introduce the subject, it is useful to consider an example. In this example, let it be desired to maintain the actual water level c in the tank as close as possible to a desired level r. The desired level will be called the system input, and the actual level the controlled variable or system output. Water flows from the tank via a valve V_o and enters the tank from a supply via a control valve V_c. The control valve is adjustable, either manually or by some type of actuator. This may be an electric motor or a hydraulic pneumatic cylinder. Very often it would be a pneumatic diaphragm actuator, in general, increasing the pneumatic pressure above the diaphragm pushes it down against a spring and increases valve opening.

Open-Loop Control

In this form of control, the valve is adjusted to make output c equal to input r, but not readjusted continually to keep the two equal. Open-loop control, with certain safeguards added, is very common. For example, in the context of sequence control, that is, guiding a process through a sequence of predetermined steps. However, for systems such as the one at hand, this form of control will normally not yield high performance. A difference between input and output, a system error $e=r-c$ would be expected to develop, due to two major effects:

1. Disturbances acting on the system
2. Parameter variations of the system

These are prime motivations for the use of feedback control. For the example, pressure variations upstream of V_c and downstream of V_o can be important disturbances affecting inflow and outflow, and hence level. In a steel rolling mill, very large disturbance torques on the drive motors of the rolls when steel slabs enter or leave affect speeds. [注5]

For the water level example, a sudden or gradual change of flow resistance of the valves due to foreign matter or valve deposits represents a system parameter variation. [注6] In a broader context, not only are the values of the parameters of a process often not precisely known, but they may also change greatly with operating condition.

In an electrical power plant, parameter value are different at 20% and 100% of full power. In a valve, the relation between pressure drop and flow rate is often nonlinear, and as a result the resistance parameter of the valve changes with flow rate. Even if all parameter variations were known precisely, it would be complex, say in the case of the level example, to schedule the valve opening to follow time-varying desired levels.

Closed-Loop Control or Feedback Control

To improve performance, the operator could continuously readjust the valve based on observation of the system error e. A feedback control system in effect automates this action, as follows:

The output c is measured continuously and fed back to be compared with the input r. The error $e=r-c$ is used to adjust the control valve by means of an actuator.

The feedback loop causes the system to take corrective action if output c (actual level) deviates from input r (desired level), whatever the reason.

A broad class of systems can be represented by the block diagram shown in Fig. 1.1. The sensor in Fig. 1.1 measures the output c and, depending on type, represents it by an electrical, pneumatic, or mechanical signal. The input r is represented by a signal in the same form. The summing junction or error junction is a device that combines the inputs to it according to the signs associated with the arrows: $e=r-c$.

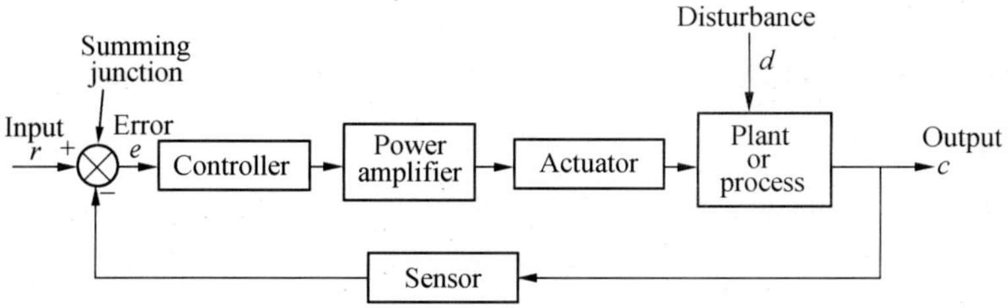

Fig. 1.1 System block diagram.

It is important to recognize that if the control system is any good, the error e will usually be small, ideally zero. Therefore, it is quite inadequate to operate an actuator. A task of the controller is to amplify the error signal. The controller output, however, will still be at a low power level. That is, voltage or pressure have been raised but current or airflow are still small. The power amplifier raises power to the levels needed for the actuator.

The plant or process has been taken to include the valve characteristics as well as the tank. In part this is selated to the identification of a disturbance d in Fig. 1. 1 as an additional input to the block diagram. For the level control, d could represent supply pressure variations upstream of the control valve.

1.4 Control System Analysis and Design

Control system analysis and design can be summarized in terms of the following two questions:

(1) Analysis: What is the performance of a given system in response to changes of inputs or disturbances?

(2) Design: If the performance is unsatisfactory, how can it be improved without changing the process, actuator, and power amplifier blocks?

It is particularly important to note the constraints imposed on the designer. The blocks indicated generally represent relatively, or very , expensive equipment, and must be considered as a fixed part of the system.[注7] The power of design techniques that will permit large changes in performance to be achieved by changing only the controller should be appreciated.[注8]

⋮

The term performance is used to summarize several aspects of the behavior. Assume that in Fig. 1. 1 a sudden change of input is applied, to a new constant value. A certain period of time will be required for transient response terms to decay and for the output to level off at the new value. One key feature of this transient period is that it should be sufficiently short. Another is that the transient response should not be excessively oscillatory or severely overshoot the final level.

The steady-state response, after the transients have decayed, is an equally important aspect of the performance. Any steady-state errors between r and c must be satisfactorily small. To a disturbance input, the output should ideally not respond at all, and in any case the steady-state value of this output should be acceptably small.

The performance of a design is also measured by its success in reducing the dynamic and steady-state effects of parameter variations in the plant on the output.

Disturbances and parameter variations were given as motivations for feedback control. However, the transient response and steady-state error characteristics can also be improved by the use of feedback, and the motivations for feedback can be listed as follows: [注9]

(1) Reducing the effects of parameter variations.

(2) Reducing the effects of disturbance inputs.

(3) Improving transient response characteristics.

(4) Reducing steady-state errors.

In fact, improvements in the first two items are usually achieved in the course of design procedures aimed at the last two.

An intuitive idea concerning these can be obtained by assuming the controller in Fig. 1.1 to be an amplifier with gain K; that is, the output of this block is K times its input. Larger K means greater amplification of the error signal e. Therefore, the errors for given output values are smaller. Hence large gains are desirable to reduce errors, that is, to improve accuracy. Also, larger gain means a larger change of valve opening for a certain change of error. This suggests a faster change of the output, and greater speed of response of the system.

On the other hand, these faster changes of output intuitively suggest increasing danger of severe overshoot and oscillations of the output following a sudden change of the input. We can show the large effect on the response to a step change of r which can easily result if the gain is increased from a rather low to a rather high value. In fact, with a further increase of gain the oscillations may grow instead of decay. The system is then unstable.

Stability is always the primary concern in feedback control design. But to be useful a system must also possess adequate relative stability; that is, the overshoot of a step response must be acceptably small, and this response must not be unduly oscillatory during the transient period.

Relative stability considerations usually impose an upper limit on gain, and hence on accuracy and speed of response. [注10] Much of control system design can be summarized as being concerned with achieving a satisfactory compromise between these features. If this is not possible with only a gain K, controller complexity is increased.

The remainder of this chapter provides a basis for the tools needed to move beyond this intuitive discussion and to answer the questions it raises. [注11]

1.5 Linearized Dynamic Models

The concept of a transfer function will be developed to describe individual blocks and their interconnections in a block diagram. This is a linear model and requires a linearized description of system dynamic behavior.

A nonlinear relation $y=f(x)$ between the input x and the output y

of a block in a block diagram could represent the force-deflection relation of a rubber spring, or the flow versus valve opening characteristic of a control valve. If the variations of x about x_0 are small enough, the non-linear curve can be approximated by its tangent at (x_0, y_0). The model is then said to be linearized about the steady-state operating point (x_0, y_0). If $\Delta x = x - x_0$, $\Delta y = y - y_0$, the linearized model of $f(x)$ about x_0 is

$$\Delta y = \left(\frac{\mathrm{d}f}{\mathrm{d}x}\right)_{x_0} \Delta x \tag{1.1}$$

where $(\mathrm{d}f/\mathrm{d}x)_{x_0}$, is the slope of the tangent at (x_0, y_0).

It may also be that the output y of a block is a nonlinear function of two or more inputs. For example, valve flow is a function of valve opening and the pressure drop across the valve. If $y = f(x, z)$, the linearized model for small variations Δx and Δz about an operating point (x_0, z_0) is

$$\Delta y = \left(\frac{\partial f}{\partial x}\right)_{x_0, z_0} \Delta x + \left(\frac{\partial f}{\partial x}\right)_{x_0, z_0} \Delta z \tag{1.2}$$

where $(\partial f/\partial x)_{x_0, z_0}$ and $(\partial f/\partial z)_{x_0, z_0}$ are partial derivatives. Note that the variables in these linearized models are not the actual values of the variables, but the deviations from those at the steady-state operating point.

It is a common practice in these linearized models to redefine the variables to represent the variations. Thus the models (1.1) and (1.2) will often be written as

$$y = Kx \qquad y = K_1 x + K_2 z \tag{1.3}$$

For a broad class of systems the dynamic behavior of the variations about operating-point values can be approximated by an nth-order linear differential equation

$$\frac{\mathrm{d}^n c}{\mathrm{d}t^n} + a_{n-1}\frac{\mathrm{d}^{n-1} c}{\mathrm{d}t^{n-1}} + \cdots + a_1 \frac{\mathrm{d}c}{\mathrm{d}t} + a_0 c = b_m \frac{\mathrm{d}^m r}{\mathrm{d}t^m} + \cdots + b_1 \frac{\mathrm{d}r}{\mathrm{d}t} + b_0 r \tag{1.4}$$

where the variations $c(t)$ and $r(t)$ of output and input are functions of time t, and a_i and b_i are real constants.

Frequently, it is sufficient to determine the dynamic behavior of the output variations $c(t)$. If the actual variables are required , the steady-state solutions at the operating point must be added, corresponding to x_0 and y_0. These can be found from the actual nonlinear equations by setting derivatives with respect to time to zero.

Example 1.5.1 Spring-Mass-Damper System

The linear case of the classical system is considered in Example 2.2.1. The differential equation(2.2) that describes the position $x(t)$ of the mass m in response to an external force $f(t)$ is

$$m\ddot{x}+c\dot{x}+kx=f$$

As discussed in Section 2.2, $-kx$ is the spring force on m, with spring constant k, and $-c\dot{x}$ the damping force, with damping coefficient c. In the linear case k and c are constant, and weight mg does not occur in the equation if $x=0$ is chosen at the position of static equilibrium, where the weight is counterbalanced by a spring force.

But often spring force does not change proportionally with x, and a nonlinear differential equation model is necessary, for example

$$m\ddot{x}+c\dot{x}+kx^3=f+mg$$

Weight mg is added to the downward force $f(t)$ and $x=0$ at the position of zero spring force.

At a steady-state operating point where $f=f_0=$constant, the solution $x=x_0=$constant, so that $kx_0^3=f_0+mg$, or $x_0=[(f_0+mg)/k]^{1/3}$. To linearize the equation for small variations $\Delta x=x-x_0$, $\Delta f=f-f_0$ about the operating point, the nonlinear term $f(x)=kx^3$ is linearized according to (1.1) as

$$kx_0^3+(\frac{df}{dx})_{x_0}\Delta x=kx_0^3+3kx_0^2\Delta x$$

Then, since $(\Delta\dot{x})=\dot{x}$, $(\Delta\ddot{x})=\ddot{x}$, the linear model is

$$m(\Delta\ddot{x})+c(\Delta\dot{x})+3kx_0^2(\Delta x)+kx_0^3=f_0+\Delta f+mg$$

Since $kx_0^3=f_0+mg$, redefining x and f to represent the variations about x_0 and f_0 gives

$$m\ddot{x}+c\dot{x}+(3kx_0^2)x=f$$

If, say to determine physical clearances, the actual positions are needed, x_0 must be added to the solution of this linear differential equation.

For linear system, the equations for actual variables and deviations are the same. For example, if $\ddot{x}+c\dot{x}+dx=y$, then substituting $x=x_0+\Delta x$, $y=y_0+\Delta y$, where x_0 and y_0 are constant, yields

$$\Delta\ddot{x}+c\Delta\dot{x}+d\Delta x+dx_0=\Delta y+y_0$$

But $dx_0=y_0$ is the steady-state solution, so the equation in terms of Δx is the same as that for x.

In Chapter 12 the state space model will be introduced. It is a description of dynamic systems in terms of a set of first-order differential equations, written compactly in matrix form. This form of model is very powerful for the study of even very large systems. But in classical control theory, systems are commonly described by means of transfer functions. These will be defined by the use of Laplace transform.

1.6 Laplace Transforms

Laplace transform theory is quite extensive, and it is therefore fortunate that only a small and isolated part of it is needed. The Laplace transform $F(s)$ of a function $f(t)$ is defined by

$$F(s) = L[f(t)] = \int_0^{\infty} f(t)e^{-st}dt \tag{1.5}$$

For the present it suffices to consider the Laplace variable s simply as a complex variable with real part σ and imaginary part ω

$$s = \sigma + j\omega \tag{1.6}$$

From (1.5), the transform changes a function of time into a function of this new variable s. The advantage will be found to be that differentiation and integration are changed into algebraic operations.

Important examples and theorems are discussed below. The solutions of the integrals, which need not be evaluated in the use that will be made of all these results, may be verified, if desired, from tables of integrals.

(1) Unit step function $u(t)$: This is a common test input to evaluate the performance of control systems. Its Laplace transform, from substitution of $f(t)=1$ into (1.5), is

$$L[u(t)] = \int_0^{\infty} (1)e^{-st}dt = \frac{1}{s} \tag{1.7}$$

For a step of magnitude A, $Au(t)$, the transform is A/s.

(2) Ramp function At: This is also a common test input, with $f(t) = At$, integration by parts in equation (1.5) yields

$$L[At] = \int_0^{\infty} Ate^{-st}dt = \frac{A}{s^2} \tag{1.8}$$

(3) Decaying exponential Ae^{-at}: In many physical systems, the transient response that follows a change of input or a disturbance decays according to this characteristic.

$$L[Ae^{-at}] = \int_0^{\infty} (Ae^{-at})e^{-st}dt = \frac{A}{s+\alpha} \tag{1.9}$$

(4) Derivatives $d^n f(t)/dt^n$ if $F(s)=L[f(t)]$

$$L\left[\frac{df(t)}{dt}\right] = \int_0^\infty \left[\frac{df(t)}{dt}\right] e^{-st} dt = e^{-st} f(t)\Big|_0^\infty + s\int_0^\infty f(t) e^{-st} dt = sF(s) - f(0)$$

(1.10)

Repeating this procedure yields for the second derivative

$$L\left[\frac{d^2 f(t)}{dt^2}\right] = s^2 F(s) - sf(0) - \frac{df(0)}{dt} \quad (1.11)$$

In general, for the n-th derivative, if the initial conditions of $f(t)$ and its derivatives are zero

$$L\left[\frac{d^n f(t)}{dt^n}\right] = s^n F(s) \quad (1.12)$$

From this it is useful to remember that taking a derivative of a function is equivalent to multiplying its transform by s.

(5) Integrals of $f(t)$ if $F(s) = L[f(t)]$: By using integration by parts in the definition (1.5), it can be shown that

$$L\left[\int_{-\infty}^{t} f(\zeta) d\zeta\right] = \frac{1}{s} F(s) + \frac{1}{s}\left[\int_{-\infty}^{t} f(\zeta) d\zeta\right]_{t=0} \quad (1.13)$$

where $\left[\int_{-\infty}^{t} f(d\xi)\right]_{t=0}$ is the initial value of the integral. For zero initial conditions

$$L[n\text{th integral of } f(t)] = \frac{F(s)}{S^n} \quad (1.14)$$

(6) The product $e^{-at} f(t)$ *if* $F(s) = L[f(t)]$

$$L[e^{-at} f(t)] = \int_0^\infty e^{-at} f(t) e^{-st} dt = \int_0^\infty f(t) e^{-(s+a)t} dt = F(s+a)$$

(1.15)

since the last integral is the definition of the transform, with s replaced by $(s+a)$. This result will be used in the following context: If $F(s+a) = 1/(s+a)^2$, then $F(s) = 1/s^2$, which from (1.8) is known to be the transform of t. Hence

$$L[te^{-at}]=\frac{1}{(s+a)^2} \tag{1.16}$$

(7) The translated function $f(t-t_d)$ if $F(s)=L[f(t)]$: $f(t-t_d)$ equals $f(t)$ translated by t_d along the t-axis, and is zero for $t<t_d$.

$$L[f(t-t_d)] = \int_0^{\infty} f(t-t_d)\mathrm{e}^{-st}\mathrm{d}t = \int_{t_d}^{\infty} f(t-t_d)\mathrm{e}^{-st}\mathrm{d}t =$$

$$\mathrm{e}^{-st_d}\int_{t_d}^{\infty} f(\tau)\mathrm{e}^{-st}\mathrm{d}t = \mathrm{e}^{-st_d}\int_0^{\infty} f(\tau)\mathrm{e}^{-st}\mathrm{d}\tau = \mathrm{e}^{-st_d}F(s)$$

where $\tau=t-t_d$.

Thus translation over t_d is equivalent to multiplying the transform by e^{-st_d}.

(8) The linearity theorem: If $F_1(s) = L[f_1(t)]$, $F_2(s) = L[f_2(t)]$, and c_1 and c_2 are independent of t and s, then

$$L[c_1f_1(t)+c_2f_2(t)]=c_1F_1(s)+c_2F_2(s) \tag{1.18}$$

(9) The final value theorem

$$\lim_{t\to\infty} f(t)=\lim_{s\to 0} sF(s) \tag{1.19}$$

This allows the final or steady-state value of $f(t)$, that is, its value as $t\to\infty$, to be found from $F(s)$. The theorem is valid only if the limit exists.

Table 1.6.1 is a table of Laplace transform pairs which includes the preceding examples. The additional entries will be considered later. The transform of a unit impulse can be obtained by a limit process in which the width of a rectangular pulse of unit area is allowed to approach zero. The left column shows the inverse Laplace transforms of the expressions on the right. The entries in the table will be used to determine the inverse transforms of more complex expressions by expanding these expressions in terms of their partial fractions.

However, it is desirable to define the concept of a transfer function first, to show how such transforms arise in the study of control systems.

Table 1.6.1 Laplace Transform Pairs

$f(t)$	$F(s)$
$u(t)$	$1/s$
At	A/s^2
Ae^{-at}	$A/(s+\alpha)$
$\vdots$	$\vdots$

1.7 Transfer Functions and System Response

Fig. 1.2(a) shows a block representing a system with input r and output c, which could also be subsystem in a block diagram. The general linearized differential equation (1.4) will be taken to relate r and c. Based on the linearity theorem in Section 1.6, its Laplace transform can be written simply by transforming each term in turn. If the initial conditions are assumed to be zero, the result is, using (1.12) or Table 1.6.1

$$(s^n+a_{n-1}s^{n-1}+\cdots+a_1s+a_0)C(s)=(b_ms^m+\cdots+b_1s+b_0)R(s) \quad (1.20)$$

where
$$C(s)=L[c(t)] \qquad R(s)=L[r(t)] \quad (1.21)$$

Equation (1.20) gives immediately the common system representation of classical control theory.

Definition. The transfer function of a (sub) system is the ratio of the Laplace transforms of its output and input, assuming zero initial condition

$$G(s)=\frac{C(s)}{R(s)} \quad (1.22)$$

From (1.20), the transfer function is given by

$$G(s)=\frac{b_ms^m+b_{m-1}s^{m-1}+\cdots+b_1s+b_0}{s^n+a_{n-1}s^{n-1}+\cdots+a_1s+a_0} \quad (1.23)$$

The representation of Fig. 1.2 (a) is now replaced by that of

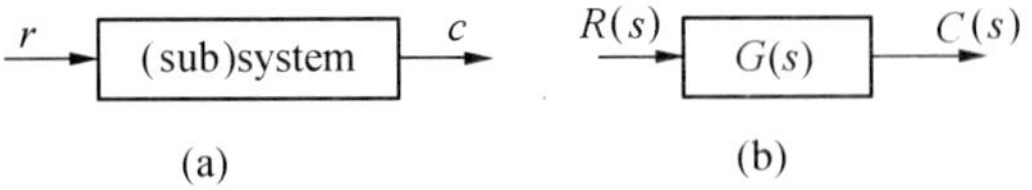

Fig. 1.2 Block in time (a) and Laplace (b) domain

Fig. 1.2(b), in terms of transforms and the transfer function. The following interpretation will often be applied

$$C(s)=G(s)R(s) \tag{1.24}$$

In words, the transform $C(s)$ of the output equals the transfer function $G(s)$ times the transform $R(s)$ of the input.

⋮

The assumption of zero initial conditions is very common in system analysis and design. It is natural for linearized equations, in which the variables are variations about operating point values. Furthermore, for linear systems the nature of the transient response is independent of the initial conditions: that is, whether or not the response is oscillatory, and if it is, whether the oscillations decay sufficiently fast. This is the type of information usually of most interest to the designer. At the same time, it is well to point out that the assumption of zero initial conditions in the definition of $G(s)$ is not a constraint. For linear systems the principle of superposition applies, which means that the total response is the sum of those to the input and to the initial conditions applied separately. Thus the initial conditions can be set to zero in determining the response to input $r(t)$, and $r(t)$ set to zero when calculating the response to initial conditions.

⋮

The above in effect provides the scenario for calculating the response $c(t)$ of a system to a given input $r(t)$ with specified initial conditions. For example, using the dot notation for derivatives, if

$$\ddot{c}+a_1\dot{c}+a_0c=r \quad c(0)=c_0 \quad \dot{c}(0)=\dot{c}_0 \tag{1.25}$$

then the transfer function is

$$G(s)=\frac{C_1(s)}{R(s)}=\frac{1}{s^2+a_1s+a_0} \tag{1.26}$$

and for a unit step input $r(t)$ $[R(s)=1/s]$ the transform of the output due to $r(t)$ is

$$C_1(s)=\frac{1}{s(s^2+a_1s+a_0)} \tag{1.27}$$

For the response to initial conditions, $r=0$ in (1.25) and this equation is transformed, using (1.10) and (1.11) or Table 1.6.1, to

$$[s^2C_2(s)-sc_0-\dot{c}_0]+a_1[sC_2(S)-c_0]+a_0C_2(s)=0$$

Rearranging yields the output transform

$$C_2(s)=\frac{(s+a_1)c_0+\dot{c}_0}{s^2+a_1s+a_0} \tag{1.28}$$

Hence the transform of the total output is

$$C(s)=C_1(s)+C_2(s) \tag{1.29}$$

Inverse Laplace transformation of these transforms will give the corresponding responses in the time domain. For very simple cases these inverses may be available directly in a table of Laplace transform pairs such as Table 1.6.1, but it is now evident that techniques are needed to invert more complex expressions. This will be considered in detail and in a broader context in Chapter 3. But, in part to help motivate the derivation of transfer functions for physical systems in Chapter 2 by showing at least one of the uses to which they can be put, the simplest case of the technique to be used is introduced here.

Inverse Transformation by Partial Fraction Expansion

[Roots of denominator of $C(s)$ assumed real and distinct.] Examples will be used to demonstrate the technique.

Example 1.7.1

Determine the response to initial conditions $c(0)=1$, $\dot{c}(0)=2$ of the system

$$\ddot{c}+7\dot{c}+6c=r \tag{1.30}$$

For the response to initial conditions, the input r can be taken to be zero, and the transform is

$$[s^2C-sc(0)-\dot{c}(0)]+7[sC-c(0)]+6C=0$$

or

$$C=\frac{(s+7)c(0)+\dot{c}(0)}{s^2+7s+6}+\frac{s+9}{s^2+7s+6}$$

For inverse transformation, the denominator is factored as $(s+1)(s+6)$, and $C(s)$ is expanded into partial fractions according to

$$C(s)=\frac{s+9}{(s+1)(s+6)}=\frac{K_1}{s+1}+\frac{K_2}{s+6}$$

with a separate term for each real root factor in the denominator of $C(s)$. These terms are of the form $A/(s+\alpha)$, for which Table 1.6.1 gives the inverse Ae^{-at}. The constants K_i are the residues at the corresponding roots. To find K_1, multiply both sides of the equation by its denominator $(s+1)$

$$(s+1)C(s)=\frac{s+9}{s+6}=K_1+\frac{K_2(s+1)}{s+6}$$

If s is permitted to approach the root -1 of $(s+1)$, the second term on the right disappears and the residue K_1 is

$$K_1=[(s+1)C(s)]_{s=-1}=(\frac{s+9}{s+6})_{s=-1}=1.6$$

Residue K_2 at root -6 is found in the same manner by multiplying through by $(s+6)$

$$K_2=[(s+6)C(s)]_{s=-6}=(\frac{s+9}{s+6})_{s=-6}=-0.6$$

The partial fraction expansion is now

$$C(s)=\frac{1.6}{s+1}-\frac{0.6}{s+6}$$

By the linearity theorem, the inverse is the sum of the inverses of the terms, so that the transient response $c(t)$ is the sum of two decaying exponentials

$$c(t)=1.6e^{-t}-0.6e^{-6t}$$

Example 1.7.2

Find the response $c(t)$ of a system with transfer function

$$G(s)=\frac{2(s+3)}{(s+1)(s+6)} \tag{1.31}$$

to a decaying exponential input $r(t)=e^{-2t}$.

From Table 1.6.1 $R(s)=1/(s+2)$, so that $C(s)$ and its partial fraction expansion can be written as follows

$$C(s)=G(s)R(s)=\frac{2(s+3)}{(s+2)(s+1)(s+6)}=\frac{K_1}{s+2}+\frac{K_2}{s+1}+\frac{K_3}{s+6}$$

The residues are calculated next

$$K_1=[(s+2)C(s)]_{s=-2}=[\frac{2(s+3)}{(s+1)(s+6)}]_{s=-2}=-0.5$$

$$K_2=[(s+1)C(s)]_{s=-1}=[\frac{2(s+3)}{(s+2)(s+6)}]_{s=-1}=+0.8$$

$$K_3=[(s+6)C(s)]_{s=-6}=[\frac{2(s+3)}{(s+1)(s+2)}]_{s=-6}=-0.3$$

The partial fraction expansion is

$$C(s)=-\frac{0.5}{s+2}+\frac{0.8}{s+1}-\frac{0.3}{s+6}$$

so that the response sought is

$$c(t)=-0.5e^{-2t}+0.8e^{-t}-0.3e^{-6t}$$

The foregoing technique for calculating residues also applies when the roots of the denominator of $C(s)$ are distinct but include complex conjugate pairs. But then the residues also include complex conjugate pairs. A vector-based method is preferable for these cases and for more complicated transforms generally. This is discussed in Chapter 3, where repeated roots are considered as well.

1.8 Block Diagram Reduction

The discussion of Section 1.7 appears to imply that if the transfer function relating input r and output c in block diagram such as Fig. 1.1 is desired, a differential equation relating these two variables must be obtained first. Fortunately, this is not necessary. The transfer function can be derived instead by certain algebraic manipulations of those of the subsystems or blocks. Some examples will show this block diagram reduction technique and provide some useful results.

Example 1.8.1

Reduce the cascade or series connection of two blocks in Fig. 1.3 to a single block G as in Fig. 1.2(b). By definition.

$$C=G_2M \qquad M=G_1R$$

hence, substituting the second into the first yields

$$C=GR \qquad G=G_1G_2 \tag{1.32}$$

By direct extension it follows that

The overall transfer function of a series of blocks equals the product of the individual transfer functions.

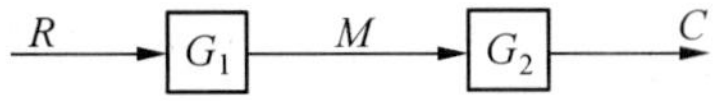

Fig. 1.3　Two-block cascade

Example 1.8.2

The configuration in Fig. 1.4 equivalent to that in Fig. 1.1, is extremely common. By definition

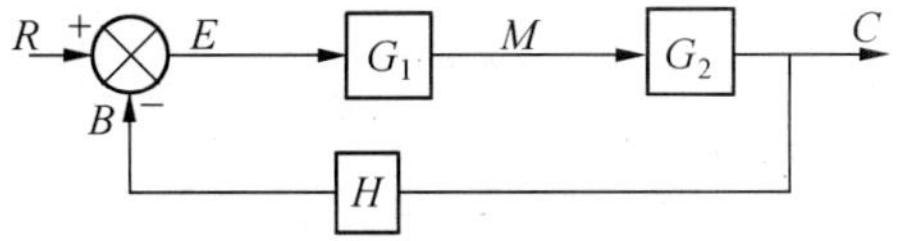

Fig. 1.4　Standard feedback loop

$$C=G_2M \qquad M=G_1R \qquad E=R-B \qquad B=HC$$

Combining each pair yields

$$C=G_1G_2E \qquad E=R-HC$$

Eliminating E gives

$$C=G_1G_2R-G_1G_2HC$$

and rearranging this, the closed-loop transfer function

$$\frac{C}{R}=\frac{G_1G_2}{1+G_1G_2H} \tag{1.33}$$

In words, and in somewhat generalized form, this important result states that

The closed-loop transfer function of the standard loop equals the pro-duct of the transfer functions in the forward path divided by the sum of 1 and the loop gain function. The loop gain function is defined as the product of the transfer functions around the loop.

Note further that, since $C=G_1G_2E$

$$\frac{E}{R}=\frac{1}{1+G_1G_2H} \tag{1.34}$$

If $H=1$, then $E=R-C$ is the system error, as in Fig. 1.1 and E/R is the input-to-error transfer function. It will permit the error response for a given input $r(t)$ to be found directly. The transfer function relating the input to any variable of interest can be found similarly.

Example 1.8.3

The configuration in Fig. 1.5(a), which includes a minor feedback

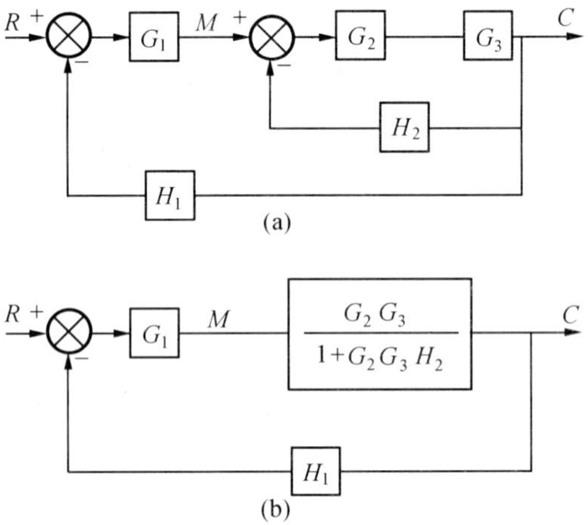

Fig. 1.5 Minor loop feedback

loop, is very common in servomechanisms. Derivation of C/R by the approach of Example 1.8.2 would be laborious, but becomes simple if the result in (1.33) is used. It is applied first to reduce the minor feedback loop C/M to a single block, as shown in Fig. 1.5(b). But (1.33) applies again to this new loop and now yields the closed-loop transfer function

$$\frac{C}{R}=\frac{G_1G_2}{1+G_1G_2H_1}=\frac{G_1G_2G_3}{1+G_2G_3H_2+G_1G_2G_3H_1} \tag{1.35}$$

Example 1.8.4

In a two-input system , the additional input D often represents a disturbance, such as a supply pressure variation in the level control example in Section 1.3. With the additional block L, the diagram models the effect of the disturbance on the system.

For linear systems the principle of superposition applies, and the total output is the sum of the outputs due to each input separately. Thus the output due to R is found as before, and while finding that due to D, R is put equal to zero.

The rule of Example 1.8.2 applies when finding the response to D, but note that the product of the transfer functions in the forward path consists, aside from L, only of G_2. Note also that for $R=0$ the minus sign for the feedback at R can be moved to the summing junction for D. Inspection now yields

$$\frac{C}{D}=\frac{G_2 L}{1+G_1 G_2 H} \tag{1.36}$$

Example 1.8.5

In Fig. 1.6 the two feedback loops interfere with each other. The rearrangements (a) and (b) are alternative first steps to make the result in (1.33) again applicable. Verify that neither changes the system, and that applying (1.33) twice to (a) or (b) yields the closed-loop transfer function

$$\frac{C}{R}=\frac{G_1 G_2}{1+G_1 H_2+G_2 H_1} \tag{1.37}$$

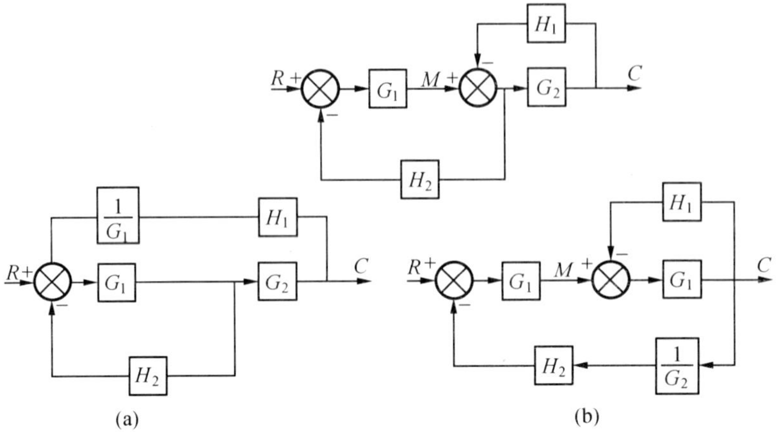

Fig. 1.6 Example 1.8.5

Signal Flow Graphs

Signal flow graphs are alternative to block diagrams. In signal flow graphs, variables are shown as nodes instead of line segments, and line segments with associated arrows and transfer functions represent the relations between variables. For complex systems, the block diagram reduction procedure can become laborious.

For signal flow graphs a general equation is available from which overall transfer functions can be obtained without graphical reductions. For a first course, the block diagram is preferable because it is closer to the physical reality of the system. Block diagrams are used in this book.

1.9 Conclusion

In this chapter a general introduction has been given first, including physical discussion of some fundamental features of control system behavior. A level control example led to a common block diagram configuration.

Laplace transforms led to the transfer function description of dynamic behavior, and block diagram reduction to the description of an interconnected system of blocks.

The application of transfer functions and transforms to calculation of the response $c(t)$ to an input $r(t)$ and initial conditions has been demonstrated for cases where the roots of the denominator of the transform $C(s)$ are real and distinct.

This provides a framework and motivation for study of the next chapter, and a basis for detailed discussion of transient response in Chapter 3. It also allows for an introductory examination of some of the effects of feedback in the problems below.

New words and phrases:

1. dynamic *a.* 动态的
2. model *n.* 模型
3. classification *n.* 分类
4. sophistication *n.* 复杂
5. relay n. 继电器
6. oscillate *v.* 振荡
7. discrete *a.* 离散的
8. inherent *v.* 属于
9. valve *n.* 阀门
10. actuator *n.* 执行器
11. hydraulic *a.* 液压的
12. pneumatic *a.* 气压的 气动的
13. cylinder *n.* 气缸
14. diaphragm *n.* 隔膜
15. mill *n.* 磨机
16. slab *n.* 坯
17. summing junction 相加点
18. performance *n.* 性能
19. level off 稳定
20. intuitive *a.* 直觉的
21. overshoot *n.* 超调
22. unduly *adv.* 过分地
23. compromise *n.* 折中
24. deflection *n.* 变形
25. versus *prep.* 相对于
26. tangent *n.* 切线
27. slope *n.* 斜率
28. partial derivative 偏导

29. differential *adj.* 微分
30. damping *n.* 阻尼
31. coefficient *n.* 系数
32. static equilibrium 静平衡
33. clearance *n.* 间隙
34. state space 状态空间
35. matrix *n.* 矩阵
36. integral *a.* 积分
37. step *n.* 阶跃
38. magnitude *n.* 幅值
39. ramp *n.* 斜坡
40. exponential *n.* 指数
41. initial *a.* 初始的
42. independent of 与……无关
43. final value theorem 终值定理
44. entry *n.* 项
45. impulse *n.* 脉冲
46. column *n.* 列
47. inverse *a.* 逆
48. superposition *n.* 叠加
49. scenario *n.* 情况
50. time domain 时域
51. denominator *n.* 分母
52. factor *n.* 因子
53. residue *n.* 留数
54. complex conjugate 复共轭
55. variable *n.* 变量
56. node *n.* 节点
57. line segment 线段

Notes:

1. This completes the framework necessary for Chapter 2, in which transfer functions are derived for a variety of physical (sub) systems.

译：这就完成了第二章所需的框架，在第二章中导出了各种物理(子)系统的传递函数。

2. Control systems exist in a virtually infinite variety, both in type of application and level of sophistication.

译：实际上，控制系统无论是在应用的种类还是复杂程度上都存在许许多多形式。

3. It must follow the system input, the angle of the steering wheel, as

closely as possible but at a much higher power level.

译：它必须尽可能地跟踪系统输入-方向盘角度，但是功率水平更高。

4. The controlled variable, or output, must be held as closed as possible to a usually constant desired value, or input, despite any disturbances.

译：尽管存在干扰，被控变量或叫输出必须尽可能保持在一个希望的常值也就是输入上。

5. In a steel rolling mill, very large disturbance torques on the drive motors of the rolls when steel slabs enter or leave affect speeds.

译：在一个钢滚磨机中，当钢坯进入或离开时作用在驱动马达上的非常大的干扰力矩影响速度。

6. For the water level example, a sudden or gradual change of flow resistance of the valves due to foreign matter or valve deposits represents a system parameter variation.

译：对于水位的例子，由于外部物质或阀门沉渣所引起的阀门流阻的突然或逐渐的变化代表系统的参数变化。

7. The blocks indicated generally represent relatively, or very , expensive equipment, and must be considered as a fixed part of the system.

译：标出的块一般表示相对或非常贵重的设备，并且必须被认为是系统的固定部分。

8. The power of design techniques that will permit large changes in performance to be achieved by changing only the controller should be appreciated.

译：只通过改变控制器而可取得大的性能改变的设计技术的作用应该得到重视。

9. Disturbances and parameter variations were given as motivations for feedback control. However, the transient response and steady-state error characteristics can also be improved by the use of feedback, and the motivations for feedback can be listed as follows:

译：干扰和参数变化被认为是使用反馈的原因。然而，通过使用反馈暂态响应与稳态误差同样能被改善，并且使用反馈的动因列出如下：

10. Relative stability considerations usually impose an upper limit on gain, and hence on accuracy and speed of response.

译：相对稳定性的考虑，通常使增益有一个上限，从而使精度和响应速度也有上限。

11. The remainder of this chapter provides a basis for the tools needed to move beyond this intuitive discussion and to answer the questions it raises.

译：本章的余下部分为超出直觉的讨论所需的工具提供一个基础并且回答它所提出的问题。

PART 1 **CHAPTER TWO**

2 Transfer Function Models of Physical Systems

2.1 Introduction

In this chapter differential equations are derived to describe the dynamic behavior of mechanical, electrical, thermal, and fluid systems. These are used to obtain transfer functions between selected variables. The same differential equations can also be formulated into state-space models. This alternative, mentioned in Section 1.5, is discussed in Chapter 12.

The chapter will concentrate on subsystem blocks, with attention to the restrictions that must be observed when separating a system into blocks. Block diagram reduction can then provide overall system transfer functions. For many systems that include feedback control, the division into blocks is far from obvious. Such system, in which all system equations and the block diagram are derived directly, are discussed in Chapter 4. Frequently, the precise nature of the feedback may be evident only from this block diagram.[注1]

It is useful to note that a model should not be expected to be evident "by inspection." Rather, it usually will emerge gradually from equations written for parts of the system.[注2]

2.2 Mechanical Systems

Fig. 2.1 shows common elements of mechanical systems with linear and rotational motion, together with the equations used to describe them. It is noted that in Fig. 2.1 and diagrams to follow, the arrows identify the positive directions of the associated variables.

(1) Springs: These occur in many design configurations and materials. For linearized models the force F (torque T) is taken to be proportional to linear deflection x (angular deflection θ), but for larger variations of deflections the behavior may be nonlinear. Note that in linearized models F and x represent the variations of force and deflection about the operating point values, and that the spring constant k for nonlinear springs changes with the operating point.

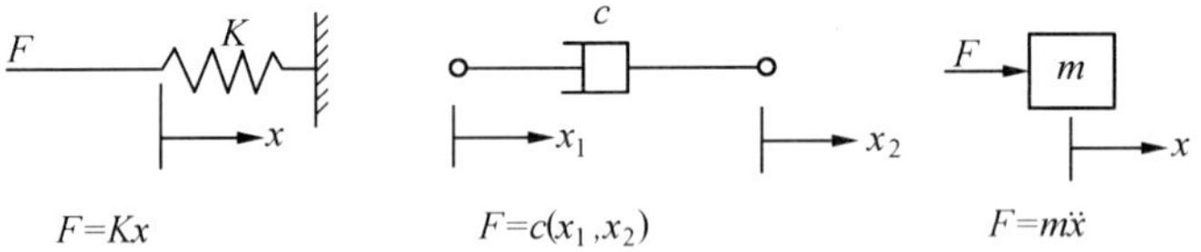

Fig. 2.1 Mechanical system elements

(2) Dampers or dashpots: These generate a damping force F (torque T) proportional to the difference $\dot{x}_1-\dot{x}_2(\dot{\theta}_1-\dot{\theta}_2)$ of the velocities across the damper, and in the opposite direction. In practice, the friction in mechanical systems may differ greatly from the viscous friction of this linear damper model. For dry friction, or Coulomb friction, the force or torque is opposite the velocity difference but independent of its magnitude. The approximate linearization of such behavior is a subject in the study of nonlinear systems.

(3) Mass and inertia: By Newton's law, force F (torque T) equals mass m (inertia J) times acceleration $\ddot{x}(\ddot{\theta})$.

(4) Lever mechanism: For small enough angles from horizontal,

the total motion y equals the sum of the motion due to x_1 with $x_2=0$ and that due to x_2 with $x_1=0$. It is useful to observe that the lever is a mechanical implementation of a summing junction in a block diagram, and is in fact often used for this purpose. If $a=b$, then $y=0.5(x_1-x_2)$ if the direction of x_2 is reversed. If input and output are available in mechanical form and are applied to x_1 and x_2, respectively, the linkage with $a=b$ and x_2 opposite implements the feedback loop as well as providing the system error $e=x_1-x_2$

(5) Gears: This very common element is often identified in terms of its gear ratio n

$$n=\frac{\text{speed of driving gear}}{\text{speed of driven gear}}=\frac{\omega_1}{\omega_2}=\frac{\dot{\theta}_1}{\dot{\theta}_2}\left(=\frac{\theta_1}{\theta_2}=\frac{\ddot{\theta}_1}{\ddot{\theta}_2}\right) \tag{2.1}$$

where $\omega_i=\dot{\theta}_i$ is the angular velocity (rad/sec) of the gear with diameter d_i. The relation $T_2=nT_1$ between the torques arises because the two gears have a common contact force, and the torque equals this force times the gear radius.

Examples incorporating these elements are considered next.

Example 2.2.1 Spring-Mass-Damper System

By Newton's law, $m\ddot{x}$ equals the resultant of all external forces on m in this example in the downward direction. To help in determining the signs of the terms in such problems, it is useful to make any assumption concerning the motion[注3]: for example, that the mass is moving downward from $x=0$. In that case the spring is stretched, so spring force kx is upward, and hence opposes downward acceleration. It therefore receives a minus sign on the right side of the equation for $m\ddot{x}$. Since the mass moves down, the damping force $c\dot{x}$ is upward, and this term must also have a minus sign. The external force $f(t)$ helps downward acceleration, and therefore has a plus sign. The resulting equation is

$$m\ddot{x}=-kx-c\dot{x}+f(t)$$

Rearranging gives the differential equation of motion in the usual form:

$$m\ddot{x}+kx+c\dot{x}=f(t) \tag{2.2}$$

It may have been observed that the effects of gravity do not appear, so that turning the system upside down will not affect the equation. This is done by choosing $x=0$ at the position of static equilibrium, where the weight mg is counterbalanced by a spring force.

For a transfer function model, assume that the response $x(t)$ to $f(t)$ is desired. With zero initial conditions, the transform of (2.2) is

$$(ms^2+cs+k)X(s)=F(s)$$

and the transfer function of interest is

$$\frac{X(s)}{F(s)}=\frac{1}{ms^2+cs+k} \tag{2.3}$$

Example 2.2.2 Two-Mass System

The system in this example can represent a dynamic absorber, where a relatively small mass m_1 is attached to a main mass m via spring k_1 and damper c_1 to reduce vibrations x due to force f. Assume, say, that m and m_1 both move to the right from the zero positions, m farther and faster than m_1. Then spring force $k(x-x_1)$ "opposes" m and "helps" m_1, and damper force $c_1(\dot{x}-\dot{x}_1)$ has the same effect. Hence the differential equations of motion become

$$m\ddot{x}=-kx-k_1(x-x_1)-c_1(\dot{x}-\dot{x}_1)+f$$

$$m_1\ddot{x}_1=k_1(x-x_1)+c_1(\dot{x}-\dot{x}_1)$$

or

$$m\ddot{x}+c_1\dot{x}+(k+k_1)x=c_1\dot{x}_1+k_1x_1+f$$
$$m_1\ddot{x}_1+c_1\dot{x}_1+k_1x_1=c_1\dot{x}_1+k_1x \tag{2.4}$$

For a transfer function model, the effect of f on x would be of interest. This requires the elimination of x_1, an algebraic operation if (2.4) are first transformed

$$(ms^2+c_1s+k+k_1)X(s)=(c_1s+k_1)X_1(s)+F(s)$$
$$(m_1s^2+c_1s+k_1)X_1(s)=(c_1s+k_1)X_1(s) \tag{2.5}$$

Solving $X_1(s)$ from the second equation, substituting it into the first, and rearranging, would give the transfer function X/F.

Example 2.2.3 Rotating Drive System

In this system, there is a drive system, with c representing a friction coupling, and torsion spring k the twisting of a long shaft due to torque. Angle θ_1 is taken to be the input and θ_3 the output. Any other variables may be introduced to facilitate the writing of the equations, such as θ_2, the angle to the right as well as the left of J_1.

The approach of the preceding examples could be used, but an alternative is often convenient. Equations are written in order, starting at the input. To help visualize signs, assume that $\theta_1>\dot{\theta}_2, \dot{\theta}_2>\theta_3$. The shaft torque $k(\theta_1-\theta_2)$ accelerates inertia J_1 and supplies the damping torque

$$k(\theta_1-\theta_2)=J_1\ddot{\theta}_2+c(\dot{\theta}_2-\dot{\theta}_3)$$

It is the damping torque which in turn accelerates inertia J_2

$$c(\dot{\theta}_2-\dot{\theta}_3)=J_2\ddot{\theta}_3$$

Rearranging yields the differential equations

$$J_1\ddot{\theta}_2+c\,\dot{\theta}_2+k\,\theta_2=c\,\dot{\theta}_3+k\,\theta_1$$
$$J_2\ddot{\theta}_3+c\,\dot{\theta}_3=c\,\dot{\theta}_2 \tag{2.6}$$

and the transformed equations

$$(J_1 s^2+cs+k)\theta_2(s)=cs\ \theta_3(s)+k\ \theta_1(s)$$

$$(J_1 s^2+cs)\theta_3(s)=cs\ \theta_2(s)$$

where $\theta_i(s)$ is the transform of $\theta_i(t)$. From the second equation

$$\theta_2(s)=(\frac{J_2}{c}s+1)\theta_3(s)$$

Substituting this into the first and rearranging gives the transfer function

$$\frac{\theta_3(s)}{\theta_1(s)}=\left(\frac{k}{(J_1J_2/c)s^3+(J_1+J_2)s^2+(J_2k/c)s+k}\right) \tag{2.7}$$

Example 2.2.4 Systems with Gears

Although not necessary, it is often convenient for analysis to replace a system with gears by a dynamically equivalent system without gears. This example shows the derivation of the equivalent inertia, spring, and damping, identified as J_e, k_e, *and* c_e, on the first shaft which can replace J, k, and c on the second shaft. In addition to the relation $T_2 = nT_1$, (2.1) is used, and the fact that $\ddot{\theta}_i=\omega_i$. Note that in each case the equivalent element is obtained by dividing the original element by the square of the speed ration n.

Example 2.2.5 Nongeared Equivalent System

Using example 2.2.4, the system in this example can be replaced immediately by its nongeared equivalent where J_e, $k_e$and c_e are as given in example 2.2.4.

2.3 Electrical Systems: Circuits

Fig. 2.2 summarizes some important results for the modeling of electrical circuits, Fig. 2. 2(a) gives the voltage-current relations of the basic elements in the time domain and the Laplace domain, assuming zero initial conditions. In the general transformed relation $V=IZ$, Z is the impedance. In an ideal voltage source, the voltage difference across the terminals is independent of the current through them, In a real voltage source, the voltage ν_s across the terminals decreases with increasing current due to the voltage drop across the internal impedance of the source, which may be a resistance R.

The use of these results and those in Fig. 2. 2(b) and (c) will be illustrated by application to the following examples. The transfer functions $E_o(s)/E_i(s)$ between inputs $e_i(t)$ and outputs $e_o(t)$ are desired. The current through the output terminals must be assumed to be negligibly small, because otherwise its value would affect e_o, and E_o/E_i would not be uniquely defined. In such a case a transfer function can be derived from differential equations written for the combination of the circuit and its load. This illustrates a key condition when subdividing a system into subsystem blocks:

The division of systems into blocks must be such that each block does not load, that is, affect the output of, the preceding block.

Example 2. 3. 1 Common Electrical Circuits (**figure omitted**)

These circuits are used extensively as controllers to improve the performance of feedback control systems. The transfer functions E_o/E_i can be found by use of the results in Fig. 2. 2(b). With no current through the output terminals, all are in effect voltage dividers, in which e_o is a fraction of the voltage e_i, determined by the current i through the input terminals caused by e_i. Consider each in turn

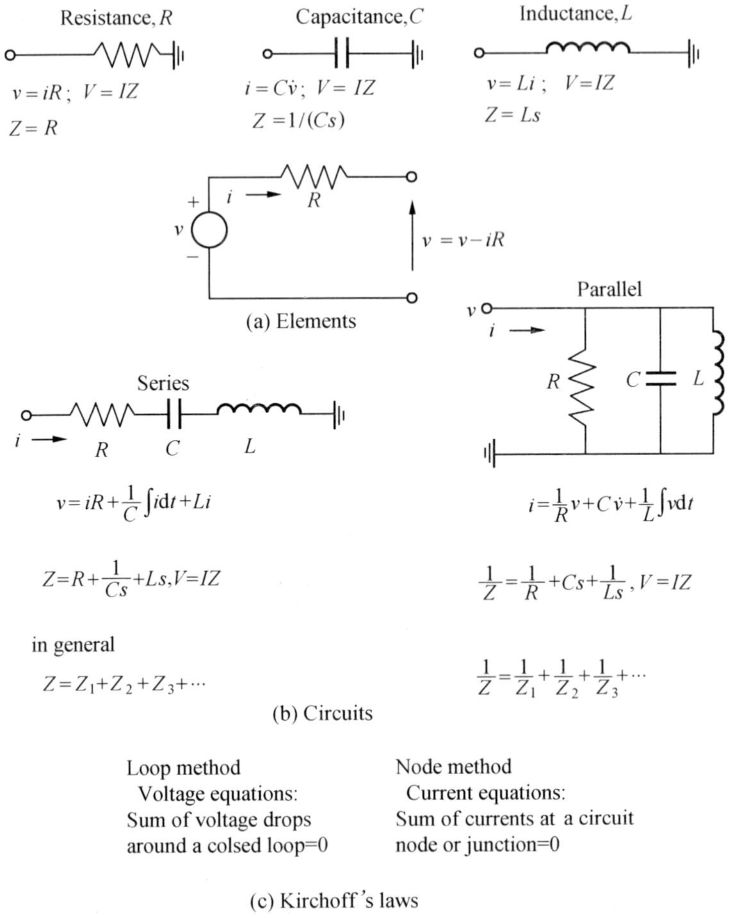

Fig. 2.2 Electrical circuit fundamentals

$$E_i = IZ = I(Z_r + Z_c) \quad Z_r = R \quad Z_c = \frac{1}{Cs}$$

$$E_i = I\left(R + \frac{1}{Cs}\right) \qquad \frac{E_o}{E_i} = \frac{1}{RCs+1} \tag{2.8a}$$

$$E_o = I\,\frac{1}{Cs}$$

$$E_i = I\left(R + \frac{1}{Cs}\right) \qquad \frac{E_o}{E_i} = \frac{RCs}{RCs+1} \tag{2.8b}$$

$$E_o = IR$$

$$E_i = I\left(R_i + R + \frac{1}{Cs}\right) \qquad \frac{E_o}{E_i} = \frac{\tau s+1}{(\tau/\alpha)s+1} \tag{2.8c}$$

$$E_o = I\left(R + \frac{1}{Cs}\right)$$

where $$\tau = RC \qquad \alpha = \frac{R}{R_1 + R}$$

$$E_i = I\left(\frac{1}{(1/R_1) + C_1 s} + R\right)$$

since from Fig. 2.2(b) the equivalent impedance Z_1 of the parallel impedances $Z_r = R_1$ and $Z_c = 1/(C_1 s)$ is given by

$$\frac{1}{Z_1} = \frac{1}{Z_r} + \frac{1}{Z_c} \quad \text{or} \quad Z_1 = 1/\left(\frac{1}{Z_r} + \frac{1}{Z_c}\right)$$

hence

$$E_i = I\left(\frac{R_1 + R + RR_1 C_1 s}{1 + R_1 C_1 s}\right) \qquad \frac{E_o}{E_i} = \alpha \frac{\tau s+1}{\alpha\tau s+1} \tag{2.8d}$$

$$E_o = IR$$

where $$\tau = R_1 C_1 \qquad \alpha = \frac{R}{R_1 + R}$$

$$E_o = I\left(\frac{1}{(1/R_1) + C_1 s} + R_2 + \frac{1}{C_2 s}\right) \qquad \frac{E_o}{E_i} = \frac{(\tau_1 s+1)(\tau_2 s+1)}{\tau_1\tau_2 s^2 + (\tau_1 + \tau_2 + \tau_{12})s + 1} \tag{2.8e}$$

$$E_o = I\left(R_2 + \frac{1}{C_2 s}\right)$$

where $$\tau_1 = R_1 C_1 \qquad \tau_2 = R_2 C_2 \qquad \tau_{12} = R_1 C_2$$

Example 2.3.2 Bridged-*T* Network

This network is often used in AC control systems, that is, systems in which signals are represented by modulation of an ac carrier. With e_o occurring inside a loop, it may be seen that the voltage-divider approach used above does not apply in equally straightforward fashion. But E_o/E_i can be obtained by the use of Kirchhoff's laws in Fig. 2. 2(c), which could also have been used in Example 2. 3. 1 E_o/E_i will be derived by both the loop and node methods.

(1) Loop method: Kirchhoff voltage equations are written for each closed loop in terms of loop current variables

$$E_i=\left(\frac{1}{Cs}+R_1\right)I_1-\frac{1}{Cs}I_2 \qquad \text{(loop 1)}$$

$$0=-\frac{1}{Cs}I_1+\left(R_2+\frac{2}{Cs}\right)I_2 \qquad \text{(loop 2)}$$

since $E_o=E_i-I_2R_2$, this set is solved for I_2 by use of Cramer's rule

$$I_2=\left.\begin{vmatrix}\frac{1}{Cs}+R_1 & E_i \\ -\frac{1}{Cs} & 0\end{vmatrix}\middle/\begin{vmatrix}\frac{1}{Cs}+R_1 & -\frac{1}{Cs} \\ -\frac{1}{Cs} & \frac{2}{Cs}+R_2\end{vmatrix}\right.=\frac{E_iCs}{1+(2R_1+R_2)Cs+R_1R_2C^2s^2}$$

then, from $E_o=E_i-I_2R_2$

$$\frac{E_o}{E_i}=\frac{1+2R_1Cs+R_1R_2C^2s^2}{1+(2R_1+R_2)Cs+R_1R_2C^2s^2} \qquad (2.8\text{f})$$

(2) Node method: Here the Kirchhoff current equations are written in terms of voltage variables at each of the circuit nodes. In this circuit the unknown node voltages are $E_a(=E_o)$ and E_b, and the equations are

$$\frac{E_a-E_i}{R_2}+\frac{E_a-E_b}{1/(Cs)}=0 \qquad \text{(node a)}$$

$$\frac{E_a-E_b}{1/(Cs)}+\frac{E_b-E_i}{1/(Cs)}+\frac{E_b}{R_1}=0 \qquad \text{(node b)}$$

Rearranging yields

$$\left(\frac{1}{R_2}+Cs\right)E_a-CsE_b=\frac{1}{R_2}E_i$$

$$-CsE_a+\left(\frac{1}{R_1}+2Cs\right)E_b=CsE_i$$

Solution for $E_a(=E_o)$ by Cramer′s rule yields E_o/E_i as in part (1), and in the case of this example in a somewhat more direct fashion.

Example 2.3.3 Ladder Network

Using the node method, current equations are written for the circuit nodes a and b

$$\frac{E_a-E_i}{L_1 s}+\frac{E_a}{R_1}+\frac{E_a-E_b}{L_2 s}=0 \qquad \frac{E_b}{R_2}+\frac{E_b-E_a}{L_2 s}=0$$

Solution for $E_b=E_o$ gives

$$\frac{E_o}{E_i}=\frac{R_1R_2}{L_1L_2s^2+(L_1R_1+L_1R_2+L_2R_1)s+R_1R_2}$$

2.4 Electromechanical Systems: Transfer Functions of Motors and Generators

Schematic diagrams of several arrangements of motors and generators are shown in Fig. 2.3. In all cases the motor load is assumed to consist of an inertia J and a damper with damping constant B. Motor shaft position θ and developed motor torque T are then related by

$$T(t)=J\,\ddot{\theta}(t)+B\,\dot{\theta}(t) \qquad T(s)=s(Js+B)\theta(s) \tag{2.9}$$

For convenience, the same variables are used in the time and Laplace domains. The identifier (t) or (s) will generally be omitted if it is evident from the context. Each of the systems in Fig. 2.3 will be considered in turn.

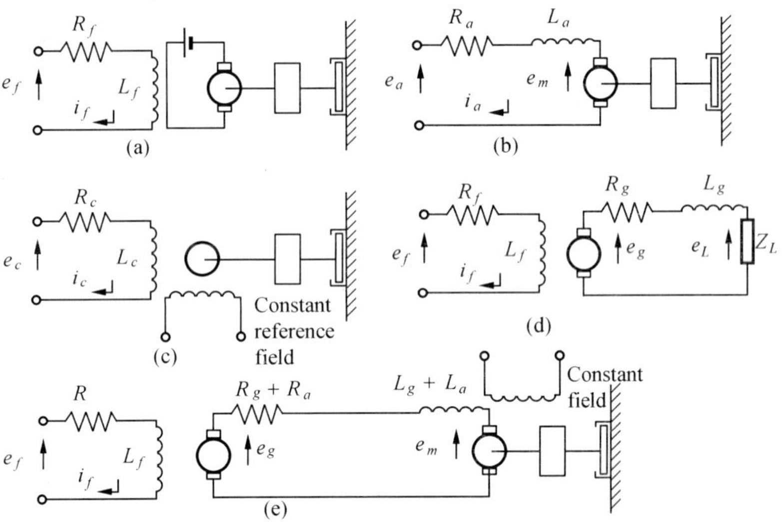

Fig. 2.3 Motors and generators: (a) field-controlled DC motor; (b) armature-controlled DC motor; (c) two-phase AC servomotor; (d) DC generator; (e) motor-generator set

Example 2.4.1 Field-Controlled DC Motor [Fig. 2.3(a)]

The equation for the field loop is

$$e_f = R_f\, i_f + L_f\, i_f \qquad E_f = (R_f + L_f\, s) I_f$$

With constant armature voltage, the developed motor torque T in (2.9) can be taken to be proportional to field current

$$T = K_t i_f \qquad T = K_t I_f \qquad K_t = \text{motor torque constant}$$

Eliminating I_f and T between these transformed equations and (2.9) yields the desired transfer function between applied field voltage e_f and shaft position θ

$$\frac{\theta}{E_f} = \frac{K_t/(R_f B)}{s(T_m s+1)(T_f\, s+1)} \tag{2.10}$$

where $\qquad T_m = J/B = \text{motor time constant}$

$$T_f=L_f/R_f=\text{field time constant}$$

often $T_f \ll T_m$, and a satisfactory approximation in the operating range of interest is

$$\frac{\theta}{E_f}=\frac{K_t/(R_f B)}{s(T_m s+1)} \tag{2.11}$$

Note that the transfer function was derived for the combination of the motor and its load. This load affects motor speed(i. e. , it loads the motor), so a series connection of two blocks with individual transfer functions would be incorrect.

The factor s in the denominator of (2. 10) and)2. 11) should be noted. From Table 1.6.1, dividing $F(s)$ by s is equivalent to integration $f(t)$. Thus the factor s represents the fact that a motor is basically an integrator: For a constant input e_f it has a shaft angle θ which increases at a constant rate, so θ is proportional to the integral of e_f.

Example 2.4.2 Armature-Controlled DC Motor [Fig. 2.3(b)]

The armature loop is described by

$$e_a=R_a i_a+L_a i_a+e_m$$

$$E_a=(R_a+L_a s)I_a+E_m$$

Here the counter emf (electromotive force) voltage can be taken to be proportional to shaft speed,[注4]

$$e_m=K_e\dot{\theta} \qquad E_m=K_e s\,\theta$$

and the developed torque proportional to current i_a

$$T=K_t i_a \qquad T=K_t I_a$$

Eliminating I_a, E_m and T between these equations and (2.9) permits the desired transfer function to be arranged in the common form

$$\frac{\theta}{E_a}=\frac{1/K_e}{s(T_aT_ms^2+(T_m+\gamma T_a)s+\gamma+1)} \tag{2.12}$$

where $T_m=JR_a/(K_eK_t)=$ motor time constant

$T_a=L_a/R_a=$ armature time constant

$\gamma=BR_a(K_eK_t)=$ damping factor

Example 2.4.3 Two-Phase AC Servomotor [Fig. 2.3(c)]

Fixed and variable magnitude AC voltages are applied to the reference and control fields, respectively. A 90° phase shift arranged between these voltages is made positive or negative depending on the desired direction of rotation. The control field is described by

$$e_c=R_ci_c+L_ci_c \quad E_c=(R_c+L_cs)I_c \tag{2.13}$$

The developed motor torque T can be taken to be proportional to i_c and to decrease proportionally with increasing speed, and is described by

$$T=K_ci_c-K_\omega\theta \qquad T=K_cI_c-K_\omega s\,\theta \tag{2.14}$$

This dependence on speed is assumed to be the same under dynamic conditions as for the steady-state torque-speed motor characteristic curves. Eliminating T and I_c between these equations and (2.9) and rearranging gives the transfer function

$$\frac{\theta}{E_c}=\frac{K}{s(T_ms+1)(T_cs+1)} \tag{2.15}$$

where $T_m=J/(B+K_\omega)=$ motor time constant

$T_c=L_c/R_c=$ electrical time constant

$K=K_c/[R_c(B+K_\omega)]=$ motor constant

Often simplification to the form (2.11) is again satisfactory: $K/[s(T_ms+1)]$.

Example 2.4.4 DC Generator [Fig 2.3(d)]

The field loop equation is

$$e_f = R_f\, i_f + L_f\, i_f \qquad E_f = (R_f + L_f s) I_f$$

The developed generator voltage e_g can be assumed to be proportional to field current

$$e_g = K_g i_f \quad E_g = K_g I_f$$

The voltage e_L across the load is given by

$E_L = Z_L I_g \quad Z_L =$ load impedance

and the generator loop is described by

$$e_g = R_g i_g + L_g i_g + e_L \qquad E_g = (L_g s + R_g + Z_L) I_g$$

Hence

$$\frac{E_g}{E_f} = \frac{K_g}{L_f\, s + R_f} \quad \frac{E_L}{E_g} = \frac{Z_L}{L_g s + R_g + Z_L} \quad \frac{E_L}{E_f} = \frac{E_L E_g}{E_g E_f} \tag{2.16}$$

Example 2.4.5 Motor-Generator Set [Fig. 2.3(e)]

The generator serves as a rotating power amplifier. $\theta/E_f = (\theta/E_g)(E_g/E_f)$ is obtained directly by appropriate substitutions in (2.12) and (2.16).

2.5 Thermal Systems

As in the preceding sections, thermal system elements are discussed first.

Thermal resistance A wall of area A separates regions with temperatures T_1 and T_2. The heat flow rate q, in units of heat per unit of time, say Btu/sec, is proportional to the temperature difference $T_1 - T_2$ and to the area A, and flows toward the lowest temperature.[注5] The constant of proportionality is the heat transfer coefficient h. In the case illustrated, this is an effective coefficient which combines the effects of heat convection at the surfaces and heat conduction through the wall. The equation would also represent heat convection across a single surface.

For heat conduction through a wall with surface temperatures T_1 and T_2 and thickness d, the heat flow is proportional to the temperature gradient $(T_1-T_2)/d$

$$q=\frac{kA(T_1-T_2)}{d}=\frac{k}{d}A(T_1-T_2) \tag{2.17}$$

where k is the thermal conductivity. Hence the equivalent heat transfer coefficient is k/d.

To identify these relations in terms of a thermal equivalent of an electrical resistance, the equation is written as

$$T_1-T_2=qR_t \quad R_t=\frac{1}{hA} \tag{2.18}$$

with T_1-T_2 analogous to voltage drop v, and q to current i, R_t becomes the thermal resistance.

Thermal capacitance. Let q be the net heat flow rate into a volume V of a material with mass density ρ and specific heat c (= heat required to raise the temperature of a unit mass by 1°). This net inflow q of heat per second must equal the change per second (i. e. the rate of change) of heat stored in V. Since the mass is ρV, the heat required for a 1° rise of temperature is ρVc, and hence the heat stored at a temperature T is ρVcT. Assuming ρ, V, and c to be constant, its rate of change is $\rho Vc\dot{T}$: hence the equation is $q=\rho Vc\dot{T}$.

From the equation $i=C\dot{v}$ in Fig. 2. 2 for an electrical capacitance follows immediately the equivalent notion of a thermal capacitance C_t

$$q = C_t \dot{T} \quad C_t = \rho V c \tag{2.19}$$

It is seen that C_t is the heat required for a 1° temperature rise.

Some examples of thermal systems follow.

Example 2.5.1 Process Control

There is a tank of volume V filled with an incompressible fluid of mass density ρ and specific heat c. Volume flow rates entering and leaving are f_i and f_o. T_i is the temperature of the inflow. It is assumed that the tank is well stirred, so that the outlet temperature equals the tank temperature T.

The tank is filled and the fluid incompressible, so $f_i = f_o$, and the mass flow rate entering and leaving is $f_i \rho$. Hence the heat inflow rate is $f_i \rho c T_i$, the outflow rate $f_i \rho c T$, and the net inflow rate $f_i \rho c(T_i - T)$. As explained, this must equal $V\rho c\dot{T}$, the rate of change of heat $V\rho cT$ stored in the tank, $V\rho c\dot{T} = f_i \rho c(T_i - T)$, or

$$\frac{V}{f_i}\dot{T} + T = T_i \tag{2.20}$$

The transform is $[(V/f_i)s+1]T(s) = T_i(s)$, so that the following simple lag transfer function relates T_i and T

$$\frac{T(s)}{T_i(s)} = \frac{1}{(V/f_i)s+1} \tag{2.21}$$

Example 2.5.2 Space Heating

In this example, let T be the difference with a constant ambient temperature. By (2.18), the heat loss q_0 to ambient can be modeled by $q_o = T/R_t$, where R_t is the thermal resistance. If q_i is the heat inflow rate from an electrical heater, the net inflow $(q_i - T/R_t)$ must equal $C_t\dot{T}$, where C_t is the thermal capacitance. Hence the behavior is modeled by the differential equation

$$R_tC_t\dot{T}+T=R_tq_i \tag{2.22}$$

Therefore, the effect of heat flow q_i on the temperature T is approximated by the transfer function

$$\frac{T(s)}{Q_i(s)}=\frac{R_t}{R_tC_ts+1} \tag{2.23}$$

As in Example 2.5.1 and the electrical RC circuit in Example 2.3.1, the behavior is described by a simple lag transfer function.

Example 2.5.3 Three-Capacitance System

Extending example 2.5.1, allowance is made for heat loss to the ambient temperature T_a via surface area A_0 with heat transfer coefficient h_o[注6] and for the heating up, via surface A_m with heat transfer coefficient h_m, of an internal space or material with capacitance C_m and uniform temperature. This temperature is measured by a sensor with a significant capacitance C_s, heated via a surface of area A_s and heat transfer coefficient h_s.

The most convenient approach is to equate the net heat flow rate to the rate of change of heat for each capacitance in turn

$$\begin{aligned}
&C_o\dot{T}_o=f\rho_oc_o(T_i-T_o)-A_oh_o(T_o-T_a)-A_mh_m(T_o-T_m)\\
&C_m\dot{T}_m=A_mh_m(T_o-T_m)\\
&C_{ss}\dot{T}_s=A_sh_s(T_m-T_s)
\end{aligned} \tag{2.24}$$

The second of these equations does not include the heat loss term $-A_sh_s(T_m-T_s)$ to the sensor, on the assumption that it is relatively negligible. The last equation immediately gives the transfer function relating T_m and its value as measured by the sensor

$$\frac{T_s(s)}{T_m(s)}=\frac{1}{\tau_s s+1} \qquad \tau_s=\frac{C_s}{A_s h_s} \tag{2.25}$$

This is again a simple lag transfer function, as is that relating T_o and T_m from the second of equations(2.24)

$$\frac{T_m(s)}{T_o(s)}=\frac{1}{\tau_m s+1} \qquad \tau_s=\frac{C_m}{A_m h_m} \tag{2.26}$$

Substituting this for T_m in the first of equations (2.24), its transform, on bringing all terms for $T_o(s)$ to one side, is

$$\left[C_o s+(f\rho_o c_o+A_o h_o)+A_m h_m\left(1-\frac{1}{\tau_m s+1}\right)\right]T_o(s)=f\rho_o c_o T_i(s)+A_o h_o T_a(s)$$

and some algebraic manipulation then yields

$$T_o(s)=\frac{(\tau_m s+1)[f\rho_o c_o T_i(s)+A_o h_o T_a(s)]}{C_o \tau_m s^2+[(f\rho_o c_o+A_o h_o)\tau_m+C_o+C_m]s+f\rho_o c_o+A_o h_o} \tag{2.27}$$

This transform reflects the condition that variations of ambient temperature T_a act as a disturbance input on the system. Thus the system has two inputs, where G is the transfer function implied by (2.27). As discussed in Section 1.8, the total output is the superposition of the outputs for each input separately with the other put equal to zero.

It should also be observed, however, that if ambient temperature variations are known to be small or slow, $T_a=0$ can be assumed in the original equations (2.24). This is because in a linearized model the variables represent variations from operating point values, so that constant variables are zero.

For $T_a=0$, the overall transfer function $T_s(s)/T_i(s)$ can now be written from (2.25) to (2.27), or represented by the series connection of blocks , which also identifies the responses $T_o(s)$ and $T_m(s)$.

2.6 Fluid Systems

Fluid system elements are defined in Fig. 2.4, again in terms of their electrical equivalents.

(1) Fluid resistance R_f: This exists in flow orifices, valves, and fluid lines. With pressure drop $p_1 - p_2$ equivalent to voltage drop and flow rate q to current, R_f is equivalent to electrical resistance. Commonly, the actual relation is nonlinear, and Fig. 2.4(a) shows linearized mod-

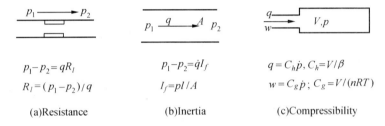

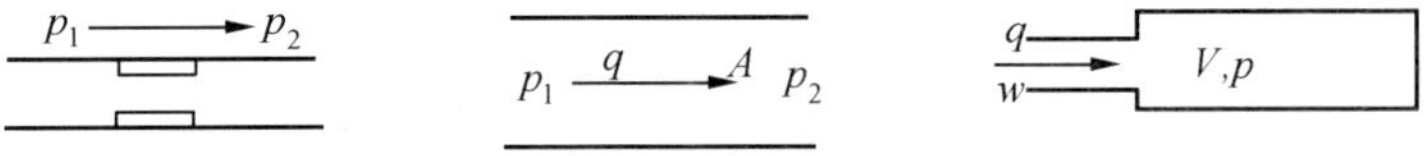

$p_1 - p_2 = qR_l$

$R_l = (p_1 - p_2)/q$

(a)Resistance

$p_1 - p_2 = \dot{q}I_f$

$I_f = pl/A$

(b)Inertia

$q = C_h\dot{p},\ C_h = V/\beta$

$w = C_g\dot{p};\ C_g = V/(nRT)$

(c)Compressibility

Fig. 2.4 Fluid system elements

el, with p_1, p_2, and q being variations about the values at an operating point used to calculate R_f. R_f may be obtained by calculation or experiment, and the units may yield either volume or mass flow rates.

(2) Fluid inertia I_f: The mass of fluid of mass density ρ in a line of length l and cross-sectional area A is ρAl. The pressure drop $p_1 - p_2$ generates a force $(p_1 - p_2)A$ to accelerate this mass. Fluid velocity v and volumetric flow rate q are related by $q = Av$, so the acceleration $\dot{v}$ can be expressed as $\dot{v} = \dot{q}/A$. Newton's law then yields $(p_1 - p_2)A = \rho Al(\dot{q}/A)$, which reduces to the equation in Fig. 2.4(b). It is equivalent to $v = L\dot{i}$ for an electrical inductance.

(3) Fluid compressibility C_h, C_g: In Fig. 2.4(c), pressure and

mass density in volume V are p and ρ. The mass in V is ρV, and its rate of change $d(\rho V)/dt$ must clearly be equal to the mass flow rate W entering V. With V constant, therefore

$$W = V\dot{\rho} \tag{2.28}$$

Liquids and gases are considered in turn.

Liquids. In high-performance hydraulic systems it is necessary to include the effect of oil compressibility.[注7] At constant temperature, near an operating point p_0, ρ_0, bulk modulus β is defined by

$$\rho - \rho_0 = \frac{\rho_0}{\beta}(p - p_0) \quad \dot{\rho} = \frac{\rho_0}{\beta}\dot{p} \tag{2.29}$$

A value $\beta \approx 200\ 000$ psi is possible theoretically, but air entrainment usually makes 100 000 psi more realistic. Substituting (2.29) into (2.28) gives

$$W = \frac{V\rho_0}{\beta}\dot{p} \tag{2.30}$$

In hydraulics, volume flow rate $q = W/\rho_0$ is more commonly used

$$q = C_h\dot{p} \quad \text{capacitance} \quad C_h = \frac{V}{\beta} \tag{2.31}$$

This is equivalent to $i = C\dot{v}$ for an electrical capacitance. The flow rate q causes a larger rate of change of pressure if the volume V is smaller or the oil stiffer (i. e., β larger).

Gases. For a polytropic process in gas described by the ideal gas law $p = \rho RT$ (T=absolute temperature; R=gas constant) the p–ρ relation is

$$p = C\rho^n \quad (\ln p = \ln C + n\ln\rho) \tag{2.32}$$

where

$$n=\begin{cases} 1 & \text{for isothermal processes} \\ k=\dfrac{C_p}{C_y} & \text{for adiabatic frictionless processes} \end{cases}$$

For the latter, where C_p and C_v are the specific heat values at constant pressure and constant volume, there is no heat exchange with the environment. Taking the derivative of (2.32) gives

$$\frac{\mathrm{d}p}{p}=\frac{n\mathrm{d}\rho}{\rho} \qquad \text{or} \qquad \dot{\rho}=\frac{\rho}{np}\dot{p}$$

and substituting into (2.28) yields

$$W=\frac{V\rho}{np}\dot{p} \tag{2.33}$$

By comparison with (2.30), this shows that

$$\beta=np=\text{bulk modulus for gases} \tag{2.34}$$

The form more common for gases

$$W=C_g\dot{p} \qquad \text{capacitance} \quad C_g=\frac{V}{nRT} \tag{2.35}$$

($n=1$: isothermal; $n=k=C_p/C_v$: adiabatic) results by substitution of $p=\rho RT$.

Example 2.6.1 Hydraulic Tank

This was the process in the level control system of Section 1.3. The net volumetric inflow rate is (q_i-q_o). This is the volume entering per unit time, so must equal the change per unit time (i. e., the rate of change) of the volume Ah in the tank

$$A\dot{h}=q_i-q_o \tag{2.36}$$

The outflow q_o depends on the pressure drop across the valve. The pressure p at depth h below the water lever is the force per unit area due to the weight of water, so equals the weight of a column of water of unit area cross section and height h: $p=\rho gh$. Here ρ is mass density and g the acceleration due to gravity. The valve resistance R is often expressed in terms of the head h instead of the pressure p.

The actual relation between h and q_o is nonlinear, but it is approximated by the linearized model

$$h=q_o R \tag{2.37}$$

with the variables representing the variations about operating-point values. R is determined as the corresponding curve from the slope of the nonlinear characteristic of h versus q_o at the operating point. Transforming these equations and substituting the second into the first yields

$$(ARs+1)H(s)=RQ_i(s)$$

and the transfer function

$$\frac{H(s)}{Q_i(s)}=\frac{R}{ARs+1} \tag{2.38}$$

Note that this again has the form of a simple lag transfer function, already encountered in electrical and thermal systems.

Example 2.6.2 Two-Tank System with Control Valve

A control valve V_c with valve opening x controls flow rate q_{i1} into the first tank from a supply with constant pressure P_s. From (2.38), the following transfer functions can be written immediately

$$\frac{H_1(s)}{Q_{i1}(s)}=\frac{R}{A_1R_1s+1} \qquad \frac{H_2(s)}{Q_{i2}(s)}=\frac{R}{A_2R_2s+1} \tag{2.39}$$

To express q_{i1} and q_{i2}, different linearized models may be used for R_1 and the control valve

$$h_1=q_{i2}R_1 \qquad q_{i1}=K_v x \tag{2.40}$$

The input to the valve model is the valve opening x, which in effect controls the valve resistance parameter. The transfer functions corresponding to (2.40) are

$$\frac{Q_{i1}(s)}{X(s)}=K_v \qquad \frac{Q_{i2}(s)}{H_1(s)}=\frac{1}{R_1} \tag{2.41}$$

Transfer functions (2.39) and (2.41) can be combined into the block diagram shown in Fig. 2.5. It should be noted that this subdivision into blocks would not apply if in this system the outflow of the first tank fed into the bottom of the second tank. The net head on R_1 would then be h_1-h_2, so the second tank would affect the output of the first. As discussed earlier, this means that the second tank loads the first, and in this case an overall transfer function must be derived directly from the equations for the combined system.

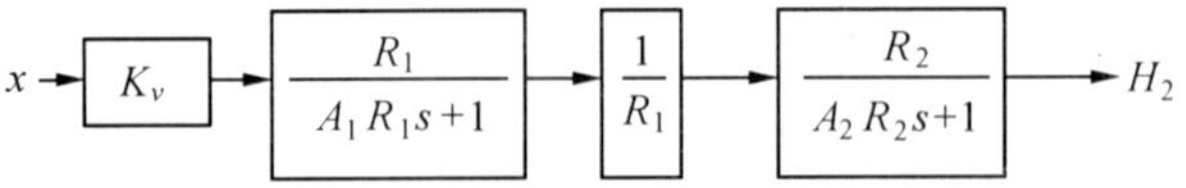

Fig. 2.5 Block diagram for system of Example 2.6.2

Example 2.6.3 Pneumatic Tank

The linearized model for subsonic flow through R can be written as

$$p_i-p_o=WR \tag{2.42}$$

From Fig. 2.4(c), this flow raises tank pressure p_o according to

$$W=C_g\dot{p}_o \qquad C_g=\text{capacitance} \tag{2.43}$$

Transforming these equations gives

$$P_i(s)-P_o(s)=W(s)R \quad W(s)=C_g sP_o(s)$$

The transfer function p_o/p_i is again a simple lag

$$\frac{P_o(s)}{P_i(s)}=\frac{1}{RC_gs+1} \tag{2.44}$$

Example 2.6.4 Pneumatically Actuated Valve

This extremely common device is the actuator in the block diagram of Fig. 1.1 assumed for the level control example.

The pneumatic line that connects control pressure p_i to pressure p above the diaphragm is represented by the linearized resistance R_g

$$p_i - p = W_a R_g \quad P_i(s) - P(s) = W_a(s) R_g \tag{2.45}$$

Diaphragm motion x is so small that the capacitance C_g of the space above it is about constant. Then W_a raises p according to

$$W_a = C_g \dot{p} \quad W_a(s) = C_g s P(s) \tag{2.46}$$

A very simplified model, by no means always acceptable, will be used for diaphragm and valve poppet motion x. [注8] The mass and friction forces of the moving parts and the fluid flow forces on the poppet will be neglected. The downward pressure force pA on the diaphragm must then be counterbalanced by the spring force kx

$$Ap = kx \qquad AP(s) = kX(s) \tag{2.47}$$

Finally, valve flow is modeled by

$$q_o = K_v x \qquad Q_o(s) = K_v X(s) \tag{2.48}$$

Eliminating W_a between (2.45) and (2.46) gives

$$\frac{P(s)}{P_i(s)} = \frac{1}{R_g C_g s + 1} \tag{2.49}$$

and this with (2.47) and (2.48) gives the overall block diagram . The overall transfer function is again a simple lag

$$\frac{Q_o(s)}{P_i(s)} = \frac{AK_v/k}{R_g C_g s + 1} \tag{2.50}$$

Note how the overall model gradually emerged from equations written for the parts of the system, and not from some form of grand view of the total system.[注9]

It is also useful to remark on the signs in (2.47) and (2.48). Remember that the variables represent changes from operating-point values. A positive change of p causes a positive change of q_o, so the signs in (2.48) must also be positive. If x had been defined as positive in upward direction, the signs in both equations would be negative on the right or left sides.

2.7 Fluid Power Control Elements

In this section the modeling of a number of very common subsystems of fluid power servos and controls is discussed by means of examples.

Example 2.7.1 Control Valves

Two common types of valves are used in this example. The supply pressure is p_s and the output pressure p. For $x = 0$ the output port is blocked off. The valve model used earlier was $q = k_v x$, where q is the volumetric flow rate. The level control example in Chapter 1 serves to show that this model is incomplete. Supply pressure variations were a major potential disturbance and a prime reason why feedback control was needed in the first place, yet their effect on valve flow is not incorporated. Valve flow increases with both x and valve pressure drop $(p_s - p)$, and an appropriate linearized valve model is $q = K_x x + K_p (p_s - p)$. In linearized models the variables represent variations about the operating point. In fluid power systems, if the supply pressure is constant, the valve model reduces to that shown in Fig. 2.6

$$q = K_x x - K_p p \tag{2.51}$$

The constants K_s and K_p are found from the slopes of the steady-state valve characteristics at the operating point(x_0, p_0).

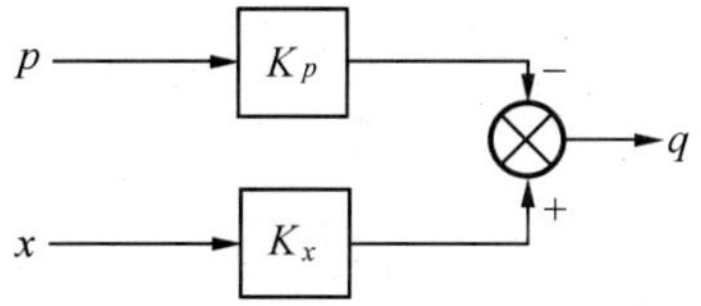

Fig. 2.6 Linearized valve model

Example 2.7.2 Hydraulic Cylinder Control

The spool-valve-controlled actuator is used extensively. For $x = 0$ the valve spool is centered, and the lands on this spool exactly block the ports of fluid lines to the ends of the cylinder, so that the piston is stopped. If the valve spool is moved slightly to the left, the ports are partially unblocked. The left side of the cylinder is now connected to the supply and the right side to a low-pressure reservoir. Thus the piston can move to the right.

Consider first the simplest possible model, in which the load connected to the piston is very small and pressure variations are negligible. Oil compressibility can then be ignored, and if the effective area A on both sides of the piston is the same, the flow rate q through both valve ports is also the same and can be modeled as

$$q = K_v x \quad Q = K_v X \tag{2.52}$$

The change $A\dot{y}$ of volume on each side of the piston per second must equal q

$$q = A\dot{y} \quad Q = AsY \tag{2.53}$$

This is modeled in Fig. 2.7, and the transfer function is

$$\frac{Y(s)}{X(s)} = \frac{K_v}{As} \tag{2.54}$$

The factor s in the denominator represents the fact that, like the electric motor, the cylinder is an integrator, since for a constant flow q the output y increases linearly.

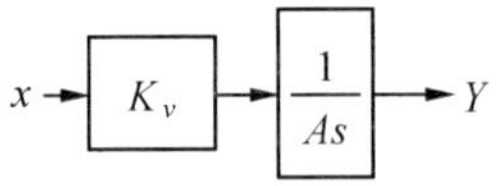

Fig. 2.7 Simple model of Example 2.7.2

Example 2.7.3 Loaded Hydraulic Cylinder Control

Let the load on the hydraulic cylinder in example 2.7.2 consist of mass m and damping b. Then if the net pressure on the piston is p, the force balance equation is

$$pA = m\ddot{y} + b\dot{y} \qquad AP(s) = (ms+b)sY(s) \tag{2.55}$$

The valve flow is modeled by (2.51)

$$q = K_x x - K_p p \qquad Q(s) = K_x X(s) - K_p P(s) \tag{2.56}$$

Equation (2.53) must be modified to include the effect of oil compressibility. From Fig. 2.4(c), near a piston position where the volume under pressure p is V, the compressibility flow associated with pressure variations is $(V/\beta)\dot{p}$. The flow q to the cylinder supplies this compressibility flow as well as the flow $A\dot{y}$ corresponding to piston velocity

$$q = A\dot{y} + \frac{V}{\beta}\dot{p} \quad Q(s) = s\left[AY(s) + \frac{V}{\beta}P(s)\right] \tag{2.57}$$

From (2.56) and (2.57)

$$K_s X - K_p P = AsY + \frac{V}{\beta}sP \qquad K_x X - AsY = \left(\frac{V}{\beta}s + K_p\right)P$$

Then substituting for P from (2.55) and rearranging yields the following improvement of the model (2.54)

$$\frac{Y(s)}{X(s)}=\frac{K_x}{s\left[\frac{mV}{\beta A}s^2+\frac{1}{A}(K_p m+\frac{V}{\beta}b)s+\frac{K_p b}{A}+A\right]} \tag{2.58}$$

Example 2.7.4 Hydraulic Motor and Hydrostatic Transmission

A constant-speed hydraulic pump supplies flow to a hydraulic motor. Motor speed can be changed by adjusting pump flow per revolution via a setting ϕ_p. Delivered pump flow is proportional to ϕ_p

$$q_p=K_p\phi_p=q_l+q_c+q_m \tag{2.59}$$

of this flow rate, a part q_l is lost in internal leakages, q_c is compressibility flow, and only part q_m causes motor rotation. Let

p = pressure drop across the motor

V = volume of oil under high pressure p

D_m = motor displacement, the volume of oil needed for 1 rad motor rotation. Then

$q_l=Lp$: leakage flow proportional to p

$q_c=\frac{V}{\beta}\dot{p}$: compressibility flow [Fig. 2.4(c)]

$q_m=D_m\dot{\theta}$: motor flow ($\dot{\theta}$ = motor speed. rad/sec)

This gives the flow equation

$$K_p\phi_p=D_m\dot{\theta}+L\,p+\frac{V}{\beta}\dot{p} \quad K_p\phi_p(s)=D_m s\theta(s)+(L+\frac{V}{\beta}s)P(s) \tag{2.60}$$

To obtain the load equation, for 100% motor efficiency its mechanical output power equals its hydraulic input power. If the developed motor torque is T, the mechanical output power is $T\dot{\theta}$. The hydraulic input power is $q_m p$. This may be verified by thinking of the motor as a cylinder of area A. With flow q_m, the piston velocity q_m is then q_m/A. and piston force pA. The power is their product, pq_m. Thus $T\dot{\theta}=q_m p=D_m\dot{\theta}p$, so that

$$T=D_m P \tag{2.61}$$

This torque accelerates inertia J and overcomes damping B, so that the load equation becomes

$$T=D_m p=J\ddot{\theta}+B\dot{\theta} \quad D_m P(s)=s(Js+B)\theta(s) \tag{2.62}$$

Substituting $P(s)$ from this into (2.60) and rearranging yields the transfer function:

$$\frac{\theta(s)}{\phi_p(s)}=\frac{K_p D_m}{s\left[\frac{VJ}{\beta}s^2+\left(\frac{VB}{\beta}+LJ\right)s+BL+D_m^2\right]} \tag{2.63}$$

2.8 Conclusion

In this chapter transfer functions were derived for a variety of physical subsystem blocks. If feedback systems consist of a connection of such blocks, overall transfer functions can now be obtained by block diagram reduction. But often such a separation into blocks and the precise nature of the feedback may become evident only when all equations for the system have been written. [注10] The modeling of such systems, and their representation by block diagrams that clarify system behavior and exhibit feedback effects, are considered in Chapters 4 and 5. The operational amplifier and some of its many uses are also discussed in Chapter 5.

First, however, it is desirable to obtain a better understanding of the nature of system transient responses. In Chapter 3 the powerful s-plane will be introduced, to provide fundamental insight into the dynamic behavior of systems described by given transfer functions, whether these describe a single block or have been obtained by block diagram reduction.

As an introduction to this, a final example is given to demonstrate the application of techniques and results of Chapters 1 and 2 to the transient analysis of a simple feedback control system.

Example 2.8.1 DC Motor Position Servo

From (2.11), let the transfer function from field voltage to shaft position of a field-controlled dc motor be

$$G(s)=\frac{0.5}{s(0.25s+1)}$$

The output of the sensor measuring shaft position is compared with a signal in the same form to obtain the error signal E. Assuming a fast response power amplifier and a constant-gain controller, the loop can be considered to be closed as shown, by an amplifier block of gain K. The closed-loop transfer function, using (1.33), is

$$\frac{C(s)}{R(s)}=\frac{2K}{s^2+4s+2K}$$

and for a unit step input $[R(s)=1/s]$, the transform of the shaft position is

$$C(s)=\frac{2K}{s(s^2+4s+2K)}$$

For $K=1$, partial fraction expansion yields the solution

$$c(t)=1-1.207e^{-0.586t}+0.207e^{-3.414t}$$

As discussed physically in Chapter 1, for larger K the motor input changes more for a given change of error and a faster response can be expected. This is confirmed by the plot for $K=1.9$, for which the solution is

$$c(t)=1-2.737e^{-1.553t}+1.737e^{-2.447t}$$

The physical discussion also suggested a danger of overcorrection and possibly severe oscillations if K is raised too high. The plot for $K=8$ exemplifies this trend. Although the speed of response is improved, a maximum overshoot of about 16% exists. In many cases this is acceptable, but not, for example, for the tool slide on an automatically controlled machine tool. It is noted that the inverse transform for this case is obtained from the corresponding entry in Table 1. 6. 1 with $\omega_n = 4$, $\xi=0.5$

$$c(t)=1-1.154e^{-2t}\sin(3.6461t+\frac{\pi}{3})$$

The steady-state or final value of the error is seen to be zero for all three values of K, as is also evident from the final value theorem:

$$c_{ss}=\lim_{t\to\infty} c(t)=\lim_{s\to 0} sC(s)=1$$

For servos, the steady-state error in following a unit ramp input [$R(s)=1/s^2$] is also an important measure of performance. For a machine tool slide moving at constant velocity, it can cause errors in part dimensions. Here application of the final value theorem to $C(s)$ yields the expected but useless result that $C_{ss}\to\infty$. The theorem is therefore applied to the error $E(s)$, as is in fact the usual practice also for step inputs. Using (1.34) yields

$$\frac{E(s)}{R(s)}=\frac{s(0.25s+1)}{0.25s^2+s+0.5K}$$

so that for $R(s)=1/s^2$.

$$e_{ss}=\lim_{t\to\infty} e(t)=\lim_{s\to 0} sE(s)=\frac{1}{0.5K}$$

As expected, this is reduced by increasing K.

New words and phrases:

1. thermal *a.* 热的，热学的
2. alternative *a.* 另外的
3. rotational *a.* 旋转的
4. spring *n.* 弹簧
5. torque *n.* 转矩，力矩
6. damper *n.* 阻尼器
7. dashpot *n.* 阻尼器
8. viscous *a.* 粘性的
9. lever *n.* 杠杆
10. reverse *v.* 颠倒
11. linkage *n.* 杆
12. stretch *v.* 伸展
13. upside down 颠倒
14. absorber *n.* 减震器
15. coupling *n.* 连接
16. torsion *n.* 扭转
17. shaft *n.* 轴
18. visualize *v.* 使具体化
19. impedance *n.* 阻抗
20. uniquely *adv.* 惟一地
21. voltage divider 分压器
22. notch *n.* 凹口
23. modulation *n.* 调制
24. carrier *n.* 载流
25. ladder *n.* 梯形
26. generator *n.* 发电机
27. schematic *a.* 示意的
28. identifier *n.* 标识符 符号
29. field *n.* 励磁
30. DC 直流
31. armature *n.* 电枢
32. area *n.* 面积
33. convection *n.* 对流
34. gradient *n.* 梯度
35. allowance *n.* 允许量，容限
36. orifice *n.* 孔，口
37. cross-sectional *a.* 横截的
38. inductance *n.* 电感
39. modulus *n.* 模数
40. stiffer *a.* 更粘
41. polytropic *a.* 多变的
42. isothermal *a.* 等温的
43. adiabatic *a.* 绝热的
44. subsonic *a.* 次声的
45. poppet *n.* 提升阀
46. spool *a.* 滑动的

47. piston *n.* 活塞

48. reservoir *n.* 容器

49. hydrostatic *a.* 流体静力的

50. displacement *n.* 排出量

Notes:

1. For many systems that include feedback control, the division into blocks is far from obvious. Such system, in which all system equations and the block diagram are derived directly, are discussed in Chapter 4. Frequently, the precise nature of the feedback may be evident only from this block diagram.

译：对于许多含有反馈的系统，分成子块不是明显的事情。在第4章中讨论所有系统方程和方块图都能直接导出的系统。通常地，反馈的精确性质只从方块图中就能明显看出。

2. It is useful to note that a model should not be expected to be evident "by inspection." Rather, it usually will emerge gradually from equations written for parts of the system.

译：应该注意到，不应期望一个模型仅通过观察(就能得到)那么明显，它通常是从对系统各部分所写的方程中逐渐得出的。

3. To help in determining the signs of the terms in such problems, it is useful to make any assumption concerning the motion.

译：为了帮助决定如此问题中各项的符号，应对运动做假设。

4. Here the counter emf (electromotive force) voltage can be taken to be proportional to shaft speed.

译：这里反电动势可以被认为与轴速成正比。

5. A wall of area A separates regions with temperatures T_1 and T_2. The

heat flow rate q, in units of heat per unit of time, say Btu/sec, is proportional to the temperature difference $T_1 - T_2$ and to the area A, and flows toward the lowest temperature.

译：一面积为 A 的墙隔离两个温度分别为 T_1 和 T_2 的区域。以单位时间的热量，例如 Btu/sec 为单位的热流速率与温差 $T_1 - T_2$ 和面积 A 成正比，并且流向最低温度。

6. Extending example 2.5.1, allowance is made for heat loss to the ambient temperature T_a via surface area A_0 with heat transfer coefficient h_0.

译：扩展例 2.5.1，规定了经面积 A_0 损失到环境温度 T_a 的允许量，面积 A_0 的热传导系数为 h_0。

7. In high-performance hydraulic systems it is necessary to include the effect of oil compressibility.

译：在高性能的液压系统中必须包括油的可压缩性的影响。

8. A very simplified model, by no means always acceptable, will be used for diaphragm and valve poppet motion x.

译：一个非常简化的模型（并不总能被接受），将被用于隔膜与提升阀的运动 x。

9. Note how the overall model gradually emerged from equations written for the parts of the system, and not from some form of grand view of the total system.

译：注意总的模型怎样从系统各部分的方程逐步得出，而不是从整个系统的整体的形式得出。

10. But often such a separation into blocks and the precise nature of the feedback may become evident only when all equations for the system have been written.

译：但是经常地，如此分成子块并且反馈的精确性质只有当系统的所有方程均被写出以后才是明显的。

PART 1	CHAPTER THREE

3 Transient Performance and The S-Plane

3.1 Introduction

In this chapter the transient behavior of systems described by given transfer functions is considered, whether these describe a single block or have been obtained by block diagram reduction. The purpose is to establish correlations and to specify requirements that ensure satisfactory performance. The use of feedback to satisfy such requirements will be considered later.

The correlations between transfer functions and response characteristics are developed in terms of the positions of the system poles and zeros in the s-plane. These are powerful concepts which will also be used in the design of feedback to improve unsatisfactory behavior.

Inverse transformation of $C(s) = G(s)R(s)$ was used in Section 1.7 to find the response $c(t)$ to an input $r(t)$, for the case where the roots of the denominator of $C(s)$ are real and distinct. The cases of repeated roots and complex conjugate pairs will now also be considered, and the s-plane will provide the basis for a graphical alternative to the analytical method of calculating the residues. This alternative enhances insight and is often preferred for more complicated transforms.

3.2 The S-Plane, Pole-Zero Patterns, and Residue Calculation

In the input-output relation $C(s) = G(s)R(s)$, each of C, G, and R is in general a ratio of polynomials in s. Definitions:

Zeros of C, G, and R are the roots of their numerator polynomials.

Poles of C, G, and R are the roots of their denominator polynomials.

System zeros and system poles are those of the system transfer function $G(S)$.

System characteristic polynomial is the name often used for the denominator polynomial of $G(s)$.

System characteristic equation identifies the result if the system characteristic polynomial is equated to zero. Evidently, its roots are the system poles.

Since the polynomials have real coefficients, poles and zeros are either real or occur in complex conjugate pairs. They are values of s and can be plotted on a complex plane called the s-plane. Because $s=\sigma+j\omega$, the real axis of this plane is the σ-axis, and frequencies are plotted along the imaginary $j\omega$-axis. It is important to note that angles in the s-plane have great significance, and therefore the scales on both axes must be identical.

Figure 3.1(a) shows this plane and the system poles and zero of the transfer function

$$G(s)=\frac{2K}{3}\frac{0.5s+1}{(1/3)s^2+(4/3)s+1}=\frac{K(s+2)}{(s+1)(s+3)} \tag{3.1}$$

This is the system pole-zero pattern. The potential power of representing all dynamic characteristics by the positions of a number of points in this manner may be appreciated.

For a unit step input $R(s)=1/s$, the pole-zero pattern of $R(s)$ consists of just a pole at the origin of the s-plane. Since $C(s)=G(s)R(s)$, the pole-zero pattern of $C(S)$ in Fig. 3.1(b) is simply the

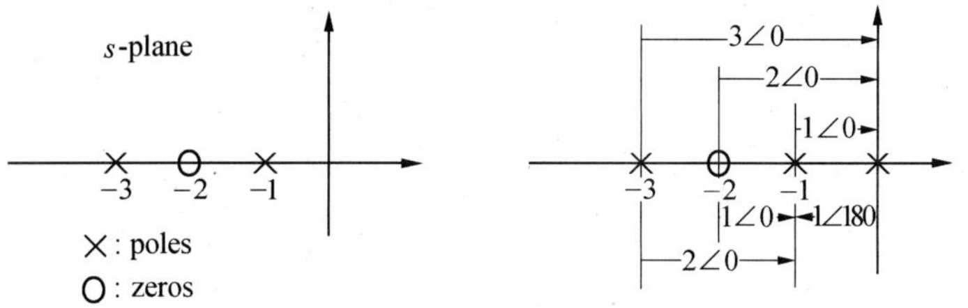

(a) (b)

Fig. 3.1 Pole-zero patterns of $G(s)$ (a) and $C(s)$ (b)

superposition of those of $G(s)$ and of $R(s)$

$$C(s)=G(s)R(s)=\frac{K(s+2)}{s(s+1)(s+3)} \tag{3.2}$$

Graphical Determination of Residues

To derive this important alternative to the analytical method in Section 1.7, it is recalled that in the partial fraction expansion

$$C(s)=\frac{K(s+2)}{s(s+1)(s+3)}=\frac{K_1}{s}+\frac{K_2}{s+1}+\frac{K_3}{s+3} \tag{3.3}$$

of the output transform, the residues are

$$K_1=\frac{K(s+2)}{(s+1)(s+3)}\bigg|_{s=0}\qquad K_2=\frac{K(s+2)}{s(s+3)}\bigg|_{s=-1}\qquad K_3=\frac{K(s+2)}{s(s+1)}\bigg|_{s=-3} \tag{3.4}$$

Vector method can help to interpret the typical factor $(s+a)\Big|_{s=b}$ in these expressions in terms of a vector in the s-plane. The factor is

$$(s+a)\big|_{s=b}=b+a=b-(-a)$$

Here b is a vector from the origin to point b in the s-plane, and $-a$ from the origin to point $-a$. The difference of these two vectors is that from $-a$ to b, and this vector can be represented by $Ae^{j\alpha}$, where A is the vector length and α the angle, measured positive counterclockwise from the direction of the positive real axis

$$(s+a)\big|_{s=b}=b+a=b-(-a)=(\text{vector from}-a\text{ to }b)=Ae^{j\alpha}=A\angle\alpha \quad (3.5)$$

Here A and α may be found by measurement or calculation from the s-plane. Now a residue of the form of the K_i in (3.4) is

$$K_i=\frac{K(s+a)}{(s+b)(s+c)}\bigg|_{s=-d}=\frac{K(A\angle\alpha)}{(B\angle\beta)(C\angle\gamma)}=\frac{KA}{BC}\angle\alpha-\beta-\gamma \quad (3.6)$$

To find K_l in (3.4), vectors as shown in the upper half of Fig. 3.1(b) are drawn to the pole $s=0$ of $C(s)$ from its zero at -2 and its other two poles at -1 and -3, and these give

$$K_1=\frac{K(2\angle 0)}{(1\angle 0)(3\angle 0)}=\frac{2}{3}K\angle 0=\frac{2}{3}K$$

The residue K_2 at the pole -2 is found from the vectors to this point, in the bottom half of Fig. 3.1(b). The vector from the pole at $s=0$ to that at -1 is in the direction of the negative real axis, so has angle $\pm180°$.

$$K_2=\frac{K(1\angle 0)}{(1\angle 180)(2\angle 0)}=\frac{1}{2}K\angle 180=-\frac{1}{2}K$$

Similarly

$$K_3=\frac{K(1\angle 180)}{(3\angle 180)(2\angle 180)}=\frac{1}{6}K\angle 180-360=-\frac{1}{6}K$$

These values of K_1, K_2 and K_3 may be verified using the analytical method, and give

$$c(t)=K\left(\frac{2}{3}-\frac{1}{2}e^{-t}-\frac{1}{6}e^{-3t}\right) \quad (3.7)$$

The gain factor K in (3.1) to (3.3) will be called the root locus gain:

The root locus gain factor of a transform or a transfer function is that which results if the coefficients of the highest powers of s in numerator and denominator are made equal to unity. [注1]

For, say,

$$C(s)=2\frac{0.5s+1}{(s+3)(0.1s+1)}=\frac{2(0.5)}{0.1}\frac{s+2}{(s+3)(s+10)}$$

the root locus gain is $2(0.5/0.1)=10$.

Reviewing the expressions for K_1, K_2 and K_3 reveals the following general rule:

The residue K_i at the $-p_i$ of $C(s)$ equals the root locus gain times the product of the vectors from all zeros of $C(s)$ to $-p_i$ divided by the product of the vectors from all other poles of $C(s)$ *to* $-p_i$.

Example 3.2.1

There is a level control system of which the process consists of the two-tank system with control valve and the level in the second tank is to be controlled. Find the unit step response of the system for $K=0.025$. The close-loop transfer function is

$$\frac{C}{R}=\frac{(0.025)5}{(0.5s+1)(0.2s+1)+(0.025)5}=\frac{1.25}{s^2+7s+11.25}=\frac{125}{(s+2.5)(s+4.5)}$$

and with $R(s)=1/s$.

$$C(s)=\frac{1.25}{s(s+2.5)(s+4.5)}=\frac{K_1}{s}+\frac{K_2}{s+2.5}+\frac{K_3}{s+4.5}$$

The pole-zero pattern of $C(s)$ and the graphical residue rule now yield

$$K_1=\frac{1.25}{(2.5\angle 0)(4.5\angle 0)}=\frac{1}{9}$$

$$K_2=\frac{1.25}{(2.5\angle 180)(2\angle 0)}=-\frac{1}{4} \tag{3.8}$$

$$K_3=\frac{1.25}{(4.5\angle 180)(2\angle 180)}=\frac{1.25}{9}$$

$$c(t)=\frac{1}{9}-\frac{1}{4}e^{-2.5t}+\frac{1.25}{9}e^{-4.5t}$$

3.3 Transient Response, Including Repeated and Complex Poles

In this section, transient responses are calculated for the cases of repeated real poles, a complex conjugate pair of poles, and combinations of distinct real poles and complex conjugate pairs.

Repeated Real Poles

Suppose that $C(s)$ has m poles at $-p_l$

$$C(s)=\frac{Z(s)}{(s+p_1)^m(s+p_2)\cdots(s+p_n)} \tag{3.9}$$

Then it can be shown that the partial fraction expansion must be written as follows

$$C(s)=\frac{K_1}{(s+p_1)^m}+\frac{K_2}{(s+p_1)^{m-1}}+\cdots+\frac{K_m}{s+p_1}+\frac{K_{m+1}}{s+p_2}+\cdots+\frac{K_{m+n-1}}{s+p_n} \tag{3.10}$$

The residues $K_{m+1},\cdots,K_{m+n-1}$ are found as before, but for the repeated root the equation is

$$K_i=\frac{1}{(i-1)!}\frac{\mathrm{d}^{i-1}}{\mathrm{d}s^{i-1}}[C(s)(s+p_1)^m]\Bigg|_{s=-p_1} \quad i=1,\cdots,m \tag{3.11}$$

Example 3.3.1

Find the response to a unit ramp input, $R(s)=1/s^2$, of the system

$$G(S)=\frac{1}{Ts+1} \quad \text{(simple lag)} \tag{3.12}$$

$$C(s)=G(s)R(s)=\frac{1}{s^2(Ts+1)}=\frac{K_1}{s^2}+\frac{K_2}{s}+\frac{K_3}{s+1/T}$$

K_1 and K_3 can be found in the usual way

$$K_3=\left[\left(s+\frac{1}{T}\right)\frac{1}{s^2(Ts+1)}\right]\Bigg|_{s=-1/T}=\frac{1}{Ts^2}\Bigg|_{s=1/T}=T$$

$$K_1=\left[s^2\frac{1}{s^2(Ts+1)}\right]=\frac{1}{Ts+1}\Bigg|_{s=0}=1$$

But if to determine K_2 the equation is multiplied by its denominator s, the first term becomes K_1/s and tends to infinity for $s\to 0$. Equation (3.11) arises by first multiplying both sides of the equation by s^2

$$s^2C(s)=K_1+K_2s+\frac{K_3s^2}{s+1/T}$$

K_1 is eliminated by differentiating both sides

$$\frac{\mathrm{d}}{\mathrm{d}s}[s^2C(s)]=K_2+K_3s\frac{2(s+1/T)-s}{(s+1/T)^2}$$

If now $s\to 0$, only K_2 remains on the right, so that, as in (3.11)

$$K_2=\frac{\mathrm{d}}{\mathrm{d}s}(s^2C)\bigg|_{s=0}=\frac{\mathrm{d}}{\mathrm{d}s}\left(\frac{1}{Ts+1}\right)\bigg|_{s=0}=-T$$

hence

$$C(s)=\frac{1}{s^2}-\frac{T}{s}+\frac{T}{s+1/T}$$

Using Table 1.6.1, the transient response is

$$c(t)=t-T+T\mathrm{e}^{-t/T}$$

Since the simple lag is so common, this response has been sketched in Fig. 3.2. The value T of the steady-state ($t\to\infty$) difference between r and c could have been found more directly by the final value theorem

$$\lim_{t\to\infty}[r(t)-c(t)]=\lim_{s\to 0}s[R(s)-C(s)]=\lim_{s\to 0}s\left[\frac{T}{s(Ts+1)}\right]=T$$

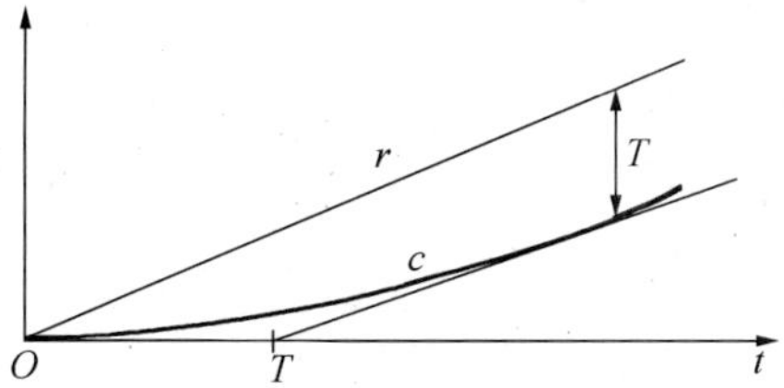

Fig. 3.2 Simple lag ramp response

Example 3.3.2 Example 3.2.1 for $K=0.045$

The response for $K=0.025$ in Example 3.2.1, with a steady-state output of 1/9 for a unit step input, so a steady-state error of 8/9, is really quite poor. For $K=0.045$ it is found that

$$\frac{C}{R}=\frac{2.25}{s^2+7s+12.25}=\frac{2.25}{(s+3.5)}$$

and for a unit step input

$$C=\frac{2.25}{s(s+3.5)^2}=\frac{K_1}{s}+\frac{K_2}{(s+3.5)^2}+\frac{K_3}{(s+3.5)}$$

$$K_1=[sC(s)]\Big|_{s=0}=\frac{9}{49}=0.187$$

$$K_2=[(s+3.5)^2C(s)]\Big|_{s=-3.5}=\frac{2.25}{s}\Big|_{s=-3.5}=-0.742\,9$$

$$K_1=\frac{\mathrm{d}}{\mathrm{d}s}(\frac{2.25}{s})\Big|_{s=-3.5}=\frac{-2.25}{s^2}\Big|_{s=-3.5}=-0.183\,7$$

hence

$$c(t)=0.183\,7-0.742\,9te^{-3.5t}-0.183\,7e^{-3.5t}$$

The steady-state error $1-0.183\,7=0.816\,3$ has been reduced, as expected with an increase of K, but is still quite large.

A Complex Conjugate Pair of Poles

The technique for distinct real poles applies also for distinct complex poles, but the residues are now complex, and the graphical approach tends to be simpler than the analytical one. [注2]

Example 3.3.3

From Table 1.6.1

$$C(s)=\frac{\omega_n^2}{s(s^2+2\zeta\omega_n s+\omega_n^2)} \tag{3.13}$$

This could be the unit impulse response of a system $G(s)=C(s)$ or the unit step response of

$$G(s)=\frac{\omega_n^2}{s^2+2\zeta\omega_n s+\omega_n^2}$$

For $\zeta<1$, the poles of $C(s)$ are

$$s_1 = 0 \quad s_2 = -\zeta\omega_n + j\omega_n\sqrt{1-\zeta^2} \quad s_3 = -\zeta\omega_n - j\omega_n\sqrt{1-\zeta^2} \tag{3.14}$$

Its partial fraction expansion

$$C(s) = \frac{K_1}{s} + \frac{K_2}{s+\zeta\omega_n - j\omega_n\sqrt{1-\zeta^2}} + \frac{K_3}{s+\zeta\omega_n + j\omega_n\sqrt{1-\zeta^2}}$$

shows that the response will be of the form

$$c(t) = K_1 + e^{-\zeta\omega_n t}[k_2 \exp(j\omega_n\sqrt{1-\zeta^2}\,t) + k_3 \exp(-j\omega_n\sqrt{1-\zeta^2}\,t)]$$

To determine the K_i, it is readily verified that the distance of s_2 and s_3 to the origin equals ω_n, and the angle ϕ is given by

$$\tan\phi = \frac{\sqrt{1-\zeta^2}}{\zeta} \tag{3.15}$$

The root locus gain is ω_n^2, and the graphical residue rule gives the following, where it is noted that angles clockwise from the positive real-axis direction are negative

$$K_1 = \frac{\omega_n^2}{(\omega_n \angle -\phi)(\omega_n \angle +\phi)} = 1$$

$$K_2 = \frac{\omega_n^2}{(\omega_n \angle \pi - \phi)(2\omega_n\sqrt{1-\zeta^2}\angle \pi/2)} = \frac{1}{2\sqrt{1-\zeta^2}} \angle -\phi - 3\pi/2 = \frac{1}{2\sqrt{1-\zeta^2}} \angle \phi + \pi/2$$

$$K_3 = \frac{\omega_n^2}{(\omega_n \angle \pi + \phi)(2\omega_n\sqrt{1-\zeta^2}\angle -\pi/2)} = \frac{1}{2\sqrt{1-\zeta^2}} \angle -\phi - \pi/2$$

Using $e^{j\pi/2} = j = -1/j$ and $e^{-j\pi/2} = -j = 1/j$, substitution into $c(t)$ yields

$$c(t) = 1 - \frac{1}{\sqrt{1-\zeta^2}} e^{-\zeta\omega_n t} \frac{1}{2j}\{\exp[j(\omega_n\sqrt{1-\zeta^2}\,t + \phi)] - \exp[-j(\omega_n\sqrt{1-\zeta^2}\,t + \phi)]\} =$$

$$1 - \frac{1}{\sqrt{1-\zeta^2}} e^{-\zeta\omega_n t} \sin(\omega_n\sqrt{1-\zeta^2}\,t + \phi)$$

This verifies the entry in Table 1.6.1.

An alternative form will actually prove much more useful when the extension to systems with more poles is considered. It is obtained by noting that

$$K_2 = \frac{1}{2\sqrt{1-\zeta^2}} \angle \theta \quad K_3 = \frac{1}{2\sqrt{1-\zeta^2}} \angle -\theta \quad \theta = \phi + \frac{\pi}{2} \tag{3.17}$$

where θ is the phase angle of residue K_2. The solution is then seen to be

$$c(t) = 1 + \frac{1}{\sqrt{1-\zeta^2}} e^{-\zeta\omega_n t} \cos(\omega_n \sqrt{1-\zeta^2}\, t + \theta) \tag{3.18}$$

Distinct Real Poles and Complex Conjugate Pairs

For distinct poles, whether real or complex, the partial fraction expansion of $C(s) = G(s)R(s)$ and the corresponding solution $c(t)$ are

$$C(s) = \frac{K_1}{s+p_1} + \frac{K_2}{s+p_2} + \cdots + \frac{K_n}{s+p_n} \tag{3.19}$$

$$c(t) = K_1 \exp(-p_1 t) + K_2 \exp(-p_2 t) + \cdots + K_n \exp(-p_n t)$$

All residues can be found by the graphical rule. Those corresponding to real poles will be real. For complex conjugate pairs, if $-p_i$ and $-p_{i+1}$ form such a pair, K_i and K_{i+1} are also complex conjugate, as in (3.17), because all poles and zeros are real or occur in pairs which are complex conjugate. Hence let

$$p_i = \zeta_i \omega_{ni} - j\omega_{ni}\sqrt{1-\zeta_i^2} \quad K_i = K_i e^{j\theta_i} = K_i \angle \theta_i \tag{3.20}$$

where K_i is the magnitude and θ_i the phase. Then

$$p_{i+1} = \zeta_i \omega_{ni} + j\omega_{ni}\sqrt{1-\zeta_i^2} \quad K_{i+1} = K_i \angle -\theta_i$$

and the corresponding terms in the inverse are

$$K_i \exp(-p_i t) + K_{i+1} \exp(-p_{i+1} t) =$$

$$K_i \exp(-\zeta\omega_{ni} t)\{\exp[j(\omega_{ni}\sqrt{1-\zeta_i^2}\, t + \theta_i)] + \exp[-j(\omega_{ni}\sqrt{1-\zeta_i^2}\, t + \theta_i)]\} =$$

$$2K_i \exp(-\zeta\omega_{ni} t)\cos(\omega_{ni}\sqrt{1-\zeta_i^2}\, t + \theta_i) \tag{3.21}$$

Thus, in general, if $C(s)$ has k real poles $-p_i$ and m complex conjugate pairs of the form of (3.20), the total response is

$$c(t)=\sum_{i=1}^{k} K_{ni}\exp(-p_i t)+2\sum_{i=1}^{m} K_i\exp(-\zeta_i\omega_{ni}t)\cos(\omega_{ni}\sqrt{1-\zeta_i^2}\,t+\theta_i) \qquad (3.22)$$

Example 3.3.4

Find the unit step response of a system with transfer function

$$G(s)=\frac{0.89}{(0.5s+1)(s^2+s+0.89)} \qquad (3.23)$$

The roots of the quadratic are $(-0.5\pm0.8j)$, and Fig. 3.3 shows the pole-zero pattern of

$$C(s)=\frac{1.78}{s(s+2)(s-0.5-0.8j)(s+0.5+0.8j)}$$

The root locus gain is 1.78, and Fig. 3.3 shows significant vector lengths and angles for determination of the residues. The residues corresponding to the poles indicated are, from the graphical rule,

$$K_1=\frac{1.78}{(2\angle 0)(0.943\angle -58°)(0.943\angle 58°)}=1$$

$$K_2=\frac{1.78}{(2\angle 180)(1.7\angle 208.1)(1.7\angle 151.9)}=-0.307$$

$$K_3=\frac{1.78}{(1.7\angle 28.1)(0.943\angle 122)(1.6\angle 90)}=0.693\angle 120$$

From (3.22), then, the response is

$$c(t)=1-0.307e^{-2t}+1.386e^{-0.5t}\cos(0.8t+120°) \qquad (3.24)$$

since

$$-\zeta\omega_n=-0.5=\text{real part of complex poles}$$

$$\omega_n\sqrt{1-\zeta^2}=0.8=\text{imaginary part}$$

Note that $C(0)=1-0.307+1.386\cos 120°=0$

The denominator of $C(s)=G(s)R(s)$ and its partial fraction expansion contain terms due to the poles of input $R(s)$ and those of the

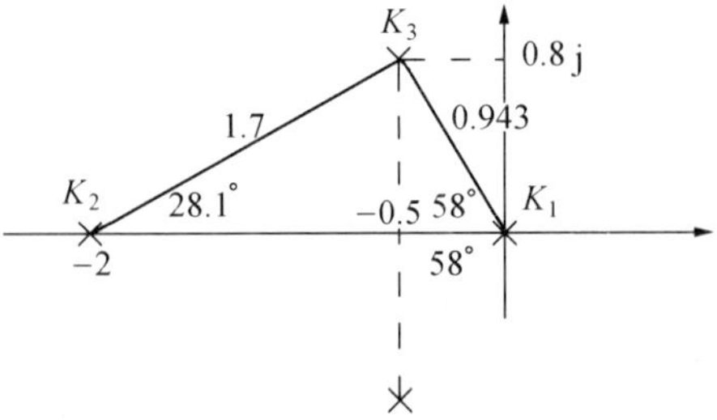

Fig. 3.3 Example 3.3.4

system $G(s)$. The terms due to $R(s)$ yield the forced solution, corresponding to the particular integral solution of a differential equation, and the system poles give the transient solution. These parts of the solution may be identified in all examples thus far.

The system poles are real or occur in complex pairs, so the transient solution, which must decay to zero for the system to be useful, is the sum of the responses for these two types, called simple lag and quadratic lag.

These two basic types of systems will now be considered in turn, with emphasis on the correlations between the nature of the response and the pole positions in the s-plane.

3.4 Simple Lag : First-Order Systems

Chapter 2 has shown that this system, with its pole-zero pattern , is very common. For a step input $R(s)=1/s$.

$$G(s)=\frac{K_1}{s}+\frac{K_2}{s+1/T}$$

$$K_1=1 \qquad K_2=-1$$

Hence the transient response is

$$c(t)=1-e^{-t/T} \tag{3.25}$$

The first term is the forced solution, due to the input, and the second the transient solution, due to the system pole. Fig. 3.4 shows this transient as well as $c(t)$. The transient is seen to be a decaying exponential. If it takes long to decay, the system response is slow, so the speed of decay is of key importance. The commonly used measure of this speed of decay is the time constant:

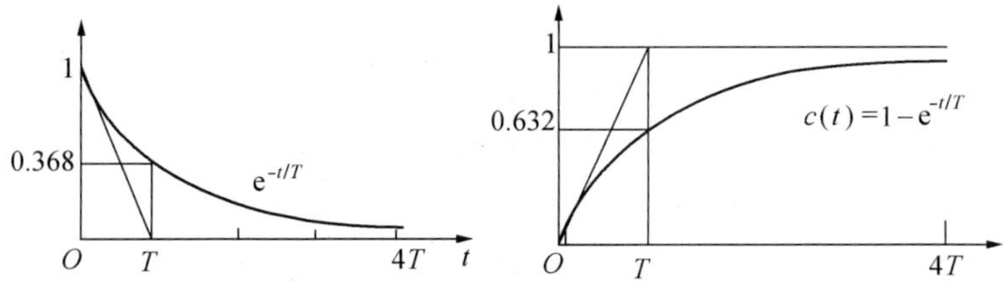

Fig. 3.4 Step response of simple lag

The time constant is the time in seconds for the decaying exponential transient to be reduced to $e^{-1}=0.368$ of its initial value. Since $e^{-t/T}=e^{-1}$ when $t=T$, it is seen that

The time constant for a simple lag $1/(Ts+1)$ is T seconds. This is, in fact, the reason a simple lag transfer function is often written in this form. The coefficient of s then immediately indicates the speed of decay. It takes 4T seconds for the transient to decay to 1.8% of its initial value. At $t=T$, $c(T)=1-0.368=0.632$.

The values at $t = T$ provide one point for sketching the curves in Fig. 3.4.

Since

$$\frac{\mathrm{d}}{\mathrm{d}t}(e^{-t/T})\bigg|_{t=0}=-\frac{1}{T}$$

it follows also that the curves are initially tangent to the dashed lines in Fig. 3.4. These two facts provide a good sketch of the response.

⋮

Now consider the correlation between this response and the pole position at $s=-1/T$. The purpose of developing such insight is that it will permit the nature of the transient response of a system to be judged by inspection of its pole-zero pattern.

For the simple lag, two features are important:

Stability

If $-1/T$ is positive, the pole lies in the right half of the s-plane. The transient $e^{-t/T}$ then grows instead of decays as t increases. The system is unstable and useless. Hence the most important rule for design:

For system stability, the system pole(s) must lie in the left half of the s-plane.

Speed of response

To speed up the response of the system (i. e., to reduce its time constant T), the pole $-1/T$ must be moved left.

How such movement is to be achieved is a problem of design, considered later. Example 2.8.1 and comparison of Examples 3.2.1 and 3.3.2 suggest, however, the use of feedback around the simple lag plant, together with an adjustable gain.

3.5 Quadratic Lag: Second-Order Systems

This very common transfer function can always be reduced to the standard form

$$G(s)=\frac{\omega_n^2}{s^2+2\zeta\omega_n s+\omega_n^2} \tag{3.26}$$

where ω_n = undamped natural frequency;

ζ = damping ratio.

The significance of these parameters will be discussed. For a unit step input $R(s)=1/s$, the transform of the output is

$$C(s)=\frac{\omega_n^2}{s(s^2+2\zeta\omega_n s+\omega_n^2)} \tag{3.27}$$

For $\zeta<1$, this is an entry in Table 1. 6. 1, verified in example 3. 3. 3. However there are three possibilities, depending on the roots of the system characteristic equation

$$s^2+2\zeta\omega_n s+\omega_n^2=0 \tag{3.28}$$

These system poles depend on ζ

$$\begin{aligned} &\zeta>1\text{, overdamped} && s_{1,2}=-\zeta\omega_n\pm\omega_n\sqrt{\zeta^2-1} \\ &\zeta=1\text{, critically damped} && s_{1,2}=-\omega_n \\ &\zeta<1\text{, underdamped} && s_{1,2}=-\zeta\omega_n\pm \mathrm{j}\omega_n\sqrt{1-\zeta^2} \end{aligned} \tag{3.29}$$

Fig. 3. 5 shows the s-plane for plotting the pole positions. For $\zeta>1$ these are on the negative real axis, on both sides of $-\omega_n$. For $\zeta=1$, both poles coincide at $-\omega_n$. For $\zeta<1$, the poles move along a circle of radius ω_n centered at the origin, as may be seen from the following expression for the distance of the poles to the origin

$$|s_{1,2}|=[(\zeta\omega_n)^2+(\omega_n\sqrt{1-\zeta^2})^2]^{1/2}=\omega_n$$

Form the geometry in Fig. 3. 5, it is seen also that $\cos\phi=\zeta\omega_n/\omega_n=\zeta$. Hence

The damping ratio $\zeta=\cos\phi$, where ϕ is the position angle of the poles with negative real axis.

An angle of $\phi=45°$ corresponds to $\zeta=0.707$, angle $\phi=60°$ to a damping ratio $\zeta=0.5$.

For $\zeta>1$, when the poles are real and distinct, the transient is a sum of two decaying exponential, each with its own time constant.

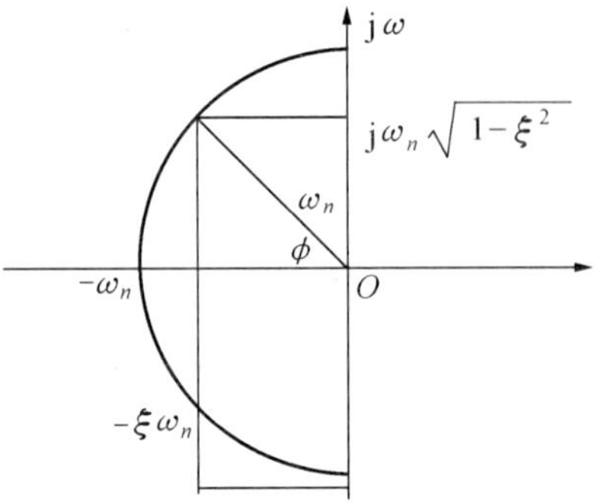

Fig. 3.5 System poles quadratic lag

Example 3.5.1

$$G(s)=\frac{2}{(s+1)(s+2)}$$

For a unit step,

$$C(s)=\frac{K_1}{s}+\frac{K_2}{s+1}+\frac{K_3}{S+2}$$

and it is found that

$$c(t)=1-2e^{-t}+e^{-2t}$$

The nature of this result, that the transient consists of exponentials with time constants $T_1=1$ and $T_2=0.5$, could have been predicted from inspection of the system pole-zero pattern . The system is a series connection of two simple lags. The exponential corresponding to the pole closest to the origin has the largest time constant and takes longest to decay. This is called the dominating pole, and to increase the speed of response it would have to be moved to the left.

For $\zeta=1$, a repeated root occurs at $-\omega_n$, and responses can be calculated as in Example 3.3.1 and 3.3.2.

For $\zeta<1$, the result in Table 1.6.1, verified by (3.15) and (3.16), applies

$$c(t)=1-\frac{1}{\sqrt{1-\zeta^2}}e^{-\zeta\omega_n t}\sin(\omega_n\sqrt{1-\zeta^2}\,t+\arctan\frac{\sqrt{1-\zeta^2}}{\zeta}) \quad (3.30)$$

The transient term is an oscillation of damped natural frequency $\omega_n\sqrt{1-\zeta^2}$, of which the amplitude decays according to $e^{-\zeta\omega_n t}$. For an underdamped second-order system

The time constant T is the time in seconds for the amplitude of oscillation to decay to e^{-1} of its initial value: $e^{-\zeta\omega_n t}=e^{-1}$. Hence

$$T=1/(\zeta\omega_n) \quad (3.31)$$

Analogous to the simple lag, the amplitude decays to 2% of its initial value in $4T$ seconds.

⋮

There are some important performance criteria of the response: Settling time T_s is the time required for the response to come permanently within a 5% or 2% band around the steady-state value.

$$T_s=3T(5\%)$$

$$T_s=4T(2\%) \quad (3.32)$$

The maximum percentage overshoot ($P.\ O$) over the steady-state response is a critical measure of performance. Equating the derivative of $c(t)$ in (3.30) to zero, to determine the extrema of the response, easily yields the equation

$$\tan\left(\omega_n\sqrt{1-\zeta^2}\,t+\arctan\frac{\sqrt{1-\zeta^2}}{\zeta}\right)=\frac{\sqrt{1-\zeta^2}}{\zeta} \quad (3.33)$$

This implies that at the peaks

$$\omega_n\sqrt{1-\zeta^2}\,t=i\pi \qquad i=1,3,\cdots$$

since then left and right sides are equal. Hence the time at the maximum peak ($i=1$), the peak time T_p, is

$$T_p = \frac{\pi}{\omega_n \sqrt{1-\zeta}} \tag{3.34}$$

If the tan of the angle in (3.33) is $\sqrt{1-\zeta^2}/\zeta$, its sin is $\pm\sqrt{1-\zeta^2}$, and substituting (3.34) into (3.30) yields

$$P.\ O. = 100\exp\left(\frac{-\pi\zeta}{\sqrt{1-\zeta^2}}\right) \tag{3.35}$$

The rise time T_r, the time at which the response first reaches the steady-state level, is closely related to peak time T_p.

It is noted that while T_s, T_p, and T_r depend on both ω_n and ζ, $P.\ O.$ depends only on the damping ratio ζ. Fig. 3.6 shows a graph of $P.\ O.$ versus damping ratio ζ. Permissible overshoot, and hence minimum acceptable ζ, depends on the application. For a machine tool slide, overshoot may cause the tool to gouge into the material being machined, so $\zeta \geqslant 1$ is required. But in most cases a limited overshoot is quite acceptable, and then $\zeta < 1$ is preferable, because it reduces peak time T_p in (3.34) and rise time T_r. For $\zeta = 0.7$ the overshoot is only 5% and the response approaches steady state much sooner.

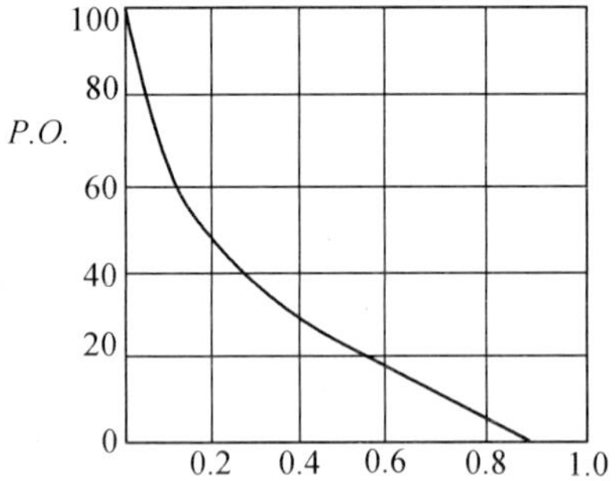

Fig. 3.6 $P.\ O.$ versus ζ

If the damping ratio could be held constant while ω_n is increased, the poles would move radially outward and both settling time and rise time would decrease. An example is given to clarify how for complex poles both of these affect the system speed of response, and also to demonstrate what constraints may exist on how the poles of a closed-loop system can be adjusted.

Example 3.5.2 DC Motor Position Servo

Fig. 3.7(a) shows the block diagram of the servo considered in

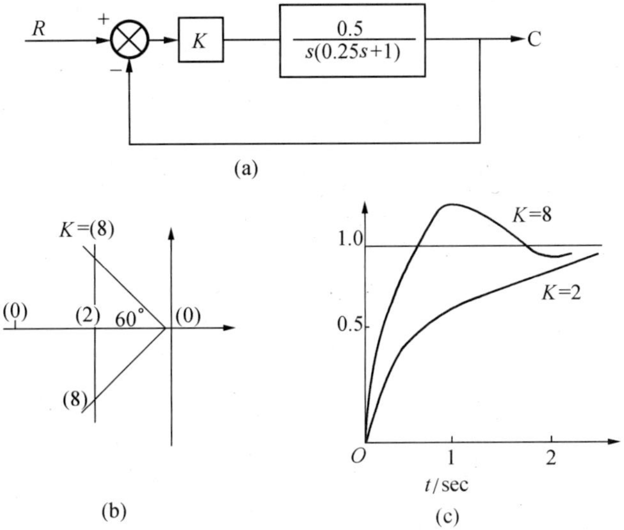

Fig. 3.7 Example 3.5.2

Example 2.8.1. The closed-loop transfer function is

$$\frac{C(s)}{R(s)}=\frac{2K}{s^2+4s+2K}$$

and the system poles are $s_{1,2}=-2\pm\sqrt{4-2K}$. For $K<2$ these poles lie along the negative real axis in the s-plane in Fig. 3.7(b). This corresponds to $\zeta>1$, and the transient is a superposition of two decaying exponential.

For $K=2$ both poles coincide at -2. By the technique used in Example 3.3.2, the unit step response, the inverse of $C(s)=4/[s(s+$

2)^2], is

$$c(t)=1-2te^{-2t}-e^{2t}$$

This is plotted in Fig. 3.7(c). Now, for $K=8$ the poles are the roots of $s^2+4s+16=0$, which corresponds to $\omega_n=4$, $\zeta=0.5$, and are located at $s_{1,2}=-2\pm3.464j$ The real part of the system poles is -2 for all $K\geqslant2$, so that the time constant and settling time are the same for $K=2$ and $K=8$. Yet clearly the plot for $K=8$ reflects a higher speed of response. The difference lies in the smaller peak time and rise time associated with the larger values of K and ω_n. The constraints on pole positions limit the poles to the real axis between 0 and -4 and the vertical at -2. This is, in fact, the root locus for the system, studied in Chapter 6.

As for the simple lag, it is again important to determine the correlations between dynamic behavior and the pole positions in the s-plane in Fig. 3.5:

Absolute stability

The real part of the pole positions is $\zeta\omega_n$. If this is positive, then from (3.30) for $c(t)$, the transient will grow instead of decay due to $e^{-\zeta\omega_n t}$. Hence, for stability the poles must lie in the left half of the s-plane.

Relative stability

To avoid excessive overshoot and unduly oscillatory behavior, damping ratio ζ must be adequate. Since $\zeta=\cos\phi$, the angle ϕ may not be close to 90°.

Settling time

Time constant and settling time are reduced by increasing the real part of the pole positions.

Frequency of transient oscillations $\omega_n\sqrt{1-\zeta^2}$

This frequency, also called the resonant frequency or damped natural frequency, equals the imaginary part of the pole positions.

Undamped natural frequency ω_n

This equals the distance of the poles to the origin. Moving the poles out radially (i. e., with ζ constant) reduces settling time, peak time, and rise time while the percentage overshoot remains constant.

Speed of response

For a constant real part, this is improved by increasing the imaginary part until ζ is reduced to a permissible level, thus reducing peak time and rise time.

3.6 Performance and Stability of Higher-Order Systems

Higher-order systems arise all too easily. For example, in mechanical drives an electric or hydraulic motor may operate a rotating system that must be modeled by a number of inertias and interconnecting torsion springs, as in Example 2.23. Each added spring-inertia combination in effect adds two poles. An analogous situation exists for multimass translating, instead of rotating, systems along the lines of Example 2.2.2. Temperature control with multiple thermal capacitances as in Example 2.5.3 augmenting the dynamics of the heat source can also involve high-order transfer functions.

Although high-order dynamics are most often caused by the process, other elements in the loop also contribute. For example, a third-order transfer function was derived in Example 2.7.3 to model a valve-controlled hydraulic cylinder with allowance for the effect of oil compressibility. In this model the mechanical displacement of the spool valve was the input. However, in high-pressure hydraulic servos the forces required for positioning this valve are quite large and are generated instead by applying hydraulic pressures to the ends of the spool. These pressures are generated in a first stage of hydraulic power amplification, with the valve itself acting as the second stage. In two-stage electrohydraulic servos, used extensively in many areas of engineering for high-performance positioning of heavy loads, the first-stage amplifier often involves an electromagnetic torque motor, and the system input is an electrical signal. For high-performance design it may be necessary to allow for the effects of motor inertia and valve spool mass as well as oil compressibility, and the transfer function from input to valve spool position can be of sixth order, raising that from input to output from order 3 to 9. [注3]

Nature of the Transient Response and Dominating Poles

Whatever the order of the transfer function, it may be stated from the preceding sections and (3.19) that, since each real pole causes a decaying exponential transient and each complex pair a decaying oscillation:

The total transient response is a superposition of exponential decays and decaying oscillations.

Repeated roots do not change this in an essential way. If all parameters are known, the response can be calculated, but its nature can also be judged without this by inspection of the pole positions. During design the parameters are not known and the aim is to use feedback which locates the poles in regions corresponding to satisfactory dynamics, that is, not too close to the imaginary axis and at a small enough angle to the negative real axis. [注4]

The dominating-poles concept is very important in this connection and simplifies design greatly. The response of many systems is dominated by one pair of complex poles relatively close to the imaginary axis, Design can therefore concentrate on locating this dominating pair satisfactorily. The fact that many systems behave approximately as second-order systems is also the reason the performance criteria for second-order systems discussed in Section 3. 5 apply to higher-order systems as well. [注5]

Absolute and Relative Stability

The foregoing relative stability conditions on the locations of the dominating poles are much more stringent than those of absolute stability. Absolute stability requires only that all roots of the system characteristic equation

$$a_n s^n + a_{n-1} s^{n-1} + \cdots + a_1 s + a_0 = 0 \tag{3.36}$$

(i. e. , the poles of its transfer function) lie in the left-half s-plane. It is known that if any of the coefficients are zero or if not all coefficients have the same sign, there will be roots on or to the right of the imaginary axis, If all coefficients are present and have the same sign, which can be taken to be positive without loss of generality, the Routh-Hurwitz criterion discussed in the next section provides a quick method for determining absolute, but not relative, stability from the coefficients, without calculating the roots. [注6]

Computer-Aided Analysis and Design

For high-order systems and for routine work on those of lower order, computational aids are indispensable for analysis and design. For example, the techniques of Section 3. 3 for transient response calculation clearly become laborious for high-order systems. Computer aids can range from batch-type programs for specific purposes, such as finding the roots of a characteristic equation or calculating the response for a given transfer function, to interactive analysis and design packages which include computer graphics. [注7]

Because computer aids are not essential to the development of concepts and techniques, it is desirable to allow for freedom of choice as to the degree to which such aids are exploited in the study of the subject. Computational aids, with examples of their use, have therefore been collected in Appendix B, and reference to particular programs will be made at appropriate points in the text.

In the context of the present chapter, Appendix B gives a program for transient response computation based on partial fraction expansion, assuming distinct poles. For closed-loop systems, the poles needed for this must usually be found from the system characteristic equation (3. 36). Appendix B gives a routine for finding the roots of polynomials that can be used for this purpose.

3.7 Routh-Hurwitz Stability Criterion

The Routh-Hurwitz stability criterion is a method for determining from the coefficients of the characteristic equation (3. 36) how many system poles are in the right-half s-plane or on the imaginary axis.

Of the Routh array below, the first two rows are produced by arranging the coefficients $a_n, \cdots, a_0$ in the order indicated by the arrows.

$$
\begin{array}{llllll}
s^n: & a_n & a_{n-2} & a_{n-4} & \cdots & 0 \\
s^{n-1}: & a_{n-1} & a_{n-3} & a_{n-5} & \cdots & 0 \\
s^{n-2}: & b_1 & b_2 & b_3 & \cdots & 0 \\
s^{n-3}: & c_1 & c_2 & c_3 & \cdots & 0 \\
\vdots & & & & & \\
s^1: & g_1 & 0 & & & \\
s^0: & h_1 & 0 & & &
\end{array}
\tag{3.37}
$$

Each of the remaining entries $b_i, c_i, \cdots$ is found from the two rows preceding it according to a pattern that can be recognized from the following equations

$$
\begin{aligned}
b_1 &= \frac{-1}{a_{n-1}} \begin{vmatrix} a_n & a_{n-2} \\ a_{n-1} & a_{n-3} \end{vmatrix} = \frac{1}{a_{n-1}}(a_{n-1}a_{n-2} - a_n a_{n-3}) \\
b_2 &= \frac{-1}{a_{n-1}} \begin{vmatrix} a_n & a_{n-4} \\ a_{n-1} & a_{n-5} \end{vmatrix} = \frac{1}{a_{n-1}}(a_{n-1}a_{n-4} - a_n a_{n-5}) \\
b_3 &= \frac{-1}{a_{n-1}} \begin{vmatrix} a_n & a_{n-6} \\ a_{n-1} & a_{n-7} \end{vmatrix} = \frac{1}{a_{n-1}}(a_{n-1}a_{n-6} - a_n a_{n-7}) \\
c_1 &= \frac{-1}{b_n} \begin{vmatrix} a_{n-1} & a_{n-3} \\ b_1 & b_2 \end{vmatrix} = \frac{1}{b_1}(b_1 a_{n-3} - b_2 a_{n-1}) \\
c_2 &= \frac{-1}{b_1} \begin{vmatrix} a_{n-1} & a_{n-5} \\ b_1 & b_3 \end{vmatrix} = \frac{1}{b_1}(b_1 a_{n-5} - b_3 a_{n-1})
\end{aligned}
\tag{3.38}
$$

Calculations in each row are continued until only zero elements remain. In each of the last two rows the second and following elements are zero. It can be shown that the elements in any row can be multiplied by an arbitrary positive constant without affecting the results below. This can be useful to simplify the arithmetic. For large n, computer algorithms can be written, based on (3.38).

The Routh-Hurwitz criterion states:

(1) A necessary and sufficient condition for stability is that there be no changes of sign in the elements of the first column of the array (3.37).

(2) The number of these sign changes is equal to the number of roots in the right-half s-plane.

(3) If the first element in a row is zero, it is replaced by a very small positive number ε, and the sign changes when $\varepsilon \to 0$ are counted after completing the array.

(4) If all elements in a row are zero, the system has poles in the right-half plane or on the imaginary axis.

Example 3.7.1

$$s^5+s^4+6s^3+5s^2+12s+20=0$$

Using (3.37) and (3.38), the Routh array is

$$\begin{array}{ccccc}
s^5 & 1 & 6 & 12 & 0 \\
s^4 & 1 & 5 & 20 & 0 \\
s^3 & 1 & -8 & 0 & \\
s^2 & 13 & 20 & 0 & \\
s^1 & \dfrac{-124}{13} & 0 & & \\
s^0 & 20 & 0 & &
\end{array}$$

There are two sign changes in the first column, first from plus to minus and then from minus to plus. Hence this characteristic equation represents an unstable system, with two poles in the right-half s-plane.

Example 3.7.2

$$s^5+s^4+5s^3+5s^2+12s+10=0$$

The zero element in the first column for s^3 in the Routh array is replaced by a small positive number ε. Then

$$c_1 \approx \frac{-2}{\varepsilon} \qquad d_1 \approx 2$$

$$\begin{array}{lcccc}
s^5 & 1 & 5 & 12 & 0 \\
s^4 & 1 & 5 & 10 & 0 \\
s^3 & \varepsilon & 2 & 0 & \\
s^2 & c_1 & 2 & 0 & \\
s^1 & d_1 & 0 & & \\
s^0 & 10 & 0 & &
\end{array}$$

Thus c_1 is a large negative number, implying two unstable poles, as in Example 3.7.1.

Example 3.7.3

For the electromechanical servo modeled in Fig. 3.8, find the limits on K for stability. The characteristic equation is $s^3+3s^2+2s+K=0$ and the Routh array is

$$\begin{array}{lccc}
s^3 & 1 & 2 & 0 \\
s^2 & 3 & K & 0 \\
s^1 & \frac{6-K}{3} & 0 & \\
s^0 & K & 0 &
\end{array}$$

Evidently, $0<K<6$ is the range of K for a stable system.

At both limits in Example 3.7.3, one row of the Routh array consists of only zero elements. It can be shown that this means that root pairs are present which are located symmetrically about the origin, usu-

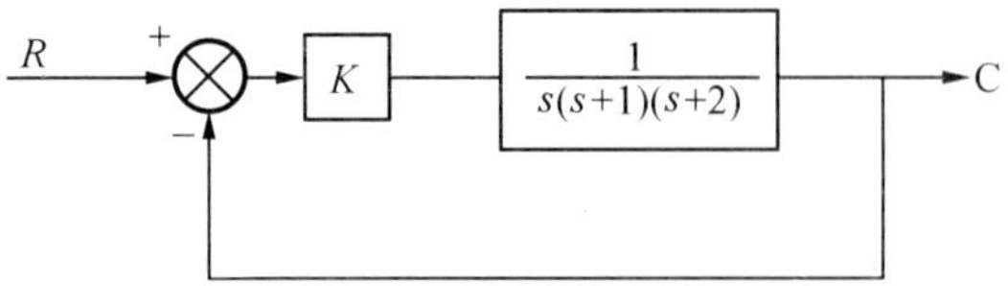

Fig. 3.8 Example 3.7.3

ally on the imaginary axis. It can also be shown that such root pairs are the roots of an auxiliary equation formulated from the elements in the row of the array which precedes that with the zeros.

For Example 3.7.3, at the upper limit $K=6$ the auxiliary equation is $3s^2+6=0$. The elements for row s^1 are zero, so it is formed from those for s^2. The highest power in the auxiliary equation is generally that of the row, and the power of successive terms reduce by 2.

The roots of the auxiliary equation are $s=\pm j\sqrt{2}=\pm 1.141j$. So at the limit $K=6$, system poles occur at these points on the imaginary axis. when several parameters vary, these techniques can be used to determine relations to be satisfied to ensure system stability.

3.8 Effect of System Zeros

Much attention has been given to system poles and the correlations between their positions in the s-plane and the nature of the transient response. A natural question is therefore what correlations exist between the response and the positions of the system zeros. The unit step response of a system with transfer function

$$G(s)=\frac{\omega_n^2}{z_1}\frac{s+z_1}{s^2+2\zeta\omega_n s+\omega_n^2} \tag{3.39}$$

will be studied to examine the effect of adding a zero to an underdamped quadratic lag.

The pole-zero pattern of $C(s)=G(s)R(s)$ is shown in Fig. 3.9. The residues K_1 and $(K_2 \angle \phi_2)$ in the solution $c(t)$ given by (3.22) are, by the graphical rule,

$$K_1 = 1$$

$$K_2 = \frac{A}{2z_1\sqrt{1-\zeta^2}} \angle (\alpha+\phi-3\pi/2)$$

and hence, by (3.22).

$$c(t) = 1 - \frac{A}{z_1\sqrt{1-\zeta^2}} e^{-\zeta\omega_n t} \sin(\omega_n \sqrt{1-\zeta^2}\, t+\phi+\alpha) \tag{3.40}$$

The geometry of Fig. 3.9 shows that if z_1 is large compared to ω_n, then $A \approx z_1$ and $\alpha = 0$. Equation (3.40) then reduces to the response for a quadratic lag given by (3.30). Thus a zero far along the axis has little effect on the transient response of the quadratic lag. But if the zero is moved to the right, it will cause a gradually increasing percentage overshoot ($P.O.$) and the peak time T_p will reduce. The proof is analogous to that of (3.33) to (3.35) for the quadratic lag: With $\phi = \arctan(\sqrt{1-\zeta^2}/\zeta)$, equating the derivative of $c(t)$ in (3.40) to zero yields

$$\tan[\omega_n \sqrt{1-\zeta^2}\, t+\alpha+\arctan(\sqrt{1-\zeta^2}/\zeta)] = \frac{\sqrt{1-\zeta^2}}{\zeta} \tag{3.41}$$

At the extrema, $\omega_n \sqrt{1-\zeta^2}\, t+\alpha = i\pi$, since then left and right sides are equal. The time T_p for the maximum peak ($i=1$) is

$$T_p = \frac{\pi-\alpha}{\omega_n \sqrt{1-\zeta^2}} \tag{3.42}$$

Since the tan of the angle in (3.41) is $\sqrt{1-\zeta^2}/\zeta$, its sin is $\pm\sqrt{1-\zeta^2}$, and using this and (3.42) in (3.40) yields the maximum overshoot

$$P.O. = 100\frac{A}{z_1}\exp\left[-\frac{(\pi-\alpha)\zeta}{\sqrt{1-\zeta^2}}\right] \tag{3.43}$$

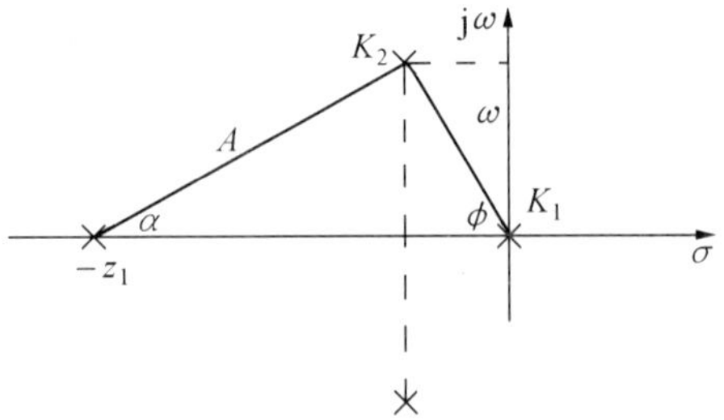

Fig. 3.9 Pole-zero pattern of $C(s)=G(s)/s$ for (3.39)

Here A and α can be measured or calculated from Fig. 3.9. Examples:

(1) If the zero is moved in from far left to the position where $\alpha=\pi/2$, (3.42) shows that the peak time is reduced by half.

(2) With $\alpha=\pi/2$ and $\phi=60$ ($\zeta=0.5$), in Fig. 3.9 $A/z_1=1.732$, and (3.43) yields an overshoot of almost 70%, a large increase over the 16% when the zero is far away.

The effect of zeros can be quite significant even if the ratio A/z_1 does not exceed 1. This is demonstrated in the next example, in which a number of feedback systems of the same structure are designed to have the same (closed-loop) poles and different zeros.

Example 3.8.1

Fig. 3.10(a) shows a control system with a simple lag process. The PI controller represents an extremely common form of control. The steady-state error for step inputs may be shown to be zero with this controller, by use of the final value theorem on $E(s)$ or $C(s)$. With a pure gain controller, this error would only approach zero for large values of gain. Except when the error E has become quite small, this would mean large process input signals (i. e., large flow rates of fluids or heat or current), implying a high cost of control.

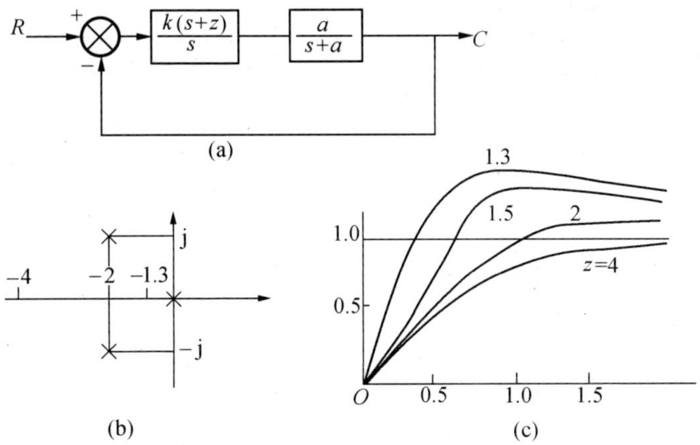

Fig. 3. 10 Example 3. 8. 1

Fig. 3. 10 (a) could model a single-tank level control (Example 2. 6. 1), a single-capacitance temperature control (Example 2. 5. 2), a pneumatic pressure control (Example 2. 6. 3), or a speed control servo, among other possibilities. For a motor speed control, the system output transform is $s\,\theta(s)$, the transform of $\dot{\theta}(s)$, and the motor transfer function in (2. 11) reduces to a simple lag. The feedback sensor could be a small generator, giving a feedback voltage proportional to shaft speed $\dot{\theta}(t)$.

The closed-loop transfer function in Fig. 3. 10(a) is

$$\frac{C(s)}{R(s)}=\frac{Ka(s+z)}{s^2+a(1+K)s+Kaz}$$

It is desired to make the closed-loop system poles equal to $-2\pm j$, that is, the denominator of C/R should be s^2+4s+5, or

$$a(1+K)=4 \qquad Kaz=5$$

Systems for which $z=4, 2, 1.5$, and 1.3, respectively, will then result for $Ka=1.25$, 2.5, $3.333\,3$, and 3.8462 with $a=2.75$, 1.5, $0.666\,7$, and $0.153\,8$. For a unit step input $R(s)=1/s$, the output transform is

$$C(s)=\frac{Ka(s+z)}{s(s^2+4s+5)}+\frac{5(1+s/z)}{s(s^2+4s+5)}$$

The pole-zero pattern is shown in Fig. 3. 10(b), and the graphical residue rule readily yields

$$c(t)=1+Ae^{-2t}\cos(t+\theta)$$

with the sets of values for (z,A,θ) equal to $(4,1.25,-216.9°)$, $(2,1.118,-153.4°)$, $(1.5,1.667,-126.9°)$, and $(1.3,2.1,-118.5°)$.

These responses are plotted in Fig. 3. 10(c). The system poles at $(-2\pm j)$ correspond to a damping ratio 0. 894, for which the overshoot is negligible and the peak time, from (3. 34), is 3. 13 sec. Moving the zero in from the left is seen to reduce the peak time and increase the overshoot. For $z=1.3$ the maximum overshoot is about 14% and occurs at about 1 sec. Thus care must be exercised in using the correlations between response and pole positions for a quadratic lag if zeros are present in relatively dominant locations.

The graphical technique for determining residues provides a particularly enlightening explanation for the effect of zeros.

Example 3. 8. 2

Find the unit step response of the system

$$G(s)=\frac{4}{a}\frac{s+a}{(s+1)(s+4)} \tag{3.44}$$

The pole-zero pattern of $C(s)=G(s)R(s)$ is shown in Fig. 3. 11. The residues are

$$K_1=1$$

$$K_2=\frac{-4(a-1)}{3a}$$

$$K_3=\frac{a-4}{3a}$$

So the unit step response is

$$c(t)=1-\frac{4(a-1)}{3a}\mathrm{e}^{-t}+\frac{a-4}{3a}\mathrm{e}^{-4t} \tag{3.45}$$

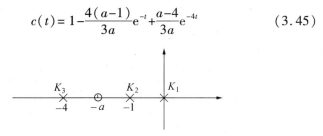

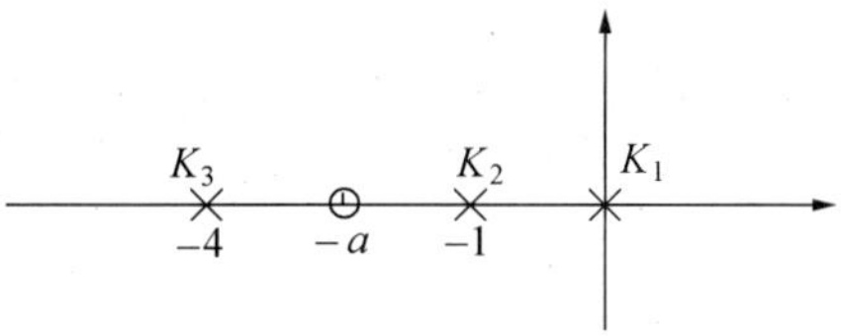

Fig. 3.11 Example 3.8.2

It is seen that if $a=1$, so if the zero coincides with, or cancels, the pole at -1, the transient corresponding to that pole is zero. Similarly, if $a=4$, the zero cancels the pole at -4, making the corresponding transient zero.

The following remarks generalize the implications of this example for the significance of the zeros in the system pole-zero pattern:

(1) A residue K_i at pole $-p_i$ corresponds to a transient term $K_i\exp(-p_it)$, so the significance of the residue is that its magnitude is the initial size of the transient corresponding to the pole.

(2) If a zero is close to a pole, the residue at the pole tends to be small, because of a short vector in the numerator, so that the corresponding transient is probably small.

(3) If the zero coincides with the pole, it cancels it, and the transient term is zero.

(4) Thus the significance of zeros is that they affect the residues at the poles, and hence the sizes of the corresponding transients.

(5) A "slow" pole (close to the imaginary axis, so with a large time constant) or a highly oscillatory pair (small damping ratio) may be acceptable if nearby zeros make the corresponding transients small.

Because pole-zero cancellation is so commonly used in design, it is important to observe that the response to initial conditions is not affected. The preceding results were based on the system transfer function, with the implied assumption of zero initial conditions. In Example 3.8.2, cross multiplication in $G(s)=C(s)/R(s)$ yield $(s^2+5s+4)C=(4+4s/a)R$. For $r=0$, the corresponding differential equation is $\ddot{c}+5\dot{c}+4c=0$. Analogous to Example 1.7.1, transformation for nonzero initial conditions gives

$$C(s)=\frac{(s+5)c(0)+\dot{c}(0)}{s^2+5s+4}$$

This initial condition response is unaffected by the numerator of $G(S)$, so by any cancellations which may have been achieved in the input-output response. [注8]

⋮

It is useful to clarify why the addition of a faraway zero does not greatly increase the sizes of residues and transients. By the final value theorem, the steady-state response of a system $G(s)=K/[(s+a)(s+b)]$ to unit step is

$$c_{ss}=\lim_{s\to 0} sG(s)R(s)=\frac{K}{ab} \tag{3.46}$$

If a zero factor $(s+z)$ or pole factor $(s+p)$ is included to change the dynamic behavior, K must be multiplied by p/z if the steady state is not to be affected also; that is, $G(s)$ should be changed to

$$G_1(s)=K\frac{p}{z}\frac{s+z}{(s+p)(s+a)(s+b)} \tag{3.47}$$

A large vector $(s+z)$, say, now in effect becomes $(1+s/z)$ and does not cause large residues.

This, as did the discussion below (3.40), again shows that the effect of faraway zeros on the transient response is small. The same is true for faraway poles, at which the residues will tend to be small. Such poles and zeros, except for their steady-state effects, are therefore often neglected on the many occasions when transfer function simplification is desirable for system analysis and design.[注9] It is fortunate that this is so, because for many system the values of such faraway poles and zeros, and even their presence and the precise form of the model, constitute the most uncertain part of the transfer function.

3.9 Conclusion

In this chapter the dynamic response characteristics corresponding to given transfer functions have been studied. The features of the response have been interpreted in terms of the locations of system poles and zeros in the s-plane.

Note, however, that except in the examples little attention has been given to feedback, and how it may be used to modify performance. Also, transient response calculations and stability determination, except by the Routh-Hurwitz criterion, of feedback systems with higher-order characteristic polynomials still requires discussion of techniques for finding their roots, the system poles. This is considered in Chapter 6, after study of the modeling, the performance, and the dynamic compensation of feedback systems.

New words and phrases:

1. transient *a.* 短暂的，暂态的
2. polynomial *n.* 多项式
3. numerator *n.* 分子
4. scale *n.* 刻度
5. origin *n.* 原点
6. counterclockwise *a.* 逆时针

7. locus *n.* 轨迹
8. residue *n.* 留数
9. sketch *n.* 草图, *v.* 画草图
10. quadratic *a.* 二次的
11. decay *v.* 衰减
12. dash lines 虚线
13. simple lag plant 纯惯性对象
14. damp *n.* 阻尼
15. coincide *v.* 重合, 一致
16. geometry *n.* 几何形状
17. dominate *v.* 主导
18. normalized *a.* 规范化的
19. oscillation *n.* 振荡
20. amplitude *n.* 幅值
21. criteria *n.* 判据
22. critical *a.* 关键的, 临界的
23. extrema *n.* 极值
24. versus *prep.* 相对于
25. slide *a.* 滑动的
26. radially *adv.* 射线地
27. excessive *a.* 过分的
28. resonant *v.* 谐振
29. inertial *n.* 惯量
30. spool *n.* 滑阀
31. electromagnetic *a.* 电磁的
32. stringent *a.* 严格的, 精确的
33. indispensable *a.* 不可缺少的
34. interactive *a.* 交互的
35. exploit *v.* 使用
36. arbitrary *a.* 任意
37. algorithm *n.* 算法
38. electromechanic *a.* 机电的
39. pneumatic *a.* 气动的, 气压的
40. compensation *n.* 补偿

Notes:

1. The root locus gain factor of a transform or a transfer function is that which results if the coefficients of the highest powers of *s* in numerator and denominator are made equal to unity.

译:一个拉氏变换或一个传递函数的根轨迹增益因子是使分子分母

中 s 的最高次幂为 1 以后所得的系数。

2. The technique for distinct real poles applies also for distinct complex poles, but the residues are now complex, and the graphical approach tends to be simpler than the analytical one.

译:对于不同复数极点,同样使用不同实数极点的技术,但是留数为复数,并且图形方法一般比解析方法更简单。

3. For high-performance design it may be necessary to allow for the effects of motor inertia and valve spool mass as well as oil compressibility, and the transfer function from input to valve spool position can be of sixth order, raising that from input to output from order 3 to 9.

译:对于高性能设计,必须考虑马达惯量和滑动阀门质量与油的可压缩性的影响,而且从输入到滑阀位置的传函为6 阶,即从输入到输出由 3 阶变为 9 阶。

4. During design the parameters are not known and the aim is to use feedback which locates the poles in regions corresponding to satisfactory dynamics, that is, not too close to the imaginary axis and at a small enough angle to the negative real axis.

译: 在设计过程中,参数未知而且目的是使用反馈将极点配置在相应于满意动态的区域,即距虚轴不要太近并且与负实轴成一足够小的角度。

5. Design can therefore concentrate on locating this dominating pair satisfactorily. The fact that many systems behave approximately as second-order systems is also the reason the performance criteria for second-order systems discussed in Section 3.5 apply to higher-order systems as

well.

译:所以设计是集中在满意地配置主导极点对上,许多系统表现近似为二阶系统的事实,同样是3.5节中讨论的二阶系统的性能指标应用于高阶系统的原因。

6. If all coefficients are present and have the same sign, which can be taken to be positive without loss of generality, the Routh-Hurwitz criterion discussed in the next section provides a quick method for determining absolute, but not relative, stability from the coefficients, without calculating the roots.

译:假如所有的系数都存在并且同号(不失一般性可以看成均为正),则下一节讨论的Routh-Hurwitz判据提供了一个无需计算根而由系数决定绝对稳定(不是相对稳定)的快速方法。

7. Computer aids can range from batch-type programs for specific purposes, such as finding the roots of a characteristic equation or calculating the response for a given transfer function, to interactive analysis and design packages which include computer graphics.

译:计算机辅助的复盖范围,从特殊目的批处理程序,诸如求特征方程的根或计算一给定传函的响应,到包括计算机图形的交互分析与设计软件包。

8. This initial condition response is unaffected by the numerator of $G(s)$, so by any cancellations which may have been achieved in the input-output response.

译:初始条件响应不受$G(s)$分子的影响,所以不受任何在输入输 出响应内可能取得对消的影响。

9. Such poles and zeros, except for their steady-state effects, are therefore often neglected on the many occasions when transfer function simplification is desirable for system analysis and design.

译:当对于系统分析与设计希望简化传函时，如此极点与零点，除了它们的稳态影响，在许多情况下经常被忽略。

PART 1 CHAPTER FOUR

4 Feedback System Modeling and Performance

4.1 Introduction

The first part of this chapter is concerned with the modeling of feedback system and the second with the motivations for the use of feedback and its effect on performance. The effect of changes of gain in the feedback loop on performance and its limitations, are considered and will motivate the discussion of dynamic system compensation in Chapter 5.

As suggested earlier, the block diagram structure of a system may be more or less immediately evident from the system schematic diagram or the nature and even the existence of feedback may be rather difficult to see by inspection. In the latter case in particular, the derivation of a "good" block diagram, which clearly identifies the feedback, is an important aid in system analysis and design. Both types are considered through examples, beginning with the first.

4.2 Feedback System Model Examples

In this section examples are given where the system structure is rather evident from the schematic diagram.

Example 4.2.1 Water Level Control System

For a first example, it is appropriate to return to the level control system in Chapter 1. It would probably operate as a process control or regulator system; that is , the desired level is usually constant and the actual level must be held near it despite disturbances. The model should therefore allow for water supply pressure variations, probably the main disturbance.

The level c is measured by means of a float and a lever is used as a summing junction to determine a measure e of the error with the desired level r. From this mechanical input, the controller and amplifier sets a pneumatic output pressure P_0 of sufficient power to operate the pneumatic actuator which adjusts the control valve opening x to control inflow q of the tank.

All subsystem transfer functions needed except that of the controller have been found in Chapter 2:

With these transfer functions and blocks, the translation to the block diagram is virtually immediate. The controller and amplifier is an off-the-shelf instrument, discussed in Chapter 5.

Example 4.2.2 Hydraulic Servo with Mechanical Feedback: Simple Model

The mechanical lever added to the hydraulic cylinder control in Example 2.7.2 acts as feedback because it causes piston motion c to affect valve position x. If, say, input r is moved to the right initially, the valve moves right, causing the piston to move left until the valve is again centered. Use of the simple valve-cylinder model in Fig. 2.7, which assumes small loads and neglects oil compressibility, now readily leads to the block diagram.

Example 4.2.3 Simple Motor Position Servo

A simple motor position servo is shown in Fig. 4.1. The motor and its load are represented by the transfer function (2.11) for a field-controlled DC motor. The time constant $T_m = J/B$, where J is the inertia and B the damping constant. A potentiometer could be used to represent shaft position by a voltage, and an operational amplifier, discussed in Chapter 5, could serve as a summing junction to determine the error voltage E with the voltage R representing desired position. Alternatively, electrical bridge circuits could be used. The controller G_c may be a simple amplifier and generates a low-power output voltage V_c. Its power is raised in a power amplifier of which the output is applied to the motor.

Example 4.2.4 Servo with Velocity Feedback

In speed or position control servomechanisms such as Example 4.2.3., design for satisfactory performance is often complicated by a

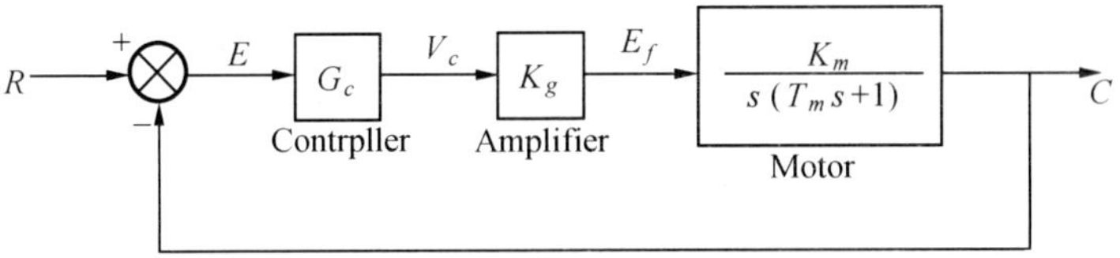

Fig. 4.1 Motor position servo

lack of adequate inherent damping in motor and load. The difficulty of positioning a large inertia J rapidly without severe overshoot in response to a step input in Fig. 4.1 if the damping constant B is small can be appreciated intuitively. One possible solution is to install a mechanical damper on the motor shaft. However, a better and more elegant solution is possible by the use of feedback. A damping torque is a torque proportional to shaft speed $\dot{c}$ and in the opposite direction. Such a torque can also be generated by mounting a small tachometer-generator on the motor shaft to obtain a signal proportional to speed

$$b=K_g\dot{c} \qquad B(s)=K_g sC(s) \tag{4.1}$$

and feeding this back negatively to the power amplifier input.

In the block diagram, this can be represented by a minor loop feedback path. In this case the minor loop is a velocity feedback. Equation

(1.35) gives the reduction of this type of diagram. Its importance may be judged from the availability of motors with integrally mounted tachometers on the shaft.

Example 4.2.5 Motor Position Servo with Load Disturbance Torques

To improve the model in Fig. 4.1 for a field-controlled dc motor position servo by making allowance for load disturbance torques T_l acting on the motor shaft, it is necessary to return to the motor equations in Example 2.4.1. Field voltage E_f and motor developed torque T are related to field current I_f by

$$E_f=(R_f+L_f s)I_f T=K_t I_f \tag{4.2}$$

where E_f and L_f are field resistance and inductance and K_t is the motor torque constant. If T_f is taken as positive in a direction opposite that of T, a net torque $(T-T_l)$ is available to accelerate motor and load inertia J and overcome their damping B

$$T-T_l=J\ddot{c}+B\dot{c} \qquad T(s)-T_l(s)=s(Js+B)C(s)$$

Hence

$$\frac{C}{T-T_l}=\frac{1}{s(Js+B)}=\frac{1/B}{s(T_m s+1)} \qquad T_m=\frac{J}{B} \tag{4.3}$$

Fig. 4.1 is now modified to the diagram in Fig. 4.2. As was noted, often the field time constant $T_f=L_f/R_f \ll T_m$ and can be neglected. The factor $1/R_f$ can then be considered to be incorporated into K_a and $E_f=I_f$ assumed in the diagram for purposes of analysis. Fig. 4.2 shows T_l as a second, disturbance, input to the block diagram. The reduction of such a diagram was discussed in Example 1.8.4. Severe disturbance torques can arise, for example, due to wind in antenna positioning systems, or in steel rolling mill speed controls when slabs enter and leave the rolls.

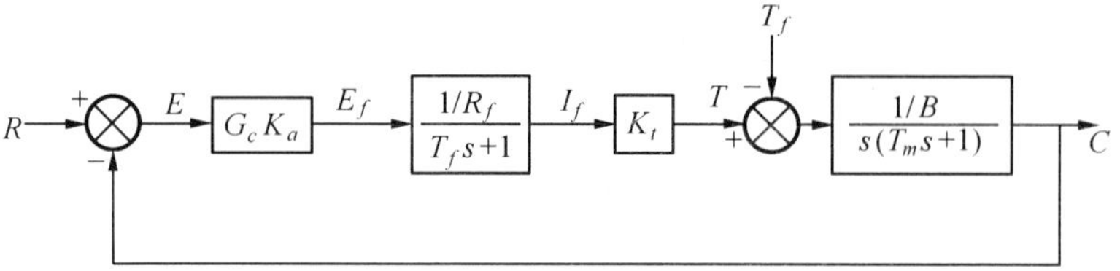

Fig. 4.2 Position servo with disturbance torque

4.3 Direct Block Diagram Modeling of Feedback Systems

In Section 4.2 feedback was realized by separate physical elements and the structure of the block diagram was easy to perceive. However, on many occasions the feedback is generated by the use of signals or physical elements which are an intrinsic part of the system. The precise nature of the feedback, or even its presence, may then be far from obvious. In such cases block diagrams can be derived directly from the system equations, and serve an important function in clarifying system behavior.

Example 4.3.1 Pneumatic Pressure Regulator

This is a very common device. Its purpose is to keep the pressure P_l to the load by the controller constant, equal to a value set by manual adjustment, despite variations of the flow W_l required by the load[注1]. Physically, the action is that a reduction of P_l reduces the pressure against the bottom of the diaphragm. This permits the spring force to push it downward to increase valve opening x, and hence increase valve flow from a suppmy with constant pressure P_s. This increase serves to raise P_l back toward the set value.

Frequently, system equations can be represented by a variety of possible block diagrams, which are all mathematically correct but not all equally useful.

A good block diagram is one that clearly identifies the components and parameters in the feedback loop.

To obtain such a diagram, the system equations are written first. This is done as in Chapter 2, for the parts of the system, taken in rather arbitrary order. Only after all have been written is consideration given to their combination into a good block diagram model on the basis of the physical operation of the system.

A linearized model is used, implying that the variables are deviations from operating point value. Hence the constant supply pressure P_s will not appear. For the weight flow W_v through the valve the linearized model (2.51) is used

$$W_v = K_x x - K_p P_l \qquad W_v(s) = K_x X(s) - K_p P_l(s) \tag{4.4}$$

The net flow entering the volume below the diaphragm, equal to V at the operating point, is $(W_v - W_l)$. This flow must equal

$$W_v - W_l = C_g \dot{P}_l - \rho A\dot{x} \qquad W_v(s) - W_l(s) = C_g\, s\dot{P}_l(s) - \rho A s X(s) \tag{4.5}$$

Here $C_g = V/(nRT)$ is the capacitance of V according to Fig. 2.4 and $C_g \dot{P}_l$ the compressibility flow. The term $\rho A\dot{x}$ is the flow rate corresponding to the change of V, equivalent to, say, (2.57) (which is in terms of volume flow rates). The minus sign arises because this example defined x as positive in the direction of decreasing volume below the diaphragm.

Force equilibrium on the moving parts, modeled as a spring-mass-damper system k, m, b, gives the equation

$$m\ddot{x}+b\dot{x}+kx=-AP_l \qquad (ms^2+bs+k)X(s)=-AP_l(s) \qquad (4.6)$$

This model is approximate because it neglects the flow forces on the poppet. The minus sign is needed because the pressure force AP_l on the bottom of the diaphragm acts in the direction of negative x.

To combine (4.4) to (4.6) into a block diagram, it is noted first that the output is the controlled variable P_l, and the input is the disturbance ,W_l the unknown flow to the load. Thus, following convention, it is desirable to show W_l at the left and P_l at the right in the diagram. The feedback should then show how changes of P_l are used to make valve flow W_v "follow" W_l. Pressure P_l determines x via (4.6), but x and P_l together determine W_v, and for model simplicity it appears preferable to eliminate W_v between (4.4) and (4.5)

$$K_xX-K_pP_l-W_l=C_gsP_l-\rho AsX$$

or

$$(C_gs+K_p)P_l=-W_l+(\rho As+K_x)X \qquad (4.7)$$

Fig. 4.3 now shows the block diagram, obtained directly from (4.6) and (4.7), in classical form. Valve flow W_v could be shown at the expense of more loops and a less simple appearance.

Example 4.3.2 Motor with IR-Drop Compensation

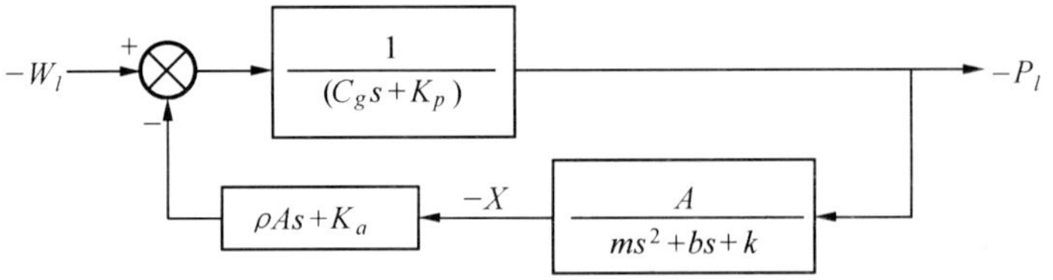

Fig. 4.3 Block diagram for Example 4.3.1

This is the armature-controlled DC motor of Fig. 2.3(b) (Example 2.4.2) with a resistance R added in the armature loop, the voltage across which is fed back as shown to the input of the power amplifier. A block diagram should clarify the nature of this feedback and allow its effect to be studied. The transfer function θ/E_a given by (2.12), with R_a replaced by R_a+R, does not show I_a, so that it is necessary to return to the equations from which it was derived. These are repeated here, with R_a replaced by R_a+R

$$E_a=(R_a+R+L_a s)I_a+E_m \quad E_m=K_e s\theta \qquad T=K_T I_a=s(Js+B)\theta \tag{4.8}$$

The additional equations are

$$E_c=E_r-I_aR \qquad E_a=K_aE_c \tag{4.9}$$

The block diagram is readily obtained from these equations, and allows the effect of the IR-drop compensation to be studied. And this diagram can be partially reduced, by replacing feedback R by a feedback $K_a R$ to the second summing junction and replacing this feedback loop around $1/[L_a s+R_a+R]$ by its closed-loop transfer function $1/[L_a s+R_a+(1+K_a)R]$. Compared to the case where $R=0$, it is seen that the armature time constant has been reduced from L_a/R_a to $L_a/[R_a+(1+K_a)R]$.

The dynamic controllers in Chapter 5 provide additional examples of direct modeling.

4.4 Effect of Feedback on Parameter Sensitivity and Disturbance Response

The motivations for the use of feedback were listed in Section 1.4:

(1) Reducing the effects of parameter variations

(2) Reducing the effects of disturbance inputs

(3) Improving transient response

(4) Reducing steady-state errors

The first two are the prime reasons why feedback is needed, and are discussed first.

Sensitivity to Parameter Variations

Consider the standard feedback loop in Fig. 4.4. G is the transfer function of the plant or process to be controlled, G_c is that of a controller which may be just a gain or dynamic as discussed in Chapter 5, and H may represent the feedback sensor. The plant model G is usually an approximation to the actual dynamic behavior, and even then the parameter values in the model are often not precisely known and may also vary widely with operating conditions. An aircraft at low level responds differently to control surface deflections than at high level. A power plant model linearized about the 30% of full power operating point has different parameter values than that linearized about the 75% point. For very wide parameter variations, adaptive control schemes, which adjust the controller parameters, may be necessary, but a prime advantage of feedback is that it can provide a strong reduction of the sensitivity without such changes of G_c.[注2]

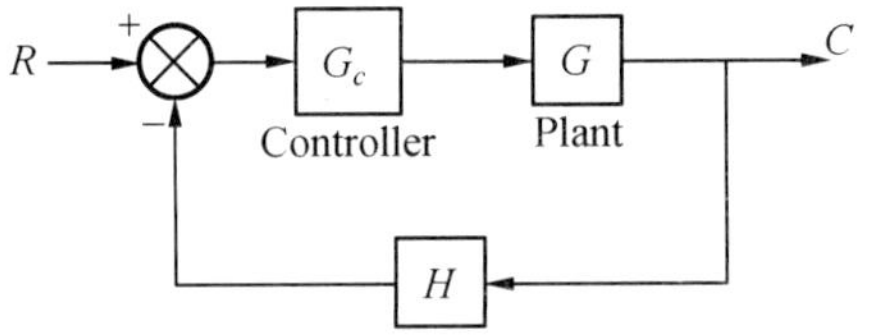

Fig. 4.4 Standard loop

These properties in Fig. 4.4 are determined primarily by the loop gain G_cGH.

G_cGH = loop gain function (i. e., the product of the transfer functions around the loop)

The closed-loop transfer function is

$$T=\frac{G_c G}{1+G_c GH} \tag{4.10}$$

and shows that if $G_c GH \gg 1$,

$$T=\frac{G_c G}{G_c GH}=\frac{1}{H} \tag{4.11}$$

Hence If the loop gain $G_c GH \gg 1$, C/R depends almost entirely on the feedback H alone, and is virtually independent of the plant and other elements in the forward path and of the variations of their parameters.

This is a major reason for the use of feedback. The feedback H must be chosen for small parameter variations, but unlike G, it is usually under the control of the designer.

Formally, the sensitivity properties can be studied by use of the sensitivity function S. For example, the sensitivity of the closed-loop transfer function T to changes in the forward path transfer function $G_f = G_c G$ is the percentage change $\partial T/T$ divided by the percentage change $\partial G_f/G_f$ of G_f which causes it

$$S=\frac{\partial T/T}{\partial G_f/G}=\frac{G_f}{T}\frac{1}{(1+G_f H)^2}=\frac{1}{1+G_f H} \tag{4.12}$$

The static sensitivity is the value of S for $s \to 0$. Dynamic sensitivities are usually calculated by replacing s by $j\omega$ and plotting S as a function of frequency ω. Such results indicate, as later work will show, how sensitivity changes with the frequency of a sinusoidal input R.

Example 4.4.1

The closed-loop transfer function is

$$T=\frac{KA}{\tau s+1+KAh}$$

The sensitivities S_a, S_h and S_τ for small changes of A, h, and τ are as follows

$$S_a=\frac{\partial T/T}{\partial A/A}=\frac{\tau s+1}{\tau s+1+KAh}$$

$$S_h=\frac{\partial T/T}{\partial h/h}=\frac{-KAh}{\tau s+1+KAh} \tag{4.13}$$

$$S_\tau=\frac{\partial T/T}{\partial \tau/\tau}=\frac{-\tau s}{\tau s+1+KAh}$$

The static sensitivity S_{as} is seen to reduce as loop gain KAh increases, but the magnitude of S_{hs} will approach 1. It is seen also that the static sensitivity $S_{\tau s}$ is zero.

Frequently, the variations of A and τ will be interrelated. From example 2.6.1, if a single-tank level control is modeled, $A=K_vR_1$, $\tau=A_1R_1$, where K_v is the control valve gain and A_1 and R_1 are the tank area and outlet valve resistance. R_1 could vary due to obstructions or inadvertent adjustment, and level sensor gain h could change due to a malfunction. To illustrate the effects, unit step responses when these parameters are halved and doubled from their nominal values will be compared, assuming that $K=9$, $K_v=1$, $A_1=1$, $R_1(\text{nom.})=1$, $h(\text{nom})=1$. Leaving R_1 and h as free parameters, the closed-loop transfer function yields the unit step response

$$c(t)=\frac{9}{9h+1/R_1}\left\{1-\exp\left[-\left(9h+\frac{1}{R_1}\right)t\right]\right\}$$

This is plotted in the corresponding Figure for the nominal parameters and when one of R_1 and h is 2 or 0.5 times the nominal value. As expected, the response is far more sensitive to h than to R_1. In view of the large parameter changes, the differences between the curves for $R_1 = 1$, 2, and 0.5 appear small. If K were reduced, reducing loop gain, these differences would be large. This trend is evident in the curves in that loop gain is smaller for $n=0.5$ and $R_1=0.5$. Accordingly, these responses differ more from the nominal plot than those for $h=2$ and $R_1=2$, respectively.

Effect of External Disturbances

Three of the examples earlier in this chapter included the modeling of disturbance inputs. These fit the model shown in Fig. 4.5, which is equivalent to Fig. 1.5 in Section 1.8, on block diagram reduction. The effect of disturbance D on output C is given by the transfer function

$$\frac{C}{D}=\frac{G_2L}{1+G_cG_1G_2H}=-\frac{E}{D} \qquad \text{for } H=1 \tag{4.14}$$

This shows the following:

If loop gain $G_cG_1G_2H \gg 1$, then

$$\frac{C}{D}=\frac{L}{G_cG_1H} \qquad \left(\approx -\frac{E}{D} \quad \text{for } H=1\right) \tag{4.15}$$

So feedback strongly reduces the effect of a disturbance D on C if the loop gain is much greater than 1 due to high gain in the feedback path between C and D.

This also shows why a system may respond well to an input R while the response to another input D is small. For $H=1$, when $C/R=1$ is desired, loop gains $G_cG_1G_2 \gg 1$ will ensure that $\frac{C}{R}=\frac{G_cG_1G_2}{1+G_cG_1G_2}$ is near 1. By locating the high gains in G_cG_1, between the points where R and D enter the loop, both requirements can be met.

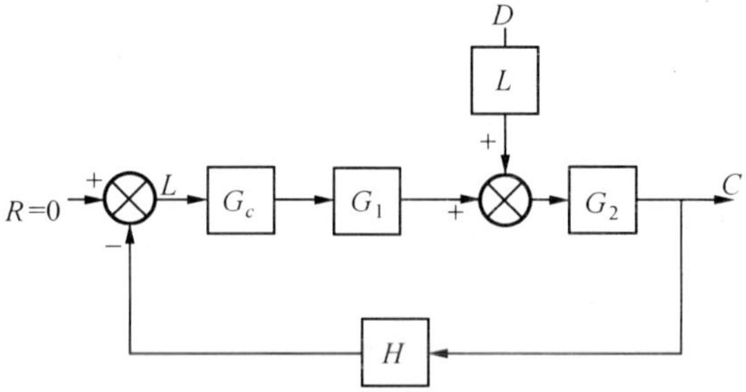

Fig. 4.5 Disturbance inputs

Disturbances may also enter the feedback path, due to the sensor measuring C. The importance of measures to avoid this is clear, since normally there will not be a high gain in the feedback between C and such disturbances to attenuate their effect. [注3]

The steady-state response, for $t \to \infty$, to a disturbance is clearly an important measure of system quality, and is readily found using the final value theorem. From (4.14), for a unit step input $D = 1/s$.

$$\lim_{t \to 0} c(t) = \lim_{s \to 0} sC(s) = \lim_{s \to 0} \frac{G_2 L}{1 + G_c G_1 G_2 H} \tag{4.16}$$

Example 4.4.2 Motor Position Control (Fig. 4.2)

For this system, from Fig. 4.2, if G_c is an amplifier with gain , $K_c G_c = K_c$, then

$$G_c G_1 = \frac{K_c K_a K_t / R_f}{T_f s + 1} \qquad L = H = 1 \qquad G_2 = \frac{1/B}{s(T_m s + 1)}$$

Hence, with the negative sign at the load disturbance torque $T_l = 1/s$.

$$\lim_{t \to \infty} c(t) = -\frac{R_f}{K_t K_a K_f} \tag{4.17}$$

High controller gain, therefore, not only makes the system less sensitive to parameter variations but also improves its stiffness against load disturbances. Note, incidentally, that the feedback to the summing junction for D in Fig. 4.5 is not positive, as the plus sign might suggest, since the minus sign at R can be moved to D when evaluation C/D. [注4]

It is useful for the sake of insight to verify the result (4.17) directly from Fig. 4.2. In the steady-state, the net torque $T-T_l$ must be zero, so if $T_l=1$, T must be 1 as well. From the diagram, this requires that $e=R_l/(K_cK_aK_l)$. Since input r is zero while considering the response to T_l, $e=r-c=-c$, so indeed $c=-R_f/(K_cK_aK_l)$.

4.5 Steady-State Errors in Feedback Systems

High loop gains were shown to be advantageous to reduce sensitivity of performance to both parameter variations and disturbance input. They will now prove equally desirable from the point of view of the reduction of steady-state errors in feedback systems. Intuitive reasoning in Section 1.4 and several examples already suggested this , and it will now be verified by consideration of the unity feedback system in Fig. 4.6. $E=R/(1+G)$, and the steady-state error e_{ss} can be found directly, without the need for inverse transformation, by the final value theorem

$$e_{ss}=\lim_{s\to 0}\frac{sR(s)}{1+G(s)} \tag{4.18}$$

For $G(s)$, the following general form assumed

$$G(s)=\frac{K}{s^n}\frac{a_ks^k+\cdots+a_1s+1}{b_ls^l+\cdots+b_1s+1} \tag{4.19}$$

In this equation:

(1) K as given, with the constant terms in numerator and denominator polynomials made unity, is formally the gain of the transfer function G. It should be distinguished from the root locus gain, defined earlier as that for which the highest power coefficients are unity, and equal to

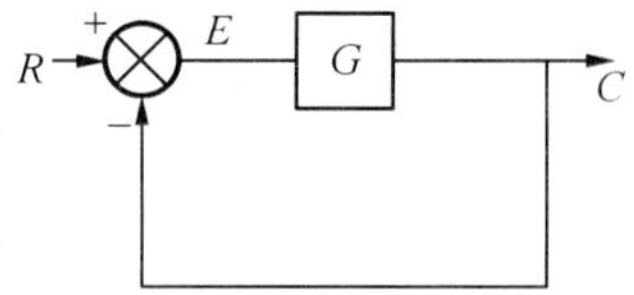

Fig. 4.6 Unity feedback system

$K\,a_k/b_l$ in (4.19).

(2) The type number of G is the value the integer n. As discussed in Example 2.4.1, a factor s in the denominator represents an integration, so the type number is the number of integrators in G.

(3) Gain $K=\lim_{s\to 0} s^n G(s)$, and a common practice associates the following names and notations with K, depending on n:

$$\begin{array}{ll} n=0 & K_p=\text{position error constant} \\ n=1 & K_v=\text{velocity error constant} \\ n=2 & K_a=\text{acceleration error constant} \end{array} \tag{4.20}$$

Equation (4.19) shows that $\lim_{s\to 0} G(s)=\lim_{s\to 0}(K/s^n)$, so that (4.18) can be written as follow

$$e_{ss}=\lim_{s\to 0}\frac{sR(s)}{1+(K/s^n)} \tag{4.21}$$

This readily yield Table 4.5.1 for the steady-state errors corresponding to different type numbers and input, of which the transforms are given in Table 1.6.1. For example, for a type 2 system with a unit ramp input

$$e_{ss}=\lim_{s\to 0}\frac{s}{s^2+K}=0$$

For insight into these result it is useful to consider Fig. 4.7, which shows type 0 and type 1 systems for $s\to 0$. For $n=0$, $C=K_pE$, so there cannot be a nonzero output without a proportional, nonzero error. If the output must increase along a ramp, the error must increase according to a ramp as well. So a type 0 system has a steady-state error for a step input and cannot follow a ramp.

For $n=1$

$$C = \frac{K_v}{s}E \qquad \text{so} \quad c(t) = K_v \int e(t)\,\mathrm{d}t$$

This means that the output cannot level off to a constant value unless the error levels off at zero. A steady-state with nonzero steady-state error cannot exist for a step input because the integrator would cause the output to change.

From a design point of view, this means that if, as is often the case, the performance specifications require zero steady-state error after a step input, the designer must ensure that the system is at least of type 1.[注5] A type 2 system would be necessary if zero steady-state errors following both steps and ramps are specified.

The hydraulic servo and motor control examples in Section 4.2 are type 1 systems, but the level control is type 0, unless it is made into type 1 via the controller.

The nonzero finite errors in Table 4.5.1 decrease as gain is increased, as do parameter sensitivity and disturbance response. As suggested in Section 1.4, for larger K a smaller error can achieve the same effect on the output.

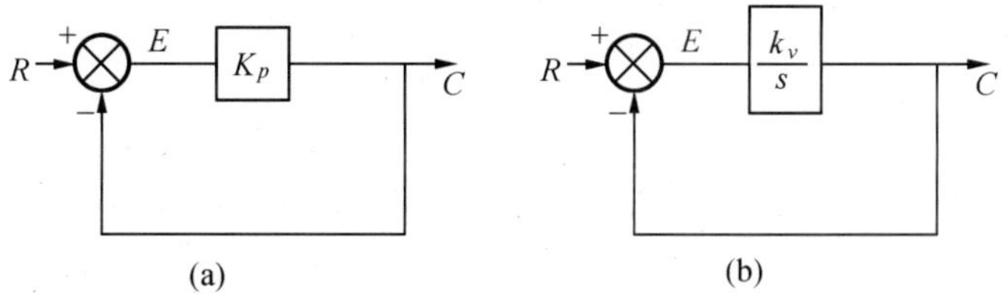

Fig. 4.7 Type 0 (a) and 1 (b) systems

Example 4.5.1

In Fig. 4.6:

$$(a)\ G(s)=\frac{K_1(as+b)}{(cs^2+ds+e)(fs+g)}:\ \text{type0 gain}\quad K_p=\frac{K_1 b}{eg}$$

$$\text{Unit step}: e_{ss}=\frac{1}{1+K_p}\qquad \text{unit ramp}: e_{ss}\to\infty$$

$$(b)\ G(s)=\frac{K_1(as+b)}{s(cs^2+ds+e)(fs+g)}:\ \text{type1 gain}\quad K_v=\frac{K_1 b}{eg}$$

$$\text{Unit step}: e_{ss}=0\qquad \text{unit ramp}: e_{ss}=\frac{1}{K_v}$$

Example 4.5.2 Steady-State Errors for Unit Steps in *R* and *D*

The system is type 1, so $e_{ss}=0$ for a step input R. For input D, the steady-state value m_{ss} of M is also zero (since otherwise e_{ss} could not be constant), but the feedback from C to D is not unity but K. [注6] For a unit value of D the condition for $m_{ss}=0$ is $1+Ke_{ss}=0$, so $e_{ss}=-1/K$. Direct application of the final value theorem to $C(s)$ will verify these results.

4.6 Transient Response versus Steady-State Errors

Preceding sections have shown that parameter sensitivity, disturbance response, and steady-state errors are all improved by increased gain. The fourth motivation for the use of feedback is to improve dynamic response.

Section 1.4 has suggested, and examples such as 2.8.1 and 3.5.2 supported this, that dynamic response considerations usually limit the permissible gain, and that feedback design is generally concerned with achieving a satisfactory compromise between relative stability and accuracy (i. e. , small errors).

Two examples will be given to show how transient response and accuracy are related. The first is unusual in that both improve with increasing gain. It is useful however in its striking demonstration of the effects of feedback.

Example 4.6.1 Proportional Control of a Simple Lag

There is a simple lag plant with a pure gain controller. This is called proportional control, or P control. The closed-loop transfer function is

$$\frac{C}{R}=\frac{KG}{1+KG}=\frac{K}{1+K}\frac{1}{[T/(1+K)]s+1} \tag{4.22}$$

Hence the close-loop system is also a simple lag, but with time constant $T/(1+K)$ instead of T. So the speed of response increases with K. Steady-state errors for a unit step input are $1/(1+K)$, since the system is type 0 with gain K, so also reduce with increasing K. The unit step response is

$$c(t)=\frac{K}{1+K}(1-\mathrm{e}^{-(1+k)t/T}) \tag{4.23}$$

It is apparent that for larger K the response not only comes to the desired value of unity, but also approaches the steady-state sooner.

The steady-state value of the output

$$C_{ss}=r-e_{ss}=\frac{K}{1+K}$$

can also be verified from (4.22), which gives

$$C_{ss}=\frac{K}{1+K}$$

Evidently, increasing gain K does in this example not reduce rela-

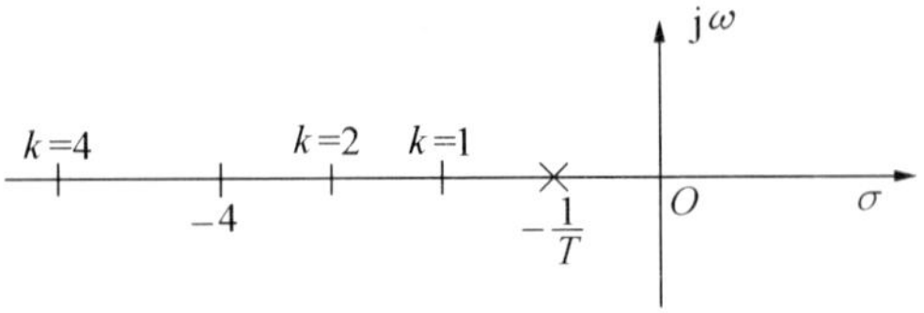

Fig. 4. 8 Example 4. 6. 1: P control

tive stability. To allow correlation of the change of transient response with change of system pole position in the s-plane, Fig. 4. 8 shows the root locus of the system. It indicates, for $T=1$, how the system pole $-(1+K)/T$ moves as K is increased from zero. This plot is in fact enough to show that there is no relative stability problem and that, because of increasing distance of the pole to the imaginary axis, the system responds faster with increasing K. [注7]

Apparently, improving the transient response can be a major motivation for the use of feedback. In this example a possibly very slow process could be made to respond at any desired speed!

However, a practical restriction should be emphasized. Changing a water level or temperature in a tank fast requires large-capacity and costly water or heat supply system. The results for the example imply the assumption of infinite capacity supplies. In practice, the use of excessive gain will cause the supplies to saturate at their maximum output levels. The system then operates in a nonlinear regime and its response changes from the predictions based on linear analysis.

Often the maximum value of K permitted by these considerations is not large enough to meet specifications on the steady-state error $1/(1+K)$. Indeed, in many cases this error is required to be zero. This motivates the use of dynamic compensation, introduced in Chapter 5, since a constant-gain controller is then no longer adequate. The results in Section 4.5 indicate that a type 1 system is required. Since the plant in Example 4.6.1 is type 0, this means that a separate factor s must be introduced into the denominator of the controller. By far the most common solution is, in fact, the PI controller $K(s+z)/s$ already introduced in Example 3.8.1 and Fig. 3.10 for the control of a simple lag plant. Figure 3.10 also presents step response curves showing the effect of the choice of the zero $-z$.

Example 4.6.2 P Control with Two Simple Lags

In Fig. 4.9(a) a second simple lag has been included in the system of Example 4.6.1. Among other possibilities, it could represent a two-tank level control as in Example 2.6.2, a temperature control with two heat capacitances in series, or a motor speed control. As in Example 4.6.1, the system is type 0 with gain K, so the steady-state error after a unit step is $1/(1+K)$. Again dynamic compensation, probably PI control, is needed if this error is required to be zero.

Consider now stability, using $T_1=1$, $T_2=0.5$ for a numerical example. The close-loop transfer function and the system characteristic equation are, respectively.

$$\frac{C}{R}=\frac{2K}{s^2+3s+2+2K} \tag{4.24}$$

The closed-loop poles are

$$s_{1,2}=-1.5\pm\sqrt{0.25-2K} \tag{4.25}$$

and a root locus showing how these pole positions in the s-plane change with K can easily be plotted in this case. The plot is shown in Fig. 4.9(c). For $K=0$ the poles coincide with those of the loop gain function, -1 and -2. As K is increased, the poles initially are still real,

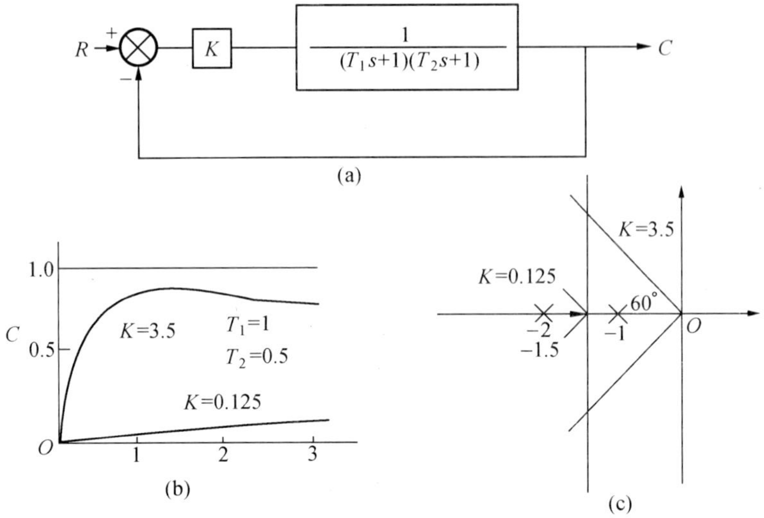

Fig. 4.9 Example 4.6.2: P control

and move together until for $K=0.125$ both are located at -1.5. For larger K the real part is constant at -1.5 and the imaginary part increases with K. The cosine of the angle of the poles with the negative real axis is the damping ratio ζ, and decreases with increasing K. Since the real part is constant, the time constant and settling time are the same for all $K\geqslant 0.125$. But as discussed in Example 3.5.2, speed of response is improved by reducing rise time, and this suggests that ζ be reduced to the lowest value for which the step response overshoot is acceptable. If this is $\zeta=0.5$, equating the characteristic equation with $s^2+2\zeta\omega_n s+\omega_n^2$ yields $\omega_n=3$, $K=3.5$.

Thus the increase of K which is desirable to increase the speed of response and to reduce steady-state errors, parameter sensitivity, and disturbance response is limited by considerations of relative stability.

The unit step response can be calculated from (4.24) and is shown in Fig. 4.9(b) for $K=0.125$ and $K=3.5$. The improvement in accuracy and speed of response for the higher gain is evident, but the steady-state error is still large and PI control, as mentioned earlier, would probably be necessary, to change the system to type 1 and achieve zero steady-state error.

Example 4.6.2 is more typical than Example 4.6.1, in that relative stability considerations usually limit the permissible gain. It is still not representative, however, of most practical systems since at least absolute stability is maintained for all K. Usually, systems actually become unstable beyond a certain value of K. As discussion of the root locus technique in Chapter 6 will show, if the vertical branches of the root locus in Fig. 4.18(c) would instead bend off to the right, then beyond a certain value of K the closed-loop poles would be located in the right-half s-plane.

The examples also motivate the use of dynamic compensation, introduced in Chapter 5, PI control $K(s+z)/s$ was mentioned as a possible solution to replace a pure gain or P control if at the maximum gain permitted by relative stability the steady-state errors are still too large.

4.7 Conclusion

In this chapter the modeling of systems with feedback in block diagram form was considered first. The examples include those where the structure of the system and the nature of the feedback are clear from the schematic diagram, as well as cases where even the existence of feedback may not be obvious. In particular in the latter case, a good block diagram is an important aid in system analysis and design.

The motivations for the use of feedback were examined next, and it was found that considerations of relative stability usually limit the gain increase desirable to increase the speed of response and to reduce sensitivity to plant parameter variations, response to disturbances, and errors. [注9]

Examples were given that motivate the use of dynamic compensation, introduced in Chapter 5, to overcome this limitation. The emphasis in Chapter 5 will be on the use of proportional plus integral plus derivative control (PID). This form is extremely common in practice, and its basic control actions are fundamental to dynamic compensation generally.

The physical realization of such controllers will also provide additional examples of the derivation of block diagrams for systems with feedback. In this context the operational amplifier mentioned in Chapter 2, and some of its applications in controller realization and system simulation, will be discussed as well.

The concept of a root locus was introduced in the examples of Section 4.6. The limitation to second-order systems, for which the roots of the characteristic equation can easily be calculated, suggests the need for more advanced techniques in practical applications. The root locus technique in Chapter 6 and the frequency response methods in Chapters 7 and 8 will fulfill this need. However, dynamic compensation is considered first because to enhance insight, it is important to introduce this subject in simple mathematical framework.

New words and phrases:

1. schematic *a.* 示意的
2. appropriate *a.* 适当的
3. pneumatic *a.* 气动的
4. off-the-shelf 流行的，现成的
5. cylinder *n.* 气缸
6. potentiometer *n.* 电位计

7. step *n.* 阶跃
8. intuitively *adv.* 直觉地
9. elegant *a.* 优美的，好的
10. field-controlled 励磁控制
11. incorporate *v.* 结合
12. antenna *n.* 天线
13. intrinsic *a.* 固有的
14. poppet *n.* 提升(阀)
15. deflection *n.* 变形
16. sinusoidal *a.* 正弦的
17. obstruction *n.* 阻塞
18. inadvertent *a.* 非故意
19. malfunction *n.* 失灵
20. nominal *a.* 名义的
21. external *a.* 外部的
22. disturbance *n.* 干扰
23. attenuate *v.* 衰减
24. amplifier *n.* 放大器
25. stiffness *n.* 刚度
26. incidentally *adv.* 顺便地
27. for the sake of 为了
28. polynomial *n.* 多项式
29. coefficient *n.* 系数
30. integrator *n.* 积分器
31. notation *n.* 符号
32. corresponding to 相应于
33. ramp *n.* 斜坡
34. level off 稳定
35. striking *a.* 惊人的
36. demonstration *n.* 证明 演示
37. saturate *v.* 饱和
38. motivation *n.* 动因　原因
39. simulation *n.* 仿真
40 enhance *v.* 提高

Notes:

1. Its purpose is to keep the pressure P_l to the load by the controller constant, equal to a value set by manual adjustment, despite variations of the flow W_l required by the load.

译：它的目的是由控制器来保持到负载的压力为常值(等于手动设定值)，尽管有由负载所要求的流量的变化。

2. For very wide parameter variations, adaptive control schemes, which adjust the controller parameters, may be necessary, but a prime ad-

vantage of feedback is that it can provide a strong reduction of the sensitivity without such changes of G_c.

译:对于较宽的参数变化，调节控制器参数的自适应控制计划可能是必要的，但是反馈的一个主要优点是，它能提供一个大的灵敏度衰减而无需改变 G_c。

3. The importance of measures to avoid this is clear, since normally there will not be a high gain in the feedback between C and such disturbances to attenuate their effect.

译：避免这样的测量的重要性是明显的，因为在 C 与如此干扰之间的反馈中一般不会有高增益来抑制它们的影响。

4. Note, incidentally, that the feedback to the summing junction for D is not positive, as the plus sign might suggest, since the minus sigh at R can be moved to D when evaluation C/D.

译：顺便提一下，到 D 处相加点的反馈并不是如正号表示的那样为正反馈，因为当计算 C/D 时，R 处的负号能被移到 D 处。

5. From a design point of view, this means that if, as is often the case, the performance specifications require zero steady-state error after a step input, the designer must ensure that the system is at lcast of type 1.

译：从设计的观点来看，如通常的情况一样，假如性能指标要求跟随阶跃输入为零稳态误差时，设计者必须保证系统至少为 1 型。

6. For input D, the steady-state value m_{ss} of M is also zero, but the feedback from C to D is not unity but K.

译：对于输入 D，M 的稳态值 m_{ss} 也是零，但从 C 到 D 的反馈不是 1 而是 K。

7. This plot is in fact enough to show that there is no relative stability

problem and that, because of increasing distance of the pole to the imaginary axis, the system responds faster with increasing K.

译：此图实际上足以表明没有相对稳定性的问题，并且因为极点到虚轴的距离的增加，系统随着 K 的增加而响应更快。

8. As discussion of the root locus technique in Chapter 6 will show, if the vertical branches of the root locus in Fig. 4.9(c) would instead bend off to the right, then beyond a certain value of K the closed-loop poles would be located in the right-half s-plane.

译：正如第 6 章讨论的根轨迹技术将表明的那样，假如图中的根轨迹分支反而弯向右面，那么超过一定的 K 值之后，闭环极点将位于 S 右半平面。

9. The motivations for the use of feedback were examined next, and it was found that considerations of relative stability usually limit the gain increase desirable to increase the speed of response and to reduce sensitivity to plant parameter variations, response to disturbances, and errors.

译：接下来研究了使用反馈的动因，并且发现相对稳定性方面的考虑通常限制了增加增益来提高响应速度，减小对对象参数变化的灵敏度、对干扰的响应及误差这方面的考虑。

PART 2	CHAPTER ONE

1 Robustness in Multivariable Control System Design

Synopsis

In this lecture, techniques are described for assessing the relative stability of a multivariable control system design. An interesting and important feature in multivariable feedback systems is that they have different stability margins at different points in their configuration.

1.1 Introduction

In the generalized Nyquist stability criterion put forward by MacFarlane, and subsequently proved by several researchers, the stability of a linear, time-invariant, multivariable, feedback system, such as is shown in Fig. 1.1, is determined from the characteristic gain loci which are a plot of the eigenvalues of the return-ratio matrix $\boldsymbol{G}(s)\boldsymbol{K}(s)$ (or equivalently the eigenvalues of the return-ratio matrix $\boldsymbol{K}(s)\boldsymbol{G}(s)$) as the Laplace transform variable s traverses the standard Nyquist D-contour[注1]. The criterion can be stated as follows:

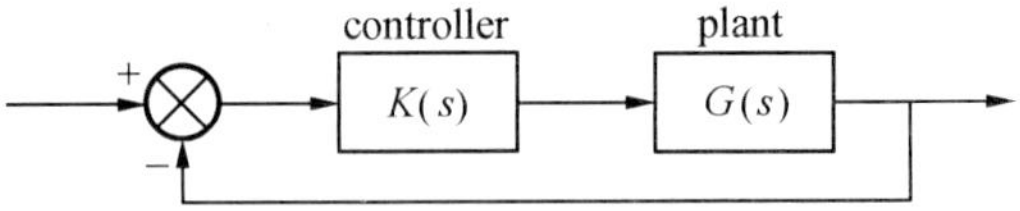

Fig. 1.1　Feedback system

Generalized Nyquist Stability Criterion. The feedback system is stable if, and only if, the number of anticlockwise encirclements of the critical point −1 by the characteristic gain loci, is equal to the number of open-loop unstable poles.

If a gain parameter k is introduced into each of the loops then closed-loop stability can be checked on the same plot for a family of parameter values k, by counting encirclements of $-1/k$. Also, in analogy, with the scalar situation, gain and phase margins can be defined from the characteristic gain loci which indicate the limiting values of the modulus and phase that k can attain before instability occurs. Although these features are very attractive the characteristic gain loci do not by themselves give reliable information concerning the robustness of the closed-loop stability property. For example, the characteristic gain loci can have infinite gain margins with respect to the gain parameter k, and only a small change in some other system parameter may make the closed-loop system unstable.

In search of a reliable means of assessing the robustness of the closed-loop stability property, Doyle and Stein introduced a gain margin concept defined in terms of the maximum singular value of an appropriate frequency-response matrix. They showed that the closed-loop system remains stable when subjected to a stable matrix perturbation $\boldsymbol{I}+\boldsymbol{P}(s)$, at any point in the configuration, providing the maximum singular value of $\boldsymbol{P}(\mathrm{j}\omega)$ multiplied by the maximum singular value of the frequencies-response matrix $[\boldsymbol{I}+\boldsymbol{T}(\mathrm{j}\omega)^{-1}]^{-1}$ is less than 1, at all frequencies, where $\boldsymbol{T}(s)$ is the return-ratio matrix for the point in question[注2]. Note that since the return-ratio matrix is generally different at different points in the configuration it follows that the robustness of the stability property will also vary around the system, and in particular it will vary before and after the plant where uncertainties are most likely to occur. Following the work of Doyle and Stein, Postlethwaite, Edmunds and MacFarlane introduced a multivariable phase margin which in conjunction with Doyle and Stein's gain margin, allows a larger class of perturbations to be identified for which the feedback system remains stable. These results are discussed in the latter half of this lecture. A system which has a large degree of stability in term of these multivariable gain and phase margins will have characteristic gain loci which although not necessarily insensitive to small perturbations will nevertheless be insensitive enough for the number of encirclements of the critical point to remain unchanged[注3]. In the first half of this lecture a direct study is made of the sensitivity of the characteristic gain loci to small perturbations. Sensitivity indices are defined in terms of the left-hand and right-hand eigenvectors of the return-ratio matrix corresponding to the point at which the system is perturbed. It follows that the characteristic gain loci are at their least sensitive when the corresponding return-ratio matrix is normal.

1.2 Sensitivity of the Characteristic Gain Loci

In this section the perturbations of the eigenvalues of a return-ratio matrix $\boldsymbol{T}(j\omega)$ are considered as the matrix is perturbed to $\boldsymbol{T}(j\omega)+\varepsilon\boldsymbol{E}(j\omega)$, where ε is a small, positive, real number. The analysis is based on two theorems due to Gerschgorin, and follows exactly the treatment given by Wilkinson in his excellent monograph on the numerical aspects of the algebraic eigenvalue problem. Because of this and in order to concentrate on the main ideas, some details and proofs will be omitted; the interested reader is strongly encouraged to study Wilkinson's book.

For convenience, the $j\omega$'s are sometimes omitted, the notation t_{ij} will be used for the ijth element of the $m\times m$ matrix $\boldsymbol{T}$, and $|t_{ij}|$ will denote the modulus of t_{ij}.

Theorem 1.2.1 (Gerschgorin)

Each eigenvalue of $\boldsymbol{T}$ lies in at least one of the discs with centres t_{ij} and radii $\sum_{i \neq j} | t_{ij} |$.

Theorem 1.2.2 (Gerschgorin)

If n of the circular discs of Theorem 1.2.1 form a connected domain which is isolated from the other discs, then there are precisely n eigenvalues of $\boldsymbol{T}$ within this connected domain.

1.2.1 Sensitivity indices

In the analysis that follows a set of quantities will be used repeatedly[注4]. They are of major importance and so will be introduced first. They are defined by the relations

$$s_i = y_i^{\mathrm{T}} x_i \qquad i = 1, 2, \cdots, m$$

where y_i^{T} is y_i transposed, and y_i, x_i are (respectively) left-hand and right-hand eigenvectors of $\boldsymbol{T}$, normalized so that the sum of the squares of the moduli of their elements is equal to unity.

As will be seen later the m numbers $| s_i |$ give a direct indication of the sensitivity of the m eigenvalues of $\boldsymbol{T}$ and will therefore be referred to as the sensitivity indices of $\boldsymbol{T}$. It is clear that the sensitivity indices range between 0 and 1.

1.2.2 Analysis

In the generic situation where $\boldsymbol{T}$ has linear elementary divisors there exists a non-singular matrix $\boldsymbol{W}$ such that

$$\boldsymbol{W}^{-1} \boldsymbol{T} \boldsymbol{W} = \mathrm{diag}(\lambda_i)$$

where the (λ_i are the eigenvalues of $\boldsymbol{T}$, and $\mathrm{diag}(\lambda_i)$ is a diagonal matrix of the λ_i. It is immediately apparent that the columns of $\boldsymbol{W}$ are a candidate set of right-hand eigenvectors for $\boldsymbol{T}$, and also that the rows of

$\boldsymbol{W}^{-1}$ are a candidate set of left-hand eigenvectors for $\boldsymbol{T}$. Further, if the column vectors of $\boldsymbol{W}$ are normalized to unity then the ith column of $\boldsymbol{W}$ can be taken to be $\boldsymbol{x}_i$, and the ith row of $\boldsymbol{W}^{-1}$ taken to be $\boldsymbol{y}_i^{\mathrm{T}}/s_i$.

With this definition for $\boldsymbol{W}$ it follows that

$$W^{-1}(T+\varepsilon E)W=\operatorname{diag}(\lambda_i)+\varepsilon\begin{bmatrix} e_{11}/s_1 & e_{12}/s_1 & \cdots & e_{1m}/s_1 \\ e_{21}/s_2 & e_{22}/s_2 & \cdots & e_{2m}/s_2 \\ \vdots & \vdots & \cdots & \vdots \\ e_{m1}/s_m & e_{m2}/s_m & \cdots & e_{mm}/s_m \end{bmatrix}$$

and the application of Theorem 1.2.1 to this shows that the perturbed eigenvalues lie in discs with centres $(\lambda_i+\varepsilon e_{ii}/s_i)$ and radii $\varepsilon\sum_{j\neq i}|e_{ij}/s_i|$. If all the eigenvalues are simple then for a sufficiently small ε all the discs are isolated and by Theorem 1.2.2 each disc contains precisely one eigenvalue. Alternatively, if there are some multiple eigenvalues, for example $\lambda_1=\lambda_2=\lambda_3$ and $\lambda_4=\lambda_5$, then there will be three Gerschgorin discs with centres $\lambda_1+\varepsilon e_{ii}/s_i$, $i=1,2,3$ and two with centres $\lambda_4+\varepsilon e_{ii}/s_i$, $i=4,5$, all with radii of order ε. For sufficiently small ε the group of three discs will be isolated from the group of two, but, in general, no claim of isolation can be made about the individual discs in a group.

From the above analysis it is clear that the sensitivity of the eigenvalues is directly related to the sensitivity indices; the larger si is, the less sensitive λ_i is to small perturbations in $\boldsymbol{T}$.

It is now demonstrated, by example, how, as $\boldsymbol{T}$ approaches a matrix having non-linear elementary divisors, the corresponding eigenvalues become increasingly sensitive. To facilitate this let $\boldsymbol{T}$ be given by

$$\boldsymbol{T}=\begin{bmatrix} t_{11} & 1 \\ 0 & t_{22} \end{bmatrix}$$

which approaches a simple Jordan submatrix as t_{11} approaches t_{22}. The eigenvalues of $\boldsymbol{T}$ are t_{11} and t_{22}, and the corresponding normalized right-hand and left-hand eigenvectors are given by

$$\boldsymbol{x}_1 = \begin{bmatrix} 1 \\ 0 \end{bmatrix}, \boldsymbol{x}_2 = \frac{1}{\sqrt{[1+(t_{11}-t_{22})^2]}} \begin{bmatrix} 1 \\ t_{22}-t_{11} \end{bmatrix}$$

$$\boldsymbol{y}_1 = \frac{1}{\sqrt{[1+(t_{11}-t_{22})^2]}} \begin{bmatrix} t_{22}-t_{11} \\ 1 \end{bmatrix}, \boldsymbol{y}_2 = \begin{bmatrix} 1 \\ 0 \end{bmatrix}$$

where for convenience t_{11} and t_{22} have been assumed real. The sensitivity indices are therefore given by

$$|s_1| = |y_1^{\mathrm{T}} x_1| = \left| (t_{11}-t_{12}) / \sqrt{1+(t_{11}-t_{12})^2} \right|$$

$$|s_2| = |y_2^{\mathrm{T}} x_2| = \left| (t_{22}-t_{11}) / \sqrt{1+(t_{11}-t_{22})^2} \right|$$

and it is seen that both indices tend to zero as t_{11} approaches t_{22}. Hence from the previous analysis both simple eigenvalues become increasingly sensitive as $\boldsymbol{T}$ tends to the simple Jordan submatrix.

1.3 Uncertainty in a Feedback System

This section considers the implications of the sensitivity results of Section 1.2 to the design of feedback systems.

For the feedback configuration of Fig. 1.1 the characteristic gain loci are the eigenvalues of the return-ratio matrix $\boldsymbol{G}(\mathrm{j}\omega)\boldsymbol{K}(\mathrm{j}\omega)$, or alternatively the eigenvalues of the return-ratio matrix $\boldsymbol{K}(\mathrm{j}\omega)\boldsymbol{G}(\mathrm{j}\omega)$. Although the eigenvalues of the two return-ratio matrices are the same, the corresponding eigenvectors will generally be different, and hence the characteristic gain loci may be sensitive to perturbations in $\boldsymbol{G}(\mathrm{j}\omega)\boldsymbol{K}(\mathrm{j}\omega)$, while insensitive to perturbations in $\boldsymbol{K}(\mathrm{j}\omega)\boldsymbol{G}(\mathrm{j}\omega)$. To see the significance of this consider the feedback configuration shown in

Fig. 1.2, where the return-ratio matrix $\boldsymbol{G}(\mathrm{j}\omega)\boldsymbol{K}(\mathrm{j}\omega)$ is assumed to have been perturbed to $\boldsymbol{G}(\mathrm{j}\omega)\boldsymbol{K}(\mathrm{j}\omega)+\varepsilon\boldsymbol{E}(\mathrm{j}\omega)$. Insofar as stability is concerned, this configuration is equivalent to that shown in Fig. 1.3, where

$$\boldsymbol{E}_{\mathrm{o}}(\mathrm{j}\omega)=\varepsilon\boldsymbol{E}(\mathrm{j}\omega)\left[\left(\boldsymbol{G}(\mathrm{j}\omega)\boldsymbol{K}(\mathrm{j}\omega)\right)\right]^{-1}$$

Therefore, the sensitivities of the eigenvalues of $\boldsymbol{G}(\mathrm{j}\omega)\boldsymbol{K}(\mathrm{j}\omega)$ give information concerning stability with respect to small perturbations (uncertainty) associated with the plant output. Note that at frequencies for which $[\boldsymbol{G}(\mathrm{j}\omega)\boldsymbol{K}(\mathrm{j}\omega)]^{-1}$ becomes very large, the moduli of the characteristic gain loci become very small, and hence their sensitivity becomes unimportant.

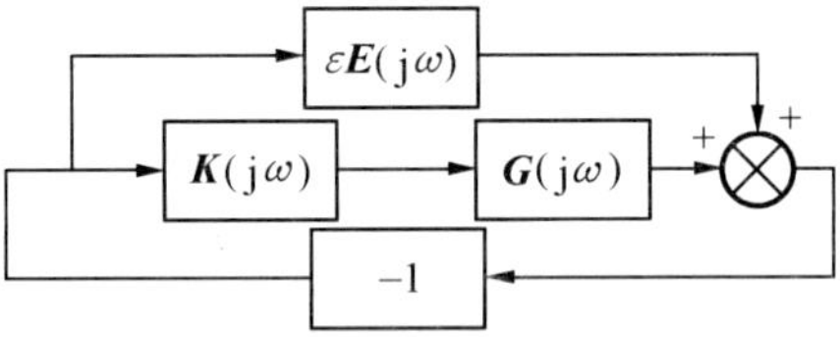

Fig. 1.2 Perturbation of return-ratio matrix $\boldsymbol{G}(\mathrm{j}\omega)\boldsymbol{K}(\mathrm{j}\omega)$

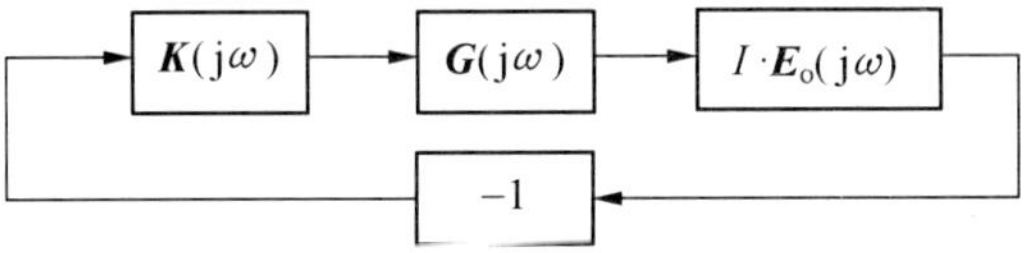

Fig. 1.3 Perturbation asociated with plant output

In an analogous fashion it can be shown that the sensitivities of the eigenvalues of $\boldsymbol{K}(\mathrm{j}\omega)\boldsymbol{G}(\mathrm{j}\omega)$ give information concerning stability with respect to small perturbations (uncertainty) associated with the plant input. For more complicated feedback configurations a return-ratio matrix can be defined at any particular point at which uncertainty is felt to be a problem and the sensitivity of the characteristic gain loci checked via the corresponding sensitivity indices. The return-ratio matrices defined for break points before and after the plant will normally be the most important, and will therefore be referred to as the input and output return-ratio matrices, denoted by $\boldsymbol{T}_{\mathrm{i}}(s)$ and $\boldsymbol{T}_{\mathrm{o}}(s)$ respectively.

The sensitivity indices are numbers between 0 and 1, and when they are all 1 it is clear that the characteristic gain loci are at their least sensitive. A class of matrices for which this is always the case is the set of normal matrices[注5].

Diagonal matrices are normal and therefore design techniques which aim to decouple the outputs from the inputs using a precompensator are well founded from the point of view of achieving robustness with respect to small perturbations at the plant output. It dose not follow, however, that such a design would necessarily be robust with respect to small perturbations at the plant input.

1.4 Relative Stability Matrices

In order to study the robustness of the closed-loop stability property with respect to large and possibly dynamic perturbations consider the feedback configuration of Fig. 1.4, where $\boldsymbol{I}+\boldsymbol{\Delta G}(s)$ represents a multiplicative perturbation of the plant from $\boldsymbol{G}(s)$ to $\boldsymbol{G}(s)+\boldsymbol{G}(s)\boldsymbol{\Delta G}(s)$. The configuration can be redrawn as shown in Fig. 1.5, where the perturbation $\boldsymbol{\Delta G}(s)$ now appears in series with a transfer function $\boldsymbol{R}_{\mathrm{i}}(s)$, given by

$$\boldsymbol{R}_{\mathrm{i}}(s)\approx[\boldsymbol{I}+(\boldsymbol{K}(s)\boldsymbol{G}(s))^{-1}]^{-1}$$

$\boldsymbol{R}_{\mathrm{i}}(s)$ will be called the relative stability matrix with respect to uncertainty at the plant input, or simply the input relative stability matrix.

For a single-input, single-output system a perturbation $1+\Delta g(s)$ commutes around the feedback loop and the relative stability function $[1+(k(s)g(s))^{-1}]^{-1}$ is the same at any point in the configuration. How-

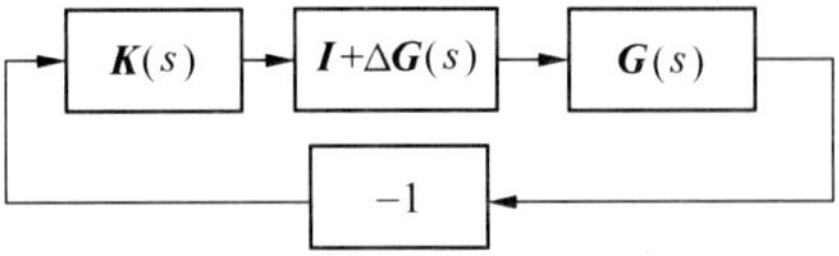

Fig. 1.4 Dynamic uncertainty at plant input

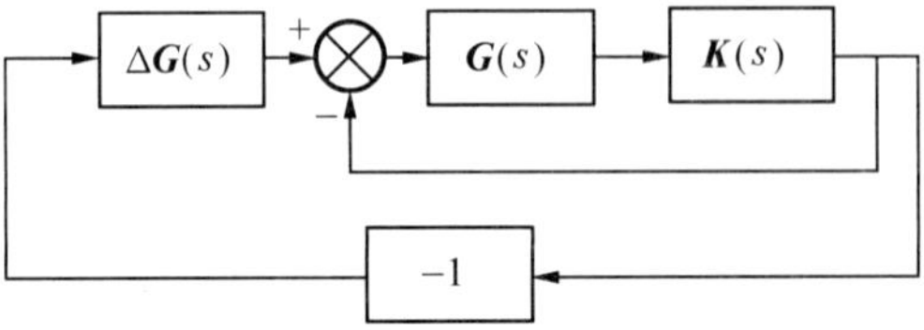

Fig. 1.5 A rearrangement of Fig. 1.4

ever, in multivariable systems this is not the case, and thus it becomes important to examine the effects of perturbations at different points in the loop. The most likely places for uncertainties to occur are at the plant input, considered above, and at the plant output. To analyse the effects of uncertainty at the output consider a multiplicative perturbation, $\boldsymbol{I}+\Delta\boldsymbol{G}(s)$, after the plant shown in Fig. 1.6. This configuration can be redrawn as shown in Fig. 1.7, where $\Delta\boldsymbol{G}(s)$ now appears in series with a transfer function $\boldsymbol{R}_{\mathrm{o}}(s)$, given by

$$\boldsymbol{R}_{\mathrm{o}}(s) \approx ([\boldsymbol{I}+(\boldsymbol{G}(s)\boldsymbol{K}(s))^{-1}]^{-1}$$

$\boldsymbol{R}_{\mathrm{o}}(s)$ will be called the relative stability matrix with respect to uncertainty at the plant output, or simply the output relative stability matrix . It is interesting to note that the input and output relative stability matrices are related by the following expression

$$\boldsymbol{R}_{\mathrm{i}}(s)=\boldsymbol{G}(s)^{-1}\boldsymbol{R}_{\mathrm{o}}(s)\boldsymbol{G}(s)$$

In the next section , it is shown how multivariable gain and phase margins can be defined in terms of the relative stability matrices thereby characterizing perturbations for which the feedback system remains stable.

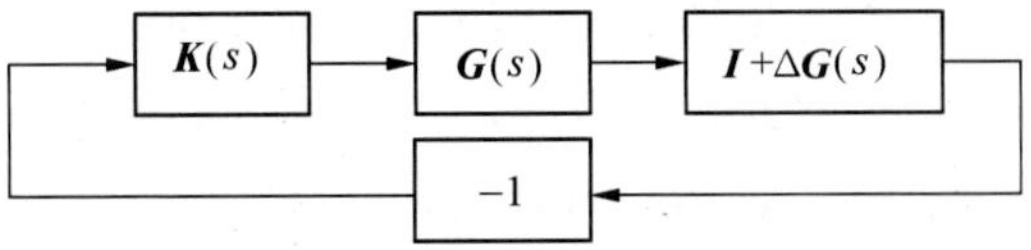

Fig. 1.6 Dynamic uncertainty at the plant output

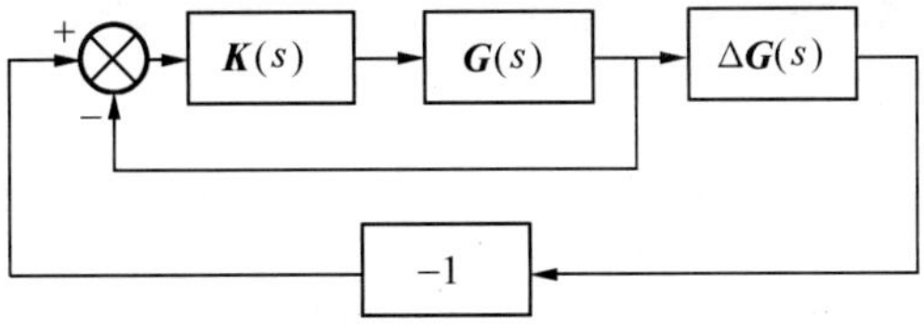

Fig. 1.7 A rearrangement of Fig. 1.6

1.5 Multivariable Gain and Phase Margins

If $\boldsymbol{R}(s)$ is the relative stability matrix corresponding to a multiplicative perturbation $\boldsymbol{I}+\Delta\boldsymbol{G}(s)$, at either the input or output of the plant, then conditions can be derived for $\Delta\boldsymbol{G}(s)$, in terms of $\boldsymbol{R}(s)$, for which the perturbed closed-loop system remains stable. The conditions are summarized in theorems 1.5.3 and 1.5.4 after first introducing some definitions and notation.

The gain and phase information from which the multivariable gain and phase margins are derived stems from the polar decomposition of a complex matrix which is now defined. Analogous to the polar form of a complex number, a complex matrix R can be represented in the forms

$$\boldsymbol{R}=\boldsymbol{U}\boldsymbol{H}_{\mathrm{R}} \tag{1.1}$$

$$\boldsymbol{R}=\boldsymbol{H}_{\mathrm{L}}\boldsymbol{U} \tag{1.2}$$

where $\boldsymbol{U}$ is unitary and $\boldsymbol{H}_{\mathrm{R}}$, $\boldsymbol{H}_{\mathrm{L}}$ are positive semidefinite Hermitian matrices. $\boldsymbol{H}_{\mathrm{R}}$, $\boldsymbol{H}_{\mathrm{L}}$ are often called right and left moduli, and are uniquely determined as $\sqrt{\boldsymbol{R}^*\boldsymbol{R}}$, $\sqrt{\boldsymbol{R}\boldsymbol{R}^*}$ respectively, where * denote complex conjugate transpose, and $\boldsymbol{U}$ is uniquely defined via (1.1) or (1.2) when $\boldsymbol{R}$ is nonsingular. Representations (1.1) and (1.2) are called Polar Decompositions of $\boldsymbol{R}$, and are easily determined from the Singular Value Decomposition of $\boldsymbol{R}$, for which there exists well tested software. If $\boldsymbol{R}$ has the singular value decomposition

$$\boldsymbol{R}=\boldsymbol{X}\Sigma\boldsymbol{V}^*,\ \boldsymbol{X},\ \boldsymbol{V}\text{ unitary, and }\Sigma\text{diagonal and}\geqslant 0$$

then

$$\boldsymbol{R}=(\boldsymbol{XV}^*)(\boldsymbol{V}(\boldsymbol{V}^*)=\boldsymbol{UH}_{\mathrm{R}}$$

and

$$\boldsymbol{R}=(\boldsymbol{X}\Sigma\boldsymbol{X}^*)(\boldsymbol{XV}^*)=\boldsymbol{H}_{\mathrm{L}}\boldsymbol{U}$$

From the polar decompositions the following key quantities are defined:

(1) The eigenvalues of $\boldsymbol{R}$ are called characteristic gains.

(2) The eigenvalues of the Hermitian part in either polar decomposi-tion of $\boldsymbol{R}$ are called principal gains, or singular values.

(3) The arguments of the eigenvalues of the unitary part of the polar decompositions of $\boldsymbol{R}$ are called principal phases.

These three quantities are related by two important uheorems.

Theorem 1.5.1 The magnitudes of the characteristic gains are bounded above and below by the maximum and minimum principal gains[注6].

Theorem 1.5.2 If the principal phases have a spread of less than π, then the arguments of the characteristic gains are bounded above and below by the maximum and minimum principal phases.

Based on these theorems Postelthwaite, Edmunds and MacFarlane derived the robustness results discussed in the remainder of this section.

Let $\boldsymbol{R}(\mathrm{j}\omega)$ have principal gains and principal phases

$$\alpha_1(\omega)\leqslant\alpha_2\leqslant(\omega)\leqslant\cdots\leqslant\alpha_m(\omega)$$

and

$$\theta_1(\omega) \leqslant \theta_2(\omega) \leqslant \cdots \leqslant \theta_m(\omega)$$

respectively; it is assumed that the $\{\theta_i(\omega)\}$ have a spread of less than π. Similarly, let the principal gains and phases of $\Delta\boldsymbol{G}(\mathrm{j}\omega)$ be

$$\delta_1(\omega) \leqslant \delta_2(\omega) \leqslant \cdots \leqslant \delta_m(\omega)$$

and

$$\varepsilon_1(\omega) \leqslant \varepsilon_2(\omega) \leqslant \cdots \leqslant \varepsilon_m(\omega)$$

respectively. Also , let the condition numbers of $\boldsymbol{R}(\mathrm{j}\omega)$ and $\Delta\boldsymbol{G}(\mathrm{j}\omega)$, using the l_2-induced norm, be $c_1(\omega)$ and $c_2(\omega)$, respectively, so that

$$c_1(\omega) \approx \alpha_m(\omega)/\alpha_1(\omega)$$

and

$$c_2(\omega) \approx \delta_m(\omega)/\delta_1(\omega)$$

and also define

$$\Psi_m(\omega) \cong \arctan\left\{\frac{[c_1(\omega)-1]c_2(\omega)}{1-[c_1(\omega)-1]c_2(\omega)}\right\}$$

which will be referred to as a phase modifier. Then the following theorems can be stated.

Theorem 1.5.3 (Small gain theorem) The perturbed closed-loop system remains stable, if

(1) $\Delta\boldsymbol{G}(s)$ is stable, and

(2) $\delta_m(\omega)\alpha_m(\omega)<1$, for all ω.

Theorem 1.5.4 (Small phase theorem) The perturbed closed-loop system remains stable, if

(1) $\Delta\boldsymbol{G}(s)$ is stable,

(2) $\{\theta_i(\omega)+\varepsilon_j(\omega):\ i, j = 1,\cdots, m\}$ have a spread of less than π, for all ω,

(3) $[c_1(\omega)-1]c_2(\omega)<1$, for all ω,

(4) $\varepsilon_1(\omega)+\theta_1(\omega)-\Psi_m(\omega)>-\pi$, for all ω, and

(5) $\varepsilon_m(\omega)+\theta_m(\omega)+\Psi_m(\omega)<\pi$, for all ω.

Corollary 1. 5. 1 By symmetry theorem 1. 5. 4 can be restated with $c_1(\omega)$ and $c_2(\omega)$ interchanged.

Corollary 1.5.2 As a consequence of theorems 1.5.3 and 1.5.4, the perturbed closed-loop system remains stable, if, for some frequency ω_b,

(1) the conditions of theorem 1.5.4 are satisfied in the frequency range $[0, \omega_b]$, and

(2) the conditions of theorem 1.5.3 are satisfied in the frequency range $[\omega_b, \infty]$.

Remark 1.5.1 Theorem 1.5.3 is exactly the small gain theorem introduced by Zames for a more general class of systems. It is also the robustness result used in the LQG-based designs of Doyle and Stein and Safonov, Laub and Hartmann.

Remark 1.5.2 Although it might be argued that theorem 1.5.3 gives an adequate characterization of the robustness of the stability property, the combination of theorems 1.5.3 and 1.5.4 allows a larger set of perturbations to be identified for which the closed-loop system remains stable.

Remark 1.5.3 If in corollary 1.5.1, $\Delta G(s)$ is simply assumed to be a phase change in each of the feedback loops, then $\Delta G(j\omega) = \mathrm{diag}\{\exp(j\omega_i)\}$ and $c_2(\omega)=1$, so that condition (3) is always satisfied, and the phase modification $\Psi_m(\omega)$ is always zero.

Remark 1.5.4 Typically a perturbation $\Delta G(s)$ representing small parameter variations and unmodelled high frequency dynamics will, at low frequencies, have a condition number of approximately 1, and small principal gains[注7]. At high frequencies its maximum principal gain will increase drastically, and the minimum principal phase will exceed 180 degrees lag. Consequently, when predicting perturbations for which the closed-loop systems remain stable, a combination of theorem 1.5.3 and 1.5.4, as in corollary 1.5.2, is useful.

Remark 1.5.5 Theorem 1.5.3 indicates that , at frequencies for which the maximum principal gain of the perturbation is large, the maximum principal gain of $\boldsymbol{R}(j\omega)$ should be designed to be small; this will normally be the case at high frequencies. At low frequencies, theorem 1.5.4 indicates that a perturbation with large gains can be tolerated providing $\boldsymbol{R}(j\omega)$ is designed to have a condition number close to 1 and a small spread of principal phases. This situation will normally be feasible at low frequencies but at high frequencies when the phase lag inevitably exceeds 180 degrees the maximum principal gain of $\boldsymbol{R}(j\omega)$ has necessarily to be made small.

From the preceding remarks it is clear that useful information concerning the robustness of the closed-loop stability property, is readily obtained from Bode plots of the principal gains and phases of the input and output relative stability matrices. Loosely speaking , in going from the scalar to multivariable case, analysis moves from studying a single Bode magnitude and phase plot to studying, for each point of uncertainty, a band of Bode plots, defined by the maximum and minimum principal gains and phases of the appropriate relative stability matrix[注8]. Also, as an indicator of the robustness of the stability property, gain and phase margins can be defined in terms of the maximum principal gain and the minimum principal phase (maximum phase lag) by considering them to be standard Bode magnitude and phase plots for a scalar system.

1.6 Conclusion

The sensitivity indices corresponding to the input and output return-ratio matrices indicate the sensitivity of the characteristic gain loci to small perturbations (uncertainties) at the input and output of the plant, respectively. The indices therefore, give crucial information concerning the possibility of closed-loop instability.

For large and possibly dynamic perturbations (uncertainties) the robustness of the closed-loop stability property is characterized by the principal gains and principal phases of the input and output relative stability matrices. From Bode-type plots of the principal values, multivariable gain and phase margins can be defined which are analogous to the classical single-loop stability margins.

New words and phrases:

1. multivariable *a.* 多变量的
2. synopsis *n.* 摘要,大纲
3. assess *v.* 估价,评定
4. stability margin 稳定裕度
5. generalized *a.* 广义的,推广的
6. time-invariant *a.* 时不变的
7. characteristic gain loci 特征增益轨迹
8. eigenvalue *n.* 本征值,特征值
9. return-ratio *n.* 回归系数
10. *D*-contour *n.* *D* 形轨线
11. critical point 临界点,驻点
12. scalar *n.* ;*a.* 标量(的)
13. singular value 奇异值
14. perturbation *n.* 扰动
15. it follows that 由此得出[可见],因此,从而
16. sensitivity index 灵敏度指数
17. left[right]-hand eigenvector 左[右]特征向量
18. normal *n.* ;*a.* 正规(的)
19. monograph *n.* 专著
20. modulus *n.* 模
21. connected domain 连通区域
22. transpose *v.* 转置
23. normalize *v.* 正规化
24. linear elementary divisor 线性初等因子
25. diagonal matrix 对角阵
26. candidate set 候选集

27. submatrix *n.* 子阵
28. decouple 解耦
29. precompensator *n.* 前置补偿器
30. multiplicative *a.* 倍增的
31. in series with 与串联
32. relative stability 相对稳定性
33. commute *v.* 变换，交换
34. polar decomposition 极(坐标)分解
35. unitary *a.* 酉(矩阵)的
36. semidefinite *a.* 半定的
37. complex conjugate transpose 复共轭转置
38. singular value decomposition 奇异值分解
39. characteristic gain 特征增益
40. principal gain (phase) 主增益[相角]
41. argument *n.* 幅角
42. spread *n.* 范围，跨距
43. condition number 条件数
44. norm *n.* 范数
45. phase modifier 相位调节器
46. corollary *n.* 推论
47. LQG (linear quadratic Gaussion) 线性二次型高斯
48. dynamic *n.* 动态
49. lag *n.* 滞后，延迟

Notes:

1. In the generalized Nyquist stability criterion put forward by MacFarlane, and subsequently proved by several researchers, the stability of a linear, time-invariant, multivariable, feedback system, such as is shown in Fig1. 1, is determined from the characteristic gain loci which are a plot of the eigenvalues of the return-ratio matrix $\boldsymbol{G}(s)\boldsymbol{K}(s)$ (or equivalently the eigenvalues of the return-ratio matrix $\boldsymbol{K}(s)\boldsymbol{G}(s)$) as the Laplace transform variable s traverses the standard Nyquist D-contour.

译：在由 MacFarlane 提出、接着被几个学者证明了的广义 Nyquist 稳

定判据中，如图 1.1 所示的一个线性时不变多变量反馈系统的稳定性是通过特征增益轨迹来确定的，特征增益轨迹是当 Laplace 变换变量 s 沿标准 Nyquist 的 D 轨线移动时，回差矩阵 $\boldsymbol{G}(s)\boldsymbol{K}(s)$ 的特征值（或者等价地，回差矩阵 $\boldsymbol{K}(s)\boldsymbol{G}(s)$ 的特征值）的曲线。

2. They showed that the closed-loop system remains stable when subjected to a stable matrix perturbation $\boldsymbol{I}+\boldsymbol{P}(s)$, at any point in the configuration, providing the maximum singular value of $\boldsymbol{P}(\mathrm{j}\omega)$ multiplied by the maximum singular value of the frequencies-response matrix $[\boldsymbol{I}+\boldsymbol{T}(\mathrm{j}\omega)^{-1}]^{-1}$ is less than 1, at all frequencies, where $\boldsymbol{T}(s)$ is the return-ratio matrix for the point in question .

译：他们指出，一闭环系统，假设在所有频率上，$\boldsymbol{P}(\mathrm{j}\omega)$ 的最大奇异值乘以频率响应矩阵 $[\boldsymbol{I}+\boldsymbol{T}(\mathrm{j}\omega)^{-1}]^{-1}$ 的最大奇异值之积小于 1（其中 $\boldsymbol{T}(s)$ 为所考虑点的回归系数矩阵），那么，当系统在结构中的任一点处受到一个稳定的矩阵扰动 $\boldsymbol{I}+\boldsymbol{P}(s)$ 时，仍能保持稳定。

3. A system which has a large degree of stability in term of these multivariable gain and phase margins will have characteristic gain loci which although not necessarily insensitive to small perturbations will nevertheless be insensitive enough for the number of encirclements of the critical point to remain unchanged.

译：在这些多变量增益和相角裕度意义上，一个具有大的稳定度的系统将有如下性质的特征增益轨迹，即该轨迹尽管对小扰动不具有必要的不敏感性，但它环绕临界点的圈数对小扰动具有足够的不敏感性，能保持不变。

4. In the analysis that follows a set of quantities will be used repeatedly.

译：在后面的分析中，一组参数将被反复使用。

5. A class of matrices for which this is always the case is the set of normal matrices.

译：总是这种情况(矩阵的灵敏度指数全为 1)的一类矩阵属于正规矩阵集合。

6. The magnitudes of the characteristic gains are bounded above and below by the maximum and minimum principal gains.

译：特征增益的幅度在上面和下面受最大和最小主增益的限制。

7. Typically a perturbation $\boldsymbol{\Delta G}(s)$ representing small parameter variations and unmodelled high frequency dynamics will, at low frequencies, have a condition number of approximately 1, and small principal gains.

译：典型地，一个代表小的参数变化和未建模高频动态的扰动 $\boldsymbol{\Delta G}(s)$，在低频处具有一个约为 1 的条件数和小的主增益。

8. Loosely speaking, in going from the scalar to multivariable case, analysis moves from studying a single Bode magnitude and phase plot to studying, for each point of uncertainty, a band of Bode plots, defined by the maximum and minimum principal gains and phases of the appropriate relative stability matrix.

译：粗略地说，在从单变量情况到多变量情况的转变中，分析方法也从研究一单个 Bode 幅值和相角图变成针对每个不确定点来研究一条 Bode 图带，这条带由适当的相对稳定性矩阵的最大、最小主增益和最大、最小主相角来定义。

PART 2	CHAPTER TWO

2 The Inverse Nyquist Array Design Method

Synopsis

The general problem of the design of multivariable control systems is considered and stability of multivariable feedback systems is examined. The concept of ' diagonal dominance' is introduced, and Rosenbrock's Inverse Nyquist Array Design Method is developed. Methods of achieving diagonal dominance are discussed and illustrated in terms of practical problems.

2.1 Introduction

The design of control systems for single-input single-output plant using the classical frequency response methods of Bode, Nyquist and Nichols is well established. However, the frequency response approach of Nyquist has been extended by Rosenbrock to deal with multi-input multi-output plant where significant interaction is present.

During the last decade, interactive computing facilities have developed rapidly and it is now possible to communicate with a digital computer in a variety of ways; e. g. graphic display systems with cursors, joysticks, and light-pens. Equally, the digital computer can present information to the user in the form of graphs on a display terminal or as hard-copy on a digital plotter. The classical frequency-response methods for single-input single-output systems rely heavily on graphical representations, and Rosenbrock's ' inverse Nyquist array' design method for multivariable systems suitably exploits the graphical output capabilities of modern digital computer system. Also, the increased complexity of multivariable systems has made it necessary to employ interactive computer-aided design facilities, such as those developed at the Control Systems

Centre, UMIST, Manchester, in order to establish an effective dialogue with the user.

2.2 The Multivariable Design Problem

In general, a multivariable control system will have m inputs and l outputs and the system can be described by an $l \times m$ transfer function matrix $\boldsymbol{G}(s)$. Since we are interested in feedback control we almost always have $l = m$.

The uncontrolled plant is assumed to be described by an rational transfer function matrix $\boldsymbol{G}(s)$ and we wish to determine a controller matrix $\boldsymbol{K}(s)$ such that when we close the feedback loops through the feedback matrix $\boldsymbol{F}$, as in Fig. 2.1, the system is stable and has suitably fast responses.

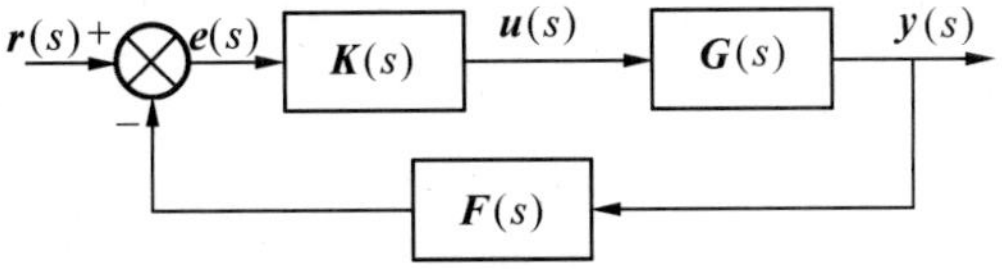

Fig. 2.1

The matrix $\boldsymbol{F}$ is assumed diagonal and independent of s, i. e.

$$\boldsymbol{F} = \mathrm{diag}\{f_i\} \tag{2.1}$$

$\boldsymbol{F}$ represents loop gains which will usually be implemented in the forward path, but which it is convenient to move into the return path[注1]. In addition, the design will have high integrity if the system remains stable as the gain in each loop is reduced.

Let us consider the controller matrix $\boldsymbol{K}(s)$ to consist of the product of two matrices $\boldsymbol{K}_p(s)$ and $\boldsymbol{K}_d$, i. e.

$$\boldsymbol{K}(s) = \boldsymbol{K}_p(s)\boldsymbol{K}_d \tag{2.2}$$

where $\boldsymbol{K}_d$ is a diagonal matrix independent of s; i. e.

$$\boldsymbol{K}_d = \mathrm{diag}\{k_i\} \qquad i = 1, \cdots, m \tag{2.3}$$

Then the system of Fig. 2. 1 can be rearranged as shown in Fig. 2. 2

where the stability of the closed-loop system is unaffected by the matrix K_d outside the loop. For convenience, we rename the matrix K_dF as F. All combinations of gains and of open or closed-loops can now be obtained by a suitable choice of the f_i, and we shall want the system to remain stable for all values of the f_i from zero up to their design values[注2].

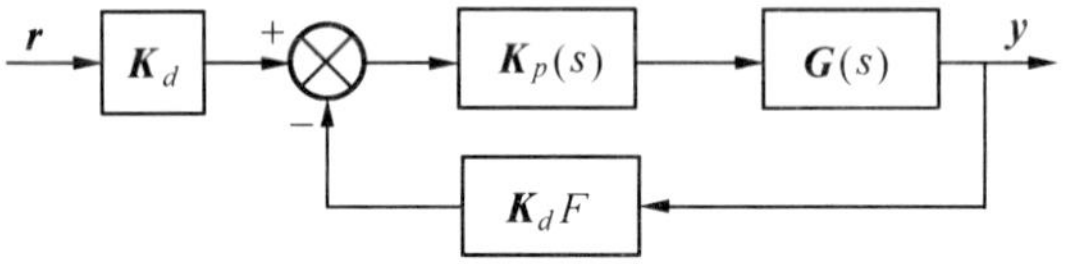

Fig. 2. 2

When $f_1 = 0$ the first loop is open, and all gains in the first loop up to the design value f_{1d} can be achieved by increasing f_1.

The elements f_i of $F = \text{diag}\{f_i\}$ can be represented by points in an m-dimensional space which can be called the gain space. That part of the gain space in which $f_i>0$, $i = 1, \cdots, m$ corresponds to negative feedback in all loops, and is the region of most practical interest. The point $\{f_1, f_2, \cdots, f_m\}$ belongs to the asymptotically stable region in the gain space if and only if the system is asymptotically stable with $F = \text{diag}\{f_i\}$[注3].

Let

$$Q(s) = G(s)K(s) \tag{2.4}$$

then the closed-loop system transfer function matrix H(s) is given by

$$H(s) = (I+Q(s)F)^{-1}Q(s) = Q(s)(I+FQ(s))^{-1} \tag{2.5}$$

Consider the open-loop system

$$Q(s) = \begin{bmatrix} \dfrac{1}{s+1} & \dfrac{2}{s+3} \\ \dfrac{1}{s+1} & \dfrac{1}{s+1} \end{bmatrix} \tag{2.6}$$

Then if $f_1 = 10$ and $f_2 = 0$, $H(s)$ has all of its poles in the open left-half plane and the system is asymptotically stable. However, for $f_1 = 10$ and

$f_2=10$, the closed-loop system $\boldsymbol{H}(s)$ is unstable, as shown in Fig. 2. 3. This situation could have been predicted by examining the McMillan form of $\boldsymbol{Q}(s)$ which is

$$\boldsymbol{M}(s)=\begin{bmatrix} \dfrac{1}{(s+1)(s+3)} & 0 \\ 0 & \dfrac{(s-1)}{(s+1)} \end{bmatrix} \tag{2.7}$$

where the poles of the McMillan form are referred to as the "poles of the system" and the zeros of the McMillan form are referred to as the "zeros of the system". If any of the "zeros" of $\boldsymbol{Q}(s)$ lie in the closed right-half plane, then it will not be possible to set up m high gain control loops around this system.

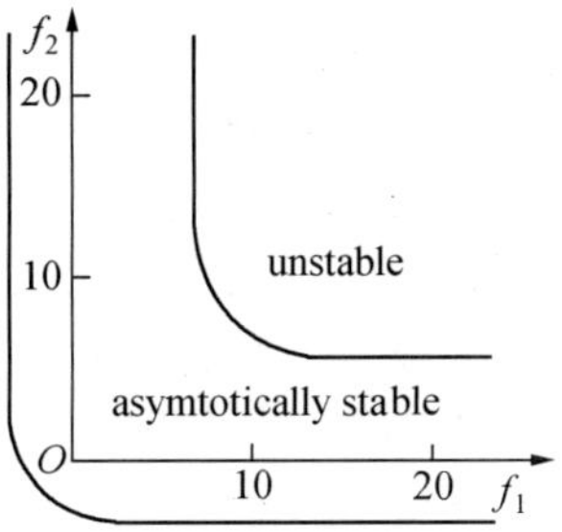

Fig. 2. 3

Consider now the gain space for the system described by

$$\boldsymbol{Q}(s)=\begin{bmatrix} \dfrac{s-1}{(s+1)^2} & \dfrac{5s+1}{(s+1)^2} \\ \dfrac{-1}{(s+1)^2} & \dfrac{s-1}{(s+1)^2} \end{bmatrix} \tag{2.8}$$

which is shown in Fig. 2. 4. Now, up to a certain point, increase of gain in one loop allows increase of gain in the other loop without instability. The McMillan form of this latter system $\boldsymbol{Q}(s)$ is

$$\boldsymbol{M}(s)=\begin{bmatrix}\dfrac{1}{(s+1)^2} & 0 \\ 0 & \dfrac{s+2}{s+1}\end{bmatrix} \tag{2.9}$$

which implies that, despite the non-minimum phase terms in the diagonal elements of $\boldsymbol{Q}(s)$, no non-minimum phase behaviour will be obtained with the feedback loops closed. It is also interesting to note that this system is stable with a small amount of positive feedback. However, this is not a high integrity system, since failure of any one loop may put the system into an unstable region of operation.

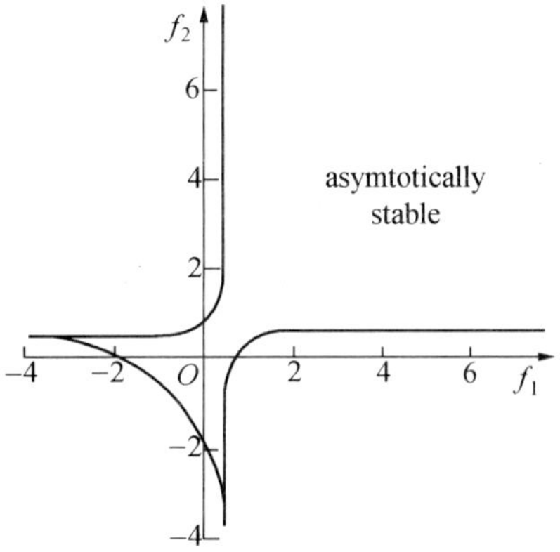

Fig. 2.4

2.3 Stability

Consider the system shown in Fig. 2.5, in which all matrices are $m \times m$; this last condition is easily relaxed. Let $\boldsymbol{Q}=\boldsymbol{LGK}$, and suppose that $\boldsymbol{G}$ arises from the system matrix

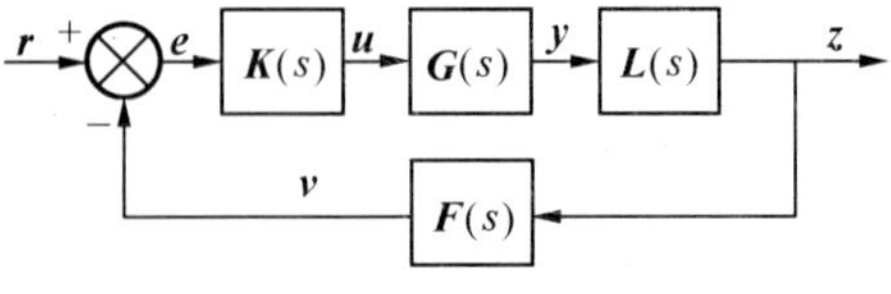

Fig. 2.5

$$P_G(s)=\begin{bmatrix} T_G(s) & U_G(s) \\ -V_G(s) & W_G(s) \end{bmatrix} \tag{2.10}$$

and similarly for $K(s)$, $L(s)$, $F(s)$. For generality, we do not require any of these system matrices to have least order. The equations of the closed-loop system can then be written as

$$\begin{bmatrix} T_K & U_K & 0 & 0 & 0 & 0 & 0 & 0 & \vdots & 0 \\ -V_K & W_K & 0 & -I_m & 0 & 0 & 0 & 0 & \vdots & 0 \\ 0 & 0 & T_G & U_G & 0 & 0 & 0 & 0 & \vdots & 0 \\ 0 & 0 & -V_G & W_G & 0 & -I_m & 0 & 0 & \vdots & 0 \\ 0 & 0 & 0 & 0 & T_L & U_L & 0 & 0 & \vdots & 0 \\ 0 & 0 & 0 & 0 & -V_L & U_L & 0 & -I_m & \vdots & 0 \\ 0 & 0 & 0 & 0 & 0 & 0 & T_F & U_F & \vdots & 0 \\ 0 & I_m & 0 & 0 & 0 & 0 & -V_F & W_F & \vdots & -I_m \\ \cdots & \cdots & \cdots & \cdots & \cdots & \cdots & \cdots & \cdots & \cdots & \cdots \\ 0 & 0 & 0 & 0 & 0 & 0 & 0 & I & \vdots & 0 \end{bmatrix} \begin{bmatrix} \bar{\xi}_K \\ -\bar{e} \\ \bar{\xi}_G \\ -\bar{u} \\ \bar{\xi}_L \\ -\bar{y} \\ \bar{\xi}_F \\ -\bar{z} \\ \cdots \\ -\bar{v} \end{bmatrix} = \begin{bmatrix} 0 \\ 0 \\ 0 \\ 0 \\ 0 \\ 0 \\ 0 \\ 0 \\ \cdots \\ -\bar{Z} \end{bmatrix} \tag{2.11}$$

Here the matrix on the left-hand side of equation (2.11) is a system matrix for the closed-loop system shown in Fig. 2.5, which we can also write as

$$P_H=\begin{bmatrix} T_H & U_H \\ -V_H & W_H \end{bmatrix} \tag{2.12}$$

The closed-loop system poles are the zeros of $|T_H(s)|$, and Rosenbrock has shown that

$$|T_H(s)| = |I_m+Q(s)F(s)|\,|T_L(s)|\,|T_G(s)|\,|T_K(s)|\,|T_F(s)| \tag{2.13}$$

As the zeros of $|T_L|\,|T_G|\,|T_K|\,|T_F|$ are the open-loop poles, we need only the following information to investigate stability:

(1) The rational function $|I_m+Q(s)F(s)|$;

(2) The locations of any open-loop poles in the closed right half-plane (crhp).

Notice that this result holds whether or not the subsystems have least order. If we apply Cauchy's theorem, (2) can be further reduced: all we need is the number p_o of open-loop poles in the crhp.

From equation (2.5)

$$|I_m+QF| = |Q(s)|/|H(s)| \tag{2.14}$$

The Nyquist criterion depends on encirclements of a critical point by the frequency response locus of the system to indicate stability. Let D be the usual Nyquist stability contour in the s-plane consisting of the imaginary axis from $-jR$ to $+jR$, together with a semi-circle of radius R in the right half plane. The contour D is supposed large enough to enclose all finite poles and zeros of $|Q(s)|$ and $|H(s)|$, lying in the closed right half plane.

Let $|Q(s)|$ map D into Γ_Q, while $|H(s)|$ maps D into Γ_H. As s goes once clockwise around D, let Γ_Q encircle the origin N_Q times clockwise, and let Γ_H encircle the origin N_H times clockwise. Then, if the open-loop system characteristic polynomial has p_o zeros in the closed right half plane, the closed-loop system is asymptotically stable if and only if

$$N-N_Q=p_o \tag{2.15}$$

This form of the stability theorem is directly analogous to the form used with single-input single-output systems, but is difficult to use since $|H(s)|$ is a complicated function of $Q(s)$[注4], namely

$$|H(s)| = |Q(s)|/|I+QF| \tag{2.16}$$

Equation (2.5)

$$H(s)=(I+Q(s)F)^{-1}Q(s)$$

shows that the relationship between the open-loop system $Q(s)$ and the closed-loop system $H(s)$ is not simple. However, if $Q^{-1}(s)$ exists then

$$H^{-1}(s)=F+Q^{-1}(s) \tag{2.17}$$

which is simpler to deal with. Instead of $H^{-1}(s)$ and $Q^{-1}(s)$ we shall write $\hat{\boldsymbol{H}}(s) = \boldsymbol{H}^{-1}(s)$ and $\hat{\boldsymbol{Q}}(s) = \boldsymbol{Q}^{-1}(s)$. Then, the $\hat{h}_{ii}(s)$ are the diagonal elements of $\boldsymbol{H}^{-1}(s)$. In general, $\hat{h}_{ii}(s) \neq h_{ii}^{-1}(s)$, where $h_{ii}^{-1}(s)$ is the inverse of the diagonal element $h_{ii}(s)$ of $\boldsymbol{H}(s)$.

We shall, in what follows, develop the required stability theorems in terms of the inverse system matrices[注5]. Also, we note that if $\boldsymbol{K}(s)$ has been chosen such that $\boldsymbol{Q}(s) = \boldsymbol{G}(s)\boldsymbol{K}(s)$ is diagonal and if $\boldsymbol{F}$ is diagonal, then we have m single loops. However, several objections to this approach can be made. In particular, it is an unnecessary extreme. Instead of diagonalising the system, we shall consider the much looser criterion of diagonal dominance.

2.3.1 Diagonal dominance

A rational $m \times m$ matrix $\hat{\boldsymbol{Q}}(s)$ is row diagonal dominant on $\boldsymbol{D}$ if

$$|\hat{q}_{ii}(s)| > \sum_{\substack{j=1 \\ j \neq i}}^{m} |\hat{q}_{ij}(s)| \tag{2.18a}$$

for $i = 1, \cdots, m$ and all s on $\boldsymbol{D}$. Column diagonal dominance is defined similarly by

$$|\hat{q}_{ii}(s)| > \sum_{\substack{j=1 \\ j \neq i}}^{m} |\hat{q}_{ji}(s)| \tag{2.18b}$$

The dominance of a rational matrix $\hat{\boldsymbol{Q}}(s)$ can be determined by a simple graphical construction. Let $\hat{q}_{ii}(s)$ map $\boldsymbol{D}$ into $\hat{\Gamma}_i$ as in Fig. 2. 6. This will look like an inverse Nyquist plot, but does not represent anything directly measurable on the physical system. For each s on $\boldsymbol{D}$ *draw a circle of radius*

$$d_i(s) = \sum_{\substack{j=1 \\ j \neq i}}^{m} |\hat{q}_{ij}(s)| \tag{2.19}$$

centred on the appropriate point of $\hat{q}_{ii}(s)$, as in Fig. 2. 6. Do the same for the other diagonal elements of $\hat{\boldsymbol{Q}}(s)$. If each of the bands so produced excludes the origin, for $i = 1, \cdots, m$, then $\hat{\boldsymbol{Q}}(s)$ is row dominant on $\boldsymbol{D}$[注6]. A similar test for column dominance can be defined by using circles of radius

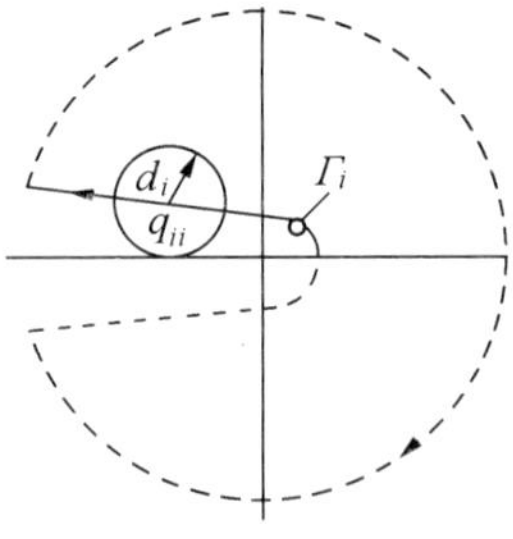

Fig. 2.6

$$d'_i(s) = \sum_{\substack{j=1 \\ j \neq i}}^{m} |\hat{q}_{ji}(s)| \tag{2.20}$$

2.3.2 Further stability theorems

If $\hat{\boldsymbol{Q}}(s)$ is row (or column) dominant on $\boldsymbol{D}$, having on it no zero of $|\hat{\boldsymbol{Q}}(s)|$ and no pole of $\hat{q}_{ii}(s)$, for $i = 1, \cdots, m$, then let $\hat{q}_{ii}(s)$ map $\boldsymbol{D}$ into $\hat{\boldsymbol{\Gamma}}_i$ and $|\hat{\boldsymbol{Q}}(s)|$ map $\boldsymbol{D}$ into $\hat{\boldsymbol{\Gamma}}_Q$. If $\hat{\boldsymbol{\Gamma}}_i$ encircles the origin $\hat{N}_i$ times and $\hat{\boldsymbol{\Gamma}}_Q$ encircles the origin $\hat{N}_Q$ times, all encirclements being clockwise, then Rosenbrock has shown that

$$\hat{N}_Q = \sum_{i=1}^{m} \hat{N}_i \tag{2.21}$$

A proof of this result is given in the Appendix.

Let $\hat{\boldsymbol{Q}}(s)$ and $\hat{\boldsymbol{H}}(s)$ be dominant on $\boldsymbol{D}$, let $\hat{q}_{ii}(s)$ map $\boldsymbol{D}$ into $\hat{\boldsymbol{\Gamma}}_{qi}$ and let $\hat{h}_{ii}(s)$ map $\boldsymbol{D}$ into $\hat{\boldsymbol{\Gamma}}_{hi}$. Let these encircle the origin $\hat{N}_{qi}$ and $\hat{N}_{hi}$ times respectively. Then with p_o defined as in (2.15), the closed-loop system is asymptotically stable if, and only if

$$\sum_{i=1}^{m} \hat{N}_{qi} - \sum_{i=1}^{m} \hat{N}_{hi} = p_o \tag{2.22}$$

This expression represents a generalized form of Nyquist's stability criterion, applicable to multivariable systems which are diagonal dominant.

For $|\boldsymbol{Q}|$

$$N_Q = -\sum_{i=1}^{m} \hat{N}_{qi} \tag{2.23}$$

and since we are considering inverse polar plots stability is determined using

$$\hat{N}_{\boldsymbol{H}}-\hat{N}_{\boldsymbol{Q}}=-p_{\mathrm{o}}+p_{\mathrm{c}} \tag{2.24}$$

where $p_{\mathrm{c}}=0$ for closed-loop stability.

Hence,

$$\hat{N}_{\boldsymbol{Q}}-\hat{N}_{N}=p_{\mathrm{o}} \tag{2.25}$$

replaces the relationship used with direct polar plots, given by equation (2.15).

2.3.3 Graphical criteria for stability

If for each diagonal element $\hat{q}_{ii}(s)$, the band swept out by its circles does not include the origin or the critical point $(-f_i, 0)$, and if this is true for $i=1, 2, \cdots, m$, then the generalized form of the inverse Nyquist stability criterion, defined by (2.25), is satisfied. In general, the $\hat{q}_{ii}(s)$ do not represent anything directly measurable on the system. However, using a theorem due to Ostrowski

$$h_i^{-1}(s) = h_{ii}^{-1}(s)-f_i \tag{2.26}$$

is contained within the band swept out by the circles centred on $\hat{q}_{ii}(s)$, and this remains true for all values of gain f_j in each other loop j between zero and $f_{j\mathrm{d}}$. Note that $h_{ii}^{-1}(s)$ is the inverse transfer function seen between input i and output i with all loops closed. The transfer function $h_i(s)$ is that seen in the ith loop when this is open, but the other loops are closed. It is this transfer function for which we must design a single-loop controller for the ith loop.

The theorems above tell us that as the gain in each other loop changes as long as dominance is maintained in the other loops, $h_{ii}^{-1}(s)$ will also change but always remains inside the ith Gershgorin band[注7]. The band within which $h_i^{-1}(s)$ lies can be further narrowed. If $\hat{\boldsymbol{Q}}$ and $\hat{\boldsymbol{H}}$ are dominant, and if

$$\phi_i(s)=\max_{\substack{j \\ j\neq i}}\frac{d_j(s)}{|f_j+\hat{q}_{jj}(s)|} \tag{2.27}$$

then $h_i^{-1}(s)$ lies wiuhin a band based on $\hat{q}_{ii}(s)$ and defined by circles of radius

$$r_i(s) = \phi_i(s) d_i(s) \qquad (2.28)$$

Thus, once the closed-loop system gains have been chosen such that stability is achieved in terms of the larger bands, then a measure of the gain margin for each loop can be determined by drawing the smaller bands, using the 'shrinking factors' $\phi_i(s)$ defined by (2.27), with circles of radius r_i. These narrower bands, known as Ostrowski bands, also reduce the region of uncertainty as to the actual location of the inverse transfer function $h_{ii}^{-1}(s)$ for each loop[注8].

2.4 Design Technique

Using the ideas developed in the previous section, the frequency domain design method proposed by Rosenbrock consists essentially of determining a matrix $\boldsymbol{K}_p(s)$ such that the product $[\boldsymbol{G}(s)\boldsymbol{K}_p(s)]^{-1}$ is diagonal dominant. When this condition has been achieved then the diagonal matrix $\boldsymbol{K}_d(s)$ can be used to implement single-loop compensators as required to meet the overall design specification. Since the design is carried out using the inverse transfer function matrix then we are essentially trying to determine an inverse precompensator $\hat{\boldsymbol{K}}_p(s)$ such that $\hat{\boldsymbol{Q}}(s) = \hat{\boldsymbol{K}}_p(s)\ \hat{\boldsymbol{G}}(s)$ is diagonal dominant. The method is well suited to interactive graphical use of a computer.

One method of determining $\hat{\boldsymbol{K}}_p(s)$ is to build up the required matrix out of elementary row operations using a graphical display of all of the elements of $\hat{\boldsymbol{Q}}(s)$ as a guide[注9]. This approach has proven successful in practice and has, in most cases considered to-date, resulted in $\boldsymbol{K}_p(s)$ being a simple matrix of real constants which can be readily realized.

Another approach which has proved useful is to choose $\hat{\boldsymbol{K}}_p = \boldsymbol{G}(0)$, if $|\boldsymbol{G}(0)|$ is nonsingular. Here again $\hat{\boldsymbol{K}}_p(s)$ is a matrix of real constants which simply diagonalizes the plant at zero frequency.

For example, Fig. 2.7 shows the inverse Nyquist array (INA) of an uncompensated system with 2 inputs and 2 outputs. An inspection of this diagram shows that element 1,2 is larger than element 1,1 at the

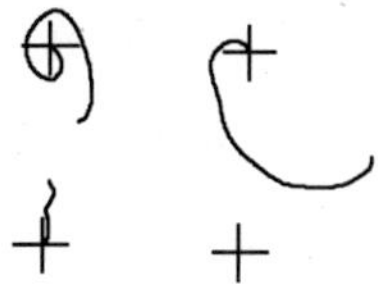

Fig. 2.7

maximum frequency considered, and similarly element 2,1 is very much larger than element 2,2 over a wide range of frequencies. Thus, the open-loop system is not row diagonal dominant, nor is it column diagonal dominant. However, by choosing $\hat{\boldsymbol{K}}_p=\boldsymbol{G}(0)$ the resulting INA of $\hat{\boldsymbol{Q}}(\mathrm{j}\omega)$ is shown in Fig. 2. 8 with the Gershgorin circles for row dominance superimposed. Both $\hat{q}_{11}$ and $\hat{q}_{22}$ are made diagonal dominant with this simple operation. The dominance of element $\hat{q}_{22}$ of this array can be further improved by another simple row operation of the form

$$R'_2=R_2+\alpha R_1 \tag{2.29}$$

where $\alpha=0.5$, in this case.

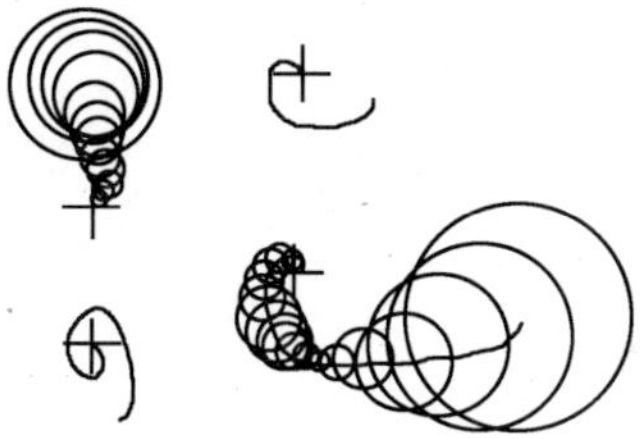

Fig. 2. 8

A further approach, which is perhaps more systematic than those mentioned above, is to determine $\hat{\boldsymbol{K}}_p$ as the 'best', in a least-mean-squares sense, wholly real matrix which most nearly diagonalizes the system $\hat{\boldsymbol{Q}}$ at some frequency $s=\mathrm{j}\omega$. This choice of $\hat{\boldsymbol{K}}_p$ can be considered as the best matrix of real constants which makes the sum of the moduli of the off-diagonal elements in each row of $\hat{\boldsymbol{Q}}$ as small as possible compared with the modulus of the diagonal element at some frequency $s=\mathrm{j}\omega$[注10]. The development of the two forms of this latter approach is given in the following paragraphs.

Consider the elements $\hat{q}_{jk}$ in some row j of $\hat{\boldsymbol{Q}}(\mathrm{j}\omega)=\hat{\boldsymbol{K}}\hat{\boldsymbol{G}}(\mathrm{j}\omega)$, i. e.

$$\hat{q}_{jk}(\mathrm{j}\omega) = \sum_{i=1}^{m} \hat{k}_{ji}\hat{g}_{ik}(\mathrm{j}\omega) = \tag{2.30}$$

$$\sum_{i=1}^{m} \hat{k}_{ji}(\alpha_{ik} + \mathrm{j}\beta_{ik}) \tag{2.31}$$

Now choose $\hat{k}_{j1}, \hat{k}_{j2}, \cdots, \hat{k}_{jm}$ so that

$$\sum_{\substack{k=1\\k\neq j}}^{m} |\hat{q}_{jk}(\mathrm{j}\omega)|^2 \tag{2.32}$$

is made as small as possible subject to the constraint that

$$\sum_{i=1}^{m} \hat{k}_{ji}^2 = 1 \tag{2.33}$$

Using a Lagrange multiplier, we minimize

$$\phi_j = \sum_{\substack{k=1\\k\neq j}}^{m} \left| \sum_{i=1}^{m} \hat{k}_{ji}(\alpha_{ik} + \mathrm{j}\beta_{ik}) \right|^2 + \lambda\left[1 - \sum_{i=1}^{m} \hat{k}_{ji}^2\right] = \tag{2.34}$$

$$\sum_{\substack{k=1\\k\neq j}}^{m} \left[\left[\sum_{i=1}^{m} \hat{k}_{ji}\alpha_{ik}\right]^2 + \left[\sum_{i=1}^{m} \hat{k}_{ji}\beta_{ik}\right]^2 + \lambda\left[1 - \sum_{i=1}^{m} \hat{k}_{ji}^2\right]\right] \tag{2.35}$$

and taking partial derivatives of ϕ_j with respect to $\hat{k}_{jl}$ (i. e. the elements of the row vector $\hat{k}_j$), we get, on setting these equal to zero

$$\frac{\partial\phi_j}{\partial k_{jl}} = \sum_{\substack{k=1\\k\neq j}}^{m} \left[2\left[\sum_{i=1}^{m} \hat{k}_{ji}\alpha_{ik}\right]\alpha_{lk} + 2\left[\sum_{i=1}^{m} \hat{k}_{ji}\beta_{ik}\right]\beta_{lk}\right] - 2\lambda\hat{k}_{jl} = 0$$

$$\text{for } l = 1, 2, \cdots, m \tag{2.36}$$

Now writing

$$\boldsymbol{A}_j = \{a_{il}^{(j)}\} = \left[\sum_{\substack{k=1\\k\neq j}}^{m} (\alpha_{ik}\alpha_{lk} + \beta_{ik}\beta_{lk})\right] \tag{2.37}$$

and

$$\hat{\boldsymbol{k}}_j = (\hat{k}_{jl}) \tag{2.38}$$

the minimization becomes

$$\boldsymbol{A}_j\hat{\boldsymbol{k}}_j^{\mathrm{T}} - \lambda\hat{\boldsymbol{k}}_j^{\mathrm{T}} = 0 \tag{2.39}$$

since

$$\sum_{\substack{k=1 \\ k \neq j}}^{m} |\hat{q}^{jk}(j\omega)|^2 = \hat{\boldsymbol{k}}_j \boldsymbol{A}_j \hat{\boldsymbol{k}}_j^{\mathrm{T}} = \boldsymbol{\lambda} \hat{\boldsymbol{k}}_j \hat{\boldsymbol{k}}_j^{\mathrm{T}} = \boldsymbol{\lambda} \tag{2.40}$$

Thus, the design problem becomes an eigenvalue/eigenvector problem where the row vector $\hat{\boldsymbol{k}}_j$, which pseudodiagonalizes row j of $\hat{\boldsymbol{Q}}$ at some frequency jω, is the eigenvector of the symmetric positive semi-definite (or definite) matrix $\boldsymbol{A}_j$ corresponding to the smallest eigenvalue of $\boldsymbol{A}_j$.

Fig. 2.9 shows the INA of a 4-input 4-output system over the frequency range 0→1 rad/sec. Although the Gershgorin circles superimposed on the diagonal elements show that the basic system is diagonal dominant, the size of these circles at the 1 rad/sec end of the frequency range indicate that the interaction in the system may be unacceptable during transient changes. Using the pseudodiagonalisation algorithm described above, at a frequency of 0.9 rad/sec in each row, a simple wholly real compensator $\hat{\boldsymbol{K}}_p$ can be determined which yields the INA shown in Fig. 2.10. Here, we can see that the size of the Gershgorin discs has in fact been considerably reduced over all of the bandwidth of interest.

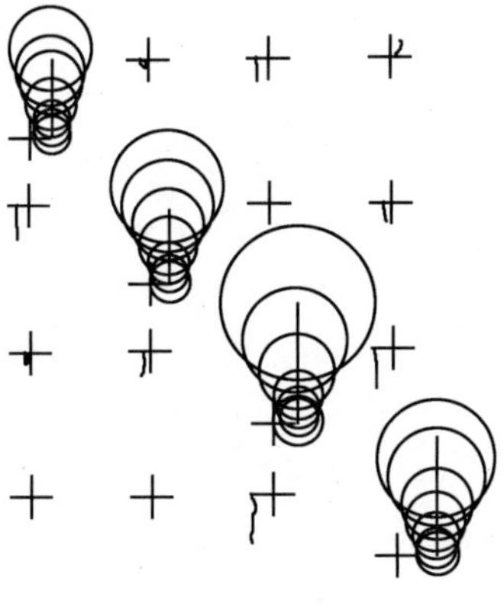

Fig. 2.9

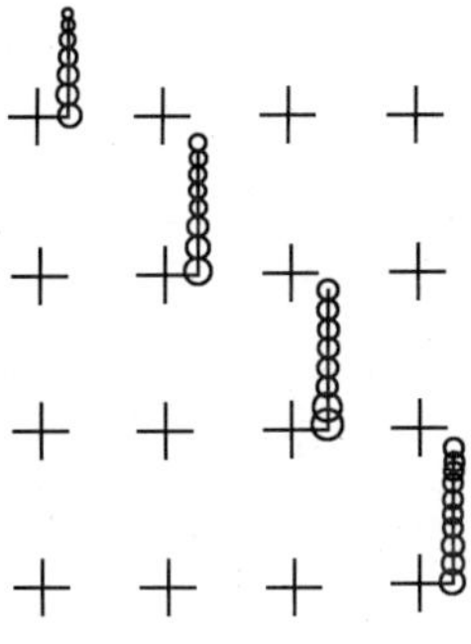

Fig. 2.10

However, in general, we may choose a different frequency ω for each row of $\hat{\boldsymbol{K}}$, and it is also possible to pseudodiagonalize each row of $\hat{\boldsymbol{Q}}$

at a weighted sum of frequencies. The formulation of this latter problem again results in an eigenvalue/eigenvector problem.

Although this form of pseudodiagonalization frequently produces useful results, the constraint that the control vector $\hat{\boldsymbol{k}}_j$ should have unit norm does not prevent the diagonal term q_{jj} from becoming very small, although the row is diagonal dominant, or vanishing altogether.

So, if instead of the constraint given by (2.33), we substitute the alternative constraint that

$$|\hat{q}_{jj}(\mathrm{j}\omega)|=1 \tag{2.41}$$

then a similar analysis leads to

$$\boldsymbol{A}_j-\boldsymbol{\lambda}\boldsymbol{E}_j\,\hat{\boldsymbol{k}}_j^{\mathrm{T}}=0 \tag{2.42}$$

where $\boldsymbol{A}_j$ is as defined by equation (2.37) and $\boldsymbol{E}_j$ is the symmetric positive semidefinite matrix

$$\boldsymbol{E}_j=\{e_{il}^{(j)}\}=[\alpha_{ij}\alpha_{lj}+\beta_{ij}\beta_{lj}] \tag{2.43}$$

Equation (2.42) now represents a generalized eigenvalue problem, since $\boldsymbol{E}_j$ can be a singular matrix, and must be solved using the appropriate numerical method.

2.5 Conclusion

The inverse Nyquist array method offers a systematic way of achieving a number of simultaneous objectives, while still leaving considerable freedom to the designer. It is easy to learn and use, and has the virtues of all frequency response methods, namely insensitivity to modelling errors including nonlinearity, insensitivity to the order of the system, and visual insight. All the results for inverse plots apply with suitable changes to direct Nyquist plots[注11]. We can also obtain multivariable generalisations of the circle theorem for systems with nonlinear, time-dependent, sector-bounded gains. Not only do the Gershgorin bands give a stability criterion; they also set bounds on the transfer function $h_{ii}(s)$ seen in the ith loop as the gains in the other loops are varied.

Several further ways of determining $\hat{\boldsymbol{K}}_p(s)$ such that $\hat{\boldsymbol{Q}}(s)$ is diagonal dominant are the subject of current research. However, several industrial multivariable control problems have already been solved using this design method.

New words and phrases:

1. inverse Nyquist array 逆奈阵列
2. diagonal dominance 对角优势
3. interactive *a.* 交互式的
4. cursor *n.* 指针,光标
5. joystick *n.* 控制杆
6. graphical representation 图形显示
7. transfer function matrix 传递函数矩阵
8. feedback matrix 反馈矩阵
9. return path 返回通道
10. asymptotically stable region 渐进稳定区域
11. open left-half plane 开左半平面(指不包含纵轴)
12. non-minimum phase terms 非最小相位项
13. unstable region of operation 不稳定工作区域
14. relax *v.* 放宽
15. hold *v.* 成立,有效,适用
16. map *A* into *B* 把 *A* 映入 *B*
17. row diagonal dominant 行对角优势的
18. inver nyquist plot 逆奈氏图
19. shrinking factor 收缩因子
20. frequency domain 频域
21. design specification 设计指标
22. pre-compensator *n.* 预补偿器
23. nonsingular *a.* 非奇异的
24. diagonalize *v.* 对角化
25. least-mean-squares *n.* 最小均方
26. Lagrange multiplier 拉格朗日乘子
27. take partial derivative of *A* with respect to *B* 取 *A* 对于 *B* 的偏导数
28. pseudo [ˈpsjuːdou] *a.* 伪的
29. symmetric *a.* 对称的
30. algorithm *n.* 算法
31. weighted sum 加权和
32. circle theorem 圆盘定理
33. time-dependent *a.* 时变的
34. sector-bounded *a.* 扇形边界的

Notes:

1. ***F*** represents loop gains which will usually be implemented in the for-

ward path, but which it is convenient to move into the return path.

译:$\boldsymbol{F}$ 代表回路增益,这个回路增益通常在前向通道实现,但移动到返回通道中是方便的(令问题简单)。

2. All combinations of gains and of open or closed-loops can now be obtained by a suitable choice of the f_i, and we shall want the system to remain stable for all values of the f_i from zero up to their design values.

译:所有的增益的组合和开环或闭环的组合现在都可通过对 f_i 的适当选择来获得,我们将要求该系统对于所有从零到设计值之间的 f_i 值都能保持稳定。

3. The point $\{f_1, f_2, \cdots, f_m\}$ belongs to the asymptotically stable region in the gain space if and only if the system is asymptotically stable with $\boldsymbol{F}=\mathrm{diag}\{f_i\}$.

译:当且仅当在 $\boldsymbol{F}=\mathrm{diag}\{f_i\}$ 时,系统为渐进稳定的条件下,点 $\{f_1, f_2, \cdots, f_m\}$ 属于增益空间中的渐进稳定区域。

4. This form of the stability theorem is directly analogous to the form used with single-input single-output systems, but is difficult to use since $|\boldsymbol{H}(s)|$ is a complicated function of $\boldsymbol{Q}(s)$.

译:稳定性定理的这个形式完全与应用于单输入单输出的形式类似,但是由于 $|\boldsymbol{H}(s)|$ 是 $\boldsymbol{Q}(s)$ 的一个复杂函数,所以用起来困难。

5. We shall, in what follows, dcvclop the required stability theorems in terms of the inverse system matrices.

译:在下文中,我们将根据逆系统矩阵来研究所需要的稳定性定理。

6. If each of the bands so produced excludes the origin, for $i=1, \cdots, m$, then $\hat{\boldsymbol{Q}}(S)$ is row dominant on $\boldsymbol{D}$.

译:如果对于 $i=1, \cdots, m$,每一个这样建立的带都不包含原点,那么 $\hat{\boldsymbol{Q}}$ 在 D 上是具有行优势的。

7. The theorems above tell us that as the gain in each other loop changes as long as dominance is maintained in the other loops, $h_{ii}^{-1}(s)$ will also change but always remains inside the ith Gershgorin band.

译:上面的定理告诉我们,随着每个其它回路中增益的变化,只要其它回路中的优势不变，$h_{ii}^{-1}(s)$也将改变，但总是仍在第 i 个 Gershgorin 带中。

8. These narrower bands, known as Ostrowski bands, also reduce the region of uncertainty as to the actual location of the inverse transfer function $h_s^{-1}(s)$ for each loop.

译：这些被称为 Ostrowski 带的更窄的带也减小了每个回路逆传递函数 $h_{ii}^{-1}(s)$的实际位置的不确定区域。

9. One method of determining $\hat{\boldsymbol{K}}_p(s)$ is to build up the required matrix out of elementary row operations using a graphical display of all of the elements of $\hat{\boldsymbol{Q}}(s)$ as a guide.

译：一个确定 $\hat{\boldsymbol{K}}_p(s)$的方法是使用 $\hat{\boldsymbol{Q}}(s)$的所有元素的图形显示作为指导，建立一个所需要的由基本行操作得到的矩阵。

10. This choice of $\hat{\boldsymbol{K}}_p$ can be considered as the best matrix of real constants which makes the sum of the moduli of the off-diagonal elements in each row of $\hat{\boldsymbol{Q}}$ as small as possible compared with the modulus of the diagonal element at some frequency $s = \mathrm{j}\omega$.

译：对 $\hat{\boldsymbol{K}}_p$ 的这一选择可以被看成是最优的实常数矩阵，它使得在某一频率 $s=\mathrm{j}\omega$ 下，$\hat{\boldsymbol{Q}}$ 的每一行的非对角线元素的模的和与对角线元素的模比较尽可能地小。

11. All the results for inverse plots apply with suitable changes to direct Nyquist plots.

译：所有对于逆乃氏图的结论，通过向直接乃氏图方式的适当转化是适用的。

PART 2	CHAPTER THREE

3 Optimal Control

Synopsis

An overview of dynamic optimization is presented which commences with a statement of the important conditions from classical theory including the Weierstrass $\boldsymbol{E}$-function and the second variation. The classical results are then reformulated in modern optimal control notation which leads immediately to a statement of Pontryagin's Minimum Principle. Necessary conditions for optimality of singular trajectories are deduced from the theory of the second variation. A description of Dynamic Programming is followed by a study of the Hamilton-Jacobi approach for the linear system/quadratic cost problem together with the associated matrix Riccati equation[注1].

3.1 The Calculus of Variations: Classical Theory

The classical problem of Bolza is that of minimizing the functional

$$\boldsymbol{J}=\boldsymbol{G}(t_0,\boldsymbol{x}(t_0),t_1,\boldsymbol{x}(t_1))+\int_{t_0}^{t_1}\boldsymbol{f}(t,\boldsymbol{x},\dot{\boldsymbol{x}})\,\mathrm{d}t$$

(where $\boldsymbol{x}$ and $\dot{\boldsymbol{x}}$ are n-vectors), subject to the differential constraints

$$\boldsymbol{\phi}_\beta(t,\boldsymbol{x},\dot{\boldsymbol{x}}) = 0 \qquad \beta=1,2,\cdots,k<n$$

and end conditions

$$\boldsymbol{\Psi}_q(t_0,\boldsymbol{x}(t_0),t_1,\boldsymbol{x}(t_1))=0 \qquad q=1,2,\cdots,\leqslant 2n+2$$

Defining a fundamental function $\boldsymbol{F}=\boldsymbol{f}+\boldsymbol{\lambda}_\beta(t)\boldsymbol{\phi}_\beta$ (note the double suffix summation is used throughout this chapter), where $\{\boldsymbol{\lambda}_\beta\}$ is a sequence of time dependent Lagrange multipliers, a number of necessary conditions for a stationary value of $\boldsymbol{J}$ can be deduced from the first variation of $\boldsymbol{J}$. These are

(1) the Euler-Lagrange equations

$$\frac{\mathrm{d}}{\mathrm{d}t}\left[\frac{\partial \boldsymbol{F}}{\partial \dot{x}_i}\right]-\frac{\partial \boldsymbol{F}}{\partial x_i}=0 \qquad i=1,2,\cdots,n \tag{3.1}$$

(2) the transversality conditions

$$\left[\left[\boldsymbol{F}-\dot{x}_i\frac{\partial \boldsymbol{F}}{\partial \dot{x}_i}\right]\mathrm{d}t+\left[\frac{\partial \boldsymbol{F}}{\partial \dot{x}_i}\right]\mathrm{d}x_i\right]_{t_0}^{t_1}+\mathrm{d}\boldsymbol{G}=0$$

$$\mathrm{d}\boldsymbol{\Psi}_q=0 \tag{3.2}$$

(3) the Weierstrass-Erdmann corner conditions

$$\frac{\partial \boldsymbol{F}}{\partial \dot{x}_i} \text{ and } \left[\boldsymbol{F}-\dot{x}_i\frac{\partial \boldsymbol{F}}{\partial \dot{x}_i}\right] \qquad i=1,2,\cdots,n \tag{3.3}$$

must be continuous across a corner of the extremal (i. e. the trajectory satisfying the necessary conditions).

(4) the Weierstrass **E**-function condition, valid for all $t\in(t_0,t_1)$

$$\boldsymbol{E}=\boldsymbol{F}(t,\boldsymbol{x},\dot{\boldsymbol{X}},\boldsymbol{\lambda})-\boldsymbol{F}(t,\boldsymbol{x},\dot{\boldsymbol{x}},\boldsymbol{\lambda})-(\dot{X}_i-\dot{x}_i)\frac{\partial \boldsymbol{F}}{\partial \dot{x}_i}(t,\boldsymbol{x},\dot{\boldsymbol{x}},\boldsymbol{\lambda})\geqslant 0 \tag{3.4}$$

where a strong variation has been employed such that the derivative $\dot{\boldsymbol{X}}$ on the variational curve may differ from the corresponding derivative $\dot{\boldsymbol{x}}$ on the extremal by an arbitrary amount[注2].

Note: If the fundamental function $\boldsymbol{F}$ does not contain the time t explicitly then a first integral of the Euler-Lagrange equations (3.1) exits and is

$$\boldsymbol{F}-\dot{\boldsymbol{x}}\frac{\partial \boldsymbol{F}}{\partial \dot{x}_i}=\text{ constant},\ t\in(t_0,\ t_1)$$

The second variation of J is given by

$$\mathrm{d}^2\boldsymbol{G}+\left[(\boldsymbol{F}_t-\dot{x}_i\boldsymbol{F}_{xi})\mathrm{d}t^2+2\boldsymbol{F}_{xi}\mathrm{d}t\right]_{t_0}^{t_1}+$$

$$\int_{t_0}^{t_1}(\boldsymbol{F}_{\dot{x}_i\dot{x}_k}\delta\dot{x}_i\delta\dot{x}_k+2\boldsymbol{F}_{\dot{x}_ix_k}\delta\dot{x}_i\delta x_k+\boldsymbol{F}_{x_ix_k}\delta x_i\delta x_k)\,\mathrm{d}t$$

which must be non-negative for all admissible variations δx_i, $\delta\dot{x}_i$, $\mathrm{d}t_0$, $\mathrm{d}t_1$, $\mathrm{d}x_i(t_0)$ and $\mathrm{d}x_i(t_1)$. This suggests a further minimization problem with the second variation as the functional and the variations δx_i and differentials $\mathrm{d}t_0$, $\mathrm{d}t_1$ as the unknowns, subject to the differential equations of constraint[注3]

$$\frac{\partial \boldsymbol{\phi}_\beta}{\partial \dot{x}_i}\delta \dot{x}_i+\frac{\partial \boldsymbol{\phi}_\beta}{\partial x_i}\delta x_i=0$$

Writing

$$\boldsymbol{\Omega}=\boldsymbol{F}_{\dot{x}_i\dot{x}_k}\delta \dot{x}_i\delta \dot{x}_k+2\boldsymbol{F}_{\dot{x}_i x_k}\delta \dot{x}_i\delta x_k+\boldsymbol{F}_{x_i x_k}\delta x_i\delta x_k+\mu_\beta\left[\frac{\partial \boldsymbol{\phi}_\beta}{\partial \dot{x}_i}\delta \dot{x}_i+\frac{\partial \boldsymbol{\phi}_\beta}{\partial x_i}\delta x_i\right]$$

the variations $\delta \boldsymbol{x}$ which minimize the second variation must satisfy the Euler-Lagrange type equations

$$\frac{\mathrm{d}}{\mathrm{d}t}\left[\frac{\partial \boldsymbol{\Omega}}{\partial \delta \dot{x}_i}\right]-\frac{\partial \boldsymbol{\Omega}}{\partial \mathrm{d}x_i}=0$$

These equations are called the accessory Euler-Lagrange equations and the new minimization problem the accessory minimum problem.

By considering the second variation it can be shown that a further necessary condition for optimality is that

$$\boldsymbol{F}_{\dot{x}_i\dot{x}_k}\delta \dot{x}_i\delta \dot{x}_k\geqslant 0$$

subject to the constraints $\frac{\partial \boldsymbol{\phi}_\beta}{\partial \dot{x}_i}\delta \dot{x}_i=0$.

3.2 The Optimal Control Problem

The general optimal control problem may be formulated as follows. To find, in a class of control variables $u_j(t)$ $(j=1, 2,\cdots, m)$ and a class of state variables $x_i(t)$ $(i=1, 2,\cdots, n)$ which satisfy differential equations

$$\dot{x}_i=f_i(\boldsymbol{x}, \boldsymbol{u}, t)$$

and end conditions

$$\boldsymbol{x}(t_0)=\boldsymbol{x}_0,\ t_0 \text{ specified}$$

$$\boldsymbol{\Psi}_q(\boldsymbol{x}(t_1), t_1)=0 \qquad q=1, 2,\cdots,\leqslant n+1$$

(t_1 may or may not be specified), that particular control vector $\boldsymbol{u}=(u_1, u_2,\cdots, u_m)^{\mathrm{T}}$ and corresponding state vector $\boldsymbol{x}=(x_1, x_2,\cdots, x_n)^{\mathrm{T}}$ which minimizes a cost functional

$$\boldsymbol{J}=\boldsymbol{G}(\boldsymbol{x}(t_1), t_1)+\int_{t_0}^{t_1}\boldsymbol{L}(\boldsymbol{x},\boldsymbol{u},t)\,\mathrm{d}t$$

The control vector $\boldsymbol{u} \in U$ where U is a control set which may be open or closed.

The essential differences between this problem and the classical one discussed earlier lies with the control vector $\boldsymbol{u}(t)$. From practical considerations we must allow the control to be discontinuous. By raising the control vector $\boldsymbol{u}$ to the status of a derivative $\dot{z}$ we may treat z as an additional state vector and use the classical theory without further modification. A second difference lies in the fact that some or all of the control variables $u_j(t)$ arising in practical problems will be constrained by inequalities of the form

$$a_j \leqslant u_j \leqslant b_j$$

where a_j, b_j are usually known constants. To use the classical theory for a problem involving such control constraints the technique of Valentine can be used. This is to introduce additional control variables $\alpha_j(t)$ such that

$$(u_j - a_j)(b_j - u_j) - \alpha_j^2 = 0$$

These new equality constraints can then be treated in the same way as the set of system equations

$$\dot{\boldsymbol{x}} = \boldsymbol{f} = (f_1 f_2, \cdots, f_n)^{\mathrm{T}}$$

Let us apply the classical theory to the control problem formulated above. The fundamental function

$$\boldsymbol{F} = \boldsymbol{L}(\boldsymbol{x}, \boldsymbol{u}, t) + \lambda_i(t)[(f_i(\boldsymbol{x}, \boldsymbol{u}, t) - \dot{x}_i)] \qquad i = 1, 2, \cdots, n \tag{3.5}$$

With $\dot{z}_j = u_j$ the Euler-Lagrange equations are

$$\frac{\mathrm{d}}{\mathrm{d}t}\left[\frac{\partial \boldsymbol{F}}{\partial \dot{x}_i}\right] = \frac{\partial \boldsymbol{F}}{\partial x_i}, \frac{\partial \boldsymbol{F}}{\partial \dot{z}_j} = \text{constant} \qquad j = 1, 2, \cdots, m \tag{3.6}$$

The transversality conditions are

$$\left[\left[\boldsymbol{F} - \dot{x}_i \frac{\partial \boldsymbol{F}}{\partial \dot{x}_i} - \dot{z}_j \frac{\partial \boldsymbol{F}}{\partial \dot{z}_j}\right]\mathrm{d}x + \frac{\partial \boldsymbol{F}}{\partial \dot{x}_i}\mathrm{d}x_j + \frac{\partial \boldsymbol{F}}{\partial \dot{z}_j}\mathrm{d}z_j\right]_{t_0}^{t_1} + \mathrm{d}\boldsymbol{G} = 0 \tag{3.7}$$

$$d\boldsymbol{\Psi}_q = 0$$

The functions $\boldsymbol{G}$ and $\boldsymbol{\Psi}_q$ do not involve the control variables explicitly. Since the variables z_j are not specified at either end point the transversality conditions yield

$$\frac{\partial \boldsymbol{F}}{\partial \dot{z}_j} = 0 \qquad j = 1, 2, \cdots, m$$

at t_0 and t_1[注4]. Then, because of the second set of Euler-Lagrange equations (3.6), we have

$$\frac{\partial \boldsymbol{F}}{\partial \dot{z}_j} \equiv \frac{\partial \boldsymbol{F}}{\partial u_j} = 0 \qquad t \in (t_0, t_1) \tag{3.8}$$

The remaining Euler-Lagrange equations (3.6) are equivalent to

$$-\dot{\lambda}_i = \frac{\partial}{\partial x_i}(\boldsymbol{L} + \lambda_i f_i) \tag{3.9}$$

Now define the Hamiltonian

$$\boldsymbol{H} = \boldsymbol{L}(\boldsymbol{x}, \boldsymbol{u}, t) + \lambda_i(t) f_i(\boldsymbol{x}, \boldsymbol{u}, t) \tag{3.10}$$

Equations (3.8) ~ (3.9) then take the form of the Pontryagin canonical equations

$$\frac{\partial \boldsymbol{H}}{\partial u_j} = 0 \qquad j = 1, 2, \cdots, m \tag{3.11}$$

$$\dot{\lambda}_i = -\frac{\partial \boldsymbol{H}}{\partial x_i} \qquad i = 1, 2, \cdots, n$$

Note that $\boldsymbol{F} - \dot{x}_i \frac{\partial \boldsymbol{F}}{\partial \dot{x}_i} = \boldsymbol{F} + \lambda_{ii} \dot{x}_i = \boldsymbol{F} + \lambda_i f_i = \boldsymbol{H}$. The transversality conditions (3.7) then reduce to

$$[\boldsymbol{H} dt - \lambda_i dx_i]_{t_0}^{t_1} + d\boldsymbol{G} = 0 \quad d\boldsymbol{\Psi}_q = 0$$

where

$$d\boldsymbol{G} = \frac{\partial \boldsymbol{G}}{\partial t_1} dt_1 + \frac{\partial \boldsymbol{G}}{\partial x_i(t_1)} dx_i(t_1)$$

and

$$d\boldsymbol{\Psi}_q = \frac{\partial \boldsymbol{\Psi}_q}{\partial t_1} dt_1 + \frac{\partial \boldsymbol{\Psi}_q}{\partial x_i(t_1)} dx_i(t_1) \qquad q = 1, 2 \cdots, \leqslant n+1$$

In particular, if $\boldsymbol{x}(t_0)$ and t_0 are specified but $\boldsymbol{x}(t_1)$ and t_1 are free, then the transversality condition yields

$$\boldsymbol{H}(t_1) = -\frac{\partial \boldsymbol{G}}{\partial t_1}$$

$$\lambda_i(t_1) = \frac{\partial \boldsymbol{G}}{\partial x_i(t_1)}$$

If, on the other hand, $\boldsymbol{x}(t_0)$ and t_1 are specified and l ($<n$) values specified at t_1 (with t_1 unspecified), e. g. $x_k(t_1)$ ($k=1, 2, \cdots, l$) specified, then the transversality conditions yield

$$\boldsymbol{H}(t_1) = -\frac{\partial \boldsymbol{G}}{\partial t_1} \text{ and } \lambda_s(t_1) = \frac{\partial \boldsymbol{G}}{\partial x_s(t_1)} \quad (s=l+1, l+2, \cdots, n)$$

In the optimal control problem the Weierstrass-Erdmann corner conditions (3.3) are that $\boldsymbol{H}$ and $\lambda_i(i=1, 2, \cdots, n)$ must be continuous at points of discontinuity in $\dot{x}_i$ and $u_j(j=1, 2, \cdots, m)$.

The Weierstrass necessary condition (3.4) may now be rewritten as

$$\boldsymbol{E}=\boldsymbol{L}(\boldsymbol{x},\dot{\boldsymbol{Z}},t)+\lambda_i(f_i(\boldsymbol{x},\dot{\boldsymbol{Z}},t)-\dot{X}_i)-\boldsymbol{L}(\boldsymbol{x},\dot{z},t)-\lambda_i(f_i(\boldsymbol{x},\dot{z},t)-\dot{x}_i)+(\dot{X}_i-\dot{x}_i)\lambda_i-(\dot{Z}_j-\dot{z}_i)\frac{\partial}{\partial \dot{z}_j}(\boldsymbol{L}+\lambda_i f_i-\lambda_i\dot{x}_i)\geqslant 0$$

On using equations (3.10) ~ (3.11), this inequality reduces to

$$\boldsymbol{L}(\boldsymbol{x},\dot{\boldsymbol{Z}},t)+\lambda_i f_i(\boldsymbol{x},\dot{\boldsymbol{Z}},t)-\boldsymbol{L}(\boldsymbol{x},\dot{z},t)-\lambda_i f_i(\boldsymbol{x},\dot{z},t)\geqslant 0$$

Writing $\dot{\boldsymbol{Z}}$, the control vector associated with a strong variation, as $\boldsymbol{u}$ and $\dot{z}$, the control vector associated with the extremal, as $\tilde{\boldsymbol{u}}$ we are led to the inequality

$$\boldsymbol{H}(\boldsymbol{x},\tilde{\boldsymbol{u}},\boldsymbol{\lambda},t)\leqslant \boldsymbol{H}(\boldsymbol{x},\boldsymbol{u},\boldsymbol{\lambda},t) \qquad t\in(t_0,t_1)$$ [注5]

Thus, the Hamiltonian $\boldsymbol{H}$ must assume its minimum value with respect to the control vector $\boldsymbol{u}$ at all points on the extremal. This is Pontryagin's Minimum Principle.

In our new notation, if the fundamental function $\boldsymbol{F}$ of (3.5) does not depend explicitly on the time t then a first integral of the Euler-Lagrange equations exists as mentioned in the Note above. This first integral is then

$$\boldsymbol{L}+\lambda_i f_i-\lambda_i\dot{x}_i+\lambda_i\dot{x}_i=\text{constant}, t\in(t_0,t_1)$$

i. e. $$\boldsymbol{H}=\text{constant}, t \in (t_0, t_1)$$

Consider a one-parameter family of control arcs $\boldsymbol{u}(t,\varepsilon)$ with the optimal control vector given by arc $\boldsymbol{u}(t,0)$. The corresponding state vector $\boldsymbol{x}$ will also be a function of t and ε with $\varepsilon=0$ along the optimal trajectory. Now introduce the notation for the state and control variations

$$\eta_i=\left[\frac{\partial x_i}{\partial \varepsilon}\right]_{\varepsilon=0} (i=1,\ 2,\cdots,n);\beta_j=\left[\frac{\partial u_i}{\partial \varepsilon}\right]_{\varepsilon=0} \qquad j=1,\ 2,\cdots,\ m \quad (3.12)$$

and, in the case where t_1 is unspecified so that $t_1=t_1(\varepsilon)$, the end-time variation

$$\xi_1=\left[\frac{\partial t_i}{\partial \varepsilon}\right]_{\varepsilon=0} \quad (3.13)$$

The second variation must again be non-negative for a minimum value of $\boldsymbol{J}$ and is given by

$$((\boldsymbol{H}_t-\dot{x}_i\boldsymbol{H}_{x_i})\boldsymbol{\xi}^2+2\boldsymbol{H}_{x_i}\boldsymbol{\xi}(\dot{x}_i\boldsymbol{\xi}+\boldsymbol{\eta}_i))_{t=t_1}+\mathrm{d}^2\boldsymbol{G}+$$

$$\int_{t_0}^{t_1}(\boldsymbol{H}_{x_ix_k}\boldsymbol{\eta}_i\boldsymbol{\eta}_k+2\boldsymbol{H}_{x_iu_j}\boldsymbol{\eta}_i\boldsymbol{\beta}_j+\boldsymbol{H}_{u_ju_h}\boldsymbol{\beta}_i\boldsymbol{\beta}_h)\,\mathrm{d}t$$

subject to

$$\mathrm{d}^2\boldsymbol{\Psi}_q=0$$

$$\dot{\eta}_i=\frac{\partial f_i}{\partial x_k}\eta_k+\frac{\partial f_i}{\partial u_j}\beta_j$$

$$\frac{\partial \boldsymbol{\Psi}_q}{\partial t_1}\xi_1+\frac{\partial \boldsymbol{\Psi}_q}{\partial x_{i1}}(\dot{x}_{i1}\xi_1+\eta_{i1})=0$$

3.3 Singular Control Problems

In the special case where the Hamiltonian $\boldsymbol{H}$ is linear in the control vector $\boldsymbol{u}$ it may be possible for the coefficient of this linear term to vanish identicallyover a finite interval of time[注6]. The Pontryagin Principle dose not furnish any information on the control during such an interval and additional necessary conditions must be used to examine such extremals, known as singular extremals.

Definition

Let u_k be an element of the control vector $\boldsymbol{u}$ on the interval $(t_2, t_3) \subset (t_0, t_1)$, which appears linearly in the Hamiltonian. Let the $(2q)$ th time derivative of $\boldsymbol{H}_{u_k}$ be the lowest order total derivative in which u_k appears explicitly with a coefficient which is not identically zero on (t_2, t_3). Then the integer q is called the order of the singular arc. The control variable u_k is referred to as a singular control.

Two necessary conditions will now be given for singular optimal control.

3.3.1 The generalized Legendre-Clebsch condition: a transformation approach

The generalized Legendre-Clebsch condition may be derived in an indirect way by first transforming the singular problem into a nonsingular one and then applying the conventional Legendre-Clebsch necessary condition. This condition for the transformed problem is the generalized Legendre-Clebsch condition for the original singular problem. We shall give Goh´s approach here which retains the full dimensionality of the original problem and is simpler in the case of vector controls. Kelley´s transformation reduces the dimension of the state space.

We have the second variation for a singular arc as

$$\boldsymbol{I}_2 = \frac{1}{2}(\boldsymbol{\eta}^{\mathrm{T}}\boldsymbol{G}_{xx}\boldsymbol{\eta})_{t_f} + \int_0^{t_f}(\frac{1}{2}\boldsymbol{\eta}^{\mathrm{T}}\boldsymbol{H}_{xx}\boldsymbol{\eta} + \boldsymbol{\beta}^{\mathrm{T}}\boldsymbol{H}_{ux}\boldsymbol{\eta})\,\mathrm{d}t \qquad (3.14)$$

subject to the equations of variation

$$\dot{\boldsymbol{\eta}} = \boldsymbol{f}_x\boldsymbol{\eta} + \boldsymbol{f}_u\boldsymbol{\beta}, \boldsymbol{\eta}(0) = 0 \qquad (3.15)$$

Write $\boldsymbol{\beta} = \dot{\boldsymbol{\zeta}}$ and, without loss of generality, put $\boldsymbol{\zeta}(0) = 0$. Now write = $\boldsymbol{\alpha} + \boldsymbol{f}_u\boldsymbol{\zeta}$ in order to eliminate $\dot{\boldsymbol{\zeta}}$ from the equations of variation. These equations become

$$\dot{\boldsymbol{\alpha}} = \boldsymbol{f}_x\boldsymbol{\alpha} + (\boldsymbol{f}_x\boldsymbol{f}_u - \dot{\boldsymbol{f}}_u)\boldsymbol{\zeta}$$

The second variation becomes

$$\boldsymbol{I}_2 = (\frac{1}{2}\boldsymbol{\alpha}^{\mathrm{T}}\boldsymbol{G}_{xx}\boldsymbol{\alpha} + \boldsymbol{\alpha}^{\mathrm{T}}\boldsymbol{G}_{xx}\boldsymbol{f}_u\boldsymbol{\zeta} + \frac{1}{2}\boldsymbol{\zeta}^{\mathrm{T}}\boldsymbol{f}_u^{\mathrm{T}}\boldsymbol{G}_{xx}\boldsymbol{f}_u\boldsymbol{\zeta})_{t_f} +$$

$$\int_0^{t_f}(\dot{\boldsymbol{\zeta}}^{\mathrm{T}}\boldsymbol{H}_{ux}(\boldsymbol{\alpha}+\boldsymbol{f}_u\boldsymbol{\zeta})+\frac{1}{2}\boldsymbol{\alpha}^{\mathrm{T}}\boldsymbol{H}_{xx}\boldsymbol{\alpha}+\boldsymbol{\zeta}^{\mathrm{T}}\boldsymbol{f}_u{}^{\mathrm{T}}\boldsymbol{H}_{xx}\boldsymbol{\alpha}+\frac{1}{2}\boldsymbol{\zeta}^{\mathrm{T}}\boldsymbol{f}_u{}^{\mathrm{T}}\boldsymbol{H}_{xx}\boldsymbol{f}_u\boldsymbol{\zeta})\,\mathrm{d}t$$

Integrate by parts the first term to eliminate $\dot{\boldsymbol{\zeta}}$ from $\boldsymbol{I}_2$. This gives

$$\boldsymbol{I}_2=(\frac{1}{2}\boldsymbol{\alpha}^{\mathrm{T}}\boldsymbol{G}_{xx}\boldsymbol{\alpha}+\boldsymbol{\alpha}^{\mathrm{T}}(\boldsymbol{G}_{xx}\boldsymbol{f}_u+\boldsymbol{H}_{xu})\boldsymbol{\zeta}+\frac{1}{2}\boldsymbol{\zeta}^{\mathrm{T}}(\boldsymbol{f}_u{}^{\mathrm{T}}\boldsymbol{G}_{xx}\boldsymbol{f}_u+\boldsymbol{H}_{ux}\boldsymbol{f}_u)\boldsymbol{\zeta})_{t_f}+$$

$$\int_0^{t_f}(\frac{1}{2}\boldsymbol{\zeta}^{\mathrm{T}}\boldsymbol{R}^*\boldsymbol{\zeta}+\boldsymbol{\zeta}^{\mathrm{T}}\boldsymbol{\Omega}^*\boldsymbol{\alpha}+\frac{1}{2}\boldsymbol{\alpha}^{\mathrm{T}}\boldsymbol{P}^*\boldsymbol{\alpha})\,\mathrm{d}t$$

We can now update $\boldsymbol{\zeta}$ to the status of a derivative since $\dot{\boldsymbol{\zeta}}$ has been eliminated completely from $\boldsymbol{I}_2$ and the equations of variation. The conventional Legendre-Clebsch condition then yields $\boldsymbol{R}^*\geqslant 0$.

Now,

$$\boldsymbol{R}^*=\boldsymbol{f}_u{}^{\mathrm{T}}\boldsymbol{H}_{xx}\boldsymbol{f}_u-\frac{\mathrm{d}}{\mathrm{d}t}\boldsymbol{H}_{ux}\boldsymbol{f}_u-2\boldsymbol{H}_{us}(\boldsymbol{f}_x\boldsymbol{f}_u-\dot{\boldsymbol{f}}_u)=-(\ddot{\boldsymbol{H}}_u)_u$$

Thus we arrive at the condition

$$-\frac{\partial}{\partial\boldsymbol{u}}\left[\frac{\mathrm{d}^2}{\mathrm{d}t^2}\boldsymbol{H}_u\right]\geqslant 0\quad t\in(t_0,t_f)\tag{3.16}$$

This inequality is a generalized Legendre-Clebsch necessary condition in that it is similar in form to the classical Legendre-Clebsch necessary condition[注7]

$$\frac{\partial}{\partial\boldsymbol{u}}\boldsymbol{H}_u\geqslant 0\qquad t\in(t_0,t_f)$$

If (3.16) is met with equality for all $t\in(t_0,t_f)$ then the functional $\boldsymbol{I}_2$ is totally singular and another transformation must be made. In this way the generalized necessary conditions are obtained

$$(-1)^q\frac{\partial}{\partial\boldsymbol{u}}\frac{\mathrm{d}^{2q}}{\mathrm{d}t^{2q}}\boldsymbol{H}_u\geqslant 0\quad t\in(t_0,t_f)\qquad q=1,2,\cdots$$

It can also be shown that

$$\frac{\partial}{\partial\boldsymbol{u}}\frac{\mathrm{d}^p}{\mathrm{d}t^p}\boldsymbol{H}_u=0\quad t\in(t_0,t_f)\quad(p\text{ an odd integer})$$

3.3.2 Jacobson's necessary condition

First adjoin the equations of variation (3.15) to the expression for the second variation (3.14) by a Lagrange multiplier vector of the form

$\boldsymbol{Q}(t)\boldsymbol{\eta}$, where $\boldsymbol{Q}$ is a $n\times n$ time-varying, symmetric matrix. Then

$$\boldsymbol{I}_2 = \frac{1}{2}(\boldsymbol{\eta}^{\mathrm{T}}\boldsymbol{G}_{xx}\boldsymbol{\eta})_{t_f} + \int_0^{t_f}(\frac{1}{2}\boldsymbol{\eta}^{\mathrm{T}}\boldsymbol{H}_{xx}\boldsymbol{\eta} + \boldsymbol{\eta}^{\mathrm{T}}\boldsymbol{Q}(\boldsymbol{f}_x\boldsymbol{\eta} + \boldsymbol{f}_u\boldsymbol{\beta} - \dot{\boldsymbol{\eta}}) + \boldsymbol{\beta}^{\mathrm{T}}\boldsymbol{H}_{ux}\boldsymbol{\eta})\,\mathrm{d}t$$

Integrate by parts the last term of the integrand to give

$$\boldsymbol{I}_2 = \frac{1}{2}(\boldsymbol{\eta}^{\mathrm{T}}(\boldsymbol{G}_{xx} - \boldsymbol{Q})\boldsymbol{\eta})_{t_f} + \int_0^{t_f}(\frac{1}{2}\boldsymbol{\eta}^{\mathrm{T}}(\dot{\boldsymbol{Q}} + \boldsymbol{H}_{xx} + \boldsymbol{f}_x^{\mathrm{T}}\boldsymbol{Q} - \boldsymbol{Q}\boldsymbol{f}_x)\boldsymbol{\eta} + \boldsymbol{\beta}^{\mathrm{T}}(\boldsymbol{H}_{ux} + \boldsymbol{f}_u^{\mathrm{T}}\boldsymbol{Q})\boldsymbol{\eta})\,\mathrm{d}t$$

Now choose $\boldsymbol{Q}$ so that $\dot{\boldsymbol{Q}} = -\boldsymbol{H}_{xx} - \boldsymbol{f}_x^{\mathrm{T}}\boldsymbol{Q} - \boldsymbol{Q}_{f_x}$

with
$$\boldsymbol{Q}(t_f) = \boldsymbol{G}_{xx}(\boldsymbol{x}(t_f), t_f) \tag{3.17}$$

Then
$$\boldsymbol{I}_2 = \int_0^{t_j}\boldsymbol{\beta}^{\mathrm{T}}(\boldsymbol{H}_{xu} + \boldsymbol{f}_u^{\mathrm{T}}\boldsymbol{Q})\boldsymbol{\eta}\,\mathrm{d}t$$

with
$$\dot{\boldsymbol{\eta}} = \boldsymbol{f}_x\boldsymbol{\eta} + \boldsymbol{f}_u\boldsymbol{\beta},\ \boldsymbol{\eta}(0) = 0$$

Now choose a special variation $\boldsymbol{\beta} = \boldsymbol{\beta}^*$, a constant for $t \in (t_1, t_1 + \Delta T)$, $0 < t_1 < t_1 + \Delta T < t_f$, and $\boldsymbol{\beta} = 0$ elsewhere. Then

$$\boldsymbol{I}_2 = \int_0^{t_1+\Delta T}\boldsymbol{\beta}^{\mathrm{T}}(\boldsymbol{H}_{ux}\boldsymbol{f}_u^{\mathrm{T}}\boldsymbol{Q})\boldsymbol{\eta}\,\mathrm{d}t,\ \boldsymbol{\eta}(t_1) = 0 \qquad (\boldsymbol{\eta}\text{ continuous})$$

By the mean value theorem,

$$\boldsymbol{I}_2 = \Delta T\boldsymbol{\beta}^{*\mathrm{T}}((\boldsymbol{H}_{ux} + \boldsymbol{f}_u^{\mathrm{T}}\boldsymbol{Q})\boldsymbol{\eta})_{t_1+\theta\Delta T} \qquad 0<\theta<1$$

Expanding in a Taylor's series

$$\boldsymbol{I}_2 = \Delta T\boldsymbol{\beta}^{*\mathrm{T}}((\boldsymbol{H}_{ux} + \boldsymbol{f}_u^{\mathrm{T}}\boldsymbol{Q})_{t_1}\boldsymbol{\eta}(t_1) + \theta\Delta T\frac{\mathrm{d}}{\mathrm{d}t}((\boldsymbol{H}_{ux} + \boldsymbol{f}_u^{\mathrm{T}}\boldsymbol{Q})\boldsymbol{\eta})_{t_1} + 0(\Delta T^2))$$

which, since $\boldsymbol{\eta}(t_1) = 0$, gives

$$\boldsymbol{I}_2 = \Delta T\boldsymbol{\beta}^{*\mathrm{T}}(\theta\Delta T(\boldsymbol{H}_{ux} + \boldsymbol{f}_u^{\mathrm{T}}\boldsymbol{Q})(\boldsymbol{f}_x\boldsymbol{\eta} + \boldsymbol{f}_u\boldsymbol{\beta})_{t_1} + 0(\Delta T^2)) = \theta\Delta T^2\boldsymbol{\beta}^{*\mathrm{T}}(\boldsymbol{H}_{ux} + \boldsymbol{f}_u^{\mathrm{T}}\boldsymbol{Q})_{t_1}\boldsymbol{f}_u(t_1)\boldsymbol{\beta}^* + 0(\Delta T^3)$$

For an optimal solution, $\boldsymbol{I}_2 \geqslant 0$. Thus

$$(\boldsymbol{H}_{ux} + \boldsymbol{f}_u^{\mathrm{T}}\boldsymbol{Q})\boldsymbol{f}_u \geqslant 0 \quad t \in (0, t_f) \tag{3.18}$$

Equations (3.17) and inequality (3.18) constitute Jacobson's condition.

3.4 Dynamic Programming

Consider the discrete system governed by the difference equations

$$x(i+1)=f^i(x(i),u(i)),x(0) \text{ specified}, \ (i=0,1,2,\cdots, N-1)$$

in which it is required to find the sequence of decisions (control vectors) $u(0)$, $u(1)$, $\cdots$, $u(N-1)$ which minimizes a cost function $\phi[x(N)]$.

The method of dynamic programming for solving such an optimal control problem is based on Bellman's Principle of Optimality. This states that an optimal policy has the property that whatever the initial state and initial decision are, the remaining decisions must constitute an optimal policy with regard to the state resulting from the first decision. In other words, having chosen $u(0)$ and determined $x(1)$, the remaining decisions, $u(1)$, $u(2)$, $\cdots$, $u(N-1)$ must be chosen so that $\phi[x(N)]$ is minimized for that particular $x(1)$. Similarly, having chosen $u(0)$, $u(1)$, $\cdots$, $u(N-2)$ and thus determined $x(N-1)$, the remaining decision $u(N-1)$ must be chosen so that $\phi[x(N)]$ is a minimum for that $x(N-1)$. Proof is by contradiction.

The principle of optimality leads immediately to an interesting computational algorithm. The basic idea is to start at the final end point $t=Nh$, where h is the step-length in time. Suppose that somehow we have determined $x(N-1)$. The choice of the final decision $u(N-1)$ simply involves the search over all valucs of $u(N-1)$ to minimize $\phi(x(N))=\phi(f^{N-1}(x(N-1),u(N-1)))$.

Suppose we denote the minimum value of $\phi(x(N))$, reached from $x(N-1)$, by $S(x(N-1),(N-1)h)$, i.e.

$$S(x(N-1),\ (N-1)h)=\min_{u(N-1)} \phi(f^{N-1}(x(N-1),\ u(N-1)))$$

Similarly, we let

$$S(x(N-2),(N-2)h)=\min_{u(N-2)}\min_{u(N-1)} \phi(x(N))=$$
$$\min_{u(N-2)} S(x(N-1),(N-1)h)=$$
$$\min_{u(N-2)} S(f^{N-2}(x(N-2),u(N-2)),(N-1)h)$$

In general, we are led to the recurrence relation

$$S(\boldsymbol{x}(n), nh) = \min_{u(n)} S(\boldsymbol{f}^n(\boldsymbol{x}(n), \boldsymbol{u}(n)), (n+1)h) \tag{3.19}$$

Using this recurrence relation and starting from $n = N - 1$ the whole process is repeated stage by stage backwards to the initial point where $\boldsymbol{x}(0)$ is specified. A sequence of optimal controls $\boldsymbol{u}^{\circ}(N-1)$, $\boldsymbol{u}^{\circ}(N-2), \cdots, \boldsymbol{u}^{\circ}(0)$ are thus generated. With the completion of this process it is possible to work forward in time from the specified point $\boldsymbol{x}(0)$ since $\boldsymbol{u}^{\circ}(0)$ will be known for that initial point. Work forward to $\boldsymbol{x}(1)$, $\boldsymbol{x}(2), \cdots$ using the optimal controls $\boldsymbol{u}^{\circ}(0)$, $\boldsymbol{u}^{\circ}(1), \cdots$ until the final end-point is reached with the final optimal control $\boldsymbol{u}^{\circ}(N-1)$.

Clearly,

$$S(\boldsymbol{x}(N), Nh) = \boldsymbol{\phi}(x(N)) \tag{3.20}$$

and this is a boundary condition on S to be used in the solution of the difference equation (3.19) for S. In solving (3.19) the minimization process is carried out first and then, having found the optimal $\boldsymbol{u}^{\circ}(n)$, S may be treated as a function depending explicitly upon $\boldsymbol{x}(n)$. By its definition the optimum cost function must satisfy equation (3.19) and, furthermore, when S has been found then, by definition, we have found the optimum cost function. Therefore, the solution of (3.19) with boundary condition (3.20) is a necessary and sufficient condition for an optimum solution. Equation (3.19) is called the Hamilton-Jacobi-Bellman equation since it is closely related to the Hamilton-Jacobi equation of classical mechanics.

As the interval h is made smaller so the discrete problem usually goes over naturally into the continuous problem. The general form of the recurrence relation (3.19), to first order terms in h, then gives rise to the equation

$$S(\boldsymbol{x}, t) = \min_{u}(S(\boldsymbol{x}, t)) + \sum_{i} \frac{\partial S}{\partial x_i} h f_i(\boldsymbol{x}, \boldsymbol{u}) + h \frac{\partial S}{\partial t})$$

Since S is not a function of $\boldsymbol{u}$ this last equation reduces to

$$\frac{\partial \boldsymbol{S}}{\partial t}+\min_{u}\left[\frac{\partial \boldsymbol{S}}{\partial x_i} f_i(\boldsymbol{x},\boldsymbol{u})\right]=0 \qquad (3.21)$$

$\boldsymbol{u}$ must be chosen to minimize the sum $f_i \dfrac{\partial \boldsymbol{S}}{\partial x_i}$ resulting in a control law $\boldsymbol{u}(\boldsymbol{x},t)$. The partial differential equation (3.21) may then be solved for $\boldsymbol{S}(\boldsymbol{x},t)$ subject to the boundary condition

$$\boldsymbol{S}(\boldsymbol{x}(t_1),\ t_1)=\boldsymbol{\phi}(\boldsymbol{x}(t_1)) \qquad (3.22)$$

3.5 The Hamilton-Jacobi Approach

This approach to the problem of optimal control is an alternative to Pontryagin's Minimum Principle. It has two advantages: (1) it eliminates the difficult two-point boundary value problem associated with the Minimum Principle, (2) it yields a closed-loop solution in the form of an optimal control law $\boldsymbol{u}^{\circ}(\boldsymbol{x},\ t)$. A disadvantage is that it gives rise to a nonlinear partial differential equation, the Hamilton-Jacobi equation, and a closed form solution has been obtained for only a few special cases[注8]. This difficulty arises since only one set of initial conditions was considered in the Pontryagin approach whereas here, by stipulating a closed-loop solution, we are seeking the solution for a whole class of initial conditions.

Let the function $\boldsymbol{S}(\boldsymbol{x},\ t)$ of (3.21) be given as the optimal cost function

$$\boldsymbol{S}(\boldsymbol{x},t)=\int_t^{t_1}\boldsymbol{L}(\boldsymbol{x}(\boldsymbol{\tau}),\boldsymbol{u}^{\circ}(\boldsymbol{x},\boldsymbol{\tau}),\boldsymbol{\tau})\,\mathrm{d}\tau \qquad (3.23)$$

i.e. $\boldsymbol{S}(\boldsymbol{x},\ t)$ is the value of the cost function evaluated along an optimal trajectory which begins at a general time t and associated state $\boldsymbol{x}(t)$. It can be shown that the partial derivatives $\partial \boldsymbol{S}/\partial x_i$ of equation (3.21) have a time behaviour identical with the Lagrange multipliers $\boldsymbol{\lambda}_i$ in the Pontryagin approach. Thus, with the cost function given in (3.23), equation (3.21) may be written as

$$\boldsymbol{H}(\boldsymbol{x},\ \nabla S(x,t),t)+\partial \boldsymbol{S}/\partial t=0 \qquad (3.24)$$

This equation is known as the Hamilton-Jacobi equation. The boundary condition (3.22) becomes

$$\boldsymbol{S}(\boldsymbol{x}(t_1),t_1)=0$$

In the case of a linear, time-invariant system

$$\dot{\boldsymbol{x}}=\boldsymbol{A}\boldsymbol{x}+\boldsymbol{B}\boldsymbol{u}$$

with a quadratic cost function

$$\int_0^{t_1}(\boldsymbol{x}^{\mathrm{T}}\boldsymbol{Q}\boldsymbol{x}+\boldsymbol{u}^{\mathrm{T}}\boldsymbol{R}\boldsymbol{u})\,\mathrm{d}t$$

($\boldsymbol{Q}$ and $\boldsymbol{R}$ constant, symmetric matrices with $\boldsymbol{R}$ positive definite) the solution of the Hamilton-Jacobi equation can be obtained in closed form. The Hamiltonian is

$$\boldsymbol{H}=\boldsymbol{x}^{\mathrm{T}}\boldsymbol{Q}\boldsymbol{x}+\boldsymbol{u}^{\mathrm{T}}\boldsymbol{R}\boldsymbol{u}+\nabla\boldsymbol{S}^{\mathrm{T}}(\boldsymbol{A}\boldsymbol{x}+\boldsymbol{B}\boldsymbol{u})$$

Assuming $\boldsymbol{u}$ is unbounded

$$\frac{\partial\boldsymbol{H}}{\partial\boldsymbol{u}}=2\boldsymbol{R}\boldsymbol{u}+\boldsymbol{B}^{\mathrm{T}}\nabla S=0$$

whence

$$\boldsymbol{u}^{\mathrm{o}}=-\frac{1}{2}\boldsymbol{R}^{-1}\boldsymbol{B}^{\mathrm{T}}\nabla S(x,t) \tag{3.25}$$

Substituting this result into equation (3.24) yields the Hamilton–Jacobi equation

$$(\nabla\boldsymbol{S})^{\mathrm{T}}\boldsymbol{A}\boldsymbol{x}-(\nabla\boldsymbol{S})^{\mathrm{T}}\boldsymbol{B}\boldsymbol{R}^{-1}\boldsymbol{B}^{\mathrm{T}}\nabla\boldsymbol{S}+\boldsymbol{x}^{\mathrm{T}}\boldsymbol{Q}\boldsymbol{x}+\frac{\partial\boldsymbol{S}}{\partial t}=0$$

It can be shown that $\boldsymbol{S}(\boldsymbol{x},t)=\boldsymbol{x}^{\mathrm{T}}\boldsymbol{P}(t)\boldsymbol{x}$ ($\boldsymbol{P}>0$) is a solution to this equation provided that the matrix $\boldsymbol{P}$ satisfies the Matrix Riccati equation

$$\dot{\boldsymbol{P}}+\boldsymbol{Q}-\boldsymbol{P}\boldsymbol{B}\boldsymbol{R}^{-1}\boldsymbol{B}^{\mathrm{T}}\boldsymbol{P}+\boldsymbol{P}\boldsymbol{A}+\boldsymbol{A}^{\mathrm{T}}\boldsymbol{P}=0 \tag{3.26}$$

with boundary condition[注9]

$$\boldsymbol{P}(t_1)=0 \tag{3.27}$$

A relatively straightforward method for solving (3.26) subject to (3.27) is a backward integration on a digital computer. Once the matrix $\boldsymbol{P}$ is known the optimal control law is found from (3.25) as

$$\boldsymbol{u}^{\mathrm{o}}(\boldsymbol{x},t)=-\boldsymbol{R}^{-1}\boldsymbol{B}^{\mathrm{T}}\boldsymbol{P}\boldsymbol{x}=-\boldsymbol{K}^{\mathrm{T}}(t)\boldsymbol{x} \qquad \text{say.}$$

The elements of matrix $\boldsymbol{K}(t)$ are known as the feedback coefficients.

In the case where the final time is infinite the matrix $\boldsymbol{P}$ is constant.

We then only have to solve a set of algebraic equations ($\dot{P}=0$ in (3.26))

$$Q-PBR^{-1}B^{\mathrm{T}}P+PA+A^{\mathrm{T}}P=0$$

the reduced or degenerate Riccati equation. Of the several possible solutions to this nonlinear equation in the elements of matrix P the one required is that yielding a positive definite P[注10].

New words and phrases:

1. optimal control 最优控制
2. second variation 二次变分
3. minimum Principle 最小原理
4. singular trajectory 奇异轨迹
5. Dynamic Programming 动态设计,动态规划
6. Riccati equation 黎卡提方程
7. calculus *n.* 微积分;计算,演算
8. *n*-vector *n. n* 维向量
9. fundamental function 特征函数,基本函数
10. suffix *n.* 下标
11. Euler-Lagrange equation 尤拉–拉格朗日方程
12. transversality condition 横截性条件
13. corner condition (隅)角条件
14. extremal *n.* 极值曲线
15. stronge variation 强变分
16. variational curve 变分曲线
17. first integral 一次积分
18. control set 控制量集合
19. inequality *n.* 不等式
20. Hamiltonian *n.* 汉密尔顿算符[函数]
21. cononical *a.* 典型的,标准的,正规的
22. notation *n.* 注释,符号表示方法
23. interval *n.* 区间;时间间隔
24. dimensionality *n.* 维数
25. without loss of generality 不失一般性
26. odd integer 奇整数
27. integrand *n.* 被积函数
28. mean value theorem 中值定理
29. Taylor′s series 泰勒级数
30. Principle of Optimality 最优性定理
31. contradiction *n.* 矛盾
32. step-length *n.* 步长
33. recurrence *n.* 递归,循环
34. partial differential equation 偏微分方程
35. two-point boundary value pro – blem 两点边界值问题
36. quadratic *a.* 二次的,二阶的

Notes:

1. A description of Dynamic Programming is followed by a study of the Hamilton-Jacobi approach for the linear system/quadratic cost problem together with the associated matrix Riccati equation.

译:在对动态规划的描述之后,研究了用于线性系统或二次型代价问题的 Hamilton-Jacobi 方法,同时研究了伴随矩阵 Riccati 方程。

2. where a strong variation has been employed such that the derivative $\dot{\boldsymbol{X}}$ on the variational curve may differ from the corresponding derivative $\dot{\boldsymbol{x}}$ on the extremal by an arbitrary amount.

译:这里已使用了一个强变分,使得变分曲线上的导数 $\dot{\boldsymbol{X}}$ 可以与极值点上的相应导数 $\dot{\boldsymbol{x}}$ 相差任意的量。

3. This suggests a further minimization problem with the second variation as the functional and the variations δx_i and differentials $\mathrm{d}t_0$, $\mathrm{d}t_1$ as the unknowns, subject to the differential equations of constraint

$$\frac{\partial \boldsymbol{\phi}_\beta}{\partial \dot{x}_i}\delta \dot{x}_i \frac{\partial \boldsymbol{\phi}_\beta}{\partial x_i}\delta x_i = 0$$

译:当二阶变分作为一个函数,并且变分 δx_i 和微分 $\mathrm{d}t_0$、$\mathrm{d}t_1$ 作为未知量时,这就提出了一个进一步的最小化问题,该问题服从约束的微分方程

$$\frac{\partial \boldsymbol{\phi}_\beta}{\partial \dot{x}_i}\delta \dot{x}_i \frac{\partial \boldsymbol{\phi}_\beta}{\partial x_i}\delta x_i = 0$$

4. Since the variables z_j are not specified at either end point the transversality conditions yield $\frac{\partial \boldsymbol{F}}{\partial \dot{z}_j} = 0$ $(j = 1, 2, \cdots, m)$ at t_0 and t_1.

译:由于变量 z_j 在两个端点都不确定,所以由横截性条件可得,在 t_0 和 t_1 时刻$\frac{\partial \boldsymbol{F}}{\partial \dot{z}_j} = 0$(其中 $j = 1, 2, \cdots, m$)。

5. Writing $\dot{\boldsymbol{Z}}$, the control vector associated with a strong variation, as $\boldsymbol{u}$ and $\dot{z}$, the control vector associated with the extremal, as $\tilde{\boldsymbol{u}}$ we are led to the inequality

$$\boldsymbol{H}(\boldsymbol{x},\tilde{\boldsymbol{u}},\boldsymbol{\lambda},t) \leqslant \boldsymbol{H}(\boldsymbol{x},\boldsymbol{u},\boldsymbol{\lambda},t) \qquad t \in (t_0,t_1)$$

译：把伴随一个强变分而产生的控制向量 $\dot{\boldsymbol{Z}}$ 记作 $\boldsymbol{u}$，并把伴随极值曲线而产生的控制向量 $\dot{z}$ 记作 $\tilde{\boldsymbol{u}}$，我们就可得到不等式

$$\boldsymbol{H}(\boldsymbol{x},\tilde{\boldsymbol{u}},\boldsymbol{\lambda},t) \leqslant \boldsymbol{H}(\boldsymbol{x},\boldsymbol{u},\boldsymbol{\lambda},t), t \in (t_0,t_1)$$

6. In the special case where the Hamiltonian $\boldsymbol{H}$ is linear in the control vector $\boldsymbol{u}$ it may be possible for the coefficient of this linear term to vanish identically over a finite interval of time.

译：在 Hamilton 函数 $\boldsymbol{H}$ 关于控制向量 $\boldsymbol{u}$ 是线性的这种特殊情况下，线性项的系数也许会在一段有限的时间间隔内同时等于零。

7. This inequality is a generalized Legendre-Clebsch necessary condition in that it is similar in form to the classical Legendre-Clebsch necessary condition

$$\frac{\partial}{\partial \boldsymbol{u}}\boldsymbol{H}_u \geqslant 0 \qquad t \in (t_0,t_f)$$

译：由于该不等式在形式上与经典的 Legendre-Clebsch 必要条件

$$\frac{\partial}{\partial \boldsymbol{u}}\boldsymbol{H}_u \geqslant 0 \qquad t \in (t_0,t_f)$$

类似，因此可以说它是一个广义的 Legendre-Clebsch 必要条件。

8. A disadvantage is that it gives rise to a nonlinear partial differential equation, the Hamilton-Jacobi equation, and a closed form solution has been obtained for only a few special cases.

译：一个缺点在于它导致了一个非线性的偏微分方程——Hamilton-Jacobi 方程，而且仅仅能对于几种特殊情况得到封闭形式的解。

9. It can be shown that $\boldsymbol{S}(\boldsymbol{x},t)=\boldsymbol{x}^{\mathrm{T}}\boldsymbol{P}(t)\boldsymbol{x}$ ($\boldsymbol{P}>0$) is a solution to this equation provided that the matrix $\boldsymbol{P}$ satisfies the Matrix Riccati equation (3.26) with boundary condition (3.27).

译：可以看出，只要矩阵 $\boldsymbol{P}$ 满足带有边界条件(3.27)的矩阵黎卡提(Riccati)方程(3.26)，那么 $\boldsymbol{S}(\boldsymbol{x},t)=\boldsymbol{x}^{\mathrm{T}}\boldsymbol{P}(t)\boldsymbol{x}$ ($\boldsymbol{P}>0$)就是这个方程的解。

10. Of the several possible solutions to this nonlinear equation in the elements of matrix $\boldsymbol{P}$ the one required is that yielding a positive definite $\boldsymbol{P}$.

译:在关于矩阵 $\boldsymbol{P}$ 的元素的非线性方程的几个可能解中,我们所需要的是使 $\boldsymbol{P}$ 为正定的一个解。

4 Optimisation in Multivariable Design

Synopsis

Three new basic algorithms to achieve diagonal dominance will be described in this paper: (1) to choose optimum permutation of input or output variables of the plant; (2) the optimal choice of scaling factors, and (3) to find a real precompensator to optimise dominance measure of the compensated plant.

4.1 Introduction

The design of multivariable systems via frequency domain based procedures has been intensively studied in the last decade and an array of significant theoretical results and design procedures have emerged. For non trivial problems the designer invariably requires the aid of a computer and in practice CAD facilities in which the designer can 'interact' with the design steps have played a significant role[注1]. As yet 'black and white' displays have proved adequate, but it seems likely that 'colour' displays will soon prove of value and that formal optimisation procedures will play an increasingly important role as a design aid.

One of our most widely used and studied design procedures employs the concept of dominance of the plant transfer function and we will mainly concentrate on the use of formal optimisation procedures in this area. Three important techniques can be employed to obtain a successful design. These are:

4.1.1 The allocation problem

Swap the inputs or outputs of the plant to obtain a better 'pairing' for subsequent precompensator design and design of single input-single output closedloops. The pairing that may emerge from physical considerations or during modelformulation is certainly not always the best from a control point of view and we will consider which pairing is ‘best’ in terms of dominance[注2]. The technique is of general value in design, and not limited to those based on dominance. We will show that modest sized problems can be solved ‘by eye’ using simple calculations, and larger problems require graph-theoretic methods.

4.1.2 The scaling problem

Scaling of inputs and outputs changes dominance, and dominance based design approaches might be criticised by not being ‘scale invariant’. As can be shown, ‘optimal’ scaling yields ‘invariant’ dominance, which can be calculated using linear programming based methods. We will describe algorithms for calculating optimal scaling.

4.1.3 Precompensation design problem

The calculation of ‘real’ compensators which are optimum over the bandwidth of the plant, has proved one of the most difficult obstacles in the application of dominance and a large number of heuristic solutions are described in the literature. As the methods we describe usually yield ‘global optima’ they usually serve in practice to settle the question of whether dominance is attainable for the given class of compensator[注3].

4.2 Problem Formulation

A matrix $\boldsymbol{Q} \in \mathbf{C}^{n \times n}$ is said to be column dominant if

$$|q_{ii}| \geqslant \delta_i^{\mathrm{c}}$$

where

$$\delta_i^{\mathrm{c}} = \sum_{\substack{j=1 \\ j \neq i}}^{n} |q_{ji}| \qquad i = 1, 2, \cdots, n$$

and row dominant if

$$|q_{ii}| \geqslant \delta_i^{\mathrm{r}}$$

where

$$\delta_i^{\mathrm{r}} = \sum_{\substack{j=1 \\ j \neq i}}^{n} |q_{ij}| \quad i = 1, 2, \cdots, n$$

The matrix $\boldsymbol{Q} \in \mathbf{C}^{n\times n}$ is said to be dominant if either of the above inequalities hold, and strictly dominant if either hold strictly. In multivariable design applications it is necessary to consider transfer function matrix $\boldsymbol{Q}(s) \in \mathbf{C}^{n\times n}$, when each of the elements are usually rational functions of a complex parameter $s \in \mathbf{C}^1$. If D is a suitable Nyquist contour in the extended complex s-plane, we say $\boldsymbol{Q}$ is (strictly) dominant on D if $\boldsymbol{Q}(s)$ is (strictly) dominant for all $s \in D$.

4.2.1 Decomposition

The simplest and most frequently used precompensator design problem can be stated as follows. Given a square transfer function matrix $\boldsymbol{G}(s) \in \mathbf{C}^{n\times n}$ find a real precompensator $\boldsymbol{K} \in \mathbf{R}^{n\times n}$ such that at frequency $s = \mathrm{j}\omega$ say,

$$\boldsymbol{Q}(\mathrm{j}\omega) = \boldsymbol{G}(\mathrm{j}\omega)\boldsymbol{K}$$

is dominant. Selecting the column dominance criteria we require

$$|q_{ii}| \geqslant \delta_i^{\mathrm{c}} \quad i = 1, 2, \cdots, n \tag{4.1}$$

Obviously

$$q_{ij} = \sum_{p=1}^{n} g_{ip}(\mathrm{j}\omega) k_{pj}$$

or in short form $q_{ij} = \boldsymbol{G}_{i*}(\mathrm{j}\omega)\boldsymbol{K}_{*j}$, where $\boldsymbol{G}_{i*}(\boldsymbol{G}_{*i})$ is the ith row (column) vector of $\boldsymbol{G}$. It is evident that the ith column of $\boldsymbol{Q}$ is determined by the ith column of $\boldsymbol{K}$ and hence we may without loss of generality separately consider the choice of each of the n columns of $\boldsymbol{K}$ when seeking to satisfy inequality (4.1). This decomposition of the problem into n separate problems is of great practical value.

4.2.2 Choice of dominance measure

We first note that both $|q_{ii}|$ and δ_i^{c} are positive first order homogeneous functions of $\boldsymbol{K}$ in the sense that for any $\lambda \neq 0$

$$|q_{ii}(\lambda \boldsymbol{K})| = |\lambda| q_{ii}(\boldsymbol{K}) \tag{4.2}$$

and

$$\delta_i^{\mathrm{c}}(\lambda \boldsymbol{K}) = |\lambda| \delta_i^{\mathrm{c}}(\boldsymbol{K}) \quad i = 1, 2, \cdots, n$$

Hence a suitable and normalised dominance measure widely adopted in the literature is

$$J_i^{\mathrm{c}} = \delta_i^{\mathrm{c}} / | q_{ii} | \tag{4.3}$$

where for dominance of column i we require $J_i^{\mathrm{c}} < 1\ (i = 1, 2, \cdots, n)$.

From equation (4.2) it is clear that J_i^{c} is independent of λ and that J_i^{c} is constant on any ray in $\mathbf{R}^n$ and indeterminate at the origin. However, in any design the magnitude of the scaling factor is determined from engineering considerations, and the sign of λ from stability considerations, and hence these indeterminacies are acceptable. To avoid computational difficulties associated with constancy of $J_i^{\mathrm{c}}(\lambda \boldsymbol{K})$ for any $\lambda \neq 0$ and the singular behaviour for $\lambda = 0$, it is usually convenient to introduce a constraint of the form $\| \boldsymbol{K} \| = 1$ say, where $\| * \|$ is any convenient norm; if we also wish to avoid ambiguity in the sign of λ then a stronger constraint such as $k_{ii} = 1$ is convenient[注4].

4.2.3 General problem

A great interest has been placed on achieving dominance over a set of frequencies $\Omega \approx \{ \omega_i ; i = 1, 2, \cdots, m \}$ usually spread through the bandwidth of the system. We need to decide a suitable form of cost function. Now design difficulties are usually reflected by the 'Worst Case' on Chebyshev measure, i. e.

$$\max_i J^{\mathrm{c}}(\omega_i)$$

there generally being little value in obtaining 'tight' dominance at one frequency ($J_i^{\mathrm{c}} \ll 1$) if we have $J_i^{\mathrm{c}} \approx 1$ at some other frequencies. Hence, for multiple frequency case we consider the decomposed problems.

$$P_0 : \min_k \max_r J^{\mathrm{c}}(\omega_r) \qquad r = 1, 2, \cdots, m$$

$$J^{\mathrm{c}}(\omega_r) = \delta_i^{\mathrm{c}}(\omega_r) / | q_i^i(\omega_r) |$$

$$\delta_i^{\mathrm{c}}(\omega_r) = \sum_{\substack{j=1 \\ j \neq i}}^{n} | q_j^i(\omega_r) |$$

$$\boldsymbol{q}^i(\omega_r) = \boldsymbol{G}(\omega_r) \boldsymbol{K}$$

where $\boldsymbol{q}^i \in \mathbf{C}^{n \times 1}$, $\boldsymbol{K} \in \mathbf{R}^{n \times 1}$ and we have, where there is no ambiguity dropped the suffix i[注5]. Although all the algorithms described have been successfully extended to multiple frequency case, we will, for reasons of space, only state the single frequency algorithms[注6].

4.3 Allocation Problem

consider a single frequency problem where we seek to permute the row (column) of a matrix to obtain (in some sense) best overall column (row) dominance of the resultant matrix. Essentially we are deciding how best to pair inputs and outputs[注7]. Although this problem is trivial for the 2×2 problems which pervade the literature, it rapidly becomes more difficult as the dimensions increase(for $n=5$ there are 120 possible permutations and for $n=10$ more than 3.6 million). Furthermore, studies indicate that correct pairing can significantly improve the design problem.

As each row permutation affects two column dominance (similarly for column permutation on row dominance), we need first to introduce a method of comparing the column dominance for any permutation. For any $\boldsymbol{Z}\in\mathbf{C}^{n\times n}$ consider a positive matrix $\boldsymbol{D}^{c}$ where

$$d_{ij}^{c} \approx \frac{\sum\limits_{\substack{p=1\\ p\neq i}}^{n} |z_{pi}|}{|z_{ij}|}$$

It is easily shown that this represents the appropriate dominance measure (analogous to J_i^{c} of equation 4.3) when rows i and j are interchanged, and hence element j of column i is moved into the diagonal position i. Following the Chebyshev norm approach we require that the optimally permuted matrix displays the smallest possible maximum dominance measure. This criteria in principle only fixes one diagonal element and the dominance measure of one column. Extending Chebyshev criteria to the choice of a second diagonal element should then minimise the maximum dominance measure of the remaining columns; proceeding in this way we see the optimum permutation will select diagonal element so as to satisfy a sequence of n minmax criteria. In short, we are required to solve a sequence of problem of the form

$$P_1 : \min_{p} \max_{i} \{ J_i^{c}[\boldsymbol{P}, \boldsymbol{Q}] \}$$

An equivalent problem to P_1 is that of choosing a set of n elements of $\boldsymbol{D}^{c}$ which form a 'perfect matching' of $\boldsymbol{D}^{c}$ and additionally minimise the maximum element in the matching. A set of n elements forms a perfect matching of $\boldsymbol{D}^{c} \in \mathbf{R}^{n\times n}$ if there is exactly one element of the set in every row and column of $\boldsymbol{D}^{c}$. A simple heuristic for finding such a set (which usually suffices for 'by eye' solution of practical problems) is as follows:

Algorithm 4.3.1 (to find $\boldsymbol{P}$)

Data: $\boldsymbol{D}^{c} \in \mathbf{R}^{n\times n}$.

Step 0: Set $\boldsymbol{P}^{1} = \boldsymbol{D}^{c}$; $l=1$.

Step 1: 'Colour' the smallest 'uncoloured' element of $\boldsymbol{P}$.

Step 2: As each additional element is coloured, check to see if the coloured set contains a perfect matching. If not, return to Step 1.

Step 3: Colour the element in $\boldsymbol{D}^{c}$ corresponding to the last element coloured in $\boldsymbol{P}^{l}$. If $l=n$, stop. Otherwise form a new matrix $\boldsymbol{P}^{l-1} \in \mathbf{R}^{(l-1)\times(l-1)}$ by removing the row and column of $\boldsymbol{P}^{l}$ containing the last coloured element. Set $l=l+1$.

Return to Step 2.

The sequence of coloured element in $\boldsymbol{D}^{c}$ is the optimal solution. To see this, consider the first time Step 3 is executed. The last element coloured is the smallest element that can be chosen in its row and column, whilst at the same time ensuring the other rows and columns can be 'covered' by the set already coloured and comprising elements of $\boldsymbol{D}^{c}$ smaller than the last element coloured[注8]. The same reasoning applies for the successively reduced matrices $\boldsymbol{P}^{l}$ each time we enter Step 3; hence we end up with a perfect cover whose elements also satisfy the sequence of minmax properties required for optimality. We note that the solution is unique if the elements of $\boldsymbol{D}^c$ are distinct.

The only step in the algorithm where difficulty can arise is in checking to see if the coloured elements contain a matching (Step 2), and usually this is possible 'by eye' for multivariable design problems ($n \leqslant 3$). For larger problems there is advantage in finding the optimum match automatically, especially since it may be required several times in a design (as shown by example later). The graph-theoretic equivalent of the problem is a minimax 'bottleneck' matching problem for which powerful algorithms exist[注9]. For instance modern bipartite graph theory matching algorithms or simple modification of the classical 'Hungarian' algorithm may be used.

4.4 Scaling Problem

Given transfer function $\boldsymbol{G} \in \mathbf{C}^{n \times n}(s)$, for a linear square system with zero initial condition

$$\boldsymbol{y}(s) = \boldsymbol{G}\boldsymbol{u}(s)$$

where $\boldsymbol{y} \in \mathbf{C}^{n \times 1}$ is the output and $\boldsymbol{u} \in \mathbf{C}^{n \times 1}$ is the input and s is the Laplace Transform. If the outputs y_i are each scaled by factor s_i respectively ($i = 1, 2, \cdots, n$), then the transfer function is simply

$$\boldsymbol{Z} = \boldsymbol{S}\boldsymbol{G}$$

where $\boldsymbol{Z} \in \mathbf{C}^{n \times n}(s)$, and $\boldsymbol{S} = \mathrm{diag}\{s_i\}, s_i > 0$. The fact that dominance is not 'scale invariant' has at least represented a philosophical criticism of dominance based approaches.

Again the problem may be easy for $n = 2$, but rapidly becomes difficult for $n > 2$. Since the worst of the column dominances represents a measure of design difficulty, it is again natural to adopt a Chebyshev norm optimality criteria and seek

$$\min_{[S]} \max_i \{J_i^c(\boldsymbol{Z})\}$$

For convenience, introducing the matrix $\boldsymbol{M}$

$$m_{ij} = |z_{ij}| / |z_{ii}| = 0 \quad \text{otherwise} \quad i \neq j$$

and define

$$\eta = \max_i \{ J_i^{c}(\boldsymbol{Z}) \}$$

(and taking into account the requirement $s_i > 0$, $i = 1, 2, \cdots, n$), we seek a solution of the problem

$$P_2: \min_{S} \{ \eta \}$$

subject to
$$\sum_{\substack{j=1 \\ j \neq i}}^{n} m_{ij} s_j \leqslant \eta s_i \qquad i = 1, 2, \cdots, n$$

$$s_i > 0 \qquad i = 1, 2, \cdots, n$$

$$\sum_{i=1}^{n} s_i = 1$$

where the last equality is introduced to remove indeterminacy with respect to scaling in $\boldsymbol{S}$.

A simple procedure for solving the optimization problem is as follows:

Algorithm 4.4.1

Data: $\varepsilon > 0$

Step 0: Set $l = 1$; $\eta_1 = \max_i \sum_{\substack{j=1 \\ j \neq i}}^{n} m_{ji}$

Step 1: Solve $\min_{S} \{ z^l \}$

Subject to:

$$(\boldsymbol{M}^{\mathrm{T}} - \boldsymbol{\eta}_l \boldsymbol{I}) \boldsymbol{S} - z^l \boldsymbol{I} \leqslant 0$$

$$\sum_{j=1}^{n} s_j = 1$$

$$s_j \geqslant 0 \qquad j = 1, 2, \cdots, n$$

$$z^l \geq 0$$

Step 2: $d = \eta_1 / 2^l$; if $d < \varepsilon$ then stop.

Step 3: If $z^l = 0$ then $n_{l+1} = n_l - d$

else $n_{l+1} = n_l + d$

Step 4: $l = l + 1$. Go to Step 1.

The scalar ε determines the absolute accuracy to which η is determined. Gershgorin's theorem ensures $\eta_1 > \hat{\eta}$ in Step 0 ($\hat{\eta}, \hat{s}$ denote optimal solution to this problem). Step 1 involves solution of a standard linear program. Step 3 represents a standard binary search procedure on the interval $[0, \eta]$ in which successive bisection search is employed to more closely locate $\hat{\eta}$.

4.5 Compensator Design

Given $\boldsymbol{Q} \in \mathbf{C}^{n \times n}$, we seek a real compensator $\boldsymbol{K} \in \mathbf{R}^{n \times n}$ such that

$$\boldsymbol{Z} = \boldsymbol{Q}\boldsymbol{K}$$

has a minimum normalised column dominance. We may without loss of generality, drop the suffix i and letting it equal to 1, consider n separate problem (P_3^0) of the form

$$P_3^0: \min_{[\boldsymbol{K}]} \{ \delta_2^c / |z_1|_2 \}$$

$$z = \boldsymbol{Q}\boldsymbol{k}$$

$$\| \boldsymbol{K} \| = 1$$

with $z \in \mathbf{C}^{n \times 1}, \boldsymbol{k} \in \mathbf{C}^{n \times 1}$ and if $z_j = \alpha_j + i\beta_j$

$$|z_j|_2 \approx \sqrt{\alpha_j^2 + \beta_j^2}, j = 1, 2, \cdots, n \quad \text{and}$$

$$\delta_2^c = \sum_{i=2}^{n} |z_j|_2$$

This is the 'single frequency' version, the multiple frequency case can be stated as

$$P_3^1: \min_{k} \max_{\omega_i} \{ \delta_2^c(\omega_i) / |z_1|_2 \}$$

where $\omega_i, i = 1, 2, \cdots, r$ represent selection frequencies covering the system bandwidth.

The single frequency problem can be trivially re-expressed

$$\mathrm{P}_3^1: \min_{[\boldsymbol{K}]} \boldsymbol{\eta}$$

$$\delta_2^c - \eta \| z_1 \| \leqslant 0 \tag{4.4a}$$

$$\boldsymbol{Z} = \boldsymbol{Q}\boldsymbol{K} \tag{4.4b}$$

$$\| \boldsymbol{K} \| = 1 \tag{4.4c}$$

A number of procedures may be used to solve this problem. A simple approach which has proved effective is

Algorithm 4. 5. 1 (**Conceptual**)

Data: $\varepsilon>0$

Step 0: Set $l=1$, $\eta_1=\delta_2^c(\bar{\boldsymbol{k}})$, $\bar{\boldsymbol{k}}_i, i=1,\cdots,n$

Step 1: If inequalities (4.4) are consistent, set $d=\eta_1/2^l$

$\eta_{l+1}=\eta_l-d$

otherwise set $\eta_{l+1}=\eta_l+d$

Step 2: If $d<\varepsilon$ stop, otherwise set $l=l+1$.

Return to Step 1.

The initial step ensures that $\eta=\eta_1$ yields a consistent set of inequalities (4.4a). Step 1 employs a simple binary search on $[0,\eta_1]$. The consistency test in Step 1 is the only difficult step. It is well known that feasible direction algorithms may be used to solve sets of inequalities such as (4.4a), but that such algorithms may be slow. A recently developed algorithm which employs both a Newton like step with quadratic convergence together with a first order step which yields finite convergence to a feasible point has been utilised with considerable success[注10]. If the Newton and the first order steps fail, we assume the inequalities are inconsistent. More reliable behaviour and faster convergence was obtained when equality constraint (4.4c) was replaced by inequality constraints $1\leqslant\|\boldsymbol{K}\|\leqslant\boldsymbol{L}$ say, where $\boldsymbol{L}\ll 1$; this is admissible in view of the optimality criteria being first order homogeneous in $\boldsymbol{K}$. Also it is always advantageous to substitute (4.4b) into (4.4a) and hence reduce the problem to checking two simple inequalities for consistency.

It should be remarked that the multiple frequency case involves a minmax criteria and that powerful methods have also been developed for this general class of design problem. These methods again utilise linear programming subroutines; for the multiple frequency case they behave like Newton methods and display quadratic convergence (whereas in the single frequency case they are analogous to steepest ascent and display only linear convergence).

Finally, mention should be made of special procedures tailored to the problem. These have proved reliable but are computationally demanding.

4.6 Design Example

Here is an example of applying these new algorithms developed earlier to Direct Nyquist Method (DNA). The linear jet engine model chosen is a 5-states, 3-inputs, 3-outputs simplified model. Only a simplified actuator dynamic is included, sensor dynamic is neglected and all output variables are assumed measurable, and the plant transfer matrix is normalised by the appropriate input/output nominal operating factors.

Achieving dominance (a multiple frequency case):

Step 1: Choose a set of frequency which will approximately cover the whole operating frequency range of the plant to be controlled.

Step 2: With A-4.3.1, to compute a permutation matrix $\boldsymbol{P}$: ($\boldsymbol{G}_1 = \boldsymbol{P}_1\boldsymbol{G}$) yields

$$\boldsymbol{P}_1 = \begin{bmatrix} 0 & 0 & 1 \\ 0 & 1 & 0 \\ 1 & 0 & 0 \end{bmatrix}$$

The origin maximum dominance before is

$$\delta_{\max}^{c} = (51.33,\ 527.4,\ 0.325)$$

The improved maximum dominance after permuting is

$$\delta_{\max}^{c} = (0.0968,\ 527.4,\ 16.06)$$

Step 3: By A-4.4.1, output scaling algorithms with the same set of frequency: ($\boldsymbol{G}_2 = \boldsymbol{S}_1\boldsymbol{G}_1\boldsymbol{S}_1^{-1}$).

The output rescaling matrix is

$$\boldsymbol{S} = \mathrm{diag}\{0.146,\ 0.913,\ 1.940\}$$

improved dominance measure is

$$\delta_{\max}^{c} = (7.92,\ 0.285,\ 7.83)$$

Step 4: Re-permuting output again: ($\boldsymbol{G}_3 = \boldsymbol{P}_2\boldsymbol{G}_2$) gives

$$\boldsymbol{P}_2 = \begin{bmatrix} 1 & 0 & 0 \\ 0 & 0 & 0 \\ 0 & 1 & 0 \end{bmatrix}$$

The improved dominance measure is

$$\delta^{c}_{\max} = (7.92,\ 6.85,\ 0.194)$$

Step 5: Rescaling again with A-4.4.1 ($\boldsymbol{G}_4 = \boldsymbol{S}_2\boldsymbol{G}_3\boldsymbol{S}_2^{-1}$) gives

$$\boldsymbol{S}_2 = \mathrm{diag}\{1.721,\ 1.141,\ 0.137\}$$

and improved dominance measure is

$$\delta^{c}_{\max} = (1.85,\ 1.85,\ 1.85)$$

Step 6: Compute a real pre-compensator by A-4.5.1 ($\boldsymbol{G}_5 = \boldsymbol{G}_4\boldsymbol{K}_1$) gives

$$\boldsymbol{K}_1 = \begin{bmatrix} 1 & 5.128E-3 & -6.257E-3 \\ 35.131 & -1 & 1.518 \\ 1 & -0.136 & 1 \end{bmatrix}$$

and the improved dominance measure is

$$\delta^{c}_{\max} = (0.9,\ 0.7,\ 0.8)$$

Up to this stage the dominance level of the jet engine is acceptable. Columns 1 and 2 are both open and closed-loop dominant, column 3 is closed-loop dominant with forward gain less than 1.5.

The process of Step 1 to Step 5 can be summarised as follows

$$\boldsymbol{G}_{\mathrm{D}} = \boldsymbol{UGL}$$

where

$$\boldsymbol{U} = \boldsymbol{S}_2\boldsymbol{P}_2\boldsymbol{S}_1\boldsymbol{P}_1 \quad \text{and} \quad \boldsymbol{L} = \boldsymbol{S}_1^{-1}\boldsymbol{S}_2^{-1}\boldsymbol{K}_1$$

with

$$\boldsymbol{U} = \begin{bmatrix} 0 & 0 & 2.520E-2 \\ 0.571 & 0 & 0 \\ 0 & 0.331 & 0 \end{bmatrix}$$

$$\boldsymbol{L} = \begin{bmatrix} 39.684 & 0.204 & -0.248 \\ 12.758 & -0.363 & 0.552 \\ 14.590 & -1.997 & 14.590 \end{bmatrix}$$

In view of steady state responses and gain margins, a combined lead-compensator and proportional–integral controller is used ($\boldsymbol{K}_c$).

$$\boldsymbol{K}_c=\text{diag}\left\{1,\frac{10(s+5)}{(s+50)}\cdot\left(1.25+\frac{1}{0.167s}\right),\left(1.2+\frac{1}{0.25s}\right)\right\}$$

The forward gain factor for stable and good responses is

$$\boldsymbol{K}_a=\text{diag}\{50,\ 0.6,\ 1.8\}$$

4.7 Discussion

The algorithms described can all be extended to

(1) Multiple frequency case.

(2) 'Parameterised' controllers $\boldsymbol{K}^c$ of forms such as

$$\boldsymbol{K}^c=\boldsymbol{K}_P+\boldsymbol{K}_I/s$$

where $\boldsymbol{K}_P$, $\boldsymbol{K}_I\in\mathbf{R}^{n\times n}$ are multivariable proportional and integral terms.

(3) Use of inequalities on K_{ij}, $1\leqslant i,j\leqslant n$.

(4) 'Sparse' controllers where we seek to satisfy the important practical criterion that the controllers should be of sample 'structure' and not employ complexly interconnected controllers.

(5) Solution of large sets of equations by 'tearing'. The 'tear' inputs and outputs can be 'compensated' using the methods described, and dominance is a key property for ensuring the convergence of iterated 'torn' equations.

Research is being undertaken in all these areas.

New words and phrases:

1. optimisation *n*. 最优化
2. scaling factor 比例因数
3. permutation *n*. 变换,(重)排列
4. precompensator *n*. 预置补偿器
5. dominance measure 优势度
6. allocation *n*. 分配
7. swap *v*. 配对,交换
8. graph-theoretic method 图解推理法
9. bandwith *n*. 带宽
10. heuristic *a*. *n*. 启发式的(研究)
11. global optima 全局最优
12. column (row) dominance 列(行)优势
13. rational *a*. 有理(数)的
14. Nyquist contour 乃奎斯特轨线

15. square matrix 方阵
16. decomposition *n*. 分解
17. homogeneous *a*. 齐次的
18. indeterminate *a*. 不确定的
19. indeterminacy *n*. 不确定性
20. norm *n*. 范数
21. ambiguity *n*. 不定性,双重性,混淆
22. cost function 代价(损失)函数
23. row permutation 行变换
24. minmax criteria 极小化最大准则
25. suffice for 足够,足以满足
26. bottleneck *n*. 难点,瓶颈
27. bipartite *a*. 双向[枝]的,由两部分构成的
28. scaling problom 定标问题
29. binary *a*. 两分的,两自由度的
30. bisention *n*. 二分;平分
31. consistent *a*. 一致的
32. first order 一阶
33. consistency *n*. 一致性
34. convergence *n*. 收敛性
35. tailor to 满足条件
36. nominal *a*. 额定的,标称的
37. operating factor 工作系数
38. lead-compensator 超前补偿器
39. forward gain 前向增益
40. sparse *s*. 稀疏的
41. tear *v*. 分开,分解
42. sample *n*. 采样

Notes:

1. For non trivial problems the designer invariably requires the aid of a computer and in practice CAD facilities in which the designer can ‘interact’ with the design steps have played a significant role.

译:对于复杂些的问题,设计者必定需要计算机的辅助,而在实际中,允许设计者与设计步骤之间交互信息的计算机辅助设计(CAD)设备已经扮演了一个重要的角色。

2. The pairing that may emerge from physical considerations or during model formulation is certainly not always the best from a control point of view and we will consider which pairing is‘best’ in terms of dominance.

译:通过物理考虑或在建立模型过程中所得到的配对,从控制的观点来看,当然并不总是最好的,我们将根据优势的概念来考虑哪个配对最好。

3. As the methods we describe usually yield 'global optima' they usually serve in practice to settle the question of whether dominance is attainable for the given class of compensator.

译:由于我们所描述的方法通常能得到'全局最优解',因此这些方法在实际中经常被用来解决下面的问题,即:对于给定的一类补偿器,优势是否可以被获得。

4. To avoid computational difficulties associated with constancy of $J_i^c(\lambda \boldsymbol{K})$ for any $\lambda \neq 0$ and the singular behaviour for $\lambda = 0$, it is usually convenient to introduce a constraint of the form $\|\boldsymbol{K}\| = 1$ say, where $\| * \|$ is anyconvenient norm; if we also wish to avoid ambiguity in the sign of λ then a stronger constraint such as $k_{ii} = 1$ is convenient.

译:要避免由 $\lambda \neq 0$ 时 $J_i^c(\lambda \boldsymbol{K})$ 的不变性和 $\lambda = 0$ 时的奇异特性所带来的计算上的困难,引入一个型为 $\|\boldsymbol{K}\| = 1$(其中的 $\| * \|$ 可以是任意合适的范数)的约束通常是有用的;如果我们还希望避免 λ 在符号(指"+""-"号)上的不定性,那么可以引入一个更强的约束,比如 $k_{ii} = 1$。

5. we have, where there is no ambiguity dropped the suffix i.

译:我们已经在不引起混淆的地方省掉下标 i。

6. Although all the algorithms described have been successfully extended to multiple frequency case, we will, for reasons of space, only state the single frequency algorithms.

译: 尽管所有上述算法都已被成功地推广到多频率情况,但由于篇幅原因,在这里只阐述单频率的算法。

7. Essentially we are deciding how best to pair inputs and outputs.

译:实质上,我们是在决定如何将输入与输出配对最好。

8. The last element coloured is the smallest element that can be chosen in its row and column, whilst at the same time ensuring the other rows and columns can be 'covered' by the set already coloured and comprising elements of $\boldsymbol{D}^c$ smaller than the last element coloured.

译:最后被染色的元素是在其所在的行和列中能被选出的最小元素,而同时,保证了其它的行和列,能被已经染色的元素集合所'覆盖’,并且包含比最后染色的元素小的 $\boldsymbol{D}^c$ 中的元素。

9. The graph-theoretic equivalent of the problem is a minimax ‘bottle-neck’ matching problem for which powerful algorithms exist.

译:这个问题在图解理论上的等价是极小化极大值匹配问题的难点,在这方面有一些非常有效的算法。

10. A recently developed algorithm which employs both a Newton like step with quadratic convergence together with a first order step which yields finite convergence to a feasible point has been utilised with considerable success.

译:一个近来发展起来的算法已经被相当成功地使用了,这种算法使用了一个具有二阶收敛性的类牛顿(Newton)步骤,同时还使用了一个对于适宜点能达到有限收敛的一阶步骤。

PART 2	CHAPTER FIVE

5 Pole Assignment

Synopsis

The problem of pole assignment using state feedback or output feedback is examined. An algorithm for the design of full rank minimum degree output-feedback compensators is presented and results in a unification of previously obtained results[注1].

5.1 Introduction

The problem of pole assignment has been extensively studied by many research workers over the last decade. It is simply concerned with moving the poles (or eigenvalues) of a given time-invariant linear system to a specified set of locations in the s-plane (subject to complex pairing) by means of state or output feedback[注2]. The state-feedback approach is well established, however the output-feedback case is still being explored as a research area.

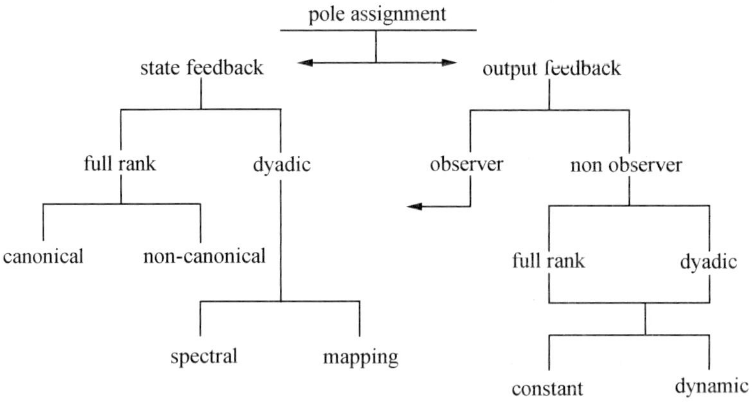

Fig. 5.1 Pole Assignment Algorithms

A large number of algorithms exist for the solution of this problem. Fortunately, these algorithms can be categorised by the characteristics of the approaches used, as shown in Fig. 5. 1. Both the state-feedback methods and the output-feedback methods result in compensator matrices which are broadly speaking either dyadic (i. e. have rank equal to one) or have full rank[注3]. Although the dyadic algorithms have considerable elegance and simplicity, the resulting closed-loop systems have poor disturbance rejection properties compared with their full-rank counterparts.

Here, we shall review several existing algorithms and then consider the development of an algorithm which uses the dyadic design mechanism to generate full-rank minimum degree output-feedback compensators, which allow arbitrary pole assignment. The approach to be presented is 'consistent' with all previously established results and provides a unifying framework. The case of state-feedback is readily shown to be a special case of output-feedback.

The problem to be considered is as follows. Given a system described in state-space form as

$$\dot{\boldsymbol{x}}=\boldsymbol{A}\boldsymbol{x}+\boldsymbol{B}\boldsymbol{u} \tag{5.1}$$

$$\boldsymbol{y}=\boldsymbol{C}\boldsymbol{x} \tag{5.2}$$

where $\boldsymbol{A}$, $\boldsymbol{B}$, $\boldsymbol{C}$ are real matrices with dimensions $n\times n$, $n\times m$, $l\times n$, respectively, or by its corresponding transfer-function matrix representation

$$\boldsymbol{G}(s)=\boldsymbol{C}(s\boldsymbol{I}-\boldsymbol{A})^{-1}\boldsymbol{B} \tag{5.3}$$

when and how can we apply feedback to this system such that the resulting closed-loop system has a desired set of arbitrary poles, or eigenvalues (subject to complex pairing). First, we consider some of the well established results, starting with the state-feedback case.

5.2 State-Feedback Algorithms

Using a feedback law of the form

$$\boldsymbol{u}=\boldsymbol{r}-\boldsymbol{K}\boldsymbol{x} \tag{5.4}$$

where $\boldsymbol{r}$ is an $m \times 1$ vector of reference inputs and $\boldsymbol{K}$ is an $m \times n$ real matrix, 'when' and 'how' can we determine $\boldsymbol{K}$ such that the resulting closed-loop system

$$\dot{\boldsymbol{x}} = (\boldsymbol{A} - \boldsymbol{B}\boldsymbol{K})\boldsymbol{x} + \boldsymbol{B}\boldsymbol{r} \tag{5.5}$$

has a desired set of eigenvalues $\{\gamma_i\}$; $i = 1, 2, \cdots, n$?

The question when was answered by Wonham and the requirement is that the pair $[\boldsymbol{A}, \boldsymbol{B}]$ is completely controllable. The question of how can be examined in several ways, as follows.

5.2.1 Dyadic designs

Under the heading of dyadic designs (see Fig. 1), the spectral approach essentially requires the calculation of the eigenvalues $\{\lambda_i\}$, and the associated eigenvectors $\{\boldsymbol{w}_i\}$ and reciprocal eigenvectors $\{\boldsymbol{v}_i^{\mathrm{T}}\}$ of the matrix $\boldsymbol{A}$. Significant contributions have been made in this area by several workers. Here, the matrix $\boldsymbol{K}$ is considered as the outer product of two vectors; i. e.

$$\boldsymbol{K} = \boldsymbol{f}\boldsymbol{m}^{\mathrm{T}} \tag{5.6}$$

where $\boldsymbol{f}$ is $m \times 1$ and $\boldsymbol{m}^{\mathrm{T}}$ is $1 \times n$.

The problem of simultaneously determining the $(m+n-1)$ free elements in $\boldsymbol{K}$ is nonlinear. However, by pre-assigning values to the elements of one vector, the determination of the remaining elements results in a linear problem. Conventionally, the vector $\boldsymbol{f}$ is chosen such that the resulting pseudo single-input system $[\boldsymbol{A}, \boldsymbol{B}\boldsymbol{f}]$ is completely controllable. Then for a desired closed-loop pole set $\{\gamma_i\}$, the vector $\boldsymbol{m}^{\mathrm{T}}$ is given by

$$\boldsymbol{m}^{\mathrm{T}} = \sum_{i=1}^{q} \boldsymbol{\delta}_i \boldsymbol{v}_i^{\mathrm{T}} \tag{5.7}$$

where q = number of poles to be altered, the $\boldsymbol{v}_i^{\mathrm{T}}$ are the reciprocal eigenvectors associated with those eigenvalues $\{\lambda_i\}$ to be altered, and the scalars δ_i are weighting factors calculated as

$$\delta_i = \frac{\prod_{j=1}^{q}(\lambda_i - \gamma_i)}{p_i \prod_{\substack{j=1 \\ j\neq i}}^{q}(\lambda_i - \lambda_j)} \tag{5.8}$$

where the scalars p_i are defined by the inner product

$$p_i = \langle \boldsymbol{v}_i, \boldsymbol{Bf} \rangle \tag{5.9}$$

We note that if the λ_i or γ_i are complex then the resulting δ_i will be complex. However, $\boldsymbol{m}^{\mathrm{T}}$ will be real if these values correspond to complex-conjugate pole-pairs.

When the open-loop system has any eigenvalues of multiplicity greater than 1, the above algorithm breaks down, since the denominator term in equation (5.8) becomes zero for certain δ_i. However, a modification to this algorithm to cater for this latter situation has been developed.

In contrast to the above method, the mapping approach (see Fig. 5.1) due to Young and Willems does not require the spectral decomposition of the open-loop system. Once the desired closed-loop system poles have been specified, the corresponding closed-loop system characteristic polynomial $\Delta_{\mathrm{d}}(s)$, where

$$\Delta_{\mathrm{d}}(s) = s^n + d_1 s^{n-1} + \cdots + d_n \tag{5.10}$$

can be calculated. If the open-loop system characteristic polynomial is defined as

$$\Delta_{\mathrm{o}}(s) = |s\boldsymbol{I} - \boldsymbol{A}| = s^n + a_1 s^{n-1} + \cdots + a_n \tag{5.11}$$

then we can define a difference polynomial $\delta(s)$ as

$$\delta(s) = \Delta_{\mathrm{d}}(s) - \Delta_{\mathrm{o}}(s) = s^n + (d_1 - a_1)s^{n-1} + \cdots + (d_n - a_n) \tag{5.12}$$

Now, if the vector $\boldsymbol{f}$ is chosen such that $[\boldsymbol{A}, \boldsymbol{Bf}]$ is completely controllable, the required vector $\boldsymbol{m}^{\mathrm{T}}$ is determined as

$$\boldsymbol{m} = [\boldsymbol{\phi}_{\mathrm{c}}^{\mathrm{T}}]^{-1} \boldsymbol{X}^{-1} \boldsymbol{\delta} \tag{5.13}$$

where
$$\boldsymbol{\delta}_{\mathrm{c}} = [\boldsymbol{Bf}, \boldsymbol{ABf}, \cdots, \boldsymbol{A}^{n-1}\boldsymbol{Bf}] \tag{5.14}$$

$$X = \begin{bmatrix} 1 & 0 & & 0 & 0 \\ a_1 & 1 & & \vdots & \vdots \\ \vdots & a_1 & & \vdots & \vdots \\ \vdots & \vdots & & \vdots & \vdots \\ \vdots & \vdots & & \vdots & \vdots \\ a_{n-2} & a_{n-3} & \cdots & 1 & \vdots \\ a_{n-1} & a_{n-2} & \cdots & a_1 & 1 \end{bmatrix} \tag{5.15}$$

and
$$\boldsymbol{\delta} = [d_1 - a_1,\ d_2 - a_2, \cdots,\ d_n - a_n]^{\mathrm{T}} \tag{5.16}$$

We note that by definition the $n \times n$ matrix $\boldsymbol{X}$ is nonsingular, and so is the controllability matrix $\boldsymbol{\phi}_{\mathrm{c}}$. Also, these need only be calculated once for a variety of closed-loop system pole specifications.

Another way of looking at this latter algorithm, which will set the scene for the results in the later sections, is from the frequency-domain point of view.

Let

$$\boldsymbol{\Gamma}(s) = \mathrm{adj}(s\boldsymbol{I} - \boldsymbol{A}) \tag{5.17}$$

and
$$\boldsymbol{b}_f = \boldsymbol{B}\boldsymbol{f} \tag{5.18}$$

then, after f has been chosen to give complete controllability in the resulting single-input system, we have

$$\boldsymbol{g}(\mathrm{s}) = \frac{1}{\Delta_{\mathrm{o}}(\mathrm{s})} \boldsymbol{\Gamma}(s) \boldsymbol{b}_f = \frac{1}{\Delta_{\mathrm{o}}(s)} \begin{bmatrix} N_1(s) \\ N_2(s) \\ \vdots \\ N_n(s) \end{bmatrix} \tag{5.19}$$

where the

$$N_i(s) = \beta_{i1} s^{n-1} + \beta_{i2} s^{n-2} + \cdots + \beta_{in} \tag{5.20}$$

and $\Delta_{\mathrm{o}}(s)$ is as defined by equation (5.11).

We also have $\Delta_{\mathrm{d}}(s)$ defined as

$$\Delta_{\mathrm{d}}(s) = |s\boldsymbol{I} - \boldsymbol{A} + \boldsymbol{B}\boldsymbol{K}| = |s\boldsymbol{I} - \boldsymbol{A} + \boldsymbol{b}_f \boldsymbol{m}^{\mathrm{T}}| =$$
$$|s\boldsymbol{I} - \boldsymbol{A}|\,|\boldsymbol{I} + (s\boldsymbol{I} - \boldsymbol{A})^{-1} \boldsymbol{b}_f \boldsymbol{m}^{\mathrm{T}}| \tag{5.21}$$

which can equally be written as

$$\Delta_d(s)=\Delta_o(s)+\boldsymbol{m}^T\boldsymbol{\Gamma}(s)\boldsymbol{b}_f \tag{5.22}$$

i. e.

$$\Delta_d(s)=\Delta_o(s)+\sum_{i=1}^{n} m_i N_i(s) \tag{5.23}$$

Using (5.12) we can consider the pole assignment problem as consisting of solving the equation

$$\sum_{i=1}^{n} m_i N_i(s)=\delta(s) \tag{5.24}$$

for the parameters of the vector $\boldsymbol{m}$.

As we shall see later, equation (5.24) is the heart of the dyadic approaches to pole assignment.

Equating coefficients of like powers in s on both sides of equation (5.24), we obtain

$$\begin{bmatrix} \beta_{11} & \cdots & \beta_{n1} \\ \vdots & & \vdots \\ \beta_{1n} & \cdots & \beta_{nn} \end{bmatrix}\begin{bmatrix} m_1 \\ \vdots \\ m_n \end{bmatrix}=\begin{bmatrix} \delta_1 \\ \vdots \\ \delta_n \end{bmatrix} \tag{5.25}$$

i. e.

$$\boldsymbol{X}\boldsymbol{m}=\boldsymbol{\delta} \tag{5.26}$$

where the difference vector $\boldsymbol{\delta}$ is defined by equation (5.16) and where the $n\times n$ matrix $\boldsymbol{X}$ always has full rank; i. e. the equations are consistent. Therefore, the desired vector $\boldsymbol{m}$ is given by

$$\boldsymbol{m}=\boldsymbol{X}^{-1}\boldsymbol{\delta} \tag{5.27}$$

for any $\boldsymbol{\delta}$.

5.2.2 Full-rank designs

The conditions under which a full-rank state-feedback compen-sator $\boldsymbol{K}$ can be designed are exactly as before; namely, that the open-loop system $[\boldsymbol{A}, \boldsymbol{B}]$ is completely controllable. Here, again, we shall consider two distinct approaches.

In the first approach we assume that the original system matrices $\boldsymbol{A}$ and $\boldsymbol{B}$ have been transformed into their so-called controllable canonical form yielding $\tilde{\boldsymbol{A}}$ and $\tilde{\boldsymbol{B}}$ defined as

$$\widetilde{A} = TAT^{-1} \tag{5.28}$$

and
$$\widetilde{B} = TBW \tag{5.29}$$

where $\boldsymbol{T}$ is a nonsingular transformation matrix formed from specifically selected and ordered columns of the system controllability matrix $[\boldsymbol{B}, \boldsymbol{AB}, \cdots, \boldsymbol{A}^{n-1}\boldsymbol{B}]$, and $\boldsymbol{Q}$ is a nonsingular matrix formed from the nonzero rows of the matrix $(\boldsymbol{TB})$.

Under this transformation, $\widetilde{\boldsymbol{A}}$has the particular block structure

$$\boldsymbol{A} = \begin{bmatrix} \boldsymbol{A}_{11} & \cdots & \boldsymbol{A}_{1m} \\ \vdots & & \vdots \\ \boldsymbol{A}_{m1} & \cdots & \boldsymbol{A}_{mm} \end{bmatrix} \tag{5.30}$$

where the diagonal block $\boldsymbol{A}_{ii}$ have the companion form

$$\boldsymbol{A}_{ii} = \begin{bmatrix} 0 & 1 & 0 & \cdots & 0 \\ 0 & 0 & 1 & \cdots & 0 \\ \vdots & \vdots & \vdots & & \vdots \\ 0 & 0 & 0 & \cdots & 1 \\ \times & \times & \times & \cdots & \times \end{bmatrix} \tag{5.31}$$

with dimensions $v_i \times v_i$, where the v_i are the controllability indices of the system; i. e.

$$\sum_{i=1}^{m} v_i = n$$

and where the off-diagonal blocks $\boldsymbol{A}_{ij}$, $i \times j$, have the form

$$\boldsymbol{A}_{ij} = \begin{bmatrix} & 0 & \\ & -------- & \\ \times & \times & \cdots & \times \end{bmatrix} \tag{5.32}$$

with dimension $v_i \times v_j$, $i, j = 1, 2, \cdots, m, i \neq j$. The matrix $\widetilde{\boldsymbol{B}}$ has the particular block structure

$$\boldsymbol{B} = \begin{bmatrix} \boldsymbol{B}_1 \\ \vdots \\ \boldsymbol{B}_m \end{bmatrix} \tag{5.33}$$

where

$$
B_i = \begin{bmatrix} & & & 0 & & & \\ \hline 0 & \cdots & 0 & \underset{\substack{\uparrow \\ \text{column } i}}{1} & 0 & \cdots & 0 \end{bmatrix} \tag{5.34}
$$

has dimensions $(v_i \times m)$. In equations (5.31)-(5.34), the ×'s may be nonzero coefficients.

Given a system in this special form, the feedback matrix $\boldsymbol{K}$ required to achieve a desired closed-loop pole set $\{\gamma_i\}$ is chosen such that $(\tilde{\boldsymbol{A}} - \tilde{\boldsymbol{B}}\tilde{\boldsymbol{K}})$ becomes block upper or lower triangular, or both, and such that the resulting diagonal blocks have nonzero coefficients which satisfy

$$
\prod_{i=1}^{m} \det[s\boldsymbol{I} - \tilde{\boldsymbol{A}}_{ii} + (\tilde{\boldsymbol{B}}\tilde{\boldsymbol{K}})_{ii}] = \prod_{i=1}^{n} (s - \gamma_i) \tag{5.35}
$$

The desired full-rank feedback matrix $\boldsymbol{K}$ in the original system basis is then given by

$$
\boldsymbol{K} = \boldsymbol{Q}^{-1}\tilde{\boldsymbol{K}}\boldsymbol{T} \tag{5.36}
$$

Consider now the situation where a full-rank feedback matrix $\boldsymbol{K}$ is to be determined as a sum of dyads; i. e. let

$$
\boldsymbol{K} = \sum_{i=1}^{\mu} \boldsymbol{f}^{(i)} \boldsymbol{m}^{(i)} \tag{5.37}
$$

where the $\boldsymbol{f}^{(i)}$ are $m \times 1$ column vectors, the $\boldsymbol{m}^{(i)}$ are $1 \times n$ row vectors, and $\mu = \min\{m, n\} = m$. $\boldsymbol{K}$ can also be expressed as the matrix product

$$
\boldsymbol{K} = \boldsymbol{F}\boldsymbol{M} \tag{5.38}
$$

where $\boldsymbol{F}$ is an $m \times m$ matrix whose columns are the $\boldsymbol{f}^{(i)}$, and $\boldsymbol{M}$ is an $m \times n$ matrix whose rows are the $\boldsymbol{m}^{(i)}$. We note that $\boldsymbol{K}$ will have full rank m, if and only if both $\boldsymbol{F}$ and $\boldsymbol{M}$ have maximum rank.

Consider the following algorithm:

(1) Suppose we choose $\boldsymbol{f}^{(1)}$ such that it selects input 1 of the given system; i. e. $\boldsymbol{f}^{(1)} = [1\ 0\ \cdots\ 0]^{\mathrm{T}}$. Then, since input 1 must influence $q_1 \geqslant 1$ poles of the system, we can determine $\boldsymbol{m}^{(1)}$ to reposition q_1 poles at desired locations.

Let the resulting closed-loop system

$$\dot{\boldsymbol{x}}=(\boldsymbol{A}-\boldsymbol{B}\boldsymbol{f}^{(1)}\boldsymbol{m}^{(1)})\boldsymbol{x}+\boldsymbol{B}\boldsymbol{r} \tag{5.39}$$

be considered as

$$\boldsymbol{x}(s)=[\boldsymbol{\Gamma}^{(1)}(s)/d^{(1)}(s)]\boldsymbol{r}(s) \tag{5.40}$$

where

$$\boldsymbol{\Gamma}^{(1)}(s)=\operatorname{adj}(\boldsymbol{A}-\boldsymbol{B}\boldsymbol{f}^{(1)}\boldsymbol{m}^{(1)}) \tag{5.41}$$

and $d^{(1)}(s)$ is the new characteristic polynomial.

(2) Since $\boldsymbol{\Gamma}^{(1)}(s)\big|_{s=\gamma_i}$ only has rank one, we can define $\boldsymbol{f}^{(2)}$ as

$$\boldsymbol{f}^{(2)}=[f_1\quad f_2\quad 0\ \cdots\ 0]^{\mathrm{T}} \tag{5.42}$$

and can solve the equations

$$\boldsymbol{\Gamma}^{(1)}(\gamma_i)\boldsymbol{f}^{(2)}=0 \tag{5.43}$$

We note that due to the system controllability properties, this choice of $\boldsymbol{f}^{(2)}$ will influence $q_2\geqslant 1$ more poles of the resulting single-input system given by $\boldsymbol{\Gamma}^{(1)}(s)\boldsymbol{f}^{(2)}$ and $d^{(1)}(s)$.

⋮

(m) Continuing in the above manner, it can be shown that this procedure allows us to shift all n poles of the original system to a desired set $\{\gamma_i\}$; $i=1,2,\cdots,n$; in steps.

We note, that at each stage, those poles which have not been rendered uncontrollable with respect to that stage of the design procedure, and which are not being moved to desired locations will move in an arbitrary manner[注4]. However, after m stages, all n poles have been moved to the desired locations.

The matrix $\boldsymbol{F}$ generated in this manner will have full rank m, and it can also be shown that the corresponding matrix $\boldsymbol{M}$ will simultaneously have full rank n. Thus, $\boldsymbol{K}$ will have full rank; a desired objective; and will also provide the appropriate pole shifting action.

5.3 Output-Feedback Algorithms

Here, we shall adopt the frequency-domain approach from the start. Thus, given a system described by the $l\times m$ transfer-function matrix

$\boldsymbol{G}(s)$, and using a feedback law

$$\boldsymbol{u}(s)=\boldsymbol{r}(s)-\boldsymbol{F}(s)\boldsymbol{y}(s) \tag{5.44}$$

when and how can the resulting closed-loop system

$$\boldsymbol{H}(s)=[\boldsymbol{I}+\boldsymbol{G}(s)\boldsymbol{F}(s)]^{-1}\boldsymbol{G}(s) \tag{5.45}$$

be made to have a pre-assigned set of poles $\{\gamma_i\}$; $i=1, 2, \cdots, n$? Complete pole assignment is only possible using output-feedback when $\boldsymbol{G}(s)$ has arisen from a least-order system[注5]; i. e. the corresponding state-space triple $[\boldsymbol{A}, \boldsymbol{B}, \boldsymbol{C}]$ is completely controllable and observable.

The following questions arise naturally at this point:

(1) What is the minimum degree of the compensator matrix $\boldsymbol{F}(s)$ which will allow arbitrary pole locations in the resulting closed-loop system?

(2) What are the parameters of this $\boldsymbol{F}(s)$?

(3) What is the rank of $\boldsymbol{F}(s)$?

Davison has shown that, using a constant feedback matrix $\boldsymbol{F}$, $\max\{m,l\}$ poles can be assigned arbitrarily close to desired values. However, the remaining $n-\max\{m,l\}$ poles move arbitrarily. Nevertheless, this result may prove useful in situations where only a few of the open-loop system poles are to be moved to more desirable locations[注6]. It is also known that by the use of a Luenberger observer of order $(n-l)$, or a Kalman-Bucy filter of order $(n+l)$, a good estimate of the system state-vector x can be reconstructed. This latter approach then allows any of the well known state-feedback algorithms to be applied using $\hat{\boldsymbol{x}}$[注7]. Further, if a dyadic state-feedback approach is to be used then we need only estimate $\hat{\alpha}=\boldsymbol{m}^{\mathrm{T}}\boldsymbol{x}$, and this can be done under favourable conditions using an observer of order $r=v_o-1$, where v_o is the observability index for the system.

For those situations where a dynamic compensator $\boldsymbol{F}(s)$ is required, Brasch and Pearson have shown that a dynamic compensator of degree

$$r = \min\{v_o - 1,\ v_c - 1\} \tag{5.46}$$

where v_c is the controllability index for the system, is sufficient (but not necessary) to allow arbitrary pole assignment. The design of an observer is implicit in this approach, and the resulting feedback is essentially dyadic. A similar result has been obtained by Chen and Hsu in the frequency-domain.

Another result, obtained by Davison and Wang results in a compensator of rank two. These authors have shown that if

$$m + l - 1 \geqslant n \tag{5.47}$$

then a constant compensator $\boldsymbol{F}$ exists which allows the closed-loop system poles to be assigned arbitrarily close to a desired set $\{\gamma_i\}$.

The final result to be considered in this section is due to Munro and Novin Hirbod which states that if $m+l-1 \geqslant n$ a full-rank constant compensator $\boldsymbol{F}$ can be determined, from a minimal sequence of dyads, to assign the closed-loop system poles arbitrarily close to a predefined set $\{\gamma_i\}$[注8]. Further, if $m+l-1<n$ then a full rank dynamic compensator $\boldsymbol{F}(s)$ with degree r given by

$$r \geqslant \left[\frac{n-(m+l-1)}{\max\{m, l\}}\right] \tag{5.48}$$

can be constructed from a minimal sequence of dyads, which will allow arbitrary pole assignment.

In the following, we shall consider the design of minimum degree dyadic dynamic feedback compensators, and finally the design of minimum degree full-rank dynamic feedback compensators[注9].

5.3.1 Dyadic designs

Given a strictly-proper $l \times m$ transfer-function matrix $\boldsymbol{G}(s)$, let the required compensator $\boldsymbol{F}(s)$ be considered as the outer product of two vectors $\boldsymbol{f}$ and $\boldsymbol{m}^{\mathrm{T}}(s)$; i. e.

$$\boldsymbol{F}(s) = \boldsymbol{f}\boldsymbol{m}^{\mathrm{T}}(s) \tag{5.49}$$

As before, the constant vector $\boldsymbol{f}$ is chosen such that

$$g(s)=G(s)f \tag{5.50}$$

is completely controllable. Let $g(s)$ be expressed as

$$g(s)=\frac{1}{\Delta_o(s)}\begin{bmatrix}N_1(s)\\ \vdots \\ N_l(s)\end{bmatrix} \tag{5.51}$$

where

$$\Delta_o(s)=s^n+a_1s^{n-1}+\cdots+a_n \tag{5.52}$$

is the characteristic polynomial of $G(s)$, and the

$$N_i(s)=\beta_{i1}s^{n-1}+\beta_{i2}s^{n-2}+\cdots+\beta_{in} \tag{5.53}$$

Now, let $m^T(s)$ have the form

$$m^T(s)=\frac{1}{\Delta_c(s)}[M_1(s)\cdots M_l(s)] \tag{5.54}$$

where
$$\Delta_c(s)=s^r+\gamma_1s^{r-1}+\cdots+\gamma_r \tag{5.55}$$

is the characteristic polynomial of $m^T(s)$, and the

$$M_i(s)=\theta_{i0}s^r+\theta_{i1}s^{r-1}+\cdots+\theta_{ir} \tag{5.56}$$

Then, Chen and Hsu have shown that the resulting closed-loop system characteristic polynomial $\Delta_d(s)$, where

$$\Delta_d(s)=s^{n+r}+d_1s^{n+r-1}+\cdots+d_{n+r} \tag{5.57}$$

is given by the relationship

$$\Delta_d(s)=\Delta_o(s)\Delta_c(s)+\sum_{i=1}^{l}N_i(s)M_i(s) \tag{5.58}$$

which is the heart of the dyadic approach to pole assignment using output-feedback.

If we now define a difference polynomial $\delta_r(s)$ as

$$\delta_r(s)=\Delta_d(s)-\Delta_o(s)s^r \tag{5.59}$$

then (5.58) can be written as

$$\left\{\sum_{i=1}^{l}N_i(s)M_i(s)\right\}+\Delta_o(s)(\Delta_c(s)-s^r)=\delta_r(s) \tag{5.60}$$

Equating coefficients of like powers of s on both sides of equation (5.60) yields the vector-matrix equations

$$X_r p_r = \delta_r \tag{5.61}$$

where X is an $(n+r)\times((r+1)(l+1)-1)$ matrix constructed from the coefficients a_i of $\Delta_o(s)$ and the β_{ij} of the $N_i(s)$, the vector p_r contains the unknown parameters γ_j and θ_{ij} defining $F(s)$, and the difference vector δ_r contains the coefficients δ_j of $\delta_r(s)$ as defined by equation (5.59)[注10]. The elements of X_r, p_r, δ_r are shown explicitly in Appendix 1.

The pole assignment problem can now be stated as when can equation (5.61) be solved for the vector p_r. A necessary and sufficient condition for equation (5.61) to have a solution for the $(l(r+1)+r)$ vector p_r is that

$$X_r X_r^{g_1} \delta_r = \delta_r \tag{5.62}$$

where $X_r^{g_1}$ is a g_1-inverse of the matrix X_r defined by

$$X_r X_r^{g_1} X_r = X_r \tag{5.63}$$

If equation (5.61) is consistent, the general solution for p_r is

$$p_r = X_r^{g_1}\delta_r + (I - X_r^{g_1} X_r) z \tag{5.64}$$

where z is an arbitrary $[l(r+1)+r]\times 1$ vector. Since z is arbitrary, it can be chosen as the zero vector yielding

$$p_r = X_r^{g_1}\delta_r \tag{5.65}$$

We note that if the consistency condition given by equation (5.62) is not satisfied for a particular g_1-inverse of X_r, then it will not be satisfied for any other g_1-inverse of X_r.

It has already been mentioned that if r is chosen as

$$r_m = \min\{v_o - 1,\ v_c - 1\} \tag{5.66}$$

then arbitrary pole assignment can be achieved. This result can now be simply explained, since for r defined by (5.66) we obtain under these special conditions[注11]

$$X_r X_r^{g_1} = I_{n+r} \tag{5.67}$$

This is due to the rank of X_r, for this particular value of r, being such that a right-inverse of X_r exists, defined by[注12]

$$X_r^{g1} = X_r^T [X_r X_r^T]^{-1} \qquad (5.68)$$

It is also interesting to note that for arbitrary pole assignment, r is bounded as

$$\left\lceil \frac{n-1}{l} \right\rceil \leqslant r_m \leqslant n-l \qquad (5.69)$$

We can now see that for the case of state-feedback, since then $l = n$, cquation(5.69) yields $r=0$; i. e. $\boldsymbol{F}$ is a constant matrix.

However, equation (5.69) does not allow for known exceptions, where arbitrary pole assignment can be achieved with a compensator $\boldsymbol{F}(s)$ of order $r<r_m$ [注13]. To allow for these situations, we state that the necessary and sufficient conditions on r are that it is chosen such that

$$\rho\{X_r\} = \rho\{X_r, \boldsymbol{\delta}_r\} \qquad (5.70)$$

where $\rho\{ * \}$ means rank.

5.3.2 Full-rank designs

Suppose that the required compensator $\boldsymbol{F}$, constant or dynamic, is constructed from a minimal sequence of dyads as

$$\boldsymbol{F} = \sum_{i=1}^{\mu} \boldsymbol{f}^{(i)} \boldsymbol{m}^{(i)} \qquad (5.71)$$

where $\boldsymbol{f}^{(i)}$ is an $m\times 1$ vector, $\boldsymbol{m}^{(i)}$ is a $1\times l$ vector, and

$$\mu = \min\{m, l\} \qquad (5.72)$$

Then, equation (5.71) can be equally written as

$$\boldsymbol{F} = \boldsymbol{F}_c \boldsymbol{F}_o \qquad (5.73)$$

where $\boldsymbol{F}_c$ is an m (m matrix whose columns are the vectors $\boldsymbol{f}^{(i)}$, and where $\boldsymbol{F}_o$ is an $m\times l$ matrix whose rows are the vectors $\boldsymbol{m}^{(i)}$.

We can ensure that for the case where $m<l$ the matrix $\boldsymbol{F}_c$ has full rank by its construction, but $\boldsymbol{F}$ will have full rank if and only if $\boldsymbol{F}_o$ and $\boldsymbol{F}_c$ both have full rank. It is tedious but straightforward to show that if $\boldsymbol{F}_c$ is generated by the method shown in the following algorithm, then the corresponding matrix $\boldsymbol{F}_o$ simultaneously has full rank. The case where $m>l$ is obtained by duality.

Algorithm:

(1) Choose $\boldsymbol{f}_c^{(1)}$ such that it picks up input 1, say, of the system; i. e. Let $\boldsymbol{f}_c^{(1)}=[1\ 0\ \cdots\ 0]^{\mathrm{T}}$; and determine the corresponding vector $\boldsymbol{f}_o^{(1)}$ to place as many poles as possible in desired locations. Since the system is completely controllable, the pseudo-input vector $\boldsymbol{b}^{(1)}=\boldsymbol{B}\,\boldsymbol{f}_c^{(1)}$ will influence n_1 modes of the system where $1\leqslant n_1\leqslant n$. Also, the system $[\boldsymbol{A},\ \boldsymbol{b}^{(1)},\ \boldsymbol{C}]$ has l_1 linearly independent outputs and one input and, in fact, only $q^1=\min\{l_1,\ n_1\}$ poles can be assigned to specific locations at this stage.

(2) For $\boldsymbol{f}_c^{(2)}=[f_1\,f_2\,0\ \cdots\ 0]^{\mathrm{T}}$, say, determine f_1 and f_2; $f_2\neq 0$; to render as many as possible of the q_1 poles assigned in stage 1 uncontrollable, and determine $\boldsymbol{f}_o^{(2)}$ to move at least one more pole to a desired location.

Let n_2 be the number of modes influenced by $\boldsymbol{b}^{(2)}=\boldsymbol{B}\,\boldsymbol{f}_c^{(2)}$ where $1\leqslant n_2\leqslant n-1$. Then, $\boldsymbol{f}_o^{(2)}$ is determined to move $q_2=\min\{l_2,\ n_2\}$ poles to desired locations by solving the equation (5.74):

$$\Delta^{(2)}(s)=\Delta^{(1)}(s)+\boldsymbol{f}_o^{(2)}\,\boldsymbol{C}[\operatorname{adj}(s\boldsymbol{I}-\boldsymbol{A}+\boldsymbol{B}\,\boldsymbol{f}_c^{(1)}\,\boldsymbol{f}_o^{(1)}\,\boldsymbol{C})]\boldsymbol{B}\,\boldsymbol{f}_c^{(2)} \tag{5.74}$$

where

$$\boldsymbol{\Delta}^{(1)}(s)=\boldsymbol{\Delta}_o(s)+\boldsymbol{f}_o^{(1)}\,\boldsymbol{C}[\operatorname{adj}(s\boldsymbol{I}-\boldsymbol{A})]\boldsymbol{B}\,\boldsymbol{f}_c^{(1)} \tag{5.75}$$

Note that the elements f_1 and f_2 of $\boldsymbol{f}_c^{(2)}$ are determined by solving

$$\boldsymbol{\Gamma}^{(1)}(s)\ +\boldsymbol{f}_c^{(2)}=0=[\operatorname{adj}(s\boldsymbol{I}-\boldsymbol{A}+\boldsymbol{B}\,\boldsymbol{f}_c^{(1)}\,\boldsymbol{f}_o^{(1)}\,\boldsymbol{C})]\boldsymbol{B}\,\boldsymbol{f}_c^{(2)} \tag{5.76}$$

at those roots of $\boldsymbol{\Delta}^{(1)}(s)$ which correspond to eigenvalues to be made uncontrollable.

⋮

(m) For $\boldsymbol{f}_c^{(m)}=[f_1\,f_2\cdots\,f_m]^{\mathrm{T}}$ determine f_1 to f_m; $f_m\neq 0$; to hold $(m-1)$ poles in desired locations, and determine $\boldsymbol{f}_o^{(m)}$ to place $\min\{l,\ n-m+1\}$ poles indesired locations.

Provided $m+l-1\geqslant n$, this procedure can always be carried out. Now, if $m+l-1<n$, the first $m-1$ stages of this procedure are carried out

as before, and then the final stage is carried out using a dynamic dyadic compensator of degree r, as defined by equation (5.48). The resulting full-rank compensator $\boldsymbol{F}(s)$ will have degree r.

5.3.3 Example

Consider a system with transfer-function matrix

$$\boldsymbol{G}(s)=\frac{1}{s^4}\begin{bmatrix} s^2(s+1) & (s+1) \\ 0 & s^2(s+1) \end{bmatrix} \tag{5.77}$$

which has eigenvalues $\{\lambda_i\}=[0,\ 0,\ 0,\ 0]$, $m=l=2$, $n=4$, and has two transmission zeros at $s=-1$.

(1) Choose $\boldsymbol{f}_c^{(1)}=[1\ 0]^{\mathrm{T}}$, then

$$\boldsymbol{g}^{(1)}(s)=\frac{1}{\Delta_1(s)}\boldsymbol{N}^{(1)}(s)=\frac{1}{s^2}\begin{bmatrix} (s+1) \\ 0 \end{bmatrix} \tag{5.78}$$

So, the system seen through input 1 has two poles at the origin and one zero at -1. Now, since $n_1=2$ and $l_1=1$, we get $q_1=1$. Thus, we determine $\boldsymbol{f}_o^{(1)}$ to move one pole to a new location at $s=-2$, say. This is achieved by $\boldsymbol{f}_o^{(1)}=[4\ 0]$; i. e.

$$\boldsymbol{F}_1=\begin{bmatrix} 4 & 0 \\ 0 & 0 \end{bmatrix} \tag{5.79}$$

which results in the closed-loop system pole set $\{\lambda_i\}=[0,\ 0,\ -2,-2]$. So, we have not just moved one pole to $s=-2$ but have in fact moved two there. This situation is fully predictable from the resulting closed-loop system root-locus plot.

(2) Now, consider $\{\lambda_i\}=[\{\gamma_i\}$ of step 1]. Since $m+l-1=3<n$, a dynamic compensator of degree $r=1$, as predicted by equation (5.48), is required. Let

$$\boldsymbol{f}^{(2)}(s)=\frac{1}{s+\gamma_1}[\theta_{10}s+\theta_{11}\ \ \theta_{20}s+\theta_{21}] \tag{5.80}$$

and determine $\boldsymbol{f}_c^{(2)}=[f_1\ \ f_2]^{\mathrm{T}}$ such that one of the poles moved to $s=-2$ in step 1 becomes uncontrollable.

After step 1, the resulting closed-loop system is

$$\boldsymbol{H}^{(1)}(s)=\frac{1}{s^2(s+2)^2}\begin{bmatrix} s^2(s+1) & (s+1) \\ 0 & (s+1)(s+2)^2 \end{bmatrix} \tag{5.81}$$

and

$$\boldsymbol{\Gamma}^{(1)}(-2)\boldsymbol{f}_c^{(2)}=0 \tag{5.82}$$

yields $\boldsymbol{f}_c^{(2)}=[1 \quad -4]^{\mathrm{T}}$, and so

$$\boldsymbol{N}^{(2)}(s)=(s+2)(s+1)\begin{bmatrix}(s-2)\\(s+2)\end{bmatrix} \tag{5.83}$$

To place the remaining poles at say $s=-1, -3, -4, -5$, the required vector $\boldsymbol{f}_c^{(2)}(s)$ is

$$\boldsymbol{f}_o^{(2)}(s)=\frac{1}{s+1}[\,(20s+37)/2 \quad (-97/8)\,] \tag{5.84}$$

i. e.

$$\boldsymbol{F}_2(s)=\frac{1}{s+1}\begin{bmatrix}(20s+37)/2 & (-97/8)\\ -2(20s+37) & (97/2)\end{bmatrix} \tag{5.85}$$

A root-locus plot of the resulting closed-loop system pole behaviour during this step of the compensator design shows that the effect of feedback on the origin poles is stabilizing, as was also the case with loop 1 determined in the first step.

The overall full-rank feedback compensator $\boldsymbol{F}(s)=\boldsymbol{F}_1+\boldsymbol{F}_2(s)$ which results in the desired closed-loop system poles is

$$\boldsymbol{F}(s)=\frac{1}{s+1}\begin{bmatrix}(28s+45)/2 & (-97/2)\\ -2(20s+37) & (97/2)\end{bmatrix} \tag{5.86}$$

5.4 Concluding Remarks

The full rank output-feedback algorithm, described in the previous section, provides a systematic and unified approach to the problem of pole assignment using state or output feedback. Both dyadic and full-rank compensators can be readily designed. The computational procedures required are straightforward, and advantage can be taken of 'singular-value decomposition' techniques to solve the resulting sets of equations.

It is also interesting to note that the same full-rank output-feedback algorithm can be directly used to design proportional-plus-integral action controllers which allow arbitrary pole assignment in the resulting closed-loop system. Here, the original system [$\boldsymbol{A}$, $\boldsymbol{B}$, $\boldsymbol{C}$]-matrices are augmented to introduce the desired integral action into the open-loop system description, and the full-rank pole assignment algorithm (of section 5.3) is then applied to the resulting noncyclic open-loop system.

Finally, it is interesting to note that although a great deal of effort has been invested in the pole assignment problem little attention has been given to the numerical properties of these algorithms. However, recently an interest has been shown in this area by numerical analysts and some new results are beginning to emerge.

New words and phrases:

1. pole assignment 极点配置
2. state feedback 状态反馈
3. output feedback 输出反馈
4. full rank 满秩的
5. minimum degree 最小阶
6. unification *n.* 统一,一致
7. categorise *v.* 把分类
8. broadly speaking 一般说来,概括地说
9. dyadic *a.* 并矢的
10. dyadic algorithm 并矢算法
11. disturbance rejection property 抗干扰性能
12. counterpart *n.* 对应物
13. canonical *a.* 规范的,标准的
14. the dyadic design mechanism 并矢设计机理
15. spectral *a.* 频谱的;*n.* 频谱分析法
16. mapping *n.* 映射
17. eigenvalue *n.* 特征值
18. under the heading of 包括在题目下
19. reciprocal eigenvector 逆特征向量
20. outer product 外积
21. scalar *n.* 标量
22. weighting factor 加权因子
23. inner product 内积
24. conjugate *a.* 共轭
25. multiplicity *n.* 重复度
26. cater for 迎合;为提供必要条件
27. spectral decomposition (频)谱分解
28. polynomial *n.* 多项式
29. controllability matrix 能控性矩阵

30. complete controllability 完全能控性
31. power *n.* 幂
32. difference vector 偏差向量
33. controllable canonical form 能控标准型
34. transformation matrix 转换矩阵
35. companion form 友矩阵形式
36. controllability index 能控性指数
37. off-diagonal *a.* 非对角线上的
38. triangular *a.* 三角形的
39. reposition *v.* 改变…的位置
40. pre-assigned *a.* 预先设定的
41. triple *n.* 三元组,三个一组
42. observability *n.* 能观性
43. strictly proper 严格正则的
44. g_1-inverse *n.* 广义逆
45. general solution 通解
46. right-inverse *n.* 右逆
47. duality *n.* 对偶(性),二重[元]性
48. pseudo-input vector 伪输入向量
49. linearly independent 线性无关的
50. transmission zero 传输零点
51. noncyclic *a.* 非周期的

Notes:

1. An algorithm for the design of full rank minimum degree output-feedback compensators is presented and results in a unification of previously obtained results.

译:提出一种用于设计满秩最小阶输出反馈补偿器的算法,导出了与前面获得的结果一致的结论。

2. It is simply concerned with moving the poles (or eigenvalues) of a given time-invariant linear system to a specified set of locations in the *s*-plane (subject to complex pairing) by means of state or output feedback.

译:它只与下面的问题有关,即通过状态或输出反馈将一给定的时变线性系统的极点(或特征值)移动到 *s*-平面中指定的一组位置上(这些位置要服从复数对条件)。

3. Both the state-feedback methods and the output-feedback methods result in compensator matrices which are broadly speaking either dyadic (i. e. have rank equal to one) or have full rank.

译:通过状态反馈方法和输出反馈方法都会得到补偿器矩阵,一般说来,这些矩阵或者是并矢式(即秩等于1)或者是满秩的。

4. We note, that at each stage, those poles which have not been rendered uncontrollable with respect to that stage of the design procedure, and which are not being moved to desired locations will move in an arbitrary manner.

译:我们注意到,在每一个阶段中,那些根据设计步骤还没有被变得不可控的极点和那些不是正被移到期望位置的极点将以一种随意的方式移动。

5. Complete pole assignment is only possible using output-feedback when $\boldsymbol{G}(s)$ has arisen from a least-order system;

译:当$\boldsymbol{G}(s)$得于一个最小阶系统时,只有使用输出反馈才有可能实现完全极点配置;

6. Nevertheless, this result may prove useful in situations where only a few of the open-loop system poles are to be moved to more desirable locations.

译:尽管如此,在只有几个开环系统极点要被移到更适当位置的情况下,这个结论就可以被证明是有用的了。

7. This latter approach then allows any of the well known state-feedback algorithms to be applied using $\hat{\boldsymbol{x}}$.

译:这后一种方法于是使得任意一种众所周知的需使用$\hat{\boldsymbol{x}}$的状态反馈算法能被应用。

8. The final result to be considered in this section is due to Munro and Novin Hirbod which states that if $m+l-1 \geqslant n$ a full-rank constant compensator $\boldsymbol{F}$ can be determined, from a minimal sequence of dyads, to assign the closed-loop system poles arbitrarily close to a predefined set $\{\gamma_i\}$.

译:在本节中将要考虑的最后一个结论是由 Munro 和 Novin Hirbod 提出的,该结论表述如下:如果$m+l-1 \geqslant n$,那么通过一个最小并矢序列可以确定一个满秩的常值补偿器,来把闭环系统极点配置得任意接近一个预先设定的集合$\{\gamma_i\}$。

9. In the following, we shall consider the design of minimum degree dyadic dynamic feedback compensators, and finally the design of minimum degree full-rank dynamic feedback compensators.

译:下面,我们将考虑最小阶并矢动态反馈补偿器的设计,并且在最后将考虑最小阶满秩动态反馈补偿器的设计。

10. Equating coefficients of like powers of s on both sides of equation (5.60) yields the vector-matrix equations (5.61), where $\boldsymbol{X}$ is an $(n+r)\times((r+1)(l+1)-1)$ matrix constructed from the coefficients a_i of $\Delta_o(s)$ and the β_{ij} of the $N_i(s)$, the vector $\boldsymbol{p}_r$ contains the unknown parameters γ_j and θ_{ij} defining $\boldsymbol{F}(s)$, and the difference vector $\boldsymbol{\delta}_r$ contains the coefficients δ_j of $\delta_r(s)$ as defined by equation (5.59).

译:令方程(5.60)两边 s 的相同次幂的系数相等可以得到向量矩阵方程(5.61),其中,$\boldsymbol{X}$ 是一个由 $\Delta_o(s)$ 的系数 a_i 和 $N_i(s)$ 的系数 β_{ij} 构成的 $(n+r)\times((r+1)(l+1)-1)$ 维的矩阵,$\boldsymbol{p}_r$ 包含用来定义 $\boldsymbol{F}(s)$ 的未知参数 γ_j 和 θ_{ij},偏差向量 $\boldsymbol{\delta}_r$ 如方程(5.59)定义的那样包含 $\delta_r(s)$ 的系数 $\boldsymbol{\delta}_j$。

11. This result can now be simply explained, since for r defined by (5.66) we obtain under these special conditions (5.67).

译:因为对于由式(5.66)所定义的 r,在这些特殊的条件下,我们可得到式(5.67),所以现在可以简单地解释这个结论。

12. This is due to the rank of $\boldsymbol{X}_r$, for this particular value of r, being such that a right-inverse of $\boldsymbol{X}_r$ exists, defined by (5.68).

译:这是由于对于 r 的这个特殊的值,$\boldsymbol{X}_r$ 的秩为使得由(5.68)所定义的 $\boldsymbol{X}_r$ 的右逆存在的值。

13. However, equation (5.69) does not allow for known exceptions, where arbitrary pole assignment can be achieved with a compensator $\boldsymbol{F}(s)$ of order $r<r_m$.

译:然而,方程(5.69)并没有考虑一些已知的例外情况,在这些情况下,任意极点配置可以用阶 $r<r_m$ 的补偿器来实现。

PART 3 CHAPTER ONE

1 Multivariable Frequency Domain Design Method for Disturbance Minimization

Abstract

A new approach is presented for the design of constant feedforward controllers which minimize the effect of an external disturbance on the output variables at specified frequencies[注1]. The multi-variable design problem is formulated in the frequency domain and treated as a classical minimization problem. It is shown here that a unique constant feedforward controller to minimize the effect of disturbances almost always exists[注2]. A numerical example is included to illustrate the application of the method.

1.1 Introduction

In state space theory, geometric concepts have served as the main tools for the investigation of the effect of external disturbances on the system state-variables or outputs of interest. Several authors have proposed state-space synthesis procedures for asymptotic disturbance localization, i. e. the condition where the system outputs approach zero as $t \to \infty$ for a given class of disturbances. More recently Shah *et al.* (1980) have reported a scheme for the design of state feedback controllers to minimize the effect of arbitrary disturbances on selected outputs. Muller and Luckel (1975) and Levin and Kriendler (1976) have also reported methods for the design of state feedback controllers to minimize the effect of a specified class of disturbances. However, no parallel design schemes for disturbance minimization have been developed using frequency domain concepts[注3].

In this paper a method is presented for the design of constant multivariable feedforward controllers which minimize the effect of specific external disturbances on the output variables. The design problem formulated as a classical minimization problem in the frequency domain and bears some similarity to the pseudo-diagonalization procedure first suggested by Rosenbrock (1970)[注4]. The proposed design procedure for feedforward controllers complements procedures for the design of feedback controllers based on frequency domain techniques such as the Nyquist array and the characteristic loci methods[注5].

1.2 Statement of the Problem

Consider the input-output description of the multivariable system shown in Fig. 1.1 The relationship between the outputs, $\boldsymbol{y}(s)$, the reference inputs, $\boldsymbol{r}(s)$, and the disturbances, $\boldsymbol{\xi}(s)$, is given by

$$\boldsymbol{y}(s)=(\boldsymbol{I}+\boldsymbol{G}(s)\boldsymbol{K}(s))^{-1}[\boldsymbol{G}(s)\boldsymbol{K}(s)\boldsymbol{r}(s)+ (\boldsymbol{G}(s)\boldsymbol{K}_{\mathrm{FF}}+\boldsymbol{G}_{\mathrm{L}}(s)\boldsymbol{\xi}(s)] \quad (1.1)$$

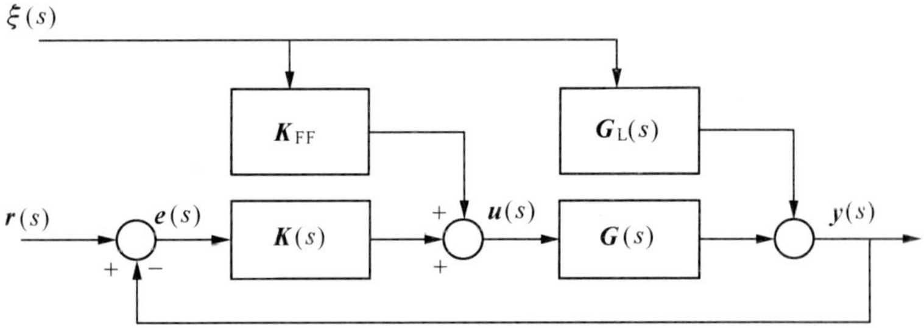

Fig. 1.1 Multivarible feedforward, feedback system configuration

From (1.1) it follows that the effect of disturbances, $\boldsymbol{\xi}(s)$, on output $\boldsymbol{y}(s)$ is minimized when the controllers $\boldsymbol{K}(s)$ and $\boldsymbol{K}_{\mathrm{FF}}$ are designed to[注6]

$$\text{Minimize}\ \{[\boldsymbol{I}+\boldsymbol{G}(s)\boldsymbol{K}(s)]^{-1}[\boldsymbol{G}(s)\boldsymbol{K}_{\mathrm{FF}}+\boldsymbol{G}_{\mathrm{L}}(s)]\} \quad (1.2)$$

In most applications the feedback controller, $\boldsymbol{K}(s)$, must be selected simultaneously to satisfy other design objectives such as stability, good servo control, etc., as well as the regulatory objective defined by (1.2). There are three basic approaches to the design problem:

(1) Design $\boldsymbol{K}(s)$ and $\boldsymbol{K}_{FF}$ simultaneously such that (1.2) and the other design criteria are optimized. The dimensionality of the problem and the difficulty in formulating an appropriate overall objective function usually make this approach impractical, so one of the following suboptimal approaches has to be used[注7].

(2) Design $\boldsymbol{K}_{FF}$ to minimize $[\boldsymbol{G}(s)\boldsymbol{K}_{FF}+\boldsymbol{G}_L(s)]$ and then design $\boldsymbol{K}(s)$ to minimize(1.2) and satisfy the other criteria such as stability.

(3) Design the feedforward controller $\boldsymbol{K}_{FF}$ to minimize $[\boldsymbol{G}(s)\boldsymbol{K}_{FF}+\boldsymbol{G}_L(s)]$ and then, in a completely separate step, design the feedback controller using any appropriate feedback design method. (It should be noted that most common methods for the design of feedback controllers do not consider the disturbances directly, nor use the information contained in $\boldsymbol{G}_L(s)$.)

The latter approach is followed in this paper. To simplify the calculations, the minimization of $[\boldsymbol{G}(s)\boldsymbol{K}_{FF}+\boldsymbol{G}_L(s)]$ is done at specific selected frequencies rather than on a global basis and for practical reasons the minimization function is formulated so that a feedforward matrix with real, constant elements is obtained[注8].

1.3 Design Scheme for Disturbance Minimization

If the (i,j)th element in the Nyquist array of $\boldsymbol{G}_L(j\omega)$ has a large magnitude at frequency ω then the disturbance ξ_j will cause a significant upset in $y_i(\omega)$. Therefore the design objective in the frequency domain is to select elements of $\boldsymbol{K}_{FF}$ such that the (i,j)th element of $|\boldsymbol{G}_L(j\omega)+\boldsymbol{G}(j\omega)\boldsymbol{K}_{FF}|^2$ is minimized where $|\cdot|^2$ denotes a matrix in which the (i,j)th element is the square of the modulus of the (i,j)th element of $(\boldsymbol{G}_L(j\omega)+\boldsymbol{G}(j\omega)\boldsymbol{K}_{FF})$[注9]. More generally, the problem can be formulated as follows

$$\text{Minimize } \sum_{i=1}^{n} \gamma_i \left| \boldsymbol{M}(\boldsymbol{G}_L(\mathrm{j}\omega_i) + \boldsymbol{G}(\mathrm{j}\omega_i)\boldsymbol{K}_{FF} \right|^2 \qquad (1.3)$$

where $\boldsymbol{M}$ and γ_i are the output weighting matrix and the frequency weights, respectively, for frequency values $\{\omega_i, i=1,\cdots,n\}$.

Case 1.3.1: Minimization at zero frequency $(\omega_1 = 0)$

For the case where it is desired to carry out the minimization at zero frequency, (1.3) has the solution given by the matrix pseudo-inverse

$$\boldsymbol{K}_{\mathrm{FF}} = -\boldsymbol{G}^{+}(\boldsymbol{\omega}_1)\boldsymbol{G}_{\mathrm{L}}(\omega_1) \qquad (1.4)$$

where $\boldsymbol{\omega}_1 = 0$ and $\boldsymbol{G}^{+}(\omega_1) = (\boldsymbol{G}^{\mathrm{T}}(\omega_1)\boldsymbol{G}(\omega_1))^{-1}\boldsymbol{G}^{\mathrm{T}}(\omega_1)$.

Note that for $\boldsymbol{\omega}_1 = 0$, $\boldsymbol{K}_{\mathrm{FF}}$ is a matrix of real numbers. However, in general, a real and optimal $\boldsymbol{K}_{\mathrm{FF}}$ cannot be evaluated using the matrix pseudoinverse approach for frequencies other than zero, i. e. $\boldsymbol{K}_{\mathrm{FF}}$ as computed by (1.4) for $\boldsymbol{\omega}_1 \neq 0$ will be complex. Therefore the following approach is suggested.

Case 1.3.2: Minimization at some frequencies $\{\omega_i \geqslant 0, i=1,2,\cdots, n\}$

For the sake of simplicity, the following development will only consider the effect of a single disturbance on all outputs. This entails no loss of generality, since each column of $\boldsymbol{K}_{\mathrm{FF}}$ corresponding to a particular disturbance can be calculated independently using the procedure outlined below[注10].

If the effect of the jth disturbance, ξ_j, on $y_1, y_2, \cdots, y_m$ is to be minimized at frequency $\boldsymbol{\omega}$, then one approach is to minimize the sum of the square of the modulus of each element of the jth column of the matrix $(\boldsymbol{G}_{\mathrm{L}}+\boldsymbol{G}\boldsymbol{K}_{\mathrm{FF}})$

$$[(g_{\mathrm{L}}(\mathrm{j}\omega)_{1j}+\boldsymbol{g}(\mathrm{j}\omega)_1^{\mathrm{T}}\boldsymbol{k}_j, (g_{\mathrm{L}}(\mathrm{j}\omega)_{2j}+\boldsymbol{g}(\mathrm{j}\omega)_2^{\mathrm{T}}\boldsymbol{k}_j), \cdots, (g_{\mathrm{L}}(\mathrm{j}\omega)_{mj}+\boldsymbol{g}(\mathrm{j}\omega)_m^{\mathrm{T}}\boldsymbol{k}_j)]^{\mathrm{T}} \qquad (1.5)$$

In the column vector of the expression (1.5), $g_{\mathrm{L}}(\mathrm{j}\omega)_{ij}, i=1,2,\cdots,m$ are elements of the jth column of $\boldsymbol{G}_{\mathrm{L}}(\mathrm{j}\omega)$, $\boldsymbol{g}(\mathrm{j}\omega)_i^{\mathrm{T}}$ is the ith row of $\boldsymbol{G}(\mathrm{j}\omega)$ and $\boldsymbol{k}_j$ is the jth column of $\boldsymbol{K}_{\mathrm{FF}}$. Let $\boldsymbol{J}(\boldsymbol{k}_j)$ be the objective function to be minimized, where

$$J(k_j)=\sum_{i=1}^{n}\gamma_i\sum_{k=1}^{m}m_k\left|g_L(j\omega_i)_{kj}+\sum_{l=1}^{r}g(j\omega_i)_{kl}k_{lj}\right|^2 \quad (1.6)$$

Let

$$g_L(j\omega_i)_{kj}=\alpha_L(\omega_i)_{kj}+j\beta_L(\omega_i)_{kj}$$

and

$$g(j\omega_i)_{kj}-\alpha(\omega_l)_{kj}+j\beta(\omega_i)_{kj} \quad (1.7)$$

Then

$$J(k_i)=\sum_{i=1}^{n}\gamma_i\sum_{k=1}^{m}m_k\{(\alpha_L(\omega_i)_{kj}+\sum_{l=1}^{r}k_{lj}\alpha(\omega_i)_{kl})^2+ \quad (1.8)$$
$$(\beta_L(\omega_i)_{kj}+\sum_{l=1}^{r}k_{lj}\ \beta(\omega_i)_{kl})^2\}$$

This is a classical, unconstrained minimization problem where the minimum for $J(k_j)$ with respect to k_{pj} is given by

$$\frac{\partial J(k_j)}{\partial k_{pj}}=0 \qquad \text{for} \qquad \frac{\partial^2 J}{\partial k_{pj}^2}>0$$

The derivative of $J(k_j)$ with respect to k_{pj} is

$$\frac{\partial J(k_j)}{\partial k_{pj}}=\sum_{i=1}^{n}\gamma_i\sum_{k=1}^{m}2m_k\{\alpha(\omega_i)_{kp}[\alpha_L(\omega_i)_{kj}+\sum_{l=1}^{r}k_{lj}\alpha(\omega_i)_{kl}]+$$
$$\beta(\omega_i)_{kp}[\beta_L(\omega_i)_{kj}+\sum_{l=1}^{r}k_{lj}\beta(\omega_i)_{kl}]\} \quad (1.9)$$

Rearrangement of (1.9) yields a set of r equations which define the r elements of the jth column of K_{FF}. Solving for $\{k_{pj},p=1,2,\cdots,r\}$ thus gives a set of r non-homogeneous equations. These are shown in matrix form in (1.10). Solutions of (1.10) yield the desired feedforward matrix, K_{FF}.

$$
\begin{bmatrix}
\sum_{i=1}^{n}\gamma_i\sum_{k=1}^{m} m_k(\alpha(\omega_i)_{k1}^2+\beta(\omega_i)_{k1}^2), & \sum_{i=1}^{n}\gamma_i\sum_{k=1}^{m} m_k(\alpha(\omega_i)_{k1}\alpha(\omega_i)_{k2}+\beta(\omega_i)_{k1}\beta(\omega_i)_{k2})\cdots \\
\sum_{i=1}^{n}\gamma_i\sum_{k=1}^{m} m_k\ \alpha(\omega_i)_{k1}\alpha(\omega_i)_{k2}+\beta(\omega_i)_{k1}\beta(\omega_i)_{k2}), & \sum_{i=1}^{n}\gamma_i\sum_{k=1}^{m} m_k(\alpha(\omega_i)_{k2}^2+\beta(\omega_i)_{k2}^2)\ \cdots \\
\vdots & \\
(\sum_{i=1}^{n}\gamma_i\sum_{k=1}^{m} m_k(\alpha(\omega_i)_{k1}\alpha(\omega_i)_{kr}+\beta(\omega_i)_{k1}\beta(\omega_i)_{kr}\cdots & (\sum_{i=1}^{n}\gamma_i\sum_{k=1}^{m} m_k(\alpha(\omega_i)_{kr}^2+\beta(\omega_i)_{kr}^2)
\end{bmatrix}
$$

$$
*\begin{bmatrix} k_{1j} \\ k_{2j} \\ k_{rj} \end{bmatrix} = -\ [(\sum_{i=1}^{n}\gamma_i\sum_{k=1}^{m} m_k(\alpha(\omega_i)_{kl}\alpha_{\mathrm{L}}(\omega_i)_{kj}+\beta(\omega_i)_{kl}\beta_{\mathrm{L}}(\omega_i)_{kj}^2)\ ,
$$

$$
(\sum_{i=1}^{n}\gamma_i\sum_{k=1}^{m} m_k(\alpha(\omega_i)_{k2}\alpha_{\mathrm{L}}(\omega_i)_{kj}+\beta(\omega_i)_{k2}\beta_{\mathrm{L}}(\omega_i)_{kj}^2)),\cdots]^{\mathrm{T}} \tag{1.10}
$$

It is interesting to note that the $r\times r$ coefficient matrix in (1.10) is symmetric, and furthermore that it can be expressed as the sum of two symmetric matrices. If $\boldsymbol{A}$ denotes the coefficient matrix, it can be shown that

$$
\boldsymbol{A} = \sum_{i=1}^{n}\gamma_i[\boldsymbol{G}_{\mathrm{R}}(\omega_i)^{\mathrm{T}}\boldsymbol{M}\boldsymbol{G}_{\mathrm{R}}(\omega_i) + \boldsymbol{G}_{\mathrm{I}}(\omega_i)^{\mathrm{T}}\boldsymbol{M}\boldsymbol{G}_{\mathrm{I}}(\omega_i)] \tag{1.11}
$$

In (1.11), $\boldsymbol{M}=\mathrm{diag}(m_1,m_2,\cdots,m_m)$ and $\boldsymbol{G}_{\mathrm{R}}(\omega_i)$ and $\boldsymbol{G}_{\mathrm{I}}(\omega_i)$ are the real and imaginary parts of the complex matrix $\boldsymbol{G}(\mathrm{j}\omega_i)$. The existence of a unique $\boldsymbol{k}_j$ follows if $\boldsymbol{A}^{-1}$ exists[注11]. In other words it must be shown that $\boldsymbol{A}$ has full rank, or that it is either positive or negative definite. The existence conditions for a unique $\boldsymbol{k}_j$ follow from the following theorem.

Theorem 1.3.1

$\boldsymbol{A}^{-1}$ always exists if (i) $\boldsymbol{M}$ is symmetric and positive definite, and (ii) $\boldsymbol{G}(\omega_i)^{-1}$ exists $\forall i\in(1,2,\cdots,n)$.

To prove the theorem we require the following lemma.

Lemma 1.3.1

Given a complex matrix, $\boldsymbol{C}=\boldsymbol{R}+\mathrm{j}\boldsymbol{X}$, where $\boldsymbol{R}$ is the matrix of the real part of $\boldsymbol{C}$ and $\boldsymbol{X}$ is the matrix of the imaginary part of $\boldsymbol{C}$, then $\boldsymbol{C}^{-1}$ only exists if $[\boldsymbol{R}^{\mathrm{T}} \quad \boldsymbol{X}^{\mathrm{T}}]^{\mathrm{T}}$ is of full rank.

Proof of Lemma 1.3.1

Let $\boldsymbol{C}^{-1}=\hat{\boldsymbol{R}}+\mathrm{j}\hat{\boldsymbol{X}}$; note $\hat{\boldsymbol{R}}\neq\boldsymbol{R}^{-1}$ and $\hat{\boldsymbol{X}}\neq\boldsymbol{X}^{-1}$ unless $\boldsymbol{R}=0$ or $\boldsymbol{X}=0$. Now $(\boldsymbol{R}\hat{\boldsymbol{R}}+\boldsymbol{X}\hat{\boldsymbol{X}})+\mathrm{j}(\boldsymbol{R}\hat{\boldsymbol{X}}+\boldsymbol{X}\hat{\boldsymbol{R}})=\boldsymbol{I}$, which in matrix form is

$$\begin{bmatrix}\boldsymbol{R} & -\boldsymbol{X}\\ \boldsymbol{X} & \boldsymbol{R}\end{bmatrix}\begin{bmatrix}\hat{\boldsymbol{R}}\\ \hat{\boldsymbol{X}}\end{bmatrix}=\begin{bmatrix}\boldsymbol{I}\\ \boldsymbol{0}\end{bmatrix}$$

Thus $\boldsymbol{C}^{-1}$ or $(\hat{\boldsymbol{R}}+\mathrm{j}\hat{\boldsymbol{X}})$ exists only if $[\boldsymbol{R}^{\mathrm{T}} \quad \boldsymbol{X}^{\mathrm{T}}]^{\mathrm{T}}$ is of full rank.

Note that the real and imaginary parts of $\boldsymbol{C}$ by themselves do not need to be nonsingular.

Proof of Theorem 1.3.1

Define $\boldsymbol{A}_i=\gamma_i[\boldsymbol{G}_{\mathrm{R}}(\omega_i)^{\mathrm{T}}\boldsymbol{M}\boldsymbol{G}_{\mathrm{R}}(\omega_i)+\boldsymbol{G}_{\mathrm{I}}(\omega_i)^{\mathrm{T}}\boldsymbol{M}\boldsymbol{G}_{\mathrm{I}}(\omega_i)]$, which in matrix form can be written as

$$\boldsymbol{A}_i=\gamma_i\,[\boldsymbol{G}_{\mathrm{R}}^{\mathrm{T}}(\omega_i)\boldsymbol{G}_{\mathrm{I}}^{\mathrm{T}}(\omega_i)]\boldsymbol{M}\begin{bmatrix}\boldsymbol{G}_{\mathrm{R}}(\omega_i)\\ \boldsymbol{G}_{\mathrm{I}}(\omega_i)\end{bmatrix}$$

Now M is symmetric and positive definite by choice. If $\boldsymbol{G}(\omega_i)^{-1}$ exists, then from Lemma 1.3.1 $[\boldsymbol{G}_{\mathrm{R}}^{\mathrm{T}}(\omega_i) \quad \boldsymbol{G}_{\mathrm{I}}^{\mathrm{T}}(\omega_i)]^{\mathrm{T}}$ is of full rank. Since $\gamma_i>0$ by choice it follows that $\boldsymbol{A}_i$ is also a positive definite matrix. If $\boldsymbol{A}_i$ is positive definite $\forall i\in(1,2,\cdots,n)$ then it is clear that the sum $\{\boldsymbol{A}_1+\boldsymbol{A}_2+\cdots+\boldsymbol{A}_n\}=\boldsymbol{A}$ is also positive definite, and thus $\boldsymbol{A}^{-1}$ exists. This completes the proof of the theorem.

In general $\boldsymbol{G}(\omega_i)^{-1}$ almost always exists and therefore it is correct to conclude that a unique $\boldsymbol{k}_j$ almost always exists.

A comment concerning the design of a feedforward controller with dynamic elements is in order here. Equation (1.7) can be expanded to facilitate computation of optimal complex elements of $\boldsymbol{K}_{\mathrm{FF}}(\mathrm{j}\omega_i)$[注12]. However for practical applications it would probably be better to compute a complex $\boldsymbol{K}_{\mathrm{FF}}(\omega_i)$ using the matrix pseudo-inverse at each frequency point of interest $\{\omega_i, i=1,2,\cdots,n\}$[注13]. The final computation of each element, $K_{pj}(s)$, of $\boldsymbol{K}_{\mathrm{FF}}(s)$ could then be done by curve-fitting lead and lag elements so that they approximate $k_{pj}(j\omega_i)$ at each frequency.

1.4 Illustrative Example

As an example, consider the two-input, two-output open-loop transfer function model of a binary distillation column (Berry 1973) with the following $\boldsymbol{G}(s)$ and $\boldsymbol{G}_L(s)$

$$\boldsymbol{G}(s)=\begin{bmatrix}\dfrac{12.8\exp(-1.0s)}{(16.7s+1)} & \dfrac{-18.9\exp(-3.0s)}{(2.10s+1)}\\ \dfrac{6.6\exp(-7.0s)}{(10.9s+1)} & \dfrac{-19.4\exp(-3.0s)}{(14.4s+1)}\end{bmatrix}\quad \boldsymbol{G}_L(s)=\begin{bmatrix}\dfrac{3.8\exp(-8.1s)}{(14.9s+1)}\\ \dfrac{4.9\exp(-3.4s)}{(13.2s+1)}\end{bmatrix}$$

The outputs, y_1, y_2 are top and bottom product compositions. The inputs, u_1, u_2 are reflux flow-rate and steam flow-rate to the reboiler. The disturbance, ξ_1, of interest is feed flow-rate to the column.

From an inspection of the Nyquist array of $\boldsymbol{G}_L(s)$ it was decided to compute $\boldsymbol{K}_{FF1}$ by minimizing expression (1.6) at $\omega_1=0$ and $\omega_2=0.06$. The output frequency weighting factors were defined as follows

$$\boldsymbol{M}=\begin{bmatrix}1.0 & 0\\ 0 & 1.0\end{bmatrix}\qquad \text{or}\qquad m_1=m_2=1.0$$

$$\gamma_1(\omega_1=0)=1.0\qquad \text{and}\qquad \gamma_2(\omega_2=0.06)=2.0$$

The values of $\boldsymbol{G}_L(j\omega)$ at $\omega_1=0$ and $\omega_2=0.06$ are

$$\boldsymbol{G}_L(0)=\begin{bmatrix}3.8\\ 4.9\end{bmatrix},\boldsymbol{G}_L(j0.06)=\begin{bmatrix}0.985,-2.655\\ 2.464,-j2.946\end{bmatrix}\tag{1.12}$$

Using (1.9) $\boldsymbol{K}_{FF1}$ is calculated to be $\boldsymbol{K}_{FF1}=[0.118, 0.30]^T$.

The resulting compensated transfer functions $\{\boldsymbol{G}(j\omega_i)\boldsymbol{K}_{FF}+\boldsymbol{G}_L(j\omega_i), i=1,2\}$ are

$$\begin{bmatrix}-0.36\\ -0.141\end{bmatrix}\ \text{at}\ \omega_1=0,\text{and}\begin{bmatrix}0.019-j0.33\\ 0.053-j0.065\end{bmatrix}\ \text{at}\ \omega_2=0.06\tag{1.13}$$

Comparison of the transfer functions in (1.12), (1.13) and Fig. 1.2 shows that the effect of the disturbances at ω_1 and ω_2 has been reduced significantly. However, the effect of disturbances in the mid-frequency range appears to have increased. Note that as ω increases, the Nyquist array of $(G(s)K_{FF1}+G_L(s)$ will eventually 'spiral' into the origin (since $G(j\omega)\to 0$ and $G_L(j\omega\to 0$ as $\omega\to\infty$). To reduce the magnitude of the compensated transfer function in the mid-frequency range, another feedforward controller, K_{FF2}, was designed this time to minimize the expression (1.3) at the four frequency points 0, 0.06, 0.6 and 1.0. The corresponding γ_i were chosen at 1, 2, 100 and 200 and $m_1 = m_2 = 1.0$ as before. The resulting feedforward controller is $F_{FF2} = [0.033 \quad 0.162]^T$.

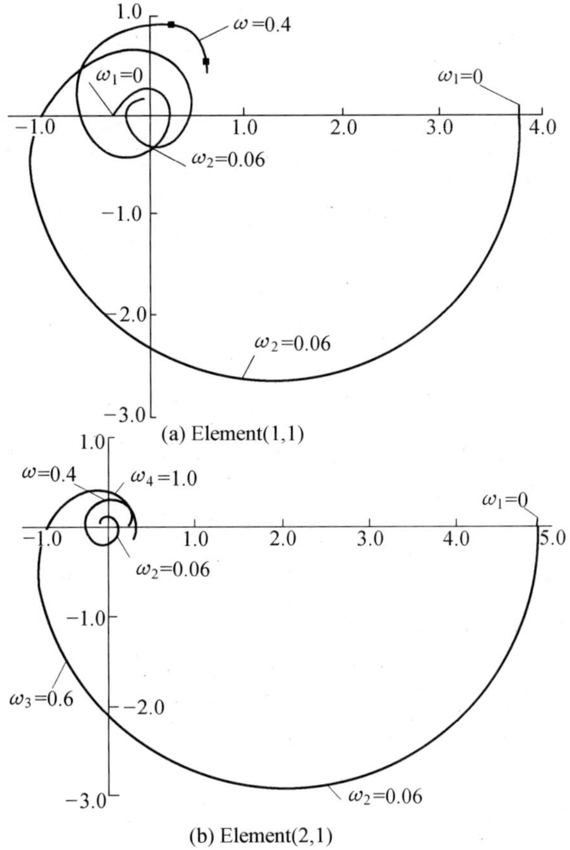

Fig. 1.2. The Nyquist array diagrams of $G_L(j\omega)$ [solid line] and $\{G(j\omega)K_{FF1}+G_L(j\omega_i)\}$ [dotted line] minimized at $\omega = 0, 0.06$

Fig. 1.3 shows the Nyquist array of $\boldsymbol{G}_{\mathrm{L}}(s)$ and $(\boldsymbol{G}(s)\boldsymbol{K}_{\mathrm{FF2}}(s))$. With this new controller, the outward spiraling effect in the mid-frequency range has now been confined. With increased weighting factors in $\boldsymbol{M}$, γ_3, γ_4 etc. the effect of high-frequency disturbances can be reduced even more. Note also that the magnitude of the closed-loop response to disturbances would be further reduced by multiplying by $(\boldsymbol{I}+\boldsymbol{G}(s)\boldsymbol{K}(s))^{-1}$ as shown in (1.1). Finally to remove zero frequency offset in the plant output in the presence of sustained disturbances, it is recommended that a little inuegral action be incorporated into the design of a pre-compensator, $\boldsymbol{K}(s)$, for the plant.

As is apparent from the above outline, the design procedure is intended to be iterative. At each step, new frequency points are addee or deleted; frequency and output weighting factors are modified until a satisfactory design is obtained. With a computer-aided frequency domain design system,! the effort required is not excessive.

1.5 Conclusions

A systematic and computationally simple scheme for tie multi-variable frequency domain design of a constant feedforward controller has been proposed[注14]. It is shown that a unique feedforward controller, $\boldsymbol{K}_{\mathrm{FF}}$, almost always exists.

The feedforward controller, $\boldsymbol{K}_{\mathrm{FF}}$,! designed here is independent of the feedback controller $\boldsymbol{K}(s)$ and the stability of the closed-loop system, and thus $\boldsymbol{K}_{\mathrm{FF}}$ can easily be field tuned. In contrast, the design of $\boldsymbol{K}_{\mathrm{FF}}$ for disturbance decoupling in the state space domain is not independent of the state feedback matrix, $\boldsymbol{K}_{\mathrm{FB}}$.

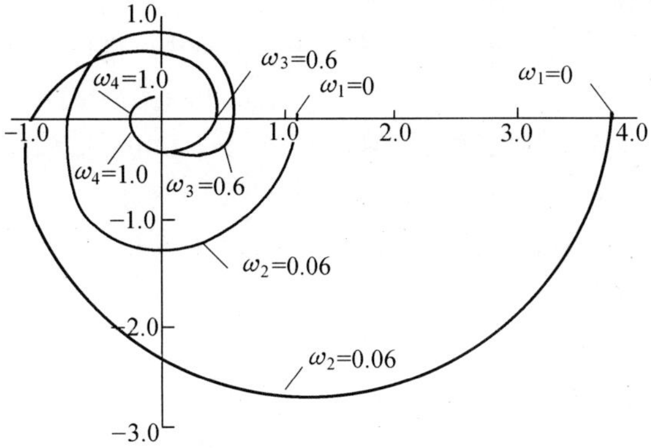

(a) Element (1,1)

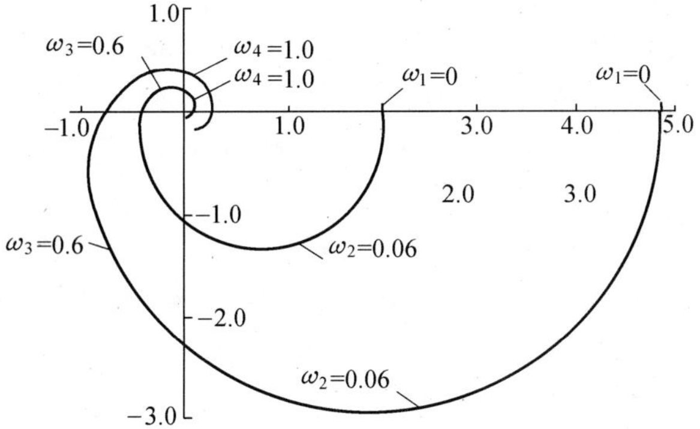

(b) Element (2,1)

Fig. 1.3 The Nyquist array diagrams of $\boldsymbol{G}_{\mathrm{L}}(\mathrm{j}\boldsymbol{\omega})$ [solid line] and $\{\boldsymbol{G}(\mathrm{j}\boldsymbol{\omega})\boldsymbol{K}_{\mathrm{FF2}}+\boldsymbol{G}_{\mathrm{L}}(\mathrm{j}\boldsymbol{\omega})\}$ [dotted line] minimized at $\boldsymbol{\omega}=0, 0.06, 0.6, 1.0$

New words and phrases:

1. formulate *vt*. (系统地)阐述,提出,表达
2. classical *a*. 典型的,经典的,标准的
3. geometric *a*. 几何(学、图形)的
4. asymptotic *a*. 渐近(线)的
5. localization *n*. 定位,探测,局部化,集中
6. parallel *a*. 同样的,类似的
7. bear *v*. 含有,负有

8. diagonalization *n.* 对角化
9. complement *n.*, *a.*, *vt.* 补充,补充的
10. follow *v.* 接受,采纳,随之而来
11. follow from 是从[是根据]… …得出的
12. dimensionality *n.* 维数
13. overall *a.* 综合的
14. suboptimal *a.* 次优的
15. upset *n.* 扰动
16. modulus *n.* 模
17. carry out 求得,完成
18. pseudo *a.* 假的,伪的
19. inverse *n.* 逆矩阵,倒数,逆元(素)
20. complex *n.* 复数
21. sake *n.* 原因,关系,目的
22. for (the) sake of 为… …起见,由于… …缘故
23. entail *vt.* 需要,要求;必然伴有,带来
24. outline *v.* 概述,提出… …的要点
25. derivative *n.* 微商,导数
26. derivative of M with respect to N M对N的微商[导数]
27. non-homogeneous *a.* 非齐次的,非均匀的
28. lemma *n.* 引理
29. (be) in order (是)完好[有条理]的,(是)适宜[必要、适用]的
30. expand *v.* 推广,展开
31. facilitate *vt.* 简化,便于
32. curve-fitting 曲线拟合(法)
33. lead *n.* 超前
34. lag *n.* 滞后
35. binary *a.* 双,二元,二分
36. distillation *n.* 蒸馏,馏出物,精华
37. column *n.* (蒸馏,萃取)塔,罐
38. binary distillation column 二分蒸馏塔
39. composition *n.* 成分,合成物
40. reflux *n.* 分馏,回流,逆流
41. reboiler *n.* 再蒸馏锅,再沸腾器
42. inspection *n.* 观察,研究
43. weighting factor 加权因子
44. dotted line 虚线
45. solid line 实线
46. significantly *adv.* 有效地,值得注意地
47. spiral *v.* 盘旋,使成螺旋线,旋进
48. incorporate into 把…包含进去
49. be intended to be 规定为,确定为
50. iterative *a.* 重复的,迭代的
51. excessive *a.* 过分的
52. computationally *adv.* 计算上地

Notes:

1. A new approach is presented for the design of constant feedforward controllers which minimize the effect of an external disturbance on the output variables at specified frequencies.

译:(本文)给出一种定常前馈控制器设计的新方法,该控制器可使外部干扰对输出变量的作用在指定频率上达到最小。

2. The multi-variable design problem is formulated in the frequency domain and treated as a classical minimization problem. It is shown here that a unique constant feedforward controller to minimize the effect of disturbances almost always exists.

译:在频域内阐述了多变量设计问题,并按古典的最小化问题进行了处理。在此可以看到,我们几乎总可以找到唯一的定常前馈控制器使得干扰作用最小化。

3. Several authors have proposed state-space synthesis procedures for asymptotic disturbance localization, i. e. the condition where the system outputs approach zero as $t \to \infty$ for a given class of disturbances. More recently Shah *et al.* (1980) have reported a scheme for the design of state feedback controllers to minimize the effect of arbitrary disturbances on selected outputs. Muller and Luckel (1975) and Levin and Kriendler (1976) have also reported methods for the design of state feedback controllers to minimize the effect of a specified class of disturbances. However, no parallel design schemes for disturbance minimization have been developed using frequency domain concepts.

译:针对渐近干扰局部化问题,即针对一类给定的干扰,使 $t \to \infty$ 时系统输出趋于零的条件,一些作者提出了状态空间综合方法。最近 Shah 等报道一种可使任意干扰信号对选定输出的作用最小化的状态反馈控制器的设计方法;Muller 等也报道一种使一特定类型干扰信号的作用达到最小的状态反馈控制器的设计方法。然而对使干扰最小化问题还没有用频域概念的类似的设计方法提出。

4. The design problem formulated as a classical minimization problem in the frequency domain bears some similarity to the pseudo-diagonalization procedure first suggested by Rosenbrock .

译:在频域内被描述成典型的最小化问题的设计问题与 Rosenbrock 首先提出的伪对角化方法有些类似。

5. The proposed design procedure for feedforward controllers complements procedures for the design of feedback controllers based on frequency domain techniques such as the Nyquist array and the characteristic loci methods.

译:(本文)提出的前馈控制器设计方法补充了基于频域方法(如乃奎斯特阵列、特征根轨迹法)的反馈控制器设计方法。

6. From (1.1) it follows that the effect of disturbances, $\xi(s)$, on output $y(s)$ is minimized when the controllers $\boldsymbol{K}(s)$ and $\boldsymbol{K}_{\mathrm{FF}}$ are designed to (1.2)

译:由式(1.1)可见当控制器 $\boldsymbol{K}(s)$、$\boldsymbol{K}_{\mathrm{FF}}$ 被设计成满足(1.2)时,干扰 $\xi(s)$ 对输出 $y(s)$ 的作用最小。

7. The dimensionality of the problem and the difficulty in formulating an appropriate overall objective function usually make this approach impractical, so one of the following suboptimal approachcs has to be used.

译:问题的维数和获得恰当的总目标函数的困难常常使得这种方法不实用,从而不得不使用下列任一种次最优方法。

8. To simplify the calculations, the minimization of $[\boldsymbol{G}(s)\boldsymbol{K}_{\mathrm{FF}}+\boldsymbol{G}_{\mathrm{L}}(s)]$ is done at specific selected frequencies rather than on a global basis and for practical reasons the minimization function is formulated so that a feedforward matrix with real, constant elements is obtained.

译:为简化计算,使 $[\boldsymbol{G}(s)\boldsymbol{K}_{\mathrm{FF}}+\boldsymbol{G}_{\mathrm{L}}(s)]$ 在指定频率(而不是所有频率)上最小化;出于实际考虑,以得到带有实定常元素的前馈矩

阵为目的来构造最小化函数。

9. Therefore the design objective in the frequency domain is to select elements of $\boldsymbol{K}_{\mathrm{FF}}$ such that the (i,j)th element of $|\boldsymbol{G}_{\mathrm{L}}(\mathrm{j}\omega)+\boldsymbol{G}(\mathrm{j}\omega)\boldsymbol{K}_{\mathrm{FF}}|^2$ is minimized where $|\cdot|^2$ denotes a matrix in which the (i,j)th element is the square of the modulus of the (i,j)th element of $(\boldsymbol{G}_{\mathrm{L}}(\mathrm{j}\omega)+\boldsymbol{G}(\mathrm{j}\omega)\boldsymbol{K}_{\mathrm{FF}})$.

译：因此频域内的设计目标是选取 $\boldsymbol{K}_{\mathrm{FF}}$ 的元素使得 $|\boldsymbol{G}_{\mathrm{L}}(\mathrm{j}\omega)+\boldsymbol{G}(\mathrm{j}\omega)\boldsymbol{K}_{\mathrm{FF}}|^2$ 的第(i,j)元素最小，其中 $|\cdot|^2$ 表示一矩阵，其第(i,j)元素是$(\boldsymbol{G}_{\mathrm{L}}(\mathrm{j}\omega)+\boldsymbol{G}(\mathrm{j}\omega)\boldsymbol{K}_{\mathrm{FF}})$的第$(i,j)$元素模的平方。

10. For the sake of simplicity, the following development will only consider the effect of a single disturbance on all outputs. This entails no loss of generality, since each column of $\boldsymbol{K}_{\mathrm{FF}}$ corresponding to a particular disturbance can be calculated independently using the procedure outlined below.

译：为简便起见，下面的推导只考虑单个干扰对所有输出的作用。这样做不失一般性，因为相应于某一种干扰 $\boldsymbol{K}_{\mathrm{FF}}$ 的每列都可以用下面简述的方法独立地计算。

11. The existence of a unique $\boldsymbol{k}_j$ follows if $\boldsymbol{A}^{-1}$ exists.

译：若 $\boldsymbol{A}^{-1}$ 存在，则 $\boldsymbol{k}_j$ 的惟一解存在。

12. A comment concerning the design of a feedforward controller with dynamic elements is in order here. Equation (1.7) can be expanded to facilitate computation of optimal complex elements of $\boldsymbol{K}_{\mathrm{FF}}(\mathrm{j}\omega_i)$.

译：在此有必要讨论一下带动态元素的前馈控制器的设计。扩展方程(1.7)以简化 $\boldsymbol{K}_{\mathrm{FF}}(\mathrm{j}\omega_i)$ 的最优复元素的计算。

13. However for practical applications it would probably be better to compute a complex $\boldsymbol{K}_{\mathrm{FF}}(\mathrm{j}\omega_i)$ using the matrix pseudo-inverse at each frequency point of interest $\{\omega_i, i=1,2,\cdots,n\}$

译：然而在实际应用中，在各个感兴趣的频率点，用伪逆矩阵来计算

复数 $\boldsymbol{K}_{\mathrm{FF}}(\mathrm{j}\omega_i)$ 可能要更好些。

14. A systematic and computationally simple scheme for the multi-variable frequency domain design of a constant feedforward controller has been proposed.

译:(本文)提出了一种在多变量频域上的系统的、计算简便的定常前馈控制器设计方法。

PART 3 **CHAPTER TWO**

2 Application of the Robust Servo-mechanism Controller to Systems with Periodic Tracking/Disturbance Signals

ABSTRACT

The following problem is considered: given a system which has tracking/disturbance signals arising from a class of periodic signals with period T, say, assume that such a periodic signal has p dominant harmonic components contained in $\{\omega_l, l=0,1,\cdots,v\}$. Then it is desired to find a finite-dimensional linear controller which gives exact robust asymptotic regulation for the case of sinusoidal signals with frequencies ω_l, $l=0,1,\cdots,v$, subject to certain controller gain magnitude constraints and/or gain margin tolerance constraints which may be imposed on the problem[注1]. This is called ' the approximate robust servomechanism problem for periodic signals of the class $\{\omega_l, l=0,1,\cdots,v\}$ '. It is to be noted that such a problem cannot in general be solved by using high gain control synthesis methods[注2]. Existence conditions and a controller design method are given to solve the problem. A number of examples is given to illustrate the type of results that may be achieved.

2.1 Introduction

The following type of problem is considered in this paper. Given a finite-dimensional linear time-invariant multivariable system, suppose that tracking/disturbance signals arise from a class of periodic signals with period T say, e. g. a triangular periodic wave. Then, unless the periodic signal $\omega(t)$ arises from the following finite-dimensional linear model: $\dot{\boldsymbol{\eta}}=\bar{\boldsymbol{A}}\boldsymbol{n}, \boldsymbol{\omega}=\bar{\boldsymbol{b}}\boldsymbol{c}$, in general, there exists no finite-dimensional linear time-invariant controller which can be applied to the system to produce exact robust asymptotic error regulation. However, it may be desired to obtain a finite-dimensional controller so that approximate robust asymptotic error regulation occurs[注3]. In this case, if one assumes that the periodic signal possesses a Fouirer series which has p dominant harmonic components contained in $\{\omega_l, l = 0, 1, \cdots, v\}$, 'approximate p mode error regulation' for the system is said to occur if there exists a finite-dimensional linear controller which produces exact robust asymptotic error regulation for sinusoidal tracking/disturbance signals of frequency $\omega_l, l=0, 1, \cdots, v$.

In solving this type of approximate problem, the following observations are to be noted.

(1) Any realistic controlled system always has restrictions imposed on the magnitude of controller gain elements which can be applied (e. g. due to possible non-linear effects, due to actuators, due to possible closed-loop instability which may arise from modeling errors, etc.).

(2) Generally, it will be the case, that at least some of the frequencies $\omega_l, l = 0, 1, \cdots, v$ which are to be regulated, are contained in the bandwidth of the system to be controlled.

(3) The system may or may not be minimum phase.

Thus, these observations give rise to the following problem: given $\{\omega_l, l=0, 1, \cdots, v\}$, find a controller, in particular, the 'simplest possible' controller, i. e. one which has minimum order, which will give exact robust error regulation for the system with disturbance/tracking signals of frequencies $\omega_l, l=0, 1, \cdots, v$, subject to specified engineering constraints imposed on the magnitude of controller gains and gain margin tolerance requirements, say. This is called the 'approximate RSP for periodic systems of the class $\{\omega_l, l=0, 1, \cdots, v\}$'[注4].

This problem can be directly solved by treating the problem as a robust servomechanism problem (RSP) using the parameter optimization method of Davison and Ferguson (1981). It is to be emphasized that in general it is impossible to satisfy the above requirements by demanding that ‘good’ regulation occurs for all $\omega \in [0, \omega_{max}]$, $\omega_{max} = \max\{\omega_1, l = 0, 1, \cdots, v\}$, since arbitrarily large controller gains are then required to satisfy this requirement.

It is the purpose of this paper to present some case studies of such a design method when applied to this type of problem. An alternative design method to this type of problem has been studied in Hara *et al.* (1985) for single-input single-output systems using an infinite-dimensional compensator, in this case no gain constraints are imposed and only sufficient conditions for a solution to exist are obtained.

2.2 Development

Consider the linear time-invariant system

$$\left.\begin{aligned} &\dot{\boldsymbol{x}} = \boldsymbol{A}\boldsymbol{x} + \boldsymbol{B}\boldsymbol{u} + \boldsymbol{E}\boldsymbol{\omega} \\ &\boldsymbol{y} = \boldsymbol{C}\boldsymbol{x} + \boldsymbol{D}\boldsymbol{u} + \boldsymbol{F}\boldsymbol{\omega}, \boldsymbol{e} = \boldsymbol{y} - \boldsymbol{y}_{ref} \\ &\boldsymbol{y}_m = \boldsymbol{C}_m\boldsymbol{X} + \boldsymbol{D}_m\boldsymbol{u} + \boldsymbol{F}_m\boldsymbol{\omega} \end{aligned}\right\} \tag{2.1}$$

where $\boldsymbol{x} \in \mathbf{R}^n$ is the state, $\boldsymbol{u} \in \mathbf{R}^m$ the inputs, $\boldsymbol{y} \in \mathbf{R}^r$ the outputs to be regulated, $\boldsymbol{y}_m \in \mathbf{R}^{rm}$ are the measurable outputs, $\omega \in \mathbf{R}^{\Omega}$ is a disturbance, and $\boldsymbol{y}_{ref} \in \mathbf{R}^r$ is the reference-input signal.

Assume that the elements of ω and $\boldsymbol{y}_{ref}$ are bounded periodic signals with period T, which satisfy the Dirichlet conditions, so that they possess a Fourier series. In particular, assume that the first p dominant harmonic components of the Fourier series for each element of $\boldsymbol{\omega}$and $\boldsymbol{y}_{ref}$ are contained in the following $v \geqslant p$ harmonic components

$$\omega_l = \frac{2l\pi}{T} \qquad l = 0, 1, \cdots, v \tag{2.2}$$

Then, if there exists a solution to the RSP for (2.1) for the case of disturbance/tracking signals poles $\pm j\omega_l, l = 0, 1, \cdots, v$, it is said that there exists an approximate p-mode solution to the RSP for (2.1), for the class of periodic signals with dominant harmonic content $(\omega_0, \omega_1, \cdots$

ω_v), or more briefly, that there exists an approximate solution to the RSP for periodic signals of the class $\{\omega_l, l=0,1,\cdots,v\}$.

The following result on the existence of a solution to the above problem is immediately obtained from Davison and Ferguson (1981).

Lemma 2.2.1

Given (2.1), there exists an approximate solution to the RSP for periodic signals of the class $\{\omega_l, l=0,1,\cdots,v\}$ if the following conditions are all satisfied:

(i) $(\boldsymbol{C}_m, \boldsymbol{A}, \boldsymbol{B})$ is stabilizable and detectable.

(ii) $(\boldsymbol{C}, \boldsymbol{A}, \boldsymbol{B}, \boldsymbol{D})$ has no transmission zeros located at $\pm \mathrm{j}\omega_l, l=0, 1,\cdots,v$.

(iii) $m \geq r$.

(iv) $\boldsymbol{y} \in \boldsymbol{y}_m$, i. e. the outputs to be regulated are measurable.

Assume that Lemma 2.2.1 holds; then a controller which solves the RSP consists of two parts, a servo-compensator and a stabilizing compensator. In the case when the system (2.1) is open-loop asymptotically stable, then there always exists a stabilizing compensator of order zero; in this case, the minimal-order controller which solves the RSP for periodic signals of the class $\{\omega_l, l=0,1,\cdots,v\}$, where $\omega_l, l=0,1,\cdots,v$, are distinct, is[注5]

$$\boldsymbol{u}=\hat{\boldsymbol{K}}_0\hat{\boldsymbol{y}}_m+\boldsymbol{K}\boldsymbol{\eta}, \hat{\boldsymbol{y}}_m=\boldsymbol{y}_m-\boldsymbol{D}_m\boldsymbol{u} \tag{2.3}$$

where $\boldsymbol{\eta} \in \mathbf{R}^{2r(v+1)}$ is the output of the servo-compensator given by $\dot{\boldsymbol{\eta}}$ = block diag

$$\left\{\begin{bmatrix}\mathbf{0}, & \boldsymbol{I}_r\\ -\omega_0^2\boldsymbol{I}_r, \mathbf{0}\end{bmatrix}, \begin{bmatrix}\mathbf{0}, & \boldsymbol{I}_r\\ -\omega_1^2\boldsymbol{I}_r, \mathbf{0}\end{bmatrix}, \cdots, \begin{bmatrix}\mathbf{0}, & \boldsymbol{I}_r\\ -\omega_v^2\boldsymbol{I}_r, \mathbf{0}\end{bmatrix}\right\}\eta+\begin{bmatrix}\boldsymbol{0}_r\\ \boldsymbol{I}_r\\ \vdots\\ \boldsymbol{0}_r\\ \boldsymbol{I}_r\end{bmatrix}(y-y_{\text{ref}}) \tag{2.4}$$

where $\boldsymbol{K}=(\boldsymbol{K}_0, \boldsymbol{K}_1, \cdots, \boldsymbol{K}_v)$ and $\boldsymbol{0}_{\mathrm{r}}$ denotes an $r \times r$ zero matrix.

The following result is now obtained directly from Davison and Ferguson (1981), relating to the existence of a controller which solves the RSP for periodic signals, subject to controller gain constraints and gain margin/time lag tolerance constraints imposed on the closed-loop system.

Theorem 2.2.1

Consider the system (2.1) and assume that $\boldsymbol{A}$ is asymptotically stable; then there exists a controller which solves the approximate RSP for periodic signals of the class $\{\omega_l, l=0,1,\cdots,v\}$ such that

(1) the controller gain elements satisfy any specified magnitude constraints $k_{max}>0$, i. e. $\|\hat{\boldsymbol{K}},\boldsymbol{K}\|<k_{max}$, where $\|\cdot\|$ is any specified norm.

(2) the resultant closed-loop system satisfies any specified gain margin and/or time lag tolerance constraints if and only if conditions (ii), (iii), (iv) of Lemma 2.2.1 all hold. Moreover, if these conditions are all satisfied, then a controller which solves the problem is given by (2.3).

Thus if a stable system satisfies Lemma 2.2.1, this implies that a controller with the structure of (2.3) can always be used to solve the approximate RSP for periodic systems. A method of designing such a controller which gives maximum speed of response, low interaction, and which satisfies the two constraints (1),(2) above, may be obtained by minimizing a performance index of the 'cheap control' type with respect to the controller parameters, $\hat{\boldsymbol{K}}\ \boldsymbol{K}$ by using non-linear programming methods[注6]. In this case, the performance index chosen for the problem is given by

$$J = \boldsymbol{E}\int_0^{\infty}(z'\boldsymbol{Q}z + \varepsilon\boldsymbol{u}'\boldsymbol{R}\boldsymbol{u})\,\mathrm{d}\tau \tag{2.5}$$

where $\boldsymbol{Q}>0, \boldsymbol{R}>0, \varepsilon\to 0$ and $z\in\mathbf{R}^r$ is the output of the servo-compensator (2.4), i. e.

$$z=[\boldsymbol{I}_r\ \boldsymbol{0}_r\ \boldsymbol{I}_r\ \boldsymbol{0}_r\cdots\boldsymbol{I}_r\ \boldsymbol{0}_r]\boldsymbol{\eta} \tag{2.6}$$

In order to carry out this parameter optimization problem, it is necessary to have a feasible initial starting point. Such an initial feasible starting point can be obtained as follows.

In (2.3), let

$$\boldsymbol{K}=\{\boldsymbol{K}_{01},\boldsymbol{K}_{02};\boldsymbol{K}_{11},\boldsymbol{K}_{12};\cdots;\boldsymbol{K}_{v1},\boldsymbol{K}_{v2}\} \tag{2.7}$$

where $\boldsymbol{K}_{ij}\in\mathbf{R}^{m\times r}$, $\forall$ i, j, and given $\{\omega_l, l=0,1,\cdots,v\}$ where $\omega_0=0,\omega_l$, $l=0,1,\cdots,v$ define $\boldsymbol{\Theta}_i\in\mathbf{R}^{2m\times 2r}$ as follows

$$\boldsymbol{\Theta}_i=\left[\begin{bmatrix}\bar{\boldsymbol{b}}_i & \boldsymbol{0}\\ \boldsymbol{0} & \bar{\boldsymbol{b}}_i\end{bmatrix}\begin{bmatrix}\bar{\boldsymbol{A}}_i & \omega_i\boldsymbol{I}\\ -\omega_i\boldsymbol{I} & \bar{\boldsymbol{A}}_i\end{bmatrix}^{-1}\begin{bmatrix}\bar{\boldsymbol{B}}_i & \boldsymbol{0}\\ \boldsymbol{0} & \bar{\boldsymbol{B}}_i\end{bmatrix}\right]^{+} \quad i=1,2,\cdots,v \tag{2.8}$$

where if $\boldsymbol{A}$ is stable and Lemma 2.2.1 holds all quantities are well defined (Davison 1976), where $\bar{\boldsymbol{A}}_i\in\mathbf{R}^{(n+2ri)\times(n+2ri)}$, $i=1,2,\cdots,v+1$ is defined recursively as follows

$$\bar{\boldsymbol{A}}_i=\begin{bmatrix}\bar{\boldsymbol{A}}_{i-1} & \bar{\boldsymbol{B}}_{i-1}\boldsymbol{K}_{i-1,1} & \bar{\boldsymbol{B}}_{i-1}\boldsymbol{K}_{i-1,2}\\ \boldsymbol{0} & \boldsymbol{0} & \boldsymbol{I}_r\\ \bar{\boldsymbol{b}}_{i-1} & -\omega_{i-1}^2\boldsymbol{I}_r & \boldsymbol{0}\end{bmatrix} \tag{2.9}$$

where $\bar{\boldsymbol{B}}_i\in\mathbf{R}^{(n+2ri)\times m}$ and $\bar{\boldsymbol{b}}_i\in\mathbf{R}^{r\times(n+2ri}$, $i=1,2,\cdots,v$ are defined by

$$\bar{\boldsymbol{B}}_i=\begin{bmatrix}\boldsymbol{B}\\ \boldsymbol{0}\end{bmatrix},\bar{\boldsymbol{b}}_i=(\boldsymbol{C},\boldsymbol{0}) \tag{2.10}$$

and

$$\bar{\boldsymbol{A}}_0=\boldsymbol{A};\quad \bar{\boldsymbol{B}}_0=\boldsymbol{B},\quad \bar{\boldsymbol{b}}_0=\boldsymbol{C}$$

The following lemma is easily established by direct evaluation.

Lemma 2.2.2

Given $\bar{\boldsymbol{b}}_i,\bar{\boldsymbol{A}}_i,\bar{\boldsymbol{B}}_i$ defined in (2.9), (2.10), assume that Lemma 2.2.1 holds; then rank $\boldsymbol{\Theta}_i=2r$, $i=1,2,\cdots,v$, where $\boldsymbol{\Theta}_i$ is given by (2.8), and on defining

$$\begin{bmatrix}\boldsymbol{\Phi}_1^i & \boldsymbol{\Phi}_2^i\\ -\boldsymbol{\Phi}_2^i & \boldsymbol{\Phi}_1^i\end{bmatrix}=\boldsymbol{\Theta}_i$$

then

$$\boldsymbol{\Phi}_1^i=\mathrm{Re}\{\bar{\boldsymbol{b}}_i(\bar{\boldsymbol{A}}_i+\mathrm{j}\omega_i\boldsymbol{I})^{-1}\bar{\boldsymbol{B}}_i\}^{+}$$

$$\Phi_2^i = \mathrm{Im}\{\bar{\boldsymbol{b}}_i(\bar{\boldsymbol{A}}_i + \mathrm{j}\omega_i \boldsymbol{I})^{-1}\bar{\boldsymbol{B}}_i\}^+$$

for $i=0,1,\cdots,v$.

The following result is now directly obtained from Davison (1976) and Lemma 2.2.2.

Theorem 2.2.2

Given the asymptotically stable system (2.1), assume that Lemma 2.2.1 holds, that a gain margin and/or time lag tolerance constraint, and controller magnitude gain constraint is specified[注7]. Then there always exist scalars $\bar{\varepsilon}_{01}>0, \bar{\varepsilon}_{02}>0, \bar{\varepsilon}_i>0, i=0,1,\cdots,v$, such that the controller (2.3) solves the approximate RSC for periodic signals of the class $\omega_l, l=0,1,\cdots,v$, using the following controller gains

$$\left.\begin{aligned} &\hat{\boldsymbol{K}}=0\\ &\boldsymbol{K}_{02}=\bar{\varepsilon}_{01}(\boldsymbol{CA}^{-1}\boldsymbol{B})^+\\ &\boldsymbol{K}_{01}=\bar{\varepsilon}_{02}\bar{\varepsilon}_{01}(\boldsymbol{CA}^{-1}\boldsymbol{B})^+\\ &\left.\begin{aligned} &\boldsymbol{K}_{i2}=2\bar{\boldsymbol{\varepsilon}}_{\mathbf{i}}(\boldsymbol{I}_m\boldsymbol{0})\boldsymbol{\Theta}_i\begin{bmatrix}\boldsymbol{I}_r\\ \boldsymbol{0}\end{bmatrix}\\ &\boldsymbol{K}_{i1}=2\bar{\varepsilon}_i\omega_i(\boldsymbol{I}_m\boldsymbol{0})\boldsymbol{\Theta}_i\begin{bmatrix}\boldsymbol{I}_r\\ \boldsymbol{0}\end{bmatrix}\end{aligned}\right\}=1,2,\cdots,v\end{aligned}\right\} \tag{2.11}$$

where $\boldsymbol{\Theta}_i$ is defined in (2.8).

This theorem forms the basis of the following algorithm which can be used to find an initial feasible starting point for the parameter optimization problem (2.5). The following definition is made. Given $(\cdot)\in\mathbf{R}^{n\times n}$, let $\mathbf{Re}[\lambda(\cdot)]=\max_{j=1,2,\cdots,n}\{\mathbf{Re}(\lambda(\cdot))\}$, where $\lambda_j, j=0,1,\cdots,n$ are the eigenvalues of $(\cdot)$.

Algorithm 2.2.1

step 1. Put $\hat{\boldsymbol{K}}=0$ and find $\bar{\varepsilon}_{01}>0$ using a one-dimensional search to stabilize $\begin{bmatrix}\boldsymbol{A} & \boldsymbol{BK}_{02}\\ \boldsymbol{C} & \boldsymbol{0}\end{bmatrix}$ such that $\min_{\bar{\varepsilon}_{01}} \mathrm{Re}\left[\lambda\begin{bmatrix}\boldsymbol{A} & \boldsymbol{BK}_{02}\\ \boldsymbol{C} & \boldsymbol{0}\end{bmatrix}\right]$ occurs, subject to the gain margin and controller gain magnitude constraint. Fix $\bar{\varepsilon}_{01}$.

step 2. Find $\bar{\varepsilon}_{02}>0$ using a one-dimensional search to stabilize $\bar{\boldsymbol{A}}_1$ such that $\min_{\bar{\varepsilon}_{02}} \mathbf{Re}[\lambda(\bar{\boldsymbol{A}}_1)]$ occurs, subject to the two constraints. Fix $\bar{\varepsilon}_{02}$.

step 3. Find $\bar{\varepsilon}_1<0$ using a one-dimensional search to stabilize $\bar{\boldsymbol{A}}_2$ such that $\min_{\bar{\varepsilon}_1} \mathbf{Re}[\lambda(\bar{\boldsymbol{A}}_2)]$ occurs, subject to the two constraints. Fix $\bar{\varepsilon}_1$.

⋮

step 4. Find $\bar{\varepsilon}_v>0$ using a one-dimensional search to stabilize $\bar{\boldsymbol{A}}_{v+1}$ such that $\min_{\bar{\varepsilon}_v} \mathbf{Re}[\lambda(\bar{\boldsymbol{A}}_{v+1}]$ occurs subject to the two constraints. Fix $\bar{\varepsilon}_v$.

It follows from Davison (1976) that all steps of this algorithm can always be carried out.

Remark 2.2.1

The assumption that the plant is open-loop asymptotically stable is made solely to ensure that an initial feasible starting point exists for the problem, given that a controller magnitude gain constraint and/or gain magnitude constraint is imposed; if no such constraints are imposed, then it is not necessary to assume the plant is opcn-loop stable.

Remark 2.2.2

It is clear that the controller (2.3) can be trivially modified to deal with the case when only a subset of the frequencies (2.2) is to be considered in the problem formulation. It is also clear that more complex stabilizing compensators (i.e. of order greater than zero) can also be considered in the problem formulation[注8].

Remark 2.2.3

There has been no attempt to consider 'perfect controllers' in the problem formulation; if this were to be done, then the stabilizing compensator of (2.3) would in general be replaced by an observer, and the vector z, defined by (2.6), would be modified to become

$$z = [\boldsymbol{\theta}_0 \boldsymbol{I}_r \boldsymbol{0}_r \boldsymbol{\theta}_1 \boldsymbol{I}_r \boldsymbol{0}_r \cdots \boldsymbol{\theta}_v \boldsymbol{I}_r \boldsymbol{0}_r]$$

where θ_i is a scalar defined by

$$\theta_i \left[\prod_{\substack{l=0 \\ \neq i}}^{v} (\omega_l^2 - \omega_i^2) \right] \qquad i = 0, 1, 2, \cdots, v$$

2.3 Numerical Examples

In the case studies to follow, the choice of $\boldsymbol{Q}=\boldsymbol{I}, \boldsymbol{R}=\boldsymbol{I}, \varepsilon = 10^{-8}$ in the performance index (2.5) was used in all examples. The algorithm of Gesing and Davison (1979) and Davison and Ferguson (1981) was used to carry out the parameter optimization procedure for (2.5). In all simulations reported, zero initials conditions are assumed on the plant and controller.

Example 2.3.1: DC motor

Consider the model of a DC motor described as in Davison and Ferguson (1981).

$$\left.\begin{aligned} \dot{\boldsymbol{x}} &= \begin{bmatrix} -\frac{B}{J}, -\frac{K_T}{J} \\ -\frac{K_e}{L}, -\frac{R}{L} \end{bmatrix} \boldsymbol{x} + \begin{bmatrix} 0 \\ \frac{1}{L} \end{bmatrix} u + \begin{bmatrix} -\frac{1}{J} \\ 0 \end{bmatrix} \omega \\ y &= (1 \ 0) \boldsymbol{x} \end{aligned}\right\} \tag{2.12}$$

where $B=0.0162$, $J=0.215$, $K_T=1.11$, $K_C=1.11$, $R=1.05$ and $L=0.0053$. This system has open-loop eigenvalues $(-5.70, -192.5)$ and no transmission zeros so that Lemma 2.2.1 holds.

Assume it is desired to solve the approximate RSP for periodic signals of the class $(0, \pi, 3\pi, 5\pi, 7\pi. 9\pi)$, using the controller (2.3), such that all elements of the gain matrices $(\hat{\boldsymbol{K}}_0, \boldsymbol{K})$ satisfy the magnitude constraint $|k_{ij}| \leqslant 10$, for all i, j.

The following solution is obtained on solving the parameter optimization problem (2.5) subject to this constraint

$$J_{\text{optimal}} = 5.36$$

$$\left.\begin{matrix}\text{Closed-loop} \\ \text{eigenvalues}\end{matrix}\right|_{\text{optimal}} = \{-6.26, -181, -2.38\pm j1.61, -1.01\pm j2.76, -0.83$$

$$\pm j9.6 -0.54\pm j16.1, -0.42\pm j22.5, -0.30\pm j28.7\}$$

$$\text{Controller gains}\,|_{\text{optimal}}$$

$$\hat{K}_0 = -2.26$$

$$\boldsymbol{K} = (\boldsymbol{K}_0, \boldsymbol{K}_1, \boldsymbol{K}_2, \boldsymbol{K}_3, \boldsymbol{K}_4, \boldsymbol{K}_5)$$

where

$$\boldsymbol{K}_0 = (-9.999, -9.999), \boldsymbol{K}_1 = (-9.999, -3.8), \boldsymbol{K}_2 = (3.8, 4.7),$$

$$\boldsymbol{K}_3 = (9.4, -4.8), \boldsymbol{K}_4 = (9.999, -5.7), \boldsymbol{K}_5 = (9.7, -5.5)$$

In this case, there are four active constraints occurring in the constrained optimization problem.

Some typical simulations of the resultant closed loop system are given in Fig. 2.1 for tracking a triangular periodic signal, and in Fig. 2.2 for regulating the system against two types of triangular periodic disturbances. It is seen that excellent tracking/disturbance rejection occurs.

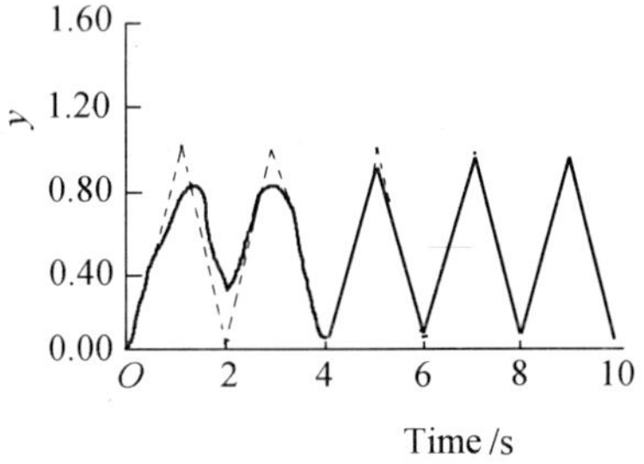

Fig. 2.1 Response of the closed-loop system of Example 2.1 for the case of tracking a periodic

A frequency response plot of the closed-loop and open-loop system's transfer function between the output y and input ω, and a frequency response plot of the closed-loop and open-loop system's transfer function between the output y and input y_{ref}, u respectively are given in Fig. 2.3. It is seen from these plots that the effect of the controller (2.3) is to selectively cause exact error attenuation to occur at the selected frequencies $(0,\pi,3\pi,5\pi,7\pi,9\pi)$.

Example 2.3.2 Unstable reactor

Consider the model of a reactor described as follows (Rosenbrock 1974)

$$\dot{\boldsymbol{x}}=\begin{bmatrix}1.38 & -0.207 & 6.715 & -5.676\\ -0.58 & -4.29 & 0 & 0.675\\ 1.067 & 4.273 & -6.654 & 5.893\\ 0.048 & 4.273 & 1.343 & -2.104\end{bmatrix}\boldsymbol{x}+\begin{bmatrix}0 & 0\\ 5.68 & 0\\ 1.14 & -3.146\\ 1.14 & 0\end{bmatrix}\boldsymbol{u}+\begin{bmatrix}1\\1\\1\\1\end{bmatrix}\omega$$

$$\boldsymbol{y}=\begin{bmatrix}1,0,0,-1\\ 0,1,0,0\end{bmatrix}\boldsymbol{x} \tag{2.13}$$

This system has open-loop eigenvalues and transmission zeros so that Lemma 2.2.1 holds, but the system is not open-loop stable.

Assume that it is desired to solve the approximate RSP for periodic signals of the class $(0,\pi,3\pi,5\pi)$ using the controller (2.3) with no constraints imposed; in this case there is no guarantee that such a controller will solve the problem. However, on noting that the system (2.13) can be stabilized by using the control $u=\hat{K}_0 y$ where $\hat{K}_0=\begin{bmatrix}0 & -2\\ 5 & 0\end{bmatrix}$, then this implies that such a minimal order controller will solve the problem.

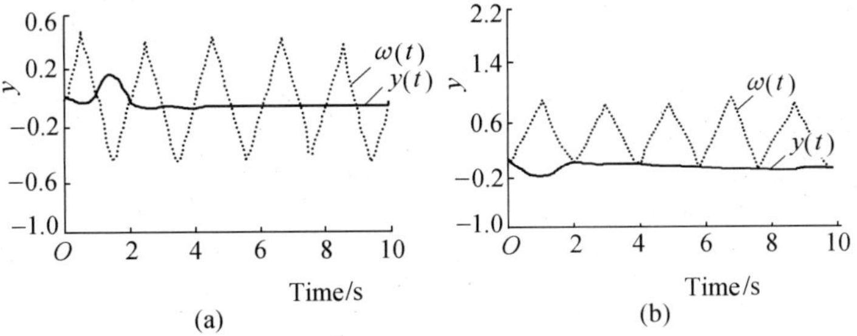

Fig. 2.2 The system response of Example 2.3.1 for the case of the disturbance rejection of two types (a), (b) of periodic trangular signals

The following solution is obtained on solving the parameter optimization problem (2.5) on using the controller $u=\begin{bmatrix}0 & -2\\ 5 & 0\end{bmatrix}y$ to prestabilize the system(2.13)

$$J_{\text{optimal}}=3.41$$

$$\left.\begin{array}{l}\text{Closed-loop}\\ \text{eigenvalues}\end{array}\right|_{\text{optimal}}=\{-1.22,-5.28,-4.26\pm j4.75,-0.901+$$
$$j2.55,\ -1.19\pm j2.44\ -1.76\pm j7.21,\ -1.75\pm j9.49,\ -2.00\pm j11.0-1.53\pm j15.9,-2.02\pm j15.1,-2.02\pm j15.1,-2.0\pm j27.0\}$$

$$\text{Controller gains}\,|_{\text{optimal}}$$

$$\hat{\boldsymbol{K}}_0=\begin{bmatrix}-4.47 & -0.145\\ 9.16 & -7.61\end{bmatrix}\quad \boldsymbol{K}=(\boldsymbol{K}_0,\boldsymbol{K}_1,\boldsymbol{K}_2,\boldsymbol{K}_3)$$

$$\boldsymbol{K}_1=\begin{bmatrix}-163 & -54 & 44 & 10\\ 241 & -182 & -65 & 21\end{bmatrix}\quad \boldsymbol{K}_2=\begin{bmatrix}-161 & -60 & -1.2 & -0.16\\ 176 & -170 & 7.8 & -6.8\end{bmatrix}$$

$$\boldsymbol{K}_3=\begin{bmatrix}-228 & -61 & -5.3 & 3.0\\ 188 & -52 & 15 & -15\end{bmatrix}$$

Some typical simulations of the resultant closed-loop system are given in Fig. 2.4 for tracking a triangular periodic wave. It is seen that excellent regulation occurs.

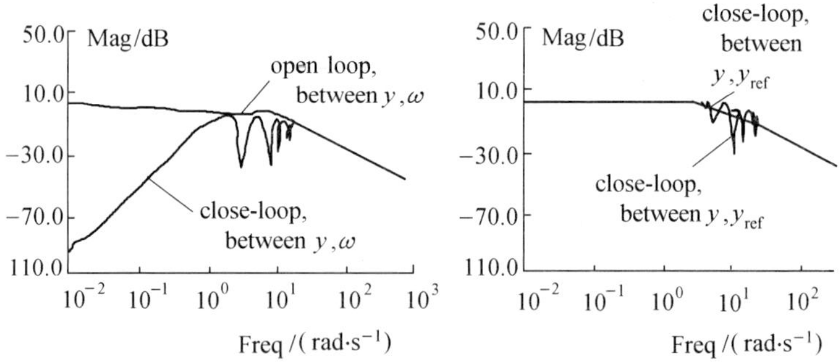

Fig. 2.3 Response of the open-loop/closed-loop system transfer function

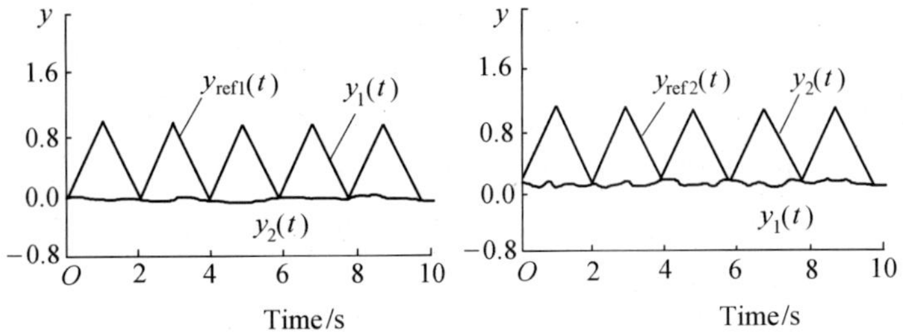

Fig. 2.4 Response of the closed-loop system transfer function for Example 2.3.2

2.4 Conclusions

This paper has considered the problem of achieving approximate robust tracking/regulation for a class of periodic signals which have a given period, by using a finite dimensional linear controller. This has been done by defining and solving the 'approximate RSP for periodic signals of the class $\{\omega_l, l=0,1,\cdots,v\}$'. In this problem formulation, it is assumed that the controller gains are constrained either directly by a controller gain magnitude constraint, or indirectly, by means of a gain margin constraint imposed on the resultant closed-loop system. Thus, this implies that any design method which uses a high-gain type of approach cannot be directly applied. Three case studies of the design method are given to illustrate the type of results that may be obtained; in all cases, excellent tracking/regulation occurs.

New words and phrases:

1. period *n*. 周期
2. periodic *a*. 周期(性)的,断续的
3. harmonic *n*. 谐波,谐波分量,谐振荡
4. sinusoidal *a*. 正弦的
5. tolerance *n*. 容限
6. triangular *n*. 三角形
7. Fourer series 傅里叶级数
8. observation *n*. 注意事项, 短评
9. give rise to 引起,导致
10. detectable *a*. 可达的
11. recursively *adv*. 递归地,循环地

12. denote *v.* 表示

13. active *a.* 常用的,有效的,实际的,快速的

14. selective *a.* 局部(部分)的,分别的,优先的

15. exact *a.* 恰当的,严格的

16. attenuation *n.* 缩减(小),降低,衰减

17. prestabilize *v.* 超前,稳定

18. cut-off frequency 截止频率

Notes:

1. The following problem is considered: given a system which has tracking/disturbance signals arising from a class of periodic signals with period T, say, assume that such a periodic signal has p dominant harmonic components contained in $\{\omega_l, l=0,1,\cdots,v\}$. Then it is desired to find a finite-dimensional linear controller which gives exact robust asymptotic regulation for the case of sinusoidal signals with frequencies $\omega_l, l=0,1,\cdots,v$ subject to certain controller gain magnitude constraints and/or gain margin tolerance constraints which may be imposed on the problem.

译:(本文)考虑下列问题:给定一带有周期性跟踪/扰动信号(周期为 T)的系统,也就是说,假设这一周期信号在$\{\omega_l, l=0,1,\cdots,v\}$上有 p 个主谐波分量,然后希望能找到一有限维线性控制器,该控制器对频率为 $\omega_l(l=0,1,\cdots,v)$的正弦信号能给出准确的鲁棒渐近调节,其中频率 ω_l 受到可能加于所讨论问题上的一定控制器增益幅值约束和/或增益余量容限的限制。

2. This is called ‘the approximate robust servomechanism problem for periodic signals of the class $\{\omega_l, l=0,1,\cdots,v\}$’. It is to be noted that such a problem cannot in general be solved by using high gain control synthesis methods.

译:这被称为周期信号$\{\omega_l, l=0,1,\cdots,v\}$的近似鲁棒伺服机构问题。注意这样的问题通常不能用高增益的控制综合方法来处理。

3. Given a finite-dimensional linear time-invariant multivariable system, suppose that tracking/disturbance signals arise from a class of periodic signals with period T say, e. g. a triangular periodic wave. Then,

unless the periodic signal $\omega(t)$ arises from the following finite-dimensional linear model: $\dot{\boldsymbol{\eta}}=\boldsymbol{An},\boldsymbol{\omega}=\boldsymbol{b\eta}$, in general, there exists no finite-dimensional linear time-invariant controller which can be applied to the system to produce exact robust asymptotic error regulation. However, it may be desired to obtain a finite-dimensional controller so that approximate robust asymptotic error regulation occurs.

译:给定一有限维线性时不变多变量系统，假设其跟踪/干扰信号由周期为 T 的周期信号产生,如周期三角波。那末,除非周期信号由如下有限维线性模型 $\dot{\boldsymbol{\eta}}=\boldsymbol{An},\boldsymbol{\omega}=\boldsymbol{b\eta}$ 产生,通常不存在有限维线性时不变控制器,它可以应用到系统中并得到准确鲁棒渐近误差调节的。然而有可能找到一有限维控制器实现近似鲁棒渐近误差调节。

4. Thus, these observations give rise to the following problem: given $\{\omega_l, l=0,1,\cdots,v\}$, find a controller, in particular, the ‘simplest possible’ controller, i. e. one which has minimum order, which will give exact robust error regulation for the system with disturbance/tracking signals of frequencies $\omega_l, l=0,1,\cdots,v$ subject to specified engineering constraints imposed on the magnitude of controller gains and gain margin tolerance requirements, say. This is called the ‘approximate RSP for periodic systems of the class, $\{\omega_l, l=0,1,\cdots, v\}$’.

译:这样,这些注意事项引起以下问题:给定$\{\omega_l,l=0,1,\cdots,v\}$，寻找一个控制器,尤其是一个最简单的可能的控制器。即一个有最小阶,且对有频率为 $\omega_l(l=0,1,\cdots,v)$ 的干扰/跟踪信号的系统可给出精确的鲁棒渐近误差调节。该控制器还受加在控制器上的增益幅值和增益裕量容限要求的特定的工程限制。这被称做“频率为 $\omega_l(l=0,1,\cdots,v)$ 的周期系统的近似鲁棒伺服机构问题(RSP)”。

5. In the case when the system (2.1) is open-loop asymptotically stable, then there always exists a stabilizing compensator of order zero;

in this case, the minimal-order controller which solves the RSP for periodic signals of the class $\{\omega_l, l=0,1,\cdots,v\}$, where $\omega_l, l=0,1,\cdots,v$, are distinct, is :⋯

译:当系统(2.1)为开环渐近稳定时,则总存在一个稳定零阶补偿器;此时,解决有周期信号$\{\omega_l, l=0,1,\cdots,v\}$(其中$\omega_l, l=0,1,\cdots,v$不同)的 RSP 问题的最小阶控制器为:⋯ ⋯

6. A method of designing such a controller which gives maximum speed of response, low interaction, and which satisfies the two constraints (i),(ii) above, may be obtained by minimizing a performance index of the 'cheap control' type with respect to the controller parameters$\hat{K}$, K by using non-linear programming methods.

译:一种能得到满足上面的(i)、(ii)两个限制,并且能给出最快响应速度、较少相互作用的控制器设计方法,可以使用非线性编程方法,通过使关于控制器参数 $\hat{K}$, K 的最经济控制类型的性能指标最小化的方法得到。

7. Given the asymptotically stable system (2.1), assume that Lemma 2.2.1 holds, that a gain margin and/or time lag tolerance constraint, and controller magnitude gain constraint is specified.

译:给定渐近稳定系统(2.1),假设引理 2.2.1 成立,增益裕量和/或时间滞后容限的限制,以及控制器幅值增益的限制均指定。

8. It is clear that the controller (2.3) can be trivially modified to deal with the case when only a subset of the frequencies (2.2) is to be considered in the problem formulation. It is also clear that more complex stabilizing compensators (i. e. of order greater than zero) can also be considered in the problem formulation.

译:很明显, 可对控制器(2.3)稍作修改以处理在问题的阐述中仅考虑有频率(2.2)的子集的情况; 也很明显的是, 更复杂的镇定补偿器(即阶次大于 0 的)也可以被考虑用到问题的阐述中。

PART 3	CHAPTER THREE

3 Regulator Design with Poles in a Specified Region

Abstract

A design method for regulators having poles in a specified region by using conformal mapping is proposed and the following two problems of regulator design are considered[注1]. The first is how to design all poles of a clos ed-loop system in a specified region by state feedback, and the other is how to design optimal regulators of which the poles may be located in a specified region, i. e. how to obtain the weighting matrices of a quadratic criterion function which yields all its poles in a specified disc with radius r and centre α within the left-half complex plane for continuous systems and in the unit circle for discrete systems. [注2]

3.1 Introduction

In designing regulators by state feedback, there are two design methods: (i) regulators based on the pole assignment, and (ii) optimal regulators minimizing a quadratic criterion function. It is known that both design methods give an asymptotically stable closed-loop system (Anderson and Moore 1971, Kwakernaak and Sivan 1972, Kuo 1980, Mita 1977, Kimura 1981)[注3].

Considering the characteristics of the closed-loop system, e. g. its stability, damping ratio, sensitivity etc., its poles are not necessarily specified at exact locations, but it is enough for them to be assigned in a region. Much research concerning this problem has been done (Bogachev *et al.* 1979, Kawasaki and Shimemura 1979, Mori and Shimemura 1980, Furuta and Kim 1987, Amin 1984, Achermann 1980, 1985).

In this paper, we also propose an alternative algorithm for designing regulators assigning closed-loop poles in a specified region by applying the concept of conformal mapping. This approach can be used in either one of the above-mentioned two methods, and they are treated individually.

The proposed concept of pole assignment by state feedback is outlined as follows: we define a new system $\tilde{\Sigma}(\boldsymbol{\Psi},\boldsymbol{\Gamma})$ which may be constructed by linear fractional transformation of the closed-loop matrix given by the system $\Sigma(\boldsymbol{A},\boldsymbol{B})$, and pole assignment is performed for the system $\tilde{\Sigma}(\boldsymbol{\Psi},\boldsymbol{\Gamma})$ by one of the well-known pole assignment methods, i. e. the state feedback law for the system $\tilde{\Sigma}(\boldsymbol{\Psi},\boldsymbol{\Gamma})$ is obtained by assigning all poles of the closed*loop system to the complex left half plane, for continuous systems, or to the unit circle, for discrete systems*[注4]*. Then, by the relationship between the state feedback laws of the original system and the transformed system, the control law of pole assignment in a specified region for the given system* $\Sigma(\boldsymbol{A},\boldsymbol{B})$ is derived. The optimal regulator problem, which is the problem of obtaining the weighting matrices $\boldsymbol{Q},\boldsymbol{R}$, $\boldsymbol{D}$ of the quadratic criterion function so that the closed-loop poles are in a specified region, may be solved in a similar way to the pole assignment problem stated above[注5]. That is, we may solve the Riccati equation for the transformed system $\tilde{\Sigma}(\boldsymbol{\Psi},\boldsymbol{\Gamma})$ and, by comparing the related properties of the Riccati equations for the given system and the transformed system, we can determine the weighting matrices $\boldsymbol{Q},\boldsymbol{R},\boldsymbol{D}$ for the given system $\Sigma(\boldsymbol{A},\boldsymbol{B})$ which satisfy our objective.

The paper is organized as follows. Section 3. 2 introduces the basic theory and concepts which are the background to our method. Section 3. 3 deals with the pole assignment problem in a specified region by using the results of section 3. 2. Section 3. 4 shows the design method for synthesizing optimal regulators which yields poles located within a specified region.

3.2 Preliminaries

In this section, we introduce the basic theory and concepts which are the background to our method of designing regulators so as to assign poles in a specified region[注6]. Consider the continuous system $\Sigma(\boldsymbol{A},\boldsymbol{B})$

$$\dot{\boldsymbol{x}}=\boldsymbol{A}\boldsymbol{x}+\boldsymbol{B}\boldsymbol{u},\boldsymbol{x}\in\boldsymbol{R}^{n},\boldsymbol{u}\in\boldsymbol{R}^{m} \tag{3.1}$$

and the discrete system $\Sigma_{D}(\boldsymbol{A},\boldsymbol{B})$

$$\boldsymbol{x}_{k+1}=\boldsymbol{A}\boldsymbol{x}_{k}+\boldsymbol{B}\boldsymbol{u}_{k},\boldsymbol{x}\in\boldsymbol{R}^{n},\boldsymbol{u}\in\boldsymbol{R}^{m} \tag{3.2}$$

where $\boldsymbol{A},\boldsymbol{B}$ are constant matrices of appropriate dimensions, and it is assumed that the pair $(\boldsymbol{A},\boldsymbol{B})$ is controllable (or reachable). For the system $\Sigma(\boldsymbol{A},\boldsymbol{B})$ and $\Sigma_{D}(\boldsymbol{A},\boldsymbol{B})$, let the state feedback control laws be given, respectively, as follows

$$\boldsymbol{u}=\boldsymbol{F}\boldsymbol{x} \tag{3.3}$$

$$\boldsymbol{u}_{k}=\boldsymbol{F}\boldsymbol{x}_{k} \tag{3.4}$$

Then, their closed-loop systems may be written as

$$\dot{\boldsymbol{x}}=(\boldsymbol{A}+\boldsymbol{B}\boldsymbol{F})\boldsymbol{x} \tag{3.5}$$

$$\boldsymbol{x}_{k}=(\boldsymbol{A}+\boldsymbol{B}\boldsymbol{F})\boldsymbol{x}_{k} \tag{3.6}$$

Here, let their poles be expressed by the following

$$\lambda_{i}(\boldsymbol{A}+\boldsymbol{B}\boldsymbol{F}) \qquad i=1,2,\cdots,n \tag{3.7}$$

Proposition 3.2.1 (Gantmacher 1960)

Let the poles of the closed-loop system for the system $\Sigma(\boldsymbol{A},\boldsymbol{B})$ or $\Sigma_{D}(\boldsymbol{A},\boldsymbol{B})$ be (3.7), and let $\phi(\mu)$ be a scalar rational function of the form

$$\phi(\mu)=\gamma_{0}\prod_{j=1}^{m}(\mu-\mu_{j})^{\sigma j} \tag{3.8}$$

where $\sigma_{j}(j=1,2,\cdots,m)$ are integers. Then $\phi(\lambda_{i}), i=1,2,\cdots,n$ are the eigenvalues of the matrix $\phi(\boldsymbol{A}+\boldsymbol{B}\boldsymbol{F})$.

Let the scalar rational function (3.8) be given by the form

$$\rho=f(\lambda)=(a\lambda+b)/(c\lambda+d), ad-bc\neq 0 \tag{3.9}$$

where a,b,c,d are scalars. Then the function (3.9) maps the λ-plane into the ρ-plane, and is called a linear fractional transformation

(Churchill *et al.* 1974). Here, the condition $ad-bc\neq0$ means that the transformation (3.9) is not constant and has conformal property. If $ad-bc=0$, then $d\rho/d\lambda=0$ and $\rho=const$. If $c\neq0$ in (3.9), it is rewritten as

$$\rho=f(\lambda)=(bc-d)/(c^2(\lambda+d/c))+a/c \tag{3.10}$$

Now, for simplicity, we express (3.9) as follows

$$\rho=f(\lambda)=\beta/(\lambda+\alpha)+\gamma \tag{3.11}$$

where

$$\alpha=d/c,\beta=(bc-ad)/c^2,\gamma=a/c \tag{3.12}$$

We are going to consider the basic concept of the proposed pole assignment problem in the case when $c\neq0$, since $f(\lambda)$ is a linear mapping when $c=0$. We make a new system which may be constructed by the linear fractional mapping of the closed-loop system of the system $\Sigma(\boldsymbol{A},\boldsymbol{B})$ or $\Sigma_D(\boldsymbol{A},\boldsymbol{B})$. Let the eigenvalues of the matrix $(\boldsymbol{A}+\boldsymbol{BF})$ be$\lambda_i, i=1,2,\cdots,n$. Since from Proposition 3.2.1, $f(\lambda_i)$ are the eigenvalues of the matrix $f(\boldsymbol{A}+\boldsymbol{BF})$ and expressed by (3.11), it is obvious that if we define the closed-loop matrix of a system $\Sigma(\boldsymbol{\Psi\Gamma})$ as

$$\boldsymbol{\Psi}+\boldsymbol{\Gamma}\hat{\boldsymbol{F}}=f(\boldsymbol{A}+\boldsymbol{BF}) \tag{3.13}$$

then its poles become $f(\lambda_i), i=1,2,\cdots,n$. Hence, from (3.12), (3.13) can be given as

$$\boldsymbol{\Psi}+\boldsymbol{\Gamma}\hat{\boldsymbol{F}}=\gamma\boldsymbol{I}+\beta(\boldsymbol{A}+\boldsymbol{BF}+\alpha\boldsymbol{I})^{-1} \tag{3.14}$$

Now, let us express the state equation of the transformed system (3.14) as follows: for the continuous systems, the system $\tilde{\Sigma}(\boldsymbol{\Psi},\boldsymbol{\Gamma})$

$$\dot{\boldsymbol{x}}_\rho=\boldsymbol{\Psi}\boldsymbol{x}_\rho+\boldsymbol{\Gamma}\boldsymbol{u}_\rho \tag{3.15}$$

and for the discrete systems, the system $\tilde{\Sigma}_D(\boldsymbol{\Psi},\boldsymbol{\Gamma})$

$$\hat{\boldsymbol{x}}_{k+1}=\boldsymbol{\Psi}\hat{\boldsymbol{x}}_k+\boldsymbol{\Gamma}\hat{\boldsymbol{u}}_k \tag{3.16}$$

and let their state feedback laws be given, respectively, by

$$\boldsymbol{u}_p=\hat{\boldsymbol{F}}\boldsymbol{x}_p \tag{3.17}$$

$$\hat{\boldsymbol{u}}_k=\hat{\boldsymbol{F}}\hat{\boldsymbol{x}}_k \tag{3.18}$$

Then, the closed-loop systems are written, respectively, as

$$\dot{\boldsymbol{x}}_\rho=(\boldsymbol{\Psi}+\boldsymbol{\Gamma}\hat{\boldsymbol{F}})\boldsymbol{x}_\rho \tag{3.19}$$

and $$\hat{\boldsymbol{x}}_{k+1}=(\boldsymbol{\Psi}+\boldsymbol{\Gamma}\hat{\boldsymbol{F}})\hat{\boldsymbol{x}}_k \tag{3.20}$$
where the system matrices $\boldsymbol{\Psi},\boldsymbol{\Gamma},\hat{\boldsymbol{F}}$ can be chosen as
$$\boldsymbol{\psi}=\gamma\boldsymbol{I}+\beta(\boldsymbol{A}+\alpha\boldsymbol{I})^{-1} \tag{3.21a}$$
$$\boldsymbol{\Gamma}=(\boldsymbol{A}+\alpha\boldsymbol{I})^{-1}\boldsymbol{B} \tag{3.21b}$$
$$\hat{\boldsymbol{F}}=-\beta\boldsymbol{F}(\boldsymbol{A}+\alpha\boldsymbol{I}+\boldsymbol{BF})^{-1}=-\beta\boldsymbol{F}(\boldsymbol{I}+(\boldsymbol{A}+\alpha\boldsymbol{I})^{-1}\boldsymbol{BF})^{-1}(\boldsymbol{A}+\alpha\boldsymbol{I}) \tag{3.21c}$$

Here, (3.21) is given by using the relation
$$(\boldsymbol{A}+\alpha\boldsymbol{I}+\boldsymbol{BF})^{-1}=(\boldsymbol{A}+\alpha\boldsymbol{I})^{-1}-(\boldsymbol{A}+\alpha\boldsymbol{I})^{-1}\boldsymbol{BF}(\boldsymbol{A}+\alpha\boldsymbol{I}+\boldsymbol{BF})^{-1} \tag{3.22}$$

Conversely, from (3.11), the linear fractional transformation which maps the ρ-plane into the λ-plane may be rewritten as
$$\lambda=g(\rho)=-\alpha+\beta/(\rho-\gamma) \tag{3.23}$$
Then, by using the linear fractional transformation (3.23) for the closed-loop matrix of the system $\tilde{\Sigma}(\boldsymbol{\Psi},\boldsymbol{\Gamma})$ or $\tilde{\Sigma}_{\mathrm{D}}(\boldsymbol{\Psi},\boldsymbol{\Gamma})$, we obtain
$$\boldsymbol{A}+\boldsymbol{BF}=\boldsymbol{g}(\boldsymbol{\Psi}+\boldsymbol{\Gamma}\hat{\boldsymbol{F}})=-\alpha\boldsymbol{I}+\beta(\boldsymbol{\Psi}+\boldsymbol{\Gamma}\hat{\boldsymbol{F}}-\gamma\boldsymbol{I})^{-1} \tag{3.24}$$
The expression in the state space of (3.24) may be interpreted as follows: the continuous system $\Sigma(\boldsymbol{A},\boldsymbol{B})$ and control law (3.3), or the discrete system $\Sigma_{\mathrm{D}}(\boldsymbol{A},\boldsymbol{B})$ and control law (3.4) respectively, and the system matrices $\boldsymbol{A},\boldsymbol{B},\boldsymbol{F}$ can have the following relationships with the system matrices $\boldsymbol{\Psi},\boldsymbol{\Gamma},\hat{\boldsymbol{F}}$ of the system $\tilde{\Sigma}(\boldsymbol{\Psi},\boldsymbol{\Gamma})$ or $\tilde{\Sigma}_{\mathrm{D}}(\boldsymbol{\Psi},\boldsymbol{\Gamma})$
$$\boldsymbol{A}=-\alpha\boldsymbol{I}+\beta(\boldsymbol{\Psi}-\gamma\boldsymbol{I})^{-1} \tag{3.25a}$$
$$\boldsymbol{B}=\boldsymbol{\beta}(\boldsymbol{\Psi}-\gamma\boldsymbol{I})^{-1}\boldsymbol{\Gamma} \tag{3.25b}$$
$$\boldsymbol{F}=-\hat{\boldsymbol{F}}(\boldsymbol{\Psi}+\boldsymbol{\Gamma}\hat{\boldsymbol{F}}-\gamma\boldsymbol{I})^{-1} \tag{3.25c}$$
which are defined similarly to (3.21).

There exist the following properties between $\Sigma(\boldsymbol{A},\boldsymbol{B})$ (or $\Sigma_{\mathrm{D}}(\boldsymbol{A},\boldsymbol{B})$) and $\tilde{\Sigma}(\boldsymbol{\Psi},\boldsymbol{\Gamma})$ (or $\tilde{\Sigma}_{\mathrm{D}}(\boldsymbol{\Psi},\boldsymbol{\Gamma})$), where α is chosen so that the matrix $(\boldsymbol{A}+\alpha\boldsymbol{I})$ is non-singular.

Theorem 3.2.1

The system $\tilde{\Sigma}(\boldsymbol{\Psi},\boldsymbol{\Gamma})$ ($\tilde{\Sigma}_{\mathrm{D}}(\boldsymbol{\Psi},\boldsymbol{\Gamma})$) is controllable (reachable) if and only if the system $\Sigma(\boldsymbol{A},\boldsymbol{B})$ (or $\Sigma_{\mathrm{D}}(\boldsymbol{A},\boldsymbol{B})$) is controllable (reachable).

Proof

If the system $\tilde{\Sigma}(\boldsymbol{\Psi},\boldsymbol{\Gamma})$ ($\tilde{\Sigma}_{\mathrm{D}}(\boldsymbol{\Psi},\boldsymbol{\Gamma})$) is controllable (reachable) then, for all ρ, it means that rank $(\rho\boldsymbol{I}-\boldsymbol{\Psi},\boldsymbol{\Gamma})=n$ and also by hypothesis, for all λ, rank$(\lambda\boldsymbol{I}-\boldsymbol{A},\boldsymbol{B})=n$. That is, for all ρ we have

$$\begin{aligned}\text{rank}(\rho\boldsymbol{I}-\boldsymbol{\Psi},\boldsymbol{\Gamma}) &= \text{rank}(\rho\boldsymbol{I}-v\boldsymbol{I}-\beta(\boldsymbol{A}+\alpha\boldsymbol{I})^{-1},(\boldsymbol{A}+\alpha\boldsymbol{I})^{-1}\boldsymbol{B} = \\ &\text{rank}(\boldsymbol{A}+\alpha\boldsymbol{I})^{-1}(v-\rho)[\gamma\boldsymbol{I}-\boldsymbol{A},(v-\rho)^{-1}\boldsymbol{B}] = \\ &\text{rank}(\lambda\boldsymbol{I}-\boldsymbol{A},\boldsymbol{B})=n \end{aligned} \tag{3.26}$$

where

$$\lambda=-\alpha+\beta/(\rho-v) \tag{3.27}$$

It follows from (3.26) that the system $\Sigma(\boldsymbol{A},\boldsymbol{B})$ ($\Sigma_{\mathrm{D}}(\boldsymbol{A},\boldsymbol{B})$) is controllable (reachable), and also its converse is satisfied.

Lemma 3.2.1

The controllability indices of the system $\tilde{\Sigma}(\boldsymbol{\Psi},\boldsymbol{\Gamma})$ $\tilde{\Sigma}_{D}(\boldsymbol{\Psi},\boldsymbol{\Gamma})$) obtained by the linear fractional transformation (3.9) of the closed-loop matrix for the given system $\Sigma(\boldsymbol{A},\boldsymbol{B})$ (or $\Sigma_{\mathrm{D}}(\boldsymbol{A},\boldsymbol{B})$) are invariant[注7].

3.3 Pole Assignment in a Specified Region

In this section, we shall consider the problem of pole assignment in a specified region by using the results of section 3.2. After considering the general pole assignment problem in section 3.3.2, an example problem will be shown in section 3.3.3.

3.3.1 Problem statement

Consider both the continuous system $\Sigma(\boldsymbol{A},\boldsymbol{B})$ and the discrete system $\Sigma_{\mathrm{D}}(\boldsymbol{A},\boldsymbol{B})$ as given in section 3.2. Then, the problem is to synthesize the state feedback control law such that the systems $\Sigma(\boldsymbol{A},\boldsymbol{B})$ and $\Sigma_{\mathrm{D}}(\boldsymbol{A},\boldsymbol{B})$ have their closed-loop poles in a specified region D. That is, we shall consider the problem such that all their closed-loop poles are elements of the following

$$\Lambda=\{\lambda_i:\lambda_i(\boldsymbol{A}+\boldsymbol{BF})\in \mathrm{D}:\text{specified region}, i=1,2,\cdots,n\} \tag{3.28}$$

where the region D is specified within the complex left half-plane for the continuous system (see Fig. 3. 1) and within the unit circle for the discrete system (see Fig. 3. 2) respectively.

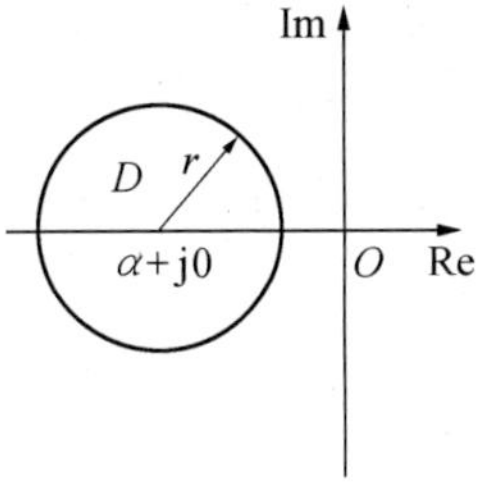

Fig. 3. 1 Disc D in the left Half of the complex plane

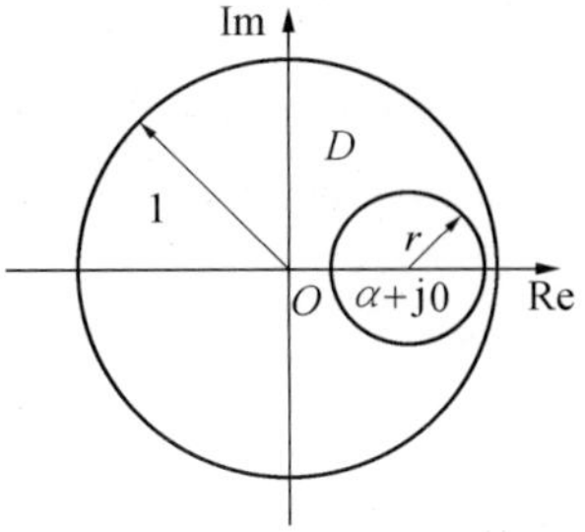

Fig. 3. 2 Disc D in the unit disc with centre at the origin

3. 3. 2 General pole assignment problems

A general pole assignment problem with its closed-loop poles in a specified region for the systems $\Sigma(\boldsymbol{A},\boldsymbol{B})$ and $\Sigma_{D}(\boldsymbol{A},\boldsymbol{B})$ is solved as follows. A region for the pole assignment D is specified so that there exists a linear fractional transformation $f(\lambda)$ mapping from a specified region D to the complex left half-plane for the continuous system and to the unit disc for the discrete system. One example of such D_s can be chosen as a disc D with centre α and radius r in the complex left half-plane for the continuous system, and also as a disc D with centre α and radius r within the unit disc for the discrete system, of which problems will be considered in section 3. 3. 3. We synthesize the state feedback control law (3. 17) [(3. 18)] which yields all closed-loop poles of the system $\tilde{\Sigma}(\boldsymbol{\Psi},\boldsymbol{\Gamma})$ [$\tilde{\Sigma}_{D}(\boldsymbol{\Psi},\boldsymbol{\Gamma})$] in the complex left half-plane (in the unit disc). Then, by using this control law in (3. 3) [(3. 4)] for the given systems $\Sigma(\boldsymbol{A},\boldsymbol{B})$ [$\Sigma_{D}(\boldsymbol{A},\boldsymbol{B})$], we may obtain the closed-loop system with its poles in the specified region D. From Theorem 3. 2. 1 it may be seen that the pole assignment problem is always possible of solution for the systems $\tilde{\Sigma}(\boldsymbol{\Psi},\boldsymbol{\Gamma})$ and $\tilde{\Sigma}_{D}(\boldsymbol{\Psi},\boldsymbol{\Gamma})$.

As an example of pole assignment for the system $\tilde{\Sigma}(\boldsymbol{\Psi},\boldsymbol{\Gamma})$, we may obtain the following theorem making use of the well-known Riccati equation, where it is assumed that the linear fractional transformation (3.11) maps the specified region D into the ρ-lane (the complex left half-plane). That is, the closed-loop poles to be assigned are elements of (3.28).

Theorem 3.3.1

Let the state feedback control law for the system $\tilde{\Sigma}(\boldsymbol{\Psi},\boldsymbol{\Gamma})$ be given by

$$\boldsymbol{u}_\rho = \hat{\boldsymbol{F}}\boldsymbol{x}_\rho = -\boldsymbol{R}^{-1}\boldsymbol{\Gamma}^{\mathrm{T}}\boldsymbol{P}\boldsymbol{x}_\rho \tag{3.29}$$

where $\boldsymbol{P}$ *is a positive definite solution of the Riccati equation*

$$\boldsymbol{P}\boldsymbol{\Psi}+\boldsymbol{\Psi}^{\mathrm{T}}\boldsymbol{P}-\boldsymbol{P}\boldsymbol{\Gamma}\boldsymbol{R}^{-1}\boldsymbol{\Gamma}^{\mathrm{T}}\boldsymbol{P} = -\boldsymbol{Q} \tag{3.30}$$

$\boldsymbol{R}$ is a positive definite matrix, and Q is a matrix such that the pair $(\boldsymbol{\Psi}, \boldsymbol{Q}^{1/2})$ is observable. Then, the closed-loop poles of the system $\Sigma(\boldsymbol{A},\boldsymbol{B})$, i.e. $\lambda_i(\boldsymbol{A}+\boldsymbol{B}\boldsymbol{F})$, $i=1,2,\cdots,n$ are located within the specified region D, where the state feedback $\boldsymbol{F}$ is given by (3.25c).

Proof

If the state feedback control (3.29) is introduced for the system $\tilde{\Sigma}(\boldsymbol{\Psi},\boldsymbol{\Gamma})$, then its closed-loop poles are within the complex left half-plane (Kwakemaak and Sivan 1972). By substituting $\hat{\boldsymbol{F}}$ (3.29) into (3.25c), all poles of the closed-loop system for the system $\Sigma(\boldsymbol{A},\boldsymbol{B})$ are located within the specified region D by Proposition 3.2.1 and the results of section 3.2.

Corollary 3.3.1

Let the state feedback control law for the systemD $\tilde{\Sigma}_{\mathrm{D}}(\boldsymbol{\Psi},\boldsymbol{\Gamma})$ be given by

$$\hat{\boldsymbol{u}}_k = \hat{\boldsymbol{F}}\hat{\boldsymbol{x}}_k = -(\boldsymbol{R}+\boldsymbol{\Gamma}^{\mathrm{T}}\boldsymbol{P}\boldsymbol{\Gamma})^{-1}\boldsymbol{\Gamma}^{\mathrm{T}}\boldsymbol{P}\boldsymbol{\Psi}\hat{\boldsymbol{x}}_k \tag{3.31}$$

where $\boldsymbol{P}$ is a positive definite solution of the Riccati equation

$$\boldsymbol{P} = \boldsymbol{\Psi}^{\mathrm{T}}\boldsymbol{P}\boldsymbol{\Psi}+\boldsymbol{Q}-\boldsymbol{\Psi}^{\mathrm{T}}\boldsymbol{P}\boldsymbol{\Gamma}(\boldsymbol{R}+\boldsymbol{\Gamma}^{\mathrm{T}}\boldsymbol{P}\boldsymbol{\Gamma})^{-1}\boldsymbol{\Gamma}^{\mathrm{T}}\boldsymbol{P}\boldsymbol{\Psi} \tag{3.32}$$

$\boldsymbol{R}$ is a positive definite matrix, and $\boldsymbol{Q}$ is a matrix such that the pair $(\boldsymbol{\Psi},$

$Q^{1/2}$) is observable. Then, the closed-loop poles of the system $\Sigma_D(A, B)$, that is $\lambda_i(A+BF)$, $i=1,2,\cdots,n$, are located within the specified region D, where the state feedback F is given by (3.25c).

3.3.3 Pole assignment for Figs. 3.1 and 3.2

Pole assignment of the type shown in Figs. 3.1 and 3.2 has been introduced by Furuta and Kim (1987), and Mori and Shimemura (1980), but in this section we shall present an alternative method derived from section 3.3.2.

Consider a linear fractional transformation of the form

$$\rho=f(\lambda)=(\lambda+r+\alpha)^{-1}(\lambda-r+\alpha) \tag{3.33}$$

In (3.33), we may see that in the case $a=1, b=\alpha-r, c=1, d=\alpha+r$ in (3.9), (3.33) maps the region D of Figs. 3.1 and 3.2 into the complex left half-plane. From Proposition 3.2.1, we have the following corollary.

Corollary 3.3.2

Let all poles of the closed-loop system for the system $\Sigma(A, B)$ $[\Sigma_D(A, B)]$ be located within the region D as shown in Figs. 3.1 and 3.2. That is, the eigenvalues of the matrix $(A+BF)$ are elements of the equation

$$\Lambda=\{\lambda_i : \lambda_i(A+BF) \in D;\ \text{centre } \alpha, \text{radius } r, i=1,2,\cdots,n\} \tag{3.34}$$

Its poles are mapped into the complex left half-plane by the linear fractional transformation (3.33).

By using (3.33) for the closed-loop matrix $(A+BF)$ of the system $\Sigma(A, B)$ $[\Sigma_D(A, B)]$, we have

$$\Psi+\Gamma\hat{F}=f(A+BF)=[A+BF+(r+\alpha)I]^{-1}[A+BF-(r-\alpha)I] \tag{3.35}$$

Let the system expression for (3.35) be the system $\bar{\Sigma}(\Psi, \Gamma)$

$$\dot{x}_\rho=\Psi x_\rho+\Gamma u_\rho \tag{3.36}$$

and let the state feedback control law be given by

$$u_\rho=\hat{F}x_\rho \tag{3.37}$$

where the system matrices $\boldsymbol{\Psi},\boldsymbol{\Gamma},\hat{\boldsymbol{F}}$ are of the form

$$\boldsymbol{\Psi}=[\boldsymbol{A}+(r+\alpha)\boldsymbol{I}]^{-1}[\boldsymbol{A}-(r-\alpha)\boldsymbol{I}] \tag{3.38a}$$

$$\boldsymbol{\Gamma}=[\boldsymbol{A}+(r+\alpha)\boldsymbol{I}]^{-1}\boldsymbol{B} \tag{3.38b}$$

$$\hat{\boldsymbol{F}}=\boldsymbol{F}\{\boldsymbol{I}-[\boldsymbol{A}+\boldsymbol{BF}+(r+\alpha)\boldsymbol{I}]^{-1}[\boldsymbol{A}+\boldsymbol{BF}-(r-\alpha)\boldsymbol{I}]\} \tag{3.38c}$$

From (3.33), we can take the following linear fractional transformation which maps the ρ-plane (the complex left half-plane) into the λ-plane (D region)

$$\lambda=g(\rho)=r(1-\rho)^{-1}(1+\rho)-\alpha \tag{3.39}$$

Then, by using (3.39) for the closed-loop matrix ($\boldsymbol{\Psi}+\boldsymbol{\Gamma}\hat{\boldsymbol{F}}$) of the system $\bar{\Sigma}(\boldsymbol{\Psi},\boldsymbol{\Gamma})$, we have

$$\boldsymbol{A}+\boldsymbol{BF}=g(\boldsymbol{\Psi}+\boldsymbol{\Gamma}\hat{\boldsymbol{F}})=r[\boldsymbol{I}-(\boldsymbol{\Psi}+\boldsymbol{\Gamma}\hat{\boldsymbol{F}})]^{-1}(\boldsymbol{I}+\boldsymbol{\Psi}+\boldsymbol{\Gamma}\hat{\boldsymbol{F}})-\alpha\boldsymbol{I} \tag{3.40}$$

Here, let the system expression of (3.40) be $\Sigma(\boldsymbol{A},\boldsymbol{B})$ and its state feedback control law be given by (3.3). Then the matrices may be given by

$$\boldsymbol{A}=r(\boldsymbol{I}-\boldsymbol{\Psi})^{-1}(\boldsymbol{I}+\boldsymbol{\Psi})-\alpha\boldsymbol{I} \tag{3.41a}$$

$$\boldsymbol{B}=r[\boldsymbol{I}+(\boldsymbol{I}-\boldsymbol{\Psi})^{-1}(\boldsymbol{I}+\boldsymbol{\Psi})]\boldsymbol{\Gamma}=2r(\boldsymbol{I}-\boldsymbol{\Psi})^{-1}\boldsymbol{\Gamma} \tag{3.41b}$$

$$\boldsymbol{F}=\frac{1}{2}\hat{\boldsymbol{F}}\{\boldsymbol{I}+(\boldsymbol{I}-\boldsymbol{\Psi}-\boldsymbol{\Gamma}\hat{\boldsymbol{F}})^{-1}(\boldsymbol{I}+\boldsymbol{\Psi}+\boldsymbol{\Gamma}\hat{\boldsymbol{F}}\boldsymbol{\Gamma})\} \tag{3.41c}$$

By Theorem 3.2.1, we have the following corollary.

Corollary 3.3.3

If the system $\Sigma(\boldsymbol{A},\boldsymbol{B})$ is controllable (reachable), then the system $\bar{\Sigma}(\boldsymbol{\Psi},\boldsymbol{\Gamma})$ is also controllable (reachable), where the matrix $[\boldsymbol{\Lambda}+(\alpha+r)\boldsymbol{I}]$ is non-singular.

Since, from Corollary 3.3.3, pole assignment for the system $\bar{\Sigma}(\boldsymbol{\Psi},\boldsymbol{\Gamma})$ is always possible, if we consider the pole assignment problem for the system $\Sigma(\boldsymbol{A},\boldsymbol{B})$ with the method shown in section 3.3.1, then we can obtain the following corollary.

Corollary 3.3.4

Let the state feedback control law for the system $\Sigma(\boldsymbol{\Psi},\boldsymbol{\Gamma})$ be given by

$$u_\rho = \hat{F}x_\rho = -R^{-1}\Gamma^{\mathrm{T}}Px_\rho \tag{3.42}$$

where P is a positive definite solution of the Riccati equation

$$P\Psi + \Psi^{\mathrm{T}}P - P\Gamma R^{-1}\Gamma^{\mathrm{T}}P = -Q \tag{3.43}$$

R is a positive definite matrix, and Q is a matrix such that the pair (Ψ, $Q^{1/2}$) is observable. Then, all poles of the closed-loop system for the system $\Sigma(A, B)$ are located within the region D as shown in Fig. 3.1, where the feedback matrix F is given by (3.41c).

We can also consider the discrete system in a similar way to the case of the continuous system above. Now, let us consider the following system $\overline{\Sigma}_{\mathrm{D}}(\Psi, \Gamma)$ instead of (3.36).

$$\hat{x}_{k+1} = \Psi\hat{x}_{k+1} + \Gamma\hat{u}_k \tag{3.36$'$}$$

Then we may obtain the following corollary.

Corollary 3.3.5

Let the state feedback control law for the system (3.36)′ be given by

$$\hat{u}_k = \hat{F}\hat{x}_k = -R^{-1}\Gamma^{\mathrm{T}}P\hat{x}_k \tag{3.44}$$

where P is a positive definite solution of the Riccati equation (3.43), and R, Q are the same as in Corollary 3.3.4. Then, all poles of the closed-loop system for the system $\Sigma_{\mathrm{D}}(A, B)$ are located within the region D shown in Fig. 3.2, where the feedback matrix F is given by (3.41c).

Remark 3.3.1

From corollary 3.3.5, it is noted that the pole assignment problem for discrete systems can be solved by the well-known method for that of continuous systems. This is an interesting point illustrated by this paper. Here, α has a value of $-1 < \alpha < 1$, and r has a value of $0 \leqslant r < 1$ in (3.33).

Example 1

Consider the following linear time-invariant system

$$\dot{x} = Ax + Bu \tag{3.45}$$

where

$$A=\begin{bmatrix}0&1&0\\0&1&0\\0&0&0\end{bmatrix}\qquad B=\begin{bmatrix}1&0\\1&0\\0&1\end{bmatrix}$$

Let α, r in (3.33) have the values $\alpha=6, r=2$, respectively. Then the matrices $\boldsymbol{\Psi}, \boldsymbol{\Gamma}$ of the system $\overline{\Sigma}(\boldsymbol{\Psi}, \boldsymbol{\Gamma})$ obtained by the linear fractional transformation $f(\lambda)$ of (3.33) is given as

$$\boldsymbol{\Psi}=\begin{bmatrix}0.5&0.056&0.0625\\0&0.56&0\\0&0&0.5\end{bmatrix}\qquad \boldsymbol{\Gamma}=\begin{bmatrix}0.111&-0.0156\\0.111&0\\0&0.125\end{bmatrix}$$

We may also obtain the state feedback matrix by solving the Riccati equation (3.43) with $\boldsymbol{Q}=\boldsymbol{I}, \boldsymbol{R}=\boldsymbol{I}$ as follows

$$\hat{\boldsymbol{F}}=\begin{bmatrix}0.389&9.807&0.0536\\130.065&-130.059&32.386\end{bmatrix}$$

Then the poles of the closed-loop system for the system $\overline{\Sigma}(\boldsymbol{\Psi}, \boldsymbol{\Gamma})$ are taken as

$$\lambda_i(\boldsymbol{\Psi}+\boldsymbol{\Gamma}\hat{\boldsymbol{F}}):\{-0.557, -0.508\pm j0.0094\}$$

By (3.41c), we obtain the feedback matrix of the system (3.45) as

$$\boldsymbol{F}=-\begin{bmatrix}0.111&6.353&0.017\\28.597&-28.596&10.695\end{bmatrix}$$

Then the closed-loop poles of the system (3.45) are located within the specified region D with centre $-6+j0$ and radius $r=2$, i.e.

$$\lambda_i(\boldsymbol{A}+\boldsymbol{B}\boldsymbol{F}):\{-5.464, -5.348\pm j0.0165\}\in D$$

3.4 Optimal Regulator with its Poles in a Specified Region

In this section, we introduce a design method for synthesizing an optimal regulator having closed-loop poles located within a specified region D. That is, this method can determine for us the weighting matrices $\boldsymbol{Q}, \boldsymbol{R}, \boldsymbol{D}$ of a quadratic criterion function so that all poles of the closed-loop system are within the disc D of Fig. 3.1 for continuous systems, and in Fig. 3.2 for discrete systems.

3.4.1 Continuous-time optimal regulator

(1) Problem statement. Consider the continuous system $\Sigma(\boldsymbol{A},\boldsymbol{B})$ (3.1). Then the state feedback control law minimizing the quadratic criterion function

$$J=\frac{1}{2}\int_0^{\infty}(\boldsymbol{x}^{\mathrm{T}}\boldsymbol{Q}\boldsymbol{x}+2x^{\mathrm{T}}\boldsymbol{D}\boldsymbol{x}\boldsymbol{u}+\boldsymbol{u}^{\mathrm{T}}\boldsymbol{R}\boldsymbol{u})\mathrm{d}t \tag{3.46}$$

is given by

$$\boldsymbol{u}(t)=\boldsymbol{F}\boldsymbol{x}(t)=-\boldsymbol{R}^{-1}(\boldsymbol{B}^{\mathrm{T}}\boldsymbol{P}+\boldsymbol{D}^{\mathrm{T}})\boldsymbol{x}(t) \tag{3.47}$$

where $\boldsymbol{Q},\boldsymbol{R}$ are positive definite matrices, $\boldsymbol{D}$ is a matrix of appropriate dimension, and $\boldsymbol{P}$ is a positive definite solution of the Riccati equation

$$0=\boldsymbol{A}^{\mathrm{T}}\boldsymbol{P}+\boldsymbol{P}\boldsymbol{A}+\boldsymbol{Q}-(\boldsymbol{P}\boldsymbol{B}+\boldsymbol{D})\boldsymbol{R}^{-1}(\boldsymbol{B}^{\mathrm{T}}\boldsymbol{P}+\boldsymbol{D}^{\mathrm{T}}) \tag{3.48}$$

Then the closed-loop poles of the system $\Sigma(\boldsymbol{A},\boldsymbol{B})$, i.e. the eigenvalues of the matrix $(\boldsymbol{A}+\boldsymbol{B}\boldsymbol{F})$

$$\lambda_i(\boldsymbol{A}+\boldsymbol{B}\boldsymbol{F})\qquad i=1,2,\cdots,n \tag{3.49}$$

are assigned in the complex left half-plane (Anderson and moore 1971).

In the next section, we shall consider the problem of determining the weighting matrices $\boldsymbol{Q},\boldsymbol{R},\boldsymbol{D}$ of (3.46) so that all closed-loop poles are located within the specified disc D with centre α and radius r. That is, the closed-loop poles of the optimal regulator are elements of

$$\boldsymbol{\Lambda}=\{\lambda_i:\lambda(\boldsymbol{A}+\boldsymbol{B}\boldsymbol{F})\in D:\text{specified disc},i=1,2,\cdots,n\} \tag{3.50}$$

(2) Determination of weighting matrices. Consider a special case of $a=1,b=-\alpha,c=0,d=r$ in (3.9). Then, the matrices $\boldsymbol{\Psi},\boldsymbol{\Gamma},\hat{\boldsymbol{F}}$ are given by

$$\boldsymbol{\Psi}=(\boldsymbol{A}+\alpha\boldsymbol{I})/r,\boldsymbol{\Gamma}=\boldsymbol{B}/r,\hat{\boldsymbol{F}}=\boldsymbol{F} \tag{3.51}$$

By the results of section 3.2 and (3.51), we may obtain the following lemma.

Lemma 3.4.1

Let the state feedback control law for the system $\overline{\Sigma}(\boldsymbol{\Psi},\boldsymbol{\Gamma})$ be given by

$$\boldsymbol{u}_\rho=\hat{\boldsymbol{F}}\boldsymbol{x}_\rho=-(\boldsymbol{R}_1+\boldsymbol{\Gamma}^{\mathrm{T}}\boldsymbol{P}_1\boldsymbol{\Gamma})^{-1}\boldsymbol{\Gamma}^{\mathrm{T}}\boldsymbol{P}_1\boldsymbol{\Psi}\boldsymbol{x}_\rho \tag{3.52}$$

where $\boldsymbol{P}_1$ is a positive definite solution of the Riccati equation

$$\boldsymbol{P}_1=\boldsymbol{\Psi}^{\mathrm{T}}\boldsymbol{P}_1\boldsymbol{\Psi}+\boldsymbol{Q}_1-\boldsymbol{\Psi}^{\mathrm{T}}\boldsymbol{P}_1\boldsymbol{\Gamma}(\boldsymbol{R}_1+\boldsymbol{\Gamma}^{\mathrm{T}}\boldsymbol{P}_1\boldsymbol{\Gamma})^{-1}\boldsymbol{\Gamma}^{\mathrm{T}}\boldsymbol{P}_1\boldsymbol{\Psi} \quad (3.53)$$

and $\boldsymbol{R}_1>0$, and $\boldsymbol{Q}_1$ and is a matrix such that $(\boldsymbol{Q}_1{}^{1/2},\boldsymbol{\Psi})$ is observable. Then, all poles of the closed-loop system for $\Sigma(\boldsymbol{A},\boldsymbol{B})$, i. e. $\lambda_i(\boldsymbol{A}+\boldsymbol{BF})$, are in the region D with centre α and radius r, where its feedback matrix $\boldsymbol{F}$ is given by $\boldsymbol{F}=\hat{\boldsymbol{F}}$.

Lemma 3.4.2

Suppose that there exists a positive definite solution $\boldsymbol{P}_1$ which satisfies (3.53), and define the following

$$\boldsymbol{Q}=\boldsymbol{Q}_w=\frac{1}{\alpha}\boldsymbol{A}^{\mathrm{T}}\boldsymbol{P}_1\boldsymbol{A}+\frac{r^2}{\alpha}\boldsymbol{Q}_1+\alpha\boldsymbol{P}_1-\frac{r^2}{\alpha}\boldsymbol{P}_1 \quad (3.54)$$

and let the matrix $\boldsymbol{Q}$ (3.54) be substituted into the Riccati equation

$$0=\boldsymbol{A}^{\mathrm{T}}\boldsymbol{P}+\boldsymbol{PA}+\boldsymbol{Q}-(\boldsymbol{PB}+\frac{1}{\alpha}\boldsymbol{A}^{\mathrm{T}}\boldsymbol{PB})\alpha(r^2\boldsymbol{R}_1+\boldsymbol{B}^{\mathrm{T}}\boldsymbol{PB})^{-1}(\boldsymbol{B}^{\mathrm{T}}\boldsymbol{P}+\frac{1}{\alpha}\boldsymbol{B}^{\mathrm{T}}\boldsymbol{PA}) \quad (3.55)$$

Then, the solution of (3.55) is positive definite and equal to the solution $\boldsymbol{P}_1$ of (3.53), where $\boldsymbol{R}_1$ is the same matrix as in (3.53).

Remark 3.4.1

It is obvious that the weighting matrix given by the positive definite solution $\boldsymbol{P}_1$ of (3.53) is positive definite, since the specified disc is within the complex left half-plane, i. e. it satisfies $\alpha\geqslant r$. Hence, this implies that in (3.54) $\boldsymbol{Q}$ is positive definite.

Theorem 3.4.1

Suppose that Lemma 3.4.1 is satisfied, and define the following matrices given by the positive definite solution $\boldsymbol{P}_1$

$$\boldsymbol{Q}=\boldsymbol{Q}_w=\frac{1}{\alpha}[\boldsymbol{A}^{\mathrm{T}}\boldsymbol{P}_1\boldsymbol{A}+r^2\boldsymbol{Q}_1+(\alpha^2-r^2)\boldsymbol{P}_1] \quad (3.56\mathrm{a})$$

$$\boldsymbol{R}=\frac{1}{\alpha}[r^2\boldsymbol{R}_1+\boldsymbol{B}^{\mathrm{T}}\boldsymbol{P}_1\boldsymbol{B}] \quad (3.56\mathrm{b})$$

$$\boldsymbol{D}=\frac{1}{\alpha}\boldsymbol{A}^{\mathrm{T}}\boldsymbol{P}_1\boldsymbol{B} \quad (3.56\mathrm{c})$$

and let these matrices be given as the weighting matrices in the Riccati equation (3.48). Then, for the system $\Sigma(\boldsymbol{A},\boldsymbol{B})$, the state feedback control law given by the solution $\boldsymbol{P}$ of (3.48), i. e. (3.47) minimizes the quadratic criterion function (3.46), and then the closed-loop system constructed by (3.47) satisfies (3.50).

Proof

From Lemma 3.4.2, we may see that the solution $\boldsymbol{P}$ obtained by the weighting matrices (3.56) is equal to that of (3.53) $\boldsymbol{P}_1$, and then the state feedback matrices $\boldsymbol{F}_1, \boldsymbol{F}$ are equal, where $\boldsymbol{F}_1$ and $\boldsymbol{F}$ are individually obtained by the solutions $\boldsymbol{P}_1$ and $\boldsymbol{P}$. This implies that from Lemma 3.4.1, all poles of the closed-loop system are elements of (3.50), and (3.47) minimizes (3.46) (Anderson and Moore 1971).

Remark 3.4.2

Since the weighting matrix $\boldsymbol{Q}$ is given by the solution of (3.53), it may be given as follows:

$$\boldsymbol{Q}=-\boldsymbol{A}^T\boldsymbol{P}_1-\boldsymbol{P}_1\boldsymbol{A}+\boldsymbol{F}_1^{\mathrm{T}}\frac{1}{\alpha}(r^2\boldsymbol{R}_1+\boldsymbol{B}^{\mathrm{T}}\boldsymbol{P}_1\boldsymbol{B})\boldsymbol{F}_1 \tag{3.57}$$

Example 2

Consider the system of Example 1. Let the specified region be a disc D with centre $-5(\alpha=5)$ and radius $r=2$ within the complex left half-plane. Then, from (3.51), the matrices $\boldsymbol{\Psi},\boldsymbol{\Gamma}$ of the system $\tilde{\Sigma}(\boldsymbol{\Psi},\boldsymbol{\Gamma})$ are given by

$$\boldsymbol{\Psi}=\begin{bmatrix}2.5 & 0.5 & 0.5\\ 0 & 3.0 & 0\\ 0 & 0 & 2.5\end{bmatrix},\quad \boldsymbol{\Gamma}=\begin{bmatrix}0.5 & 0\\ 0.5 & 0\\ 0 & 0.5\end{bmatrix}$$

We can obtain the following $\boldsymbol{P}_1$ and $\boldsymbol{F}_1$ by solving the Riccati equation (3.53) with $\boldsymbol{Q}_1=\boldsymbol{I},\boldsymbol{R}_1=\boldsymbol{I}$

$$\boldsymbol{P}_1=\begin{bmatrix}2477.839 & -2475.839 & 584.41\\ -2475.839 & 2508.074 & -584.206\\ 584.41 & -584.206 & 160.081\end{bmatrix} \tag{3.58}$$

$$F_1 = \begin{bmatrix} 0.167 & 5.026 & 0.034 \\ 17.808 & -17.808 & 8.44 \end{bmatrix} \tag{3.59}$$

Making use of the solution P_1(3.58) for the matrices Q, R, D in Theorem 3.4.1, calculation gives

$$Q = \begin{bmatrix} 10\ 407.722 & -10\ 398.525 & 2\ 454.520 \\ -103\ 98.525 & 10\ 541.556 & -2\ 453.265 \\ 2\ 454.520 & -2\ 453.265 & 1\ 168.707 \end{bmatrix}$$

$$R = \begin{bmatrix} 7.647 & 0.041 \\ 0.041 & 32.816 \end{bmatrix}, \quad D = \begin{bmatrix} 0 & 0 \\ 6.847 & 0.041 \\ 0.400 & 1\ 16.882 \end{bmatrix}$$

which enables us to obtain the solution P of (3.48) equivalent to that of (3.58) P_1. Then the poles of the closed-loop system are elements of

$$\lambda_i(A+BF): \{-4.22\pm j0.027, -4.327\} \in D \tag{3.60}$$

Therefore, by (3.60) we can see that all poles of the closed-loop system are located within the specified disc D with centre -5 and radius 2.

3.4.2 Discrete-time optimal regulator

(1) Problem statement. Consider the discrete-time system $\Sigma_D(A, B)$ of (3.2). The state feedback control law for the system $\Sigma_D(A, B)$ minimizing the quadratic criterion function

$$J = \frac{1}{2}\sum_{k=0}^{\infty}(x_k^T Q x_k + 2x_k^T D u_k + u_k^T R u_k \tag{3.61}$$

is given by

$$u_k = Fx_k = -(R+B^T PB)^{-1}(B^T PA+D^T)x_k \tag{3.62}$$

where Q, R are positive definite, D is a matrix of appropriate dimension, and P is a positive definite solution of the Riccati equation

$$P = A^T PA + Q - (A^T PB + D)(R + B^T PB)^{-1}(B^T PA + D^T) \tag{3.63}$$

Then, the closed-loop poles of the system $\Sigma_D(A, B)$, i.e. the eigenvalues of the matrix $(A+BF)$

$$\lambda_i(A+BF) \qquad i = 1, 2, \cdots, n \tag{3.64}$$

are assigned in the unit disc (Kuo 1980).

In the next section, we consider the problem of finding the weighting matrices $\boldsymbol{Q},\boldsymbol{R},\boldsymbol{D}$ of (3.61) that yield all poles of the optimal regulator located within the specified disc D with centre α and radius r in the unit circle. This problem is one of obtaining matrices such that the poles of the optimal regulator are elements of

$$\Lambda=\{\lambda_i : \lambda_i(\boldsymbol{A}+\boldsymbol{BF})\in D : \text{specified disc}, i=1,2,\cdots n\} \quad (3.65)$$

(2) Determination of weighting matrices. Suppose that the matrices $\boldsymbol{\Psi},\boldsymbol{\Gamma}$ of the system $\tilde{\Sigma}(\boldsymbol{\Psi},\boldsymbol{\Gamma})$ are the same as in section 3.4.1(2). Then we can obtain similar results to section 3.4.1(2) as follows.

Lemma 3.4.3

Let the state feedback control law for the system $\tilde{\Sigma}_{\mathrm{D}}(\boldsymbol{\Psi},\boldsymbol{\Gamma})$ be given by

$$\hat{\boldsymbol{u}}_k=\hat{\boldsymbol{F}}\hat{\boldsymbol{x}}_k=-(\boldsymbol{R}_1+\boldsymbol{\Gamma}^{\mathrm{T}}\boldsymbol{P}_1\boldsymbol{\Gamma})^{-1}\boldsymbol{\Gamma}^{\mathrm{T}}\boldsymbol{P}_1\boldsymbol{\Psi}\boldsymbol{x}_k \quad (3.66)$$

where $\boldsymbol{P}_1$ is a positive definite solution of the Riccati equation (3.53), and $\boldsymbol{R}_1,\boldsymbol{Q}_1$ are the same as given in Lemma 3.4.1. Then, all poles of the closed-loop system for the system $\Sigma_{\mathrm{D}}(\boldsymbol{A},\boldsymbol{B})$ are elements which satisfy (3.65), where the state feedback matrix is given by $\boldsymbol{F}=\hat{\boldsymbol{F}}$.

Using the above results, consider the problem of synthesizing the discrete-time optimal regulator which satisfies our objective mentioned in section 3.4.2.(1).

Lemma 3.4.4

Suppose that there exists a positive definite solution $\boldsymbol{P}_1$ satisfying (3.53), and define the following matrix, which may be obtained from this solution $\boldsymbol{P}_1$

$$\boldsymbol{Q}=\boldsymbol{Q}_w=\boldsymbol{P}_1+r^2\boldsymbol{Q}_1+\alpha(\boldsymbol{P}_1\boldsymbol{A}+\boldsymbol{A}^{\mathrm{T}}\boldsymbol{P}_1)+\alpha^2\boldsymbol{P}_1-r^2\boldsymbol{P}_1 \quad (3.67)$$

If we use (3.67) in the Riccati equation

$$\boldsymbol{P}=\boldsymbol{A}^{\mathrm{T}}\boldsymbol{PA}+\boldsymbol{Q}-(\boldsymbol{A}^{\mathrm{T}}\boldsymbol{PB}+\alpha\boldsymbol{PB})(r^2\boldsymbol{R}_1+\boldsymbol{B}^{\mathrm{T}}\boldsymbol{PB})^{-1}(\boldsymbol{B}^{\mathrm{T}}\boldsymbol{PA}+\alpha\boldsymbol{B}^{\mathrm{T}}\boldsymbol{P}) \quad (3.68)$$

then the solution $\boldsymbol{P}$ of (3.68) is equal to that of (3.53) $\boldsymbol{P}_1$, and it is a positive definite solution, where $\boldsymbol{R}_1$ is the same as given in (3.53).

From Lemma 3.4.3 and 3.4.4, we obtain the following result.

Theorem 3.4.2

Suppose that Lemma 3.4.4 is satisfied. Let the following matrices, given in terms of the solution $\boldsymbol{P}_1$ satisfying (3.53)

$$\boldsymbol{Q}=\boldsymbol{Q}_w=\boldsymbol{P}_1+r^2\boldsymbol{Q}_1+\alpha(\boldsymbol{P}_1\boldsymbol{A}+\boldsymbol{A}^{\mathrm{T}}\boldsymbol{P}_1)+(\alpha^2-r^2)\boldsymbol{P}_1 \quad (3.69\mathrm{a})$$

$$\boldsymbol{R}=r^2\boldsymbol{R}_1 \quad (3.69\mathrm{b})$$

$$\boldsymbol{D}=\boldsymbol{D}_1=\alpha\boldsymbol{P}_1\boldsymbol{B} \quad (3.69\mathrm{c})$$

be given as the weighting matrices of the Riccati equation (3.63). Then, the state feedback control law (3.62) minimizes (3.61), and all poles of the closed-loop system constructed by (3.62) are located within the disc D with centre α and radius r in the unit circle.

Remark 3.4.3

Since the matrix $\boldsymbol{Q}$ is given by the solution $\boldsymbol{P}_1$ of (3.53), it may be taken as

$$\boldsymbol{Q}=\boldsymbol{P}_1+\boldsymbol{F}_1^{\mathrm{T}}(r^2\boldsymbol{R}_1+\boldsymbol{B}^{\mathrm{T}}\boldsymbol{P}_1\boldsymbol{B})\boldsymbol{F}-\boldsymbol{A}^{\mathrm{T}}\boldsymbol{P}_1\boldsymbol{A} \quad (3.70)$$

Now, let us consider the case $\alpha=0$ in (3.51), i.e.

$$\boldsymbol{\Psi}=\boldsymbol{A}/r,\boldsymbol{\Gamma}=\boldsymbol{B}/r,\hat{\boldsymbol{F}}=\boldsymbol{F} \quad (3.71)$$

Here, by the results shown above, we can consider the problem of minimizing the criterion function in place of (3.61):

$$J=\frac{1}{2}\sum_{k=0}^{\infty}(\boldsymbol{x}_k^{\mathrm{T}}\boldsymbol{Q}\boldsymbol{x}_k+\boldsymbol{u}_k^{\mathrm{T}}\boldsymbol{R}\boldsymbol{u}_k) \quad (3.72)$$

Then the state feedback control law minimizing (3.72) may be given by

$$\boldsymbol{u}_k=\boldsymbol{F}\boldsymbol{x}_k=-(\boldsymbol{R}+\boldsymbol{B}^{\mathrm{T}}\boldsymbol{P}\boldsymbol{B})^{-1}\boldsymbol{B}^{\mathrm{T}}\boldsymbol{P}\boldsymbol{A}\boldsymbol{x}_k \quad (3.73)$$

where $\boldsymbol{Q},\boldsymbol{R}$ are positive definite, and $\boldsymbol{P}$ is a positive definite solution of the Riccati equation

$$\boldsymbol{P}=\boldsymbol{A}^{\mathrm{T}}\boldsymbol{P}\boldsymbol{A}+\boldsymbol{Q}-\boldsymbol{A}^{\mathrm{T}}\boldsymbol{P}\boldsymbol{B}(\boldsymbol{R}+\boldsymbol{B}^{\mathrm{T}}\boldsymbol{P}\boldsymbol{B})^{-1}\boldsymbol{B}^{\mathrm{T}}\boldsymbol{P}\boldsymbol{A} \quad (3.74)$$

From the above Lemma 3.4.4 and Theorem 3.4.2, the following corollary may be satisfied.

Corollary 3.4.1

Consider the Riccati equation

$$P_1 = \Psi^T P_1 \Psi + Q_1 - \Psi^T P_1 \Gamma (R_1 + \Gamma^T P_1 \Gamma)^{-1} \Gamma^T P_1 \Psi \tag{3.75}$$

where $R_1 > 0$, and Q_1 is a matrix such that $(Q_1^{1/2}, \Psi)$ is observable, and it is assumed that there is a positive definite solution satisfying (3.75). Let the following matrices given by the solution P_1 of (3.75)

$$Q = Q_w = P_1 + r^2 Q_1 - r^2 P_1 \tag{3.76a}$$

$$R = r^2 R_1 \tag{3.76b}$$

be taken as the weighting matrices of (3.74). Then the solution P is equal to that of (3.74) P_1, and the state feedback control law for the system $\Sigma(A, B)$, i. e.

$$u_k = F x_k = -(R + B^T P B)^T B^T P A x_k \tag{3.77}$$

minimizes (3.72), and then all poles of the closed-loop system constructed by (3.77) are located within the disc D defined in (3.65).

Example 3

Consider the discrete-time system

$$x_{k+1} = A x_k + B u_k \tag{3.78}$$

where the matrices A, B are the same as given in Example 1. The specified region is a disc with centre $\alpha = 0.5$ and radius $r = 0.5$ within the unit circle. Then the matrix Ψ, Γ of the system $\tilde{\Sigma}(\Psi, \Gamma)$ is given by

$$\Psi = \begin{bmatrix} -1.0 & 2.0 & 2.0 \\ 0 & 1.0 & 0 \\ 0 & 0 & -1.0 \end{bmatrix}, \quad \Gamma = \begin{bmatrix} 2.0 & 0 \\ 2.0 & 0 \\ 0 & 2.0 \end{bmatrix}$$

By solving the Riccati equation (3.53) with $Q_1 = 1$, $R_1 = 1$, we can obtain the following

$$P_1 = \begin{bmatrix} 1.86 & -0.96 & -1.81 \\ -0.96 & 2.28 & 2.01 \\ -1.81 & 2.01 & 5.04 \end{bmatrix} \tag{3.79}$$

$$F_1 = \begin{bmatrix} -0.196 & 0.646 & 0.391 \\ 0.178 & -0.177 & -0.833 \end{bmatrix} \tag{3.80}$$

Calculating the weighting matrices Q, R, D in Theorem 3.4.2 by using P_1, we have

$$Q=\begin{bmatrix} 2.11 & -1.141 & -2.74 \\ -1.141 & 1.21 & 2.39 \\ -2.74 & 2.39 & 7.10 \end{bmatrix} \qquad R=\begin{bmatrix} 0.25 & 0 \\ 0 & 0.25 \end{bmatrix},$$

$$D=\begin{bmatrix} -0.451 & 0.904 \\ -0.661 & -1.003 \\ -0.098 & -2.518 \end{bmatrix}$$

which yield, for the solution $\boldsymbol{P}$ of (3.48), a matrix equal to that of (3.53) $\boldsymbol{P}_1$. Then the poles of the closed-loop system for (3.78) are located as

$$\lambda_i(\boldsymbol{A}+\boldsymbol{BF}):\ \{0.416\pm j0.066, 0.552\} \in D$$

which shows that all closed-loop poles are within the disc D with centre 0.5 and radius 0.5.

3.5 Conclusion

In this paper, we have presented a new method of designing regulators with poles in a specified region by applying the concept conformal mapping. This method is divided into two approaches, i. e. (a) regulators based on the pole assignment problem, and (b) optimal regulators minimizing a criterion function. They are treated individually.

It has been shown that pole assignment can easily be done in the specified region by using the linear fractionally transformed system. The design approach is first to transform the original system by linear fractional mapping, then, secondly, to determine the control law of the transformed system by assigning poles so that the closed-loop system is stable. Thirdly, the inverse mapping of the control law, i. e. the control law of the original system, is derived. The algorithm is simple and practical, since an intrinsically robust control law is obtained.

New words and phrases:

conformal *a.* 保留的

conformal mapping 保角映射

so as to 以便,以致

proposition *n*. 命题，主题，定理，计划
linear fractional transformation 线性分式变换
corollary *n*. 推论，系
appropriate *a*. 恰当的，相当的，相应的

Notes:

1. A design method for regulators having poles in a specified region by using conformal mapping is proposed and the following two problems of regulator design are considered.

译：本文提出了一种用保角映射将极点设置到指定区域的调节器设计方法，并讨论了如下两个调节器设计问题。

2. The first is how to design all poles of a closed-loop system in a specified region by state feedback, and the other is how to design optimal regulators of which the poles may be located in a specified region, i.e. how to obtain the weighting matrices of a quadratic criterion function which yields all its poles in a specified disc with radius r and centre (within the left-half complex plane for continuous systems and in the unit circle for discrete systems.

译：第一个问题是怎样通过状态反馈将闭环系统的所有极点都设计到指定区域；另一个问题是怎样设计极点可在指定区域的最优调节器，即怎样得到二次标准型函数的加权矩阵，使得连续系统的所有极点均在复平面的左半部，半径为 r、中心为 α 的指定圆内；离散系统的则在单位圆内。

3. In designing regulators by state feedback, there are two design methods: (i) regulators based on the pole assignment, and (ii) optimal regulators minimizing a quadratic criterion function. It is known that both design methods give an asymptotically stable closed-loop system.

译：在用状态反馈设计调节器时，有两种设计方法：(i)基于极点配置的调节器；(ii)使二次标准型函数最小化的最优调节器。大家知道，这两种设计方法都能给出渐近稳定的闭环系统。

4. The proposed concept of pole assignment by state feedback is outlined as follows: we define a new system $\tilde{\Sigma}(\boldsymbol{\Psi},\boldsymbol{\Gamma})$ which may be construc-

ted by linear fractional transformation of the closed-loop matrix given by the system $\Sigma(\boldsymbol{A},\boldsymbol{B})$, and pole assignment is performed for the system $\tilde{\Sigma}(\boldsymbol{\Psi},\boldsymbol{\Gamma})$ by one of the well-known pole assignment methods, i.e. the state feedback law for the system $\tilde{\Sigma}(\boldsymbol{\Psi},\boldsymbol{\Gamma})$ is obtained by assigning all poles of the closed-loop system to the complex left half-plane, for continuous systems, or to the unit circle, for discrete systems.

译:本文提出的用状态反馈进行极点配置的方法概述如下:我们定义一个新系统 $\tilde{\Sigma}(\boldsymbol{\Psi},\boldsymbol{\Gamma})$,该系统可用原系统 $\Sigma(\boldsymbol{A},\boldsymbol{B})$ 的闭环矩阵的线性分式变换来构造;通过任意一种常见的极点配置方法,对新系统 $\tilde{\Sigma}(\boldsymbol{\Psi},\boldsymbol{\Gamma})$ 进行极点配置,或者说,通过将连续系统的所有闭环极点配置到复平面的左半部,或者将离散系统的所有闭环极点配置到单位圆内来得到系统 $\tilde{\Sigma}(\boldsymbol{\Psi},\boldsymbol{\Gamma})$ 的状态反馈规律。

5. The optimal regulator problem, which is the problem of obtaining the weighting matrices $\boldsymbol{Q},\boldsymbol{R},\boldsymbol{D}$ of the quadratic criterion function so that the closed-loop poles are in a specified region, may be solved in a similar way to the pole assignment problem stated above.

译:最优调节器问题(即如何得到二次标准型函数的加权矩阵 $\boldsymbol{Q},\boldsymbol{R},\boldsymbol{D}$ 以使闭环极点在指定的区域内)可以用与上述极点配置问题相类似的方法来解决。

6. In this section, we introduce the basic theory and concepts which are the background to our method of designing regulators so as to assign poles in a specified region.

译:本节引入一些基本理论和概念,它们是文中提出的将极点配置到指定区域的调节器设计方法的基础。

7. The controllability indices of the system $\tilde{\Sigma}(\boldsymbol{\Psi},\boldsymbol{\Gamma})$ ($\tilde{\Sigma}_D(\boldsymbol{\Psi},\boldsymbol{\Gamma})$) obtained by the linear fractional transformation (3.9) of the closed-loop matrix for the given system $\Sigma(\boldsymbol{A},\boldsymbol{B}$ (or $\Sigma_D(\boldsymbol{A},\boldsymbol{B})$) are invariant.

译:对给定系统 $\Sigma(\boldsymbol{A},\boldsymbol{B})$ (或 $\Sigma_D(\boldsymbol{A},\boldsymbol{B})$),通过其闭环矩阵的线性分式变换(3.9)得到的系统 $\tilde{\Sigma}(\boldsymbol{\Psi},\boldsymbol{\Gamma}$,($\tilde{\Sigma}_D(\boldsymbol{\Psi},\boldsymbol{\Gamma})$ 的能控性指标是不变的。

PART 3	CHAPTER FOUR

4 Direct Adaptive Output Tracking Control Using Multilayered Neural Networks[注1]

Abstract

Multilayered neural networks are used to construct nonlinear learning control systems for a class of unknown nonlinear systems in a canonical form. An adaptive output tracking architecture is proposed using the outputs of the two three-layered neutral networks which are trained to approximate the unknown nonlinear plant to any desired degree of accuracy by using the modified back-propagation technique[注2]. A weight-learning algorithm is presented using the gradient descent method with a dead-zone function, and the descent and convergence of the error index during weight learning are shown[注3]. The closed-loop system is proved to be stable, with the output tracking error converging to the neighborhood of the origin. The effectiveness of the proposed control scheme is illustrated through simulations.

Indexing terms

Adaptive tracking, Neural networks, Nonlinear control systems, Weight learning

4.1 Introduction

The control of systems with complex, unknown, and nonlinear dynamics has become a topic of considerable importance in the literature. In conventional nonlinear control design, so far, three main approaches have been proposed: adaptive control, Lyapunov-based control and variable structure control[注4]. And the feedback linearisation techniques of the nonlinear systems are especially appealing from the point view of the nonlinear control design. To achieve the objective of either stabilization or tracking, however, some strict assumptions were introduced regarding the structure of the uncertainties based on the completely known nonlinear models.

Advances in the area of artificial neural networks have provided the potential for new approaches to the control of systems with complex, unknown and nonlinear dynamics. The main potentials of the neural networks for control applications can be summarized as: they can be used to approximate any continuous mapping, they perform this approximation through learning, and parallel processing and fault tolerance are easily accomplished. One of the most popular of the neural network architectures for control purposes is the multilayered neural network (MNN) with the error back-propagation (BP) algorithm. It is proved that a three-layered neural network using the back-propagation algorithm can approximate a wide range of nonlinear functions to any desired degree of accuracy[注5]. To avoid modeling difficulties, a number of multilayered neural network based controllers have been proposed. If a control system is regarded as a mapping of control inputs into observation outputs, an appropriate mapping is realized by a MNN which is trained so that the desired response is obtained[注6]. For such kinds of adaptive learning control systems using the MNN, the weights of the network need to be updated using the network's output error index, and the learning control law is constructed based on the output of the MNN. Therefore, the main research topics in the field of the neural network control methods are the convergence of the weight-learning schemes and the stability of the closed-loop control systems.

4.2 Nonlinear Control Formulation

Assume that a single-input and single-output nonlinear system is given in a canonical form as

$$z^{(n)}+f(z,z^{(1)},\cdots,z^{(n-1)})=g(z,z^{(1)},\cdots,z^{(n-1)})u$$

$$y=z \tag{4.1}$$

where $z \in \boldsymbol{R}$ is a physical state, $u \in \boldsymbol{R}$ is the output. Let $\boldsymbol{x} = (x_1, x_2, \cdots, x_n)^{\mathrm{T}} = (z, z^{(1)}, \cdots, z^{(n-1)})^{\mathrm{T}}$ be the state vector, then the system of eqn. 4.1 can be represented as a state space model

$$\begin{cases} \dot{x}_1 = x_2 \\ \dot{x}_2 = x_3 \\ \vdots \\ \dot{x}_n = -f(\boldsymbol{x}) + g(\boldsymbol{x})u \\ y = x_1 \end{cases} \tag{4.2}$$

Let the desired output $y_d = y_d(t)$ be a continuously differentiable function on $[0, +\infty)$, and its first n derivatives $y_d^{(1)}, \cdots, y_d^{(n)}$ be uniformly bounded. The problem to be addressed consists of finding a control $u(t)$ that will force the output $y(t)$ to track asymptotically the desired output $y_d(t)$; that is

$$\lim_{t \to \infty}(y(t) - y_d(t)) = 0 \tag{4.3}$$

Since $g(\boldsymbol{x})$ in the system eqn. 4.2 is bounded away from zero, its inverse is well defined and the most convenient structure for a nonlinear feedback control is the one in which the input variable u is set to equal[注7]

$$u = \frac{-\sum_{k=1}^{n} c_{k-1}x_k + f(\boldsymbol{x}) + v}{g(\boldsymbol{x})} = \alpha(\boldsymbol{x}) + \beta(\boldsymbol{x})v \tag{4.4}$$

where

$$\alpha(\boldsymbol{x}) = \frac{-\sum_{k=1}^{n} c_{k-1}x_k + f(\boldsymbol{x})}{g(\boldsymbol{x})} \tag{4.5}$$

$$\beta(\boldsymbol{x}) = \frac{1}{g(\boldsymbol{x})} \tag{4.6}$$

and v is new control input to be designed for the purpose of output tracking. Since the nonlinear feedback control law (eqn. 4.4) linearises the state equation (eqn. 4. 2), it can be easily verified that the system of eqn. 4. 2 is transformed into the linear system as follows

$$\begin{cases} \dot{x}_1 = x_2 \\ \dot{x}_2 = x_3 \\ \vdots \\ \dot{x}_n = -\sum_{k=1}^{n} c_{k-1} x_k + v \\ y = x_1 \end{cases} \tag{4.7}$$

Let $e(t) = y(t) - y_d(t)$ be the output tracking error, and the new control v be chosen as

$$v = \sum_{k=1}^{n} c_k \frac{\mathrm{d}^k y_d}{\mathrm{d}t^k} = \sum_{k=1}^{n} c_k y_d^{(k)} \tag{4.8}$$

where $c_n = 1$. The output tracking error $e(t)$ satisfies the following linear error equation

$$e^{(n)} + c_{n-1} e^{(n-1)} + \cdots + c_0 e = 0 \tag{4.9}$$

If one chooses real numbers $c_0, , c_1, \cdots, c_{n-1}$ such that all the roots of the polynomial

$$N(s) = s^n + c_{n-1} s^{n-1} + \cdots + c_0 \tag{4.10}$$

have a negative real part, then the desired output $y_d(t)$ and its derivatives $y_d^{(1)}(t), \cdots, y_d^{(n-1)}(t)$ are asymptotically tracked. One can set $\boldsymbol{\Delta x} = (\Delta x_1, \Delta x_2, \cdots, \Delta x_n)^{\mathrm{T}} = (e, e^{(1)}, \cdots, e^{(n-1)})^{\mathrm{T}}$. Then, the error equation (eqn. 4. 9) can be rewritten as

$$\boldsymbol{\Delta \dot{x}} = \boldsymbol{C} \boldsymbol{\Delta x} \tag{4.11}$$

where

$$\boldsymbol{C} = \begin{bmatrix} 0 & 1 & 0 & \cdots & 0 \\ 0 & 0 & 1 & \cdots & 0 \\ & & & \ddots & \\ -c_0 & -c_1 & -c_2 & \cdots & -c_{n-1} \end{bmatrix} \tag{4.12}$$

is a Hurwitz matrix. We define the following Lyapunov function

$$\boldsymbol{V}_0(\Delta x) = \boldsymbol{\Delta x}^{\mathrm{T}} \boldsymbol{P}_0 \Delta x \tag{4.13}$$

where $\boldsymbol{P}_0$ is a symmetric, positive definite matrix solution of the following Lyapunov equation

$$\boldsymbol{P}_0\boldsymbol{C}+\boldsymbol{C}^{\mathrm{T}}\boldsymbol{P}_0=1 \tag{4.14}$$

Evaluating its time derivative along the state trajectories of the error system (eqn. 4.11), one obtains[注8]

$$\dot{\boldsymbol{V}}_0=-\boldsymbol{\Delta x}^{\mathrm{T}}\boldsymbol{\Delta x} \tag{4.15}$$

Remark

Another interesting nonlinear control strategy is the so called ‘sliding mode’ control law

$$v=\sum_{k=1}^{n} c_k\frac{\mathrm{d}^k y_d}{\mathrm{d}t_k}+c_0 y+\lambda\,\mathrm{sign}(S) \tag{4.16}$$

and

$$u=\frac{1}{g(\boldsymbol{x})}\left\{\sum_{k=2}^{n} c_{k-1}\left[\frac{\mathrm{d}^{k-1}y_d}{\mathrm{d}t^{k-1}}-x_k\right]+\left[\frac{\mathrm{d}^n y_d}{\mathrm{d}t^n}+f(\boldsymbol{x})\right]+\lambda\,\mathrm{sign}(S)\right\} \tag{4.17}$$

where $\lambda>0$, and the sliding manifold S is defined as

$$S(e)=\sum_{k=0}^{n-1} c_{k+1}\frac{\mathrm{d}^k e}{\mathrm{d}t^k}=\sum_{k=0}^{n-1} c_{k+1}e^k \tag{4.18}$$

The error equation (eqn. 4.9) is then replaced by

$$e^{(n)}+c_{n-1}e^{(n-1)}+\cdots+\lambda\,\mathrm{sign}(S)=0 \tag{4.19}$$

Furthermore, if the Lyapunov function is chosen as

$$V_1=\frac{1}{2}SS \tag{4.20}$$

then by eqns. 4.16 and 4.18 one obtains

$$\dot{V}_1=-\lambda S\mathrm{sign}(S)<0 \tag{4.21}$$

4.3 Adaptive Tracking Using Multilayered Neural Networks

Recently, several studies have independently found that a three-layered neural network using the back-propagation algorithm can approximate a wide range of nonlinear functions to any desired degree of accuracy. In this section, multilayered neural networks are used to construct a nonlinear controller for the purpose of adaptively tracking the desired output $y_d(t)$. Suppose that the continuous functions $f(\boldsymbol{x})$ and $g(\boldsymbol{x})$ are unknown. Let the nonlinear system (eqn. 4.1) be modelled by the neural network

$$\begin{cases} \dot{x}_1^* = x_2^* \\ \dot{x}_2^* = x_3^* \\ \vdots \\ \dot{x}_n^* = -\hat{f}(\boldsymbol{x},\boldsymbol{w}) + \hat{g}(\boldsymbol{x},\boldsymbol{l})\boldsymbol{u} \\ y^* = x_1^* \end{cases} \tag{4.22}$$

In the case that eqn. 4.22 is a three-layered neural network as shown on Fig. 4.1, $\hat{f}(\boldsymbol{x},\boldsymbol{w})$ $\hat{g}(\boldsymbol{x},\boldsymbol{l})$ and can be represented as

$$\hat{f}(\boldsymbol{x},\boldsymbol{w}) = \sum_{i=1}^{p} w_i H\left[\sum_{i=1}^{n} w_{ij}x_j + \hat{w}_i\right] \tag{4.23}$$

$$\hat{g}(\boldsymbol{x},\boldsymbol{l}) = \sum_{i=1}^{q} l_i H\left[\sum_{i=1}^{n} l_{ij}x_j + \hat{l}_i\right] \tag{4.24}$$

where

$$\begin{cases} \boldsymbol{w} = [(\boldsymbol{w}^2)^{\mathrm{T}}, (\boldsymbol{w}^2)^{\mathrm{T}}, (\boldsymbol{w}^3)^{\mathrm{T}}]^{\mathrm{T}} \\ \boldsymbol{w}^1 = [w_1, w_2, \cdots, w_p]^{\mathrm{T}} \\ \boldsymbol{w}^2 = [w_{11}, w_{21}, \cdots, w_{p1}, \cdots, w_{1n}, w_{2n}, \cdots, w_{pn}]^{\mathrm{T}} \\ \boldsymbol{w}^3 = [\hat{w}_1, \hat{w}_2, \cdots, \hat{w}_p]^{\mathrm{T}} \end{cases} \tag{4.25}$$

and

$$\begin{cases} \boldsymbol{l} = [(\boldsymbol{l}^1)^{\mathrm{T}}, (\boldsymbol{l}^2)^{\mathrm{T}}, (\boldsymbol{l}^3)^{\mathrm{T}}]^{\mathrm{T}} \\ \boldsymbol{l}^1 = [l_1, l_2, \cdots, l_q]^{\mathrm{T}} \\ \boldsymbol{l}^2 = [l_{11}, l_{21}, \cdots, l_{q1}, \cdots l_{1n}, l_{2n}, \cdots, l_{qn}]^{\mathrm{T}} \\ \boldsymbol{l}^3 = [\hat{l}_1, \hat{l}_2, \cdots, \hat{l}_q]^{\mathrm{T}} \end{cases} \tag{4.26}$$

are the weights of the three-layered neural networks shown on Fig 4.1. The p and q are the number of nonlinear hidden neurons of the neural networks corresponding to $\hat{f}(\boldsymbol{x},\boldsymbol{w})$ and $\hat{g}(\boldsymbol{x},\boldsymbol{l})$, respectively. The function H in eqns. 4.23 and 4.24 is the hyperbolic tangent function, which is similar to a smoothed step function.

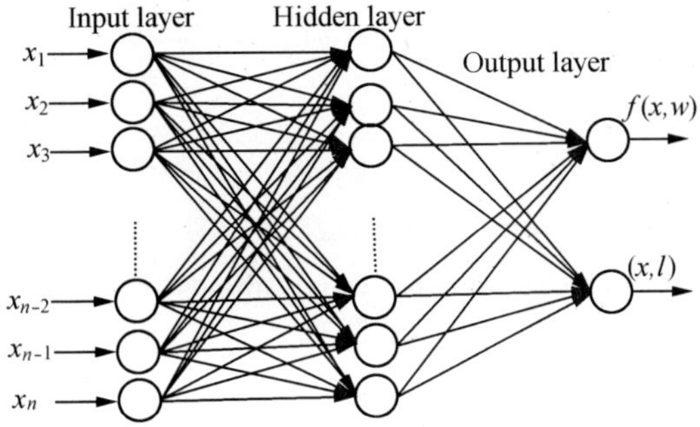

Fig. 4.1 Three-layer neural networks

$$H(x)=\frac{e^x-e^{-x}}{e^x+e^{-x}} \tag{4.27}$$

Based on the analytic results of Hecht-Nielsen about the capability of layered neural networks to approximate nonlinear functions, one can guarantee that $\hat{f}(\boldsymbol{x},\boldsymbol{w})$ and $\hat{g}(\boldsymbol{x},\boldsymbol{l})$ are complex enough (that is, they contain enough neurons) to be able to approximate $f(\boldsymbol{x})$ and $g(\boldsymbol{x})$ to the desired accuracy. The weights w and l are unknown, and $\boldsymbol{w}(t)$ and $\boldsymbol{l}(t)$ represent the estimates of $\boldsymbol{w}$ and $\boldsymbol{l}$. To better define the error index relative to the weight learning, the estimated nonlinear system using the neural networks is represented as

$$\begin{cases}\dot{x}_1^*=x_2^*\\ \dot{x}_2^*=x_3^*\\ \vdots\\ \dot{x}_n^*=-\hat{f}(x,w(t))+\hat{g}(x,l(t))u\\ y^*=x_1^*\end{cases} \tag{4.28}$$

Let the error index of the output of the neural networks be defined as

$$e^*=y^{*(n)}-y_d^{(n)}=-\hat{f}(\boldsymbol{x},\boldsymbol{w}(t))+\hat{g}(\boldsymbol{x},\boldsymbol{l}(t))u-y_d^{(n)} \tag{4.29}$$

Then, $\boldsymbol{w}(t)$ and $\boldsymbol{l}(t)$ can be adjusted using a gradient search method such that $e^*(t)$ can be reduced. Let $\boldsymbol{\pi}(t)=[\boldsymbol{w}^{\mathrm{T}}(t),\boldsymbol{l}^{\mathrm{T}}(t)]^{\mathrm{T}}$ be the estimated weight coefficient of the neural network model (eqn. 4.24).

Then the updating rule of the weights is easily given as

$$\pi(t+\delta t)=\pi(t)-\eta\frac{\partial e^{*}}{\partial\pi} \tag{4.30}$$

where

$$\frac{\partial e^{*}}{\partial \pi}=\begin{bmatrix}-\partial\hat{f}(\boldsymbol{x},\boldsymbol{w}(t))/\partial\boldsymbol{w}(t)\\ \partial\hat{g}(\boldsymbol{x},\boldsymbol{l}(t))/\partial\boldsymbol{l}(t)\end{bmatrix}$$

and η is the step-size parameter which affects the rate of convergence of the weights during learning. On the other hand, it is well known that the major disadvantage of the gradient method is that the rate of convergence of the iterative proceeding near the minimum will be very slow. To improve the rate of convergence near the minimum using a simpler method, one can employ a dead-zone algorithm for updating the weights, proposed by Chen, Khalil. Let the error $e^{*}(t)$ be applied as the input to a dead-zone function $D(e^{*})$.

$$D(e^{*})=\begin{cases}0 & \text{if} \quad |e^{*}|\leqslant d_0\\ e^{*}-d_0 & \text{if} \quad e^{*}>d_0\\ e^{*}+d_0 & \text{if} \quad e^{*}<-d_0\end{cases}$$

Then, the output of the dead-zone function is used in the following updating rule

$$\pi(t+\delta t)=\pi(t)-\eta D(e^{*})\frac{\partial e^{*}}{\partial\pi} \tag{4.31}$$

and the estimated nonlinear feedback law as shown in Fig. 4. 2 is designed as

$$\hat{u}=\hat{\alpha}(\boldsymbol{x},\boldsymbol{w}(t),\boldsymbol{l}(t))+\beta(\boldsymbol{x},\boldsymbol{l}(t))v \tag{4.32}$$

where

$$\hat{\alpha}(\boldsymbol{x},\boldsymbol{w}(t),\boldsymbol{l}(t))=\frac{-\sum_{k=1}^{n}c_{k-1}x_k+\hat{f}(\boldsymbol{x},\boldsymbol{w}(t))}{\hat{g}(\boldsymbol{x},\boldsymbol{l}(t))} \tag{4.33}$$

$$\hat{\beta}(\boldsymbol{x},\boldsymbol{l}(t))=\frac{1}{\hat{g}(\boldsymbol{x},\boldsymbol{l}(t))} \tag{4.34}$$

4.4 Results on Convergence of Weight Learning

For convenience, let $\pi_k = \pi(t+k\delta t)$. The following theorem shows that the error index e^* is descent towards the direction of the origin using the weight iterative proceeding (eqn. 4.31).

Theorem 4.4.1

If there is a weight π_k such that $|e^*(\pi_k)| > d_0$, then, there exists a number $\eta > 0$ such that

$$[e^*(\pi_k + \Delta\pi) - e^*(\pi_k)]\operatorname{sign}(e^*(\pi_k)) < 0 \tag{4.35}$$

where $\Delta\pi_k = -\eta D(e^*)\partial e^* / \partial \pi$.

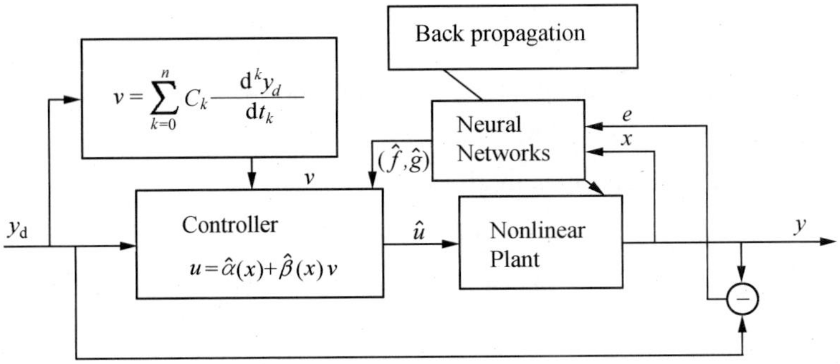

Fig. 4.2 Adaptive nonlinear tracking using MNN

The proof appears in the proof procedure of the following Theorem 4.4.2 which provides sufficient condition for the convergence in the case where a $|e^*| \leqslant d_0$ can not be reached in a finite number of learning iterations[注9].

Theorem 4.4.2

If the limit of the sequence $\{\pi_k\}$ of eqn. 4.31 is π^*, then

$$|e^*(\pi^*)| \leqslant d_0$$

Proof

The proof is by contradiction. Assume that $e^*(\pi^*) > d_0$. Then there exist numbers $\mu > 0$ and $\eta > 0$ such that

$$D(e^*)\left[\frac{\partial e^*(\pi_1)}{\partial \pi}\right]^{\mathrm{T}}\left[\frac{\partial e^*(\pi_2)}{\partial \pi}\right] \geqslant \mu > 0 \qquad (4.36)$$

for all $\boldsymbol{\pi}_1$ and $\boldsymbol{\pi}_2$ in some neighborhood of $\boldsymbol{\pi}^*$; If $\boldsymbol{\pi}_k$ is a point in this neighborhood, then so is $\boldsymbol{\pi}_{k+1}$, where

$$\boldsymbol{\pi}_{k+1} = \boldsymbol{\pi}_k - \eta D(e^*)\frac{\partial e^*}{\partial \pi} \qquad (4.37)$$

On the other hand, by the first mean-value theorem, one can imply

$$e^*(\boldsymbol{\pi}_{k+1}) - e^*(\boldsymbol{\pi}_k) = -\boldsymbol{\eta} D(e^*)\left[\frac{\partial e^*(\boldsymbol{\pi}_k)}{\partial \boldsymbol{\pi}}\right]^{\mathrm{T}}\left[\frac{\partial e^*(\boldsymbol{\pi}_k - \boldsymbol{\theta}\Delta\boldsymbol{\pi}_k)}{\partial \boldsymbol{\pi}}\right]$$

$$0 \leqslant \theta \leqslant 1 \qquad (4.38)$$

In this equation, the coefficient of $-\eta$ is at least μ from eqns. 4.36 and 4.37. Thus, in moving from $\boldsymbol{\pi}_k$ to $\boldsymbol{\pi}_{k+1}$, the value of $e^*(\pi)$ is decreased by at least $\eta\mu$, but there are an infinite number of terms of the sequence $\{\boldsymbol{\pi}_k\}$ in any neighborhood of $\boldsymbol{\pi}^*$, since

$$\lim_{k \to \infty} \boldsymbol{\pi}_k = \boldsymbol{\pi}^* \qquad (4.39)$$

Hence, by repeating the above argument for successive values of k, one finds that $e^*(\boldsymbol{\pi}^*) \to \infty$, which contradicts the fact that $\partial e^*(\boldsymbol{\pi}^*)/\partial \boldsymbol{\pi}$ exists. The original assumption that $e^*(\boldsymbol{\pi}^*) > d_0$ is therefore false. By the same proof proceeding, one can show that $e^*(\boldsymbol{\pi}^*) < -d_0$ is false, too, and the theorem is proven.

4.5 Results on Feedback Stability

To analyze the local stability of the closed-loop system the following assumptions about the nonlinear plant (eqn. 4.1) and the desired output $y_d(t)$ are required.

Assumption 4.5.1

For any $x \in \mathbf{R}^*$

$$0 < k_1 \leqslant |g(\boldsymbol{x})| \qquad (4.40)$$

Assumption 4.5.2

For any $t \in [0, +\infty)$, the desired output $y_d(t)$ and its first n derivatives $y_d^{(1)}, \cdots, Y_d^n$ are uniformly bounded; that is

$$|y_d^{(i)}(t)| \leqslant m_i \qquad i=0,1,\cdots,n \tag{4.41}$$

The following assumption is given based on the analytic results of Hecht–Nielsen about the capability of the MNNs to approximate nonlinear functions using the back-propagation technique.

Assumption 4.5.3

There exist weight coefficients $\boldsymbol{w}$ and $\boldsymbol{l}$ such that $\hat{f}(\boldsymbol{x}, \boldsymbol{w})$ and $\hat{g}(\boldsymbol{x}, \boldsymbol{l})$ approximate the continuous functions $f(\boldsymbol{x})$ and $g(\boldsymbol{x})$ with accuracy ε on Σ, a compact subset of $\mathbf{R}^n$, that is $\exists\ \boldsymbol{w}, \boldsymbol{l}$ such that

$$\max|\hat{f}(\boldsymbol{x}, \boldsymbol{w}) - f(\boldsymbol{x})| \leqslant \varepsilon \tag{4.42}$$

$$\max|\hat{g}(\boldsymbol{x}, \boldsymbol{l}) - g(\boldsymbol{x})| \leqslant \varepsilon \qquad \forall \boldsymbol{x} \in \Sigma \tag{4.43}$$

Lemma 4.5.1 ~ 4.5.3 will show that the MNNs with the hyperbolic tangent function in the hidden layer satisfy some algebraic properties on the compact set Σ.

Lemma 4.5.1

The hyperbolic tangent function $H(\boldsymbol{x})$ satisfies the following properties:

(a) $H(\boldsymbol{x})$ is strictly increasing; for each x_1, $x_2 \in \boldsymbol{R}$ such that $x_1 < x_2$ it is true that $H(x_1) < H(x_2)$;

(b) $H(\boldsymbol{x})$ is uniformly linear growth; there exists a constant $\beta_1 > 0$ such that $|H(\boldsymbol{x})| \leqslant \beta_1 |\boldsymbol{x}|$ for all $\boldsymbol{x} \in \boldsymbol{R}$.

Proof

One can easily show that the first part is a true based on the definition of the function $H(\boldsymbol{x})$. Since $H(\boldsymbol{x})$ is uniformly Lipschita, there exists a constant $\beta_1 > 0$ such that for all x_1, $x_2 \in \mathbf{R}$

$$|H(x_1) - H(x_2)| \leqslant \beta_1 (x_1 - x_2) \tag{4.44}$$

Hence

$$|H(x_1)| - |H(x_2)| \leqslant |H(x_1) - H(x_2)| \leqslant \beta_1 |x_1 - x_2| \tag{4.45}$$

Note that $H(0) = 0$. If one sets $x_2 = 0$, then the second part is implied.

Lemma 4.5.2

There exist constants $\beta_{1w},\beta_{2w}>0$ and $\beta_{1l},\beta_{2l}>0$ such that the neural network models (eqns. 4.23 and 4.24) on Σ, a compact subset of $\boldsymbol{R}^n$, satisfy the following conditions

$$|\hat{f}_1(\boldsymbol{x},\boldsymbol{w})|\leqslant\beta_{1w}\|\boldsymbol{x}\|+\beta_{2w} \tag{4.46}$$

$$|\hat{g}_1(\boldsymbol{x},\boldsymbol{l})|\leqslant\beta_{1l}\|\boldsymbol{x}\|+\beta_{2l}\qquad\forall\boldsymbol{x}\in\Sigma \tag{4.47}$$

Proof

By Lemma 4.5.1,

$$|\hat{f}_1(\boldsymbol{x},\boldsymbol{w})|\leqslant\sum_{i=1}^{p}|w_i|\left|H\left[\sum_{i=1}^{n}w_{ij}x_j+\hat{w}_i\right]\right|\leqslant$$

$$\sum_{i=1}^{p}|w_i|\left[\beta_1\left|\sum_{i=1}^{n}w_{ij}x_j^2+\hat{w}_i\right|\right]\leqslant \tag{4.48}$$

$$\sum_{i=1}^{p}|w_i|(\beta_1(\|\overline{w}_i\|\|x\|+|\hat{w}_i|)=$$

$$\beta_{1w}\|\boldsymbol{x}\|+\beta_{2w}\qquad\forall\boldsymbol{x}\in\mathbf{R}^n$$

where $\overline{\boldsymbol{w}}_i=(w_{i1},w_{i2},\cdots,w_{in})^{\mathrm{T}}$, and

$$\beta_{1w}=\sum_{i=1}^{p}|w_i||\beta_1|\|\overline{w}_i\| \tag{4.49}$$

$$\beta_{2w}=\sum_{i=1}^{p}|w_i|\beta_1)|\hat{w}_i| \tag{4.50}$$

Hence, the proof is complete.

Lemma 4.5.3

There exist constants $\hat{k}_1,\hat{k}_2>0$ such that the neural network $\hat{g}(\boldsymbol{x},\boldsymbol{l})$ on the compact set Σ of $\mathbf{R}^n$ satisfies

$$0<\hat{k}_1\leqslant|\hat{g}_1(\boldsymbol{x},\boldsymbol{l})|\leqslant\hat{k}_2\qquad\forall x\in\Sigma \tag{4.51}$$

Proof

Note that

$$\hat{g}_1(\boldsymbol{x},\boldsymbol{l})\neq0\qquad\forall\boldsymbol{x}\in\Sigma \tag{4.52}$$

This implies that $\hat{g}_1(\boldsymbol{x},\boldsymbol{l}\gg0$, or $\hat{g}_1(\boldsymbol{x},\boldsymbol{l})\ll0$ for all $\boldsymbol{x}\in\Sigma$. Since $\hat{g}_1(\boldsymbol{x},\boldsymbol{l})$ is the continuous function on the compact set Σ. Hence, there exist the nonzero maximum and minimum of $\hat{g}(\boldsymbol{x},\boldsymbol{l})$ onon Σ, which means that eqn. 4.51 is true.

The following theorem will give the local stability of the adaptive learning control system on the compact set Σ.

Theorem 4.5.3

Under the assumptions 4.5.1 ~ 4.5.3, there exists a constant $\delta = \delta(\varepsilon)$ such that the output tracking error of the nonlinear system (eqn. 4.1) on the compact set Σ using the neural network control law (eqn. 4.32) is confined to a neighborhood of the origin defined by $\|\Delta x^*\| \leqslant \delta$.

Proof

The error dynamics of the system under the neural network control law $\hat{u}$ can be obtained as

$$\Delta\dot{\boldsymbol{x}} = \boldsymbol{C}\Delta\boldsymbol{x} + b_1(\boldsymbol{x},\boldsymbol{w},\boldsymbol{l}) + b_2(\boldsymbol{x},\boldsymbol{l})v \tag{4.53}$$

where $\Delta\boldsymbol{x} = (e, e^{(1)}, \cdots, e^{n-1})^{\mathrm{T}}$, and

$$b_1(\boldsymbol{x},\boldsymbol{w},\boldsymbol{l}) = \begin{bmatrix} 0 \\ 0 \\ \vdots \\ g(\boldsymbol{x})(\hat{\alpha}(\boldsymbol{x},\boldsymbol{w},\boldsymbol{l}) - \alpha(\boldsymbol{x})) \end{bmatrix} \tag{4.54}$$

$$b_2(\boldsymbol{x},\boldsymbol{l}) = \begin{bmatrix} 0 \\ 0 \\ \vdots \\ g(\boldsymbol{x})(\hat{\beta}(\boldsymbol{x},\boldsymbol{l}) - \beta(\boldsymbol{x})) \end{bmatrix} \tag{4.55}$$

Computing the time derivative of Lyapunov function V_0 along the state trajectories of the error dynamics (eqn. 4.53),

$$\begin{aligned} \dot{V}_0 &= \langle dV_0, C\Delta\boldsymbol{x} + b_1(\boldsymbol{x},\boldsymbol{w},\boldsymbol{l}) + b_2(\boldsymbol{x},\boldsymbol{l})v \rangle = \\ &\langle dV_0, C\Delta\boldsymbol{x} \rangle + \langle dV_0, b_1(\boldsymbol{x},\boldsymbol{w},\boldsymbol{l}) \rangle + \langle dV_0, b_2(\boldsymbol{x},\boldsymbol{l})v \rangle \leq \\ &-\Delta\boldsymbol{x}^{\mathrm{T}}\Delta\boldsymbol{x} + 2\|P_0\|\,\|\Delta\boldsymbol{x}\|\,|g(\boldsymbol{x})(\hat{\alpha}(\boldsymbol{x},\boldsymbol{w},\boldsymbol{l}) - \alpha(\boldsymbol{x}))| + \\ &2\|P_0\|\,\|\Delta\boldsymbol{x}\|\,|g(\boldsymbol{x})(\hat{\beta}(\boldsymbol{x},\boldsymbol{l}) - \beta(\boldsymbol{x}))|\,|v| \end{aligned} \tag{4.56}$$

On the other hand, by assumption 4.5.3 and lemmas 4.5.2 and 4.5.3,

$$|g(\boldsymbol{x})(\hat{\alpha}(\boldsymbol{x},\boldsymbol{w},\boldsymbol{l})-\alpha(\boldsymbol{x}))|=$$

$$\left|g(\boldsymbol{x})\left[\frac{-\sum_{k=1}^{n}c_{k-1}x_k+\hat{f}(\boldsymbol{x},\boldsymbol{w})}{\hat{g}(\boldsymbol{x},\boldsymbol{l})}+\frac{\sum_{k=1}^{n}c_{k-1}x_k-f(\boldsymbol{x})}{g(\boldsymbol{x})}\right]\right|\leqslant$$

$$\frac{\sum_{k=1}^{n}|c_{k-1}x_k||\hat{g}(\boldsymbol{x},\boldsymbol{l})-g(\boldsymbol{x})|}{|\hat{g}(\boldsymbol{x},\boldsymbol{l})|}+\frac{|\hat{f}(\boldsymbol{x},\boldsymbol{w})||\hat{g}(\boldsymbol{x},\boldsymbol{l})-g(\boldsymbol{x})|}{|\hat{g}(\boldsymbol{x},\boldsymbol{l})|}+$$

$$\frac{|\hat{g}(\boldsymbol{x},\boldsymbol{l})||\hat{f}(\boldsymbol{x},\boldsymbol{w})-f(\boldsymbol{x})|}{|\hat{g}(\boldsymbol{x},\boldsymbol{l})|}\leqslant\frac{\sum_{k=1}^{n}|c_{k-1}x_k|+|\hat{f}(\boldsymbol{x},\boldsymbol{w})|+|\hat{g}(\boldsymbol{x},\boldsymbol{l})|}{|\hat{g}(\boldsymbol{x},\boldsymbol{l})|}\varepsilon\leqslant$$

$$\frac{\|c\|\ \|\boldsymbol{x}\|+\beta_{1w}\|\boldsymbol{x}\|+\beta_{2w}+\beta_{1l}\|\boldsymbol{x}\|+\beta_{21}}{\hat{k}_1}\varepsilon\leqslant$$

$$\|\Delta\dot{\boldsymbol{x}}\|\delta_1\varepsilon+\delta_2\varepsilon \tag{4.57}$$

and

$$|g(\boldsymbol{x})(\hat{\beta}(\boldsymbol{x},\boldsymbol{l})-\beta(\boldsymbol{x}))|=\left|g(\boldsymbol{x})\left[\frac{1}{\hat{g}(\boldsymbol{x},\boldsymbol{l})}-\frac{1}{g(\boldsymbol{x})}\right]\right|=$$

$$\frac{|\hat{g}(\boldsymbol{x},\boldsymbol{l})-g(\boldsymbol{x})|}{|\hat{g}(\boldsymbol{x},\boldsymbol{l})|}\leqslant\frac{\varepsilon}{\hat{k}_1} \tag{4.58}$$

where

$$\delta_1=\frac{\|c\|+\beta_{1w}+\beta_{1l}}{\hat{k}_1} \tag{4.59}$$

$$\delta_2=\delta_1\|Y_d\|+\frac{\beta_{2w}+\beta_{2l}}{\hat{k}_1} \tag{4.60}$$

and

$$c=(c_0,c_1,\cdots,c_{n-1})^{\mathrm{T}}$$

$$Y_d=(y_d,y_d^{(1)},\cdots,y_d^{(n-1)})^{\mathrm{T}}$$

therefore

$$\dot{V}_0\leqslant-\|\Delta\boldsymbol{x}\|(\|\Delta\boldsymbol{x}\|\delta_3-\delta_4) \tag{4.61}$$

where

$$\delta_3=1-2\|P_0\|\delta_1\varepsilon \tag{4.62}$$

$$\delta_4=2\|P_0\|\varepsilon\left[\delta_2+\frac{|v|}{\hat{k}}\right] \tag{4.63}$$

Thus V_0 can be assured to be nonincreasing whenever $\| \Delta x \| \geqslant \delta \equiv \delta_4 / \delta_3$, so that the output tracking error is confined to be a neighborhood of $\Delta \boldsymbol{x}=0$ defined by $\| \Delta \boldsymbol{x} \| \leqslant \delta$, which can be arbitrarily small as $\varepsilon \to 0$.

4.6 Simulation Results

In this section, the preceding nonlinear learning control scheme is illustrated using a second order SISO nonlinear plant. Consider a single-link manipulator described by

$$\pi(t)=ml^2\ddot{\theta}(t)+v\,\dot{\theta}(t)+m\,g\,l\cos\,\theta(t) \qquad (4.64)$$

where the length, mass and friction coefficient are $l=1$ m, $m=2.0$ kg and $v=1.0$ kg · m^2/s, respectively. Let the coefficients of the error equation (eqn. 4.9) be chosen as $c_1=8$ and $c_0=30$. The $\hat{f}$ network has 20 hidden neurons, the $\hat{g}$ network has five hidden neurons, the parameters of the weight updating law (eqn. 4.31) are set at $\eta=0.005$ and $d_0=0.001$, and the initial values of all weights of the $\hat{f}$ and $\hat{g}$ networks are chosen as 0.5. The simulations are performed using a fourth-order, fixed-stepsize Runge-Kutta algorithm with $\Delta t=0.01$ s. The output tracking trajectories obtained by applying four different desired outputs, step, sine, square, sawtooth, are shown in Fig. 4.3, where it is seen that the satisfactory output tracking performance has been achieved through the proposed control scheme. Meanwhile, the simulation results show that the system output response and the convergence of the learning control law are sensitive to the number of the hidden neurons and the initial values of the weights.

4.7 Concluding Remarks

We have used multilayered neural networks to construct a nonlinear learning control law for a class of unknown SISO nonlinear control systems, and it is straightforward to extend the developed MNN controller to the MIMO nonlinear control systems. The two main results given in this paper are:

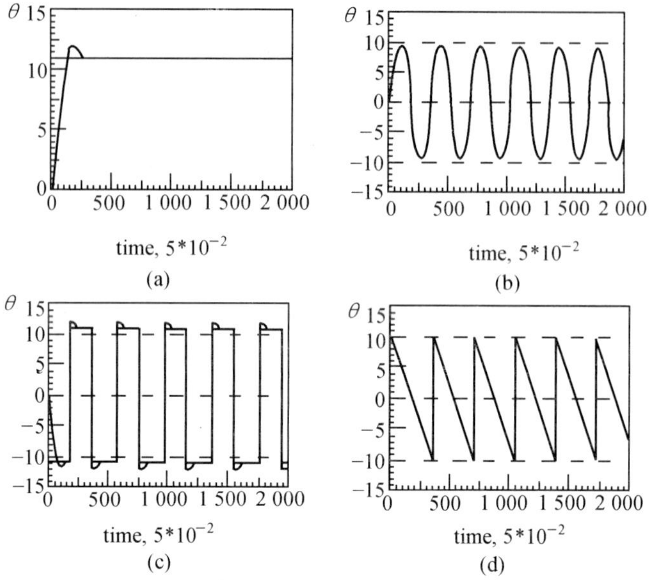

Fig. 4. 3　Simulation results of output tracking control

(a)　Tracking desired step output

(b)　Tracking desired sine output

(c)　Tracking desired square output

(d)　Tracking desired sawtooth output

(1) The three-layered neural networks were introduced to approximate the unknown nonlinear models using the modified error back propagation and a weight-learning algorithm with a dead-zone function discussed.

(2) The convergence of the weight-learning law is guaranteed through the theorems proved in Section 4.4. The stability of the closed-loop is shown as follows: If there are enough neurons in nonlinear hidden layers of the three-layer neural networks to be able to approximate $f(\boldsymbol{x})$ and $g(\boldsymbol{x})$ to the desired accuracy, the output tracking error will converge to a neighborhood of the origin, which can be arbitrarily small as well as the desired accuracy of the network learning.

New words and phrases:

1. canonical *a.* 标准的
2. gradient descent method 梯度下降法
3. dead-zone function 死区函数
4. convergence *n.* 收敛
5. multilayered neural network 多层神经网络
6. Back-propagation algorithm 反向传播算法
7. variable structure control 变结构控制
8. appealing *a.* 引人入胜的,吸引人的
9. update *v.* 更新
10. differentiable *a.* 可微的
11. trajectory *n.* 轨迹
12. sliding mode control law 滑动模控制律
13. manifold *a.* 多样的,许多的
14. hyperbolic *a.* 双曲(线)的,夸大的
15. tangent *n.* 正切
16. gradient *n.* 梯度
17. step-size *n.* 步长
18. compact set 紧集
19. uniformly bounded 一致有界

Notes

1. Direct adaptive output tracking control using multilayered neural networks.

译:利用多层神经网络的直接自适应输出跟踪控制。

2. An adaptive output tracking architecture is proposed using the outputs of the two three-layered neutral networks which are trained to approximate the unknown nonlinear plant to any desired degree of accuracy by using the modified back-propagation technique.

译:(本文)提出一种利用两个三层神经网络的输出建立的自适应输出跟踪结构。该网络借助改进的反向传播方法被训练成可以以任意期望精度逼近未知非线性对象。

3. A weight-learning algorithm is presented using the gradient descent method with a dead-zone function, and the descent and convergence of the error index during weight learning are shown.

译:利用带死区函数的梯度下降法给出了一种权值学习算法,并指出了权值学习时误差指标的减少和收敛情况。

4. In conventional nonlinear control design, so far, three main approaches have been proposed: adaptive control, Lyapunov-based control and variable structure control.

译:迄今有三种传统的非线性控制设计方法:自适应控制、基于李雅普诺夫的控制、变结构控制。

5. One of the most popular of the neural network architectures for control purposes is the multilayered neural network (MNN) with the error back-layered neural network using the back-propagation algorithm can approximate a wide range of nonlinear functions to any desired degree of accuracy.

译:用于控制的最常见的神经网络结构之一是带误差反向传播的多层神经网络,用反向传播算法可在任意期望的精度上趋近很多非线性函数。

6. If a control system is regarded as a mapping of control inputs into observation outputs, an appropriate mapping is realised by a MNN which is trained so that the desired response is obtained.

译:如果一个控制系统被看做是控制输入到观测输出的映射,则通过所训练的多层神经网络可以实现这样一个满足期望响应的恰当映射。

7. Since $g(x)$ in the system eqn. 4.2 is bounded away from zero, its inverse is well defined and the most convenient structure for a nonlinear feedback control is the one in which the input variable u is set to equal eqn. (4.4).

译:由于系统方程(4.2)中的函数 $g(x)$ 的边界设定使其不等于零,其逆存在,所以对一个非线性反馈控制来说最方便的结构是令其输入变量 u 按式(4.4)选取。

8. Evaluating its time derivative along the state trajectories of the error system (eqn. 4.11), one obtains…

译:沿着误差系统的状态轨迹估计其时间导数,可以得到… …

9. The proof appears in the proof procedure of the following Theorem 4.4.2 which provides sufficient condition for the convergence in the case where a $|e_*| \leq d_0$ can not be reached in a finite number of learning iterations.

译:定理4.4.2 提供了在$|e^*| \leq d_0$ 的情况下收敛的充分条件,但其证明过程中的证明在有限次迭代学习中不能达到。

PART 3	CHAPTER FIVE

5 Genetic Algorithms-A Robust Optimization Tool

Abstract

This paper presents an introduction to the workings of genetic algorithms and discusses their application capabilities. Applications of genetic algorithms to problem domains relevant to aerospace system optimization are discussed. Also, many references relevant to these problems are presented. Genetic algorithms are parameter search procedures based upon the mechanics of natural genetics. They combine a Darwinian survival-of-the-fittest with a random, yet structured information exchange among a population of artificial chromosomes[注1]. Robustness of genetic algorithms is reflected in their applications to a variety of problems in engineering, science, economics, finance, etc.

5.1 Introduction

Techniques that are used today for general optimization can be broadly classified under either calculus-based or direct-search methods[注2]. The calculus-based techniques work well on problems where ① the gradients (and in some cases the second derivatives) are well defined; ② the search space is unimodal; and ③ order of the search space is small. Thus, calculus-based methods lack robustness over the broad spectrum of functions that arise in engineering optimization[注3]. In the recent past, direct search techniques, which are problem-independent, have been proposed as panacea for the difficulties associated with the traditional techniques. These types, which in general require only function information, can handle non-convex and discontinuous functions. Main drawback of these schemes is that they require a trade-off between available computer time and accuracy of the optimal solution.

One of these techniques, namely, genetic algorithm (GA), has become popular among engineers from varying fields. Genetic algorithms are search procedures based on the mechanics of natural genetics. All natural species survive by adapting themselves to the environment. This natural adaptation is the underlying theme of GA. In using genetic algorithms, the usual goal is to find solutions that are closer to the globally optimal point (if not the optimal, since it is difficult to prove existence or uniqueness of the global solution for many problems of interest).

Genetic algorithms were originally developed by Holland[1] and have been analyzed and extended further by De Jong[2], Goldberg[3], and others. De Jong's empirical investigations established the robustness of GA compared to the traditional optimization techniques. Application of GA to aerospace-related engineering problems can be found in Bramlette and Cusin[4] (design and manufacture of aeronautical systems), Hajela and Lin[6] (automated structural synthesis), Krishnakumar and Goldberg[7] (aircraft control system optimization), Schmitendorf and Benson[8] (system stabilization), Montgomery et al[9] (structural control optimization), Seywald et al[10] (trajectory optimization), and Whitley et al[11], KrishnaKumar[12] (neural networks).

The main emphasis of this paper is to introduce genetic algorithm as a viable alternative search strategy for aerospace optimization problems. The rest of the paper begins with an introduction into the workings of a genetic algorithm and three of its variations. Also, a review of aerospace-related genetic algorithm optimization literature is presented.

5.2 Genetic Algorithms

Genetic algorithms are different from normal search methods encountered in engineering optimization in the following ways:

(1) GAs work with a coding of the parameter set, not the parameters themselves.

(2) GAs search from a population of points, not a single point.

(3) GAs use probabilistic transition rules, not deterministic transition rules.

Genetic algorithms require the natural parameter set of the optimization problem to be coded as a finite-length string. As an example, a parameter optimization problem with two parameters is chosen. For this optimization problem, the two parameters are discretized by mapping from a smallest possible parametric set $\boldsymbol{K}_{min}$ to a largest possible parametric set $\boldsymbol{K}_{max}$. This mapping uses a 10-bit binary unsigned integer for both $\boldsymbol{K}_1$, and $\boldsymbol{K}_2$. In this coding a string code 0000000000 maps to $\boldsymbol{K}_{min}$ and a 1111111111 maps to $\boldsymbol{K}_{max}$ with a linear mapping in between. Next, the two 10-bit sets are chained together to form a 20-bit string representing a particular controller design (see Fig. 5.1). A single 20-bit string represents one of the $2^{20} = 1,048,576$ alternative solutions.

	CODING		POPULATION(SIZE=5)	
	$\boldsymbol{K}_{min}$	$\boldsymbol{K}_{max}$	$\boldsymbol{K}_1$	$\boldsymbol{K}_2$
$\boldsymbol{K}_1$	0	25	1100110011	0011001100
			1010101010	1010111101
$\boldsymbol{K}_2$	−25	25	1110001110	0001101101
			1100111111	0000011011
	0000000000	1111111111	1011100011	0001101010

Fig. 5.1 The concept of coding and population

Genetic algorithms work iteration by iteration, generating and testing a population of strings. This population-by-population approach is similar to a natural population of biological organisms where each generation successively evolves into the next generation by being born and raised until it is ready to reproduce. This approach is very different from classical search methods, where movement is from one point in the search space to another point based on some transition rule. Another important difference between GA and the classical approaches is in the selection of the transition rules. In classical methods of optimization the transition rule is deterministic. In contrast, GA uses probabilistic operators to guide their search.

GA operators

A simple genetic algorithm is composed of three operators: ① selection, ② crossover, and ③ mutation. Selection is a process where an old string is carried through into a new population depending on the performance index (i. e., fitness) values. Due to this move strings with better fitness values get larger numbers of copies in the next generation. Selecting good strings for this operation can be implemented in many different ways. A simple way is to let strings with higher fitness values "F" get a proportionally higher probability of selection based on $P(\text{select}) = F_i / \sum F_i$; where i = string index (see Fig. 5.2).

This strategy, in which good strings get more copies in the next generation, emphasizes the survival-of-the-fittest concept of genetic algorithms. There are many other equivalent selection techniques. References 3 and 14 present comparison studies of selection schemes currently in use. In conjunction with the above mentioned selection procedures, the good strings can either be allowed to change (pure selection) or retained in to the next evolution (elite selection).

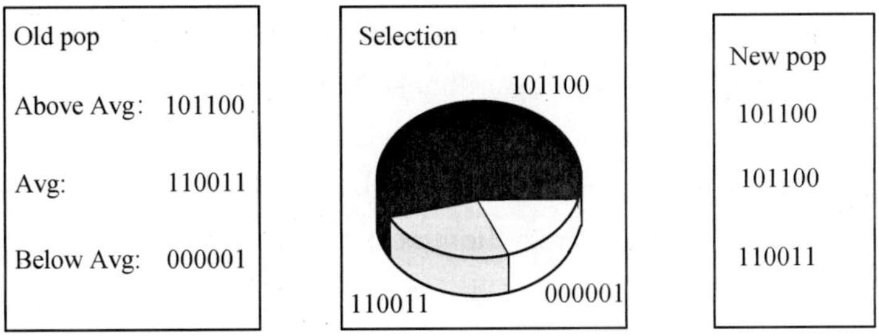

Fin. 5.2 Roulette Wheel selection

A simple crossover follows selection in three steps. First, the newly selected strings are paired together at random. Second, an integer position "n" along every pair of strings is selected uniformly at random. Finally, based on a probability of crossover, the paired strings undergo crossing over at the integer position "n" along the string. This results in new pairs of strings that are created by swapping all the characters between characters 1 and "n" inclusively. Fig. 5.3 presents illustrations of 1 point and 2 point crossovers. Although the crossover operation is a randomized event, when combined with selection it becomes an effective means of exchanging information and combining portions of good quality solutions. Selection and crossover give GA most of their search power.

Crossover(Random Information Exchange)

1 point crossover:			2 point crossover:		
0000 000000	→	0000 111111	000 000 000	→	000 111 000
1111 111111		1111 000000	111 111 111		111 000 111

Mutation(Improves the Global Search)

000 0 000000 → 000 1 000000

Fig. 5.3 Crossover and Mutation

The third operator, mutation, is simply an occasional random alteration of a string position (based on probability of mutation). In a binary code, this involves changing a 1 to a 0 and vice versa. The mutation operator helps in avoiding the possibility of mistaking a local minimum for a global minimum. When mutation is used sparingly (about one mutation per thousand bit transfers) with selection and crossover, it improves the global nature of the genetic algorithm search[注4].

A GA's performance is usually measured in terms of on-line performance and off-line performance. On-line performance is the average performance measure (average fitness value) of all the tested strings over the course of the search. Off-line performance is the average of all the generation-based best performance strings. A good choice of GA parameters is population size = 100; probability of crossover = 0.7; and probability of mutation = 0.001.

Holland's schema theorem[1,3] places the theory of genetic algorithms on rigorous footing. The processing power of GA is understood in more rigorous terms by examining the growth rates of the various schemata of similarity templates contained in a population. It is very important to understand the concepts of schemata to better understand the GA. Some of the ideas of schemata are summarized below:

(1) A schema matches a string if at every location in the schema a "1" matches a "1", a "0" matches a "0", or a" * " matches either.

Ex: Consider a string A = 101; The following schemata convey the same information: A1 = 10 *; A2 = * 01; A3 = * * *; and A4 = 1 * *.

(2) For alphabets of cardinal "k", there are $(k+1)^l$ schemata (l = length of the string).

(3) A population of size N contains somewhere between 2^l and $N * 2^l$ schemata.

(4) Order of a schema, $\boldsymbol{O}(H)$, is defined as the number of 0's and 1's in a schema. The defining length, $\delta(H)$, of a schema is the distance between the first and the last specific digit.

Ex: Consider a schema A1 = 1 * * 1; $\boldsymbol{O}(A1) = 2$ and $\boldsymbol{\delta}(A1) = 3$.

(5) Holland's[1,3] schema theorem: Low order, short defining length schema that are also fit (known as building blocks) increase exponentially in the population. His estimate of the number of schemata processed in a population of n strings is $\boldsymbol{O}(n^3)$. This processing power gives the GA the computational advantage over the other traditional techniques.

Genetic algorithm implementation considerations

Fig. 5.4 presents a computational flow chart of a simple genetic algorithm. One of the benefits of genetic algorithm is the problem-independent characteristic of the search scheme. This enables a black-box treatment of the GA code. That is, the GA supplies the parameters to the optimization problem at hand and in return the specific problem-dependent software provides the fitness function. This fitness function is then utilized by the GA to evolve to the next generation.

Convergence of the GA search can be ascertained by either examining the variance of the population fitness (known as phenotype convergence) or by examining bit-wise convergence (known as genotype convergence). Zero population fitness variance implies absolute convergence. Since this is not always possible to achieve, the search can be terminated when the population variance is below a threshold value. In problems where computational time is a factor, the best string can be retained without any modifications (elite selection). This way, if the user decides to terminate the search, a best-so-far solution to the optimization problem is always available.

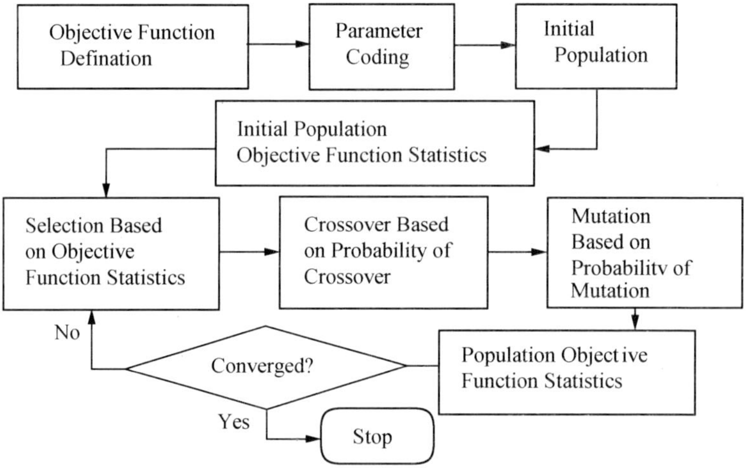

Fig. 5.4 Computational flow chart

The GA coding addressed here is binary. Recently, real-valued encoding has found good success in several applications. Here the operators act on both the integer part and the decimal part independently.

An example

An example GA optimization problem with two control system feedback gains as the parameters for the search is chosen (see Reference 7 for more details). To solve this problem a simple GA was chosen with the following operators: (a) roulette wheel selection (b) simple crossover, and (c) mutation. Each gain in the gain set $[\boldsymbol{K}_1, \boldsymbol{K}_2]$ was represented by a ten-bit string. The strings were concatenated to produce a 20-bit string, each string representing one feedback design. For the mapping chosen for this example, 0000000000 represents a predetermined minimum value for the gains and 1111111111 represents a predetermined maximum value for the gains. Note here that the mapping of the gain set on to the 10-bit string can be different for different gains depending on the desired range and resolution of the gain values.

Fig. 5.5 displays the search evolution of the GA and compares it to a Powell's conjugate direction technique. Also, the search space is illus-

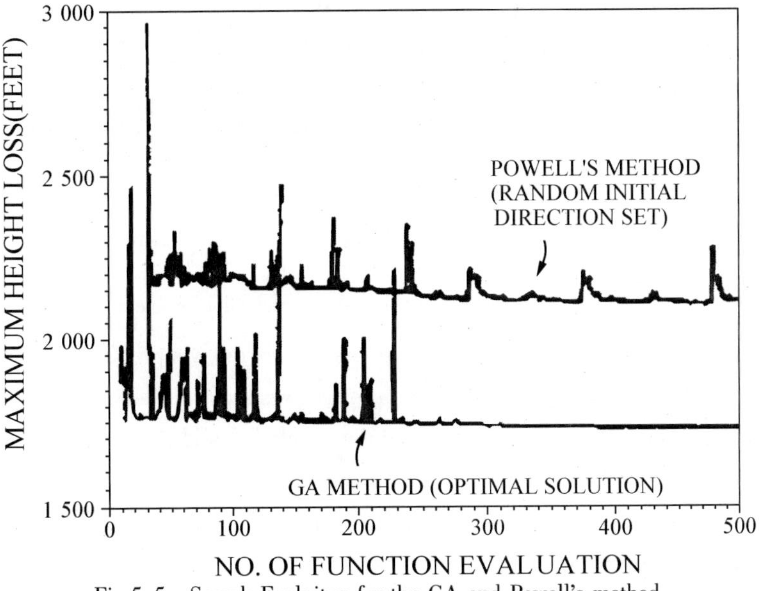

Fig 5.5 Search Evoluiton for the GA and Powell's method

trated in Fig. 5.6. The following observations are made: ① the search space is multi-modal; ② GA's search begins as a random distribution of search points; ③ due to selection pressure, the search reaches the global optimum; and ④ due to multiple optima, the Powell's method gets trapped in a local optimum.

Variations in a Simple Genetic Algorithm

There are several variations of the simple three-operator GA that are currently being used by GA researchers. Three of these techniques which the author is familiar with (and has found good success with) are reviewed next.

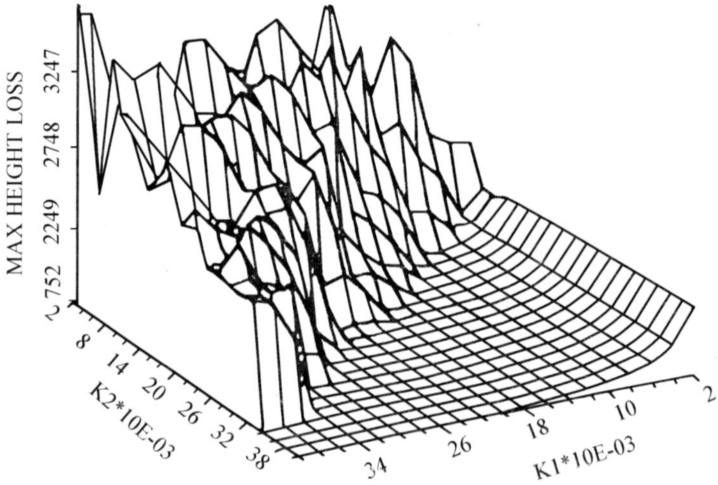

Fig. 5.6 Search surface of the optimization problem

Micro-genetic algorithms μGA[17]: Just as in the simple GA (SGA), the woks with binary coded population. The major difference between SGA and the μGA comes in the population choice and the way new information is brought in to the evolution process. In the μGA, the population size is fixed at less than ten. It is a known fact that GA generally does poor with very small population due to insufficient information processing and early convergence to non-optimal results. The key to success with small population is in bringing in new strings in regular intervals into the population. Fig. 5.7 presents a μGA implementation and details can be found in reference 17.

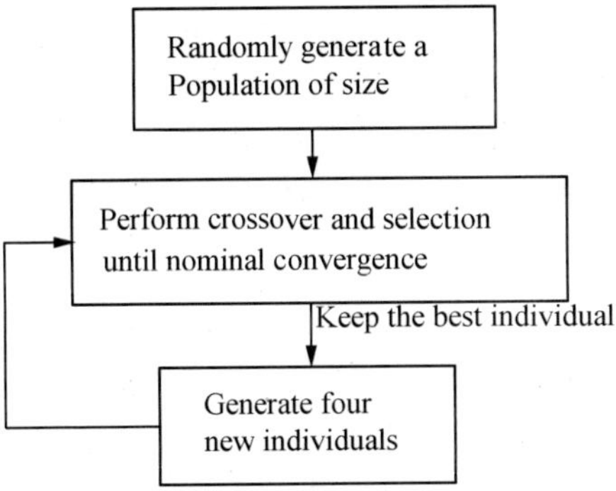

Fig. 5.7 Micro-GA implementation

The assumption that maximum real-time schema (information) processing yields maximum performance is supported by empirical results and this maximum schema processing is achieved in the μGA implementation by constant infusion of new schema at regular intervals. SGA is known to reach premature convergence forcing the search process to rely entirely on the mutation operator for new information. In the case of μGA the "start and restart" procedure helps in avoiding the premature convergence and the μGA is always looking for better strings. In implementing μGA, our interest is purely to find the optimum as quickly as possible and not in the average behavior of the population. In other words, our performance measure for μGA should be based on the best-so-far string rather than on any average performance.

Fuzzy genetic algorithms[18]: In a simple GA, the fitness value of a string is interpreted as the probability of that particular string receiving a certain fraction of the total population for crossover and mutation[注5]. To achieve faster convergence, one could interpret fitness values in the following sense: if one has prior knowledge of the maximum, then it can be inferred from the fitness values of any pair of chromosomes how close one of them is to the maximum than the other. Since there is no a priori knowledge of the actual maximum, the obvious choice is to use the best estimate of maximum at the current generation. Thus, at the kth generation, if $f(x_1), \cdots, f(x_N)$ are the fitness values, then a subjective characteristic function may be

$$\Omega[f(x_i)] = 1/\{1+[f(x^*)-f(x_i)]^2\}$$

where $f(x^*) = \max[f(x_1), \cdots, f(x_N)]$. The characteristic function after normalizing is used to apply selection pressure as in a simple GA. This technique ensures quick convergence but does not ensure optimality of the converged solution. In order to increase the information processed, higher mutation levels and/or higher population sizes should be used.

Genetic algorithms vs. other AI techniques:

It is relevant at this point to compare GA to other so called artificial intelligence (AI) techniques that are currently in use for the design and optimization of control systems. These AI techniques include, but not limited to, artificial neural networks (ANN), knowledge based systems (KBS), fuzzy-logic systems (FLS), and simulated annealing (SA). KBS and FLS applications in control rely on a priori knowledge of the problem to be solved and therefore cannot be classified under techniques that learn from past performance. On the other hand, ANNs learn through repeated exposure to desired input-output relationships.

The last technique listed above, namely, simulated annealing is a combinatorial optimization technique that has attracted attention recently for optimizing problems of large scale. SA draws its strength from exploiting the statistical optimization. In a recent review[21], the performance of GA, SA, and ANN were compared for the traveling salesman problem and it was shown that the GA delivered some of the best performance in the context of this review. The connections between GA and SA have also been explored by Goldberg[22]. The distinct difference between GA and

SA lies in the fact that the GA focuses on the importance of recombination and other operators found in living systems. This gives GA the potential to expand once the operators found in nature are better understood.

5.3 GA in Aerospace System Optimization

Genetic algorithms can be utilized to solve many problems which are difficult to solve using traditional techniques. In this section, several potential GA application areas are discussed. Previous researches related to these suggestions are cited.

Control system optimization: In referance 7, two feedback control systems were designed using GAs. The performances of these feedback control systems were compared with traditional approaches. Currently many complex and highly non-linear control systems are fine tuned using heuristic approaches. These practices can be augmented using GAs.

Robust feedback control system design: Reference 8 presents a simultaneous stabilization technique using the multiple model approach and a GA. The population approach to optimization provides another way by which feedback systems can be designed for uncertain systems. If the system parameters are known to have certain probability distribution, then in every generation parameters randomly drawn based on the known probability distribution can be used to simulate the system[注6]. This way the converged solution will contain a controller which will provide a robust performance under certain conditions.

Non-linear programming: Aircraft and spacecraft trajectory optimizations are usually conducted using non-linear programming techniques. Two of the popular techniques are multiple shooting (indirect optimization) and collocation techniques (direct optimization). In multiple shooting technique the two-point boundary value problem which results from the solution of the optimal control problem is solved. The solution requires using a second algorithm to determine the initial value of the states. The genetic algorithm can be utilized successfully in determining the initial conditions. Since the GA can evaluate the goodness of the search points based on partial information, the optimization procedure can be conducted even without "shooting" to the final boundary. References 10 and 19 present two applications of GA to trajectory optimization problems.

In a typical collocation technique the control variables are represented as nth order polynomials with time-varying coefficients. The coefficients are optimized using a parameter optimization technique. Here also GA can be easily used as a parameter optimization technique for solving the problem.

Adaptive control: Simple Genetic Algorithms (SGA) discussed earlier, have been shown to be useful tools for many function optimization problems. One present drawback of SGA is the time penalty involved in evaluating the fitness functions (performance indices) for large populations, generation after generation. In reference 17 it was shown that μGA implementation reaches the near-optimal region much earlier than the SGA implementation. Also the superior performance of the μGA in the presence of multimodality and their merits in solving non-stationary function optimization problems were demonstrated. References 17 and 20 present non-stationary function optimization using the μGA approach. In reference 17 a wind-shear controller was adaptively fine-tuned using the μGA and in Reference 20 the μGA technique was used to design an adaptive cart-pole controller.

Fuzzy logic controller (FLC) optimization: In reference 5 the concept of fine-tuning human-defined fuzzy logic sets for control was demonstrated using genetic algorithms. Using two aerospace examples, it was shown that the fuzzy logic controller sets can be designed to any desired performance. Since FLCs have been shown to work well under noisy conditions the power of fine-tuning the FLC sets for optimal performance will be useful. Reference 20 also presents the application of GA in FLC design.

Composite structure design: In reference 13 the GA was integrated with laminate design by: (a) mapping the design variables to binary forms or bit strings, and (b) formulating a fitness function. The research to date has used the fiber or lamina orientations and stacking sequences as the design variables while the fitness function was chosen to maximize laminate strength and or stiffness to weight ratios for multiple load cases. The fitness functions used to date are presented in detail in reference 13. Two of these are: (a) maximize laminate strength for a fixed number of plies; and (b) maximize the laminate strength-to-weight or stiffness-to-weight ratios.

Neural network design: References 25 and 11 present overviews and applications of combinations of genetic algorithms and neural networks. GAs can be used to optimize the weight space and the connection space of neural networks. Also, several sub networks can be combined to form optimized neural networks[12].

Multiple-objective optimization: In problems where multiple-objective optimization is required, the GA approach can be modified to provide a technique to solve such problems. Such approaches were suggested by Schaffer[23], KrishnaKumar[14], and Hajela and Lin[6].

5.4 Summary and Discussion

This paper was primarily written to motivate and educate engineers who are not currently exposed to the potentials of genetic algorithms as an optimization technique. There are several papers written and published regularly in this area. A good source for finding more information is the book by Goldberg[3] and recent genetic algorithm conference proceedings[26~29]. Currently many areas of aerospace-related optimization problems can be solved using the simple genetic algorithm. Many complex and non-linear systems are fine tuned using heuristic approaches. These practices can be augmented with genetic algorithms, which are relatively insensitive to the complexities of the optimization problem and provide a robust search method. Although more work is necessary, genetic algorithms should provide a useful weapon in the arsenal of system optimization.

There are several improvements that would make the simple genetic algorithm more useful. Some of these include alternate selection schemes, alternate coding schemes, and advanced operators such as inversion, dominance. Goldberg's book and the four GA conference proceedings should provide excellent reference materials for these topics.

References

1 Holland J. Adaptive in Natural and Artificial Systems. The Univ. of Michigan Press, Michigan, 1975

2 De Jong K A. An Analysis of the Behavior of Genetic Adaptive Systems. Dissertation Abstracts International, 1975,41(9): 3503b

3 Goldberg D E. Genetic Algorithm in Search, Optimization, and Machine Learing. Addision Weslely Publishing Company, 1989

4 Bramlette M F, Cusin R. A Comarative Evaluation of Esearch Methods Applied to Parametric Design. Proc. of the Third Int. Conf. on Genetic Algorithms, 1989. 213 ~ 218

5 Freeman L M, Krishnakumar K et al. Tuning Fuzzy Logic Controllers Using Genetic Algorithms-Aerospace Applications. Proc of the AAAIC '90 Conf, Dayton, Ohio, Oct. 1990. 351 ~ 358

6 Hajela P, Lin C Y. Genetic Sarch Strategies in Multicriterion Optimal Design. AIAA–91–1040–CP

7 KrishnaKumar K, Goldberg D E. Genetic Algorithms in Control System Optimization, J. Of Guidance, Control and Dynamics, May-July,

1992. 735 ~740
8 Schmitendorf W, And Benson R. Simultaneous Stabilization Using Genetic Algorithms. AIAA Guidance, Navigation, and Control Conference, Aug, New Orleans, Louisiana, 1991
9 Montaomery L, KrishnaKumar K. Structural Control Using Connectionist Learning Procedures. AIAA Guidance, Navigation, and Control Conference, Aug. Hilton Head, SC, 1992
10 Seywald H, Kumar R R. A Genetic Algorithm Approach to Soving Trajectory Optimization Problems with Linearly Appearing Controls. AIAA Guidance, Navigation, and Control Conference, Aug. Hilton Head, SC, 1992
11 Whitley D, Starkweather T. Genetic Algorithms and Neural Networks: Optimizing Connections and Connectivity. Parallel Computing, 1990, 14:347 ~361
12 Krishnakumar K. Immunized Neurocontrol: Concepts and Initial Results, Int. Workshop on Combinations of Genetic Algorithm and Neural Networks. IEEE Computer Society Press, COGANN'92, Baltimore, MD, June, 1992
13 Callahan K J, Weeks G E. Optimum Design of Composite Laminates Using Genetic Algorithms. Composite Engineering, 1992, 2(3): 149 ~160
14 Goldberg D E, Deb K. A Comparative Analysis of Selection Schemes Used in Genetic Algorithms (TCGA Report No. 90007). Univ. of Alabama, The Clearinghouse for Genetic Algorithms, 1990
15 Press W et al. Numerical Recipes. Cambridge Univ. Press, New York, 1989. 294 ~301
16 Goldberg D E, Deb K. Messy Genetic Algorithms: Motivation, Analysis, and First Results. Complex Systems, 1989, 3: 493 ~530
17 Krishnakumar, K, Micro-Genetic Algorithms for Stationary and Nonstationary Function Optimization. Proc. of the SPIE's Intelligent Con-

trol and Adaptive Systems Conference, 1989. 289 ~ 296

18 Krishnakumar K et al. Variations in a Simple Genetic Algorithm based on Maximizing Entropy and Maximizing Information. Proc. of the Second Workshop on Nueral Network, Auburn, Alabama, 1991. 687 ~ 693

19 Neidhoefer J, Krishnakumar K. Soving Two-point Boundary Value Problems Using a Genetic Algorithm aided Shooting Technique. Document in preparation, Dept. of Aerospace Engineering, The U. of Alabama, Tuscaloosa, AL

20 Karr C L. Design of an Adaptive Fuzzy Logic Controller Using a Genetic Algorithm. Proc. of the 4th Int. Conf. on Genetic Algorithms, San Digo, California, 1991

21 Petersen C. Parallel Distributed Approaches to Combinatorial Optimization. Neural Computation, 1990,2(3): 261 ~ 269

22 Goldberg D E. A Note on Boltzmann Tournament Selection for Genetic Algorithms and Population-orienred Simulated Annealing. TCGA Report No. 90003, U. of Alabama. The Clearinghouse for Genetic Algorithms, 1990

23 Schaffer J D. Multiple Objective Optimization with Vector Evaluated Genetic Algorithm. Proc. of the 1st Int. Conf. on Genetic Algorithms, 1985. 93 ~ 100

24 KrishnaKumar K. Genetic Algorithms: An Introduction and an Overview of their Capabilities. AIAA Guidance, Navigation, and Control Conference, Aug. Hilton Head, SC,1992

25 Schaffer J D et al. Combinations of Genetic Algorithms and Neural Networks: A Survey of the State of the Art, 1992. Proc. of the Int. Workshop on Conbinations of Genetic Algorithms and Neural Networks, IEEE Computer Society Press, COGANN ′92, Baltimore, MD, June, 1992

26 Proc. of the First Int. Conf. on GA, Morgan Kauffman, San Mateo,

1985
27 Proc. of the Second Int. Conf. on GA, Morgan Kauffman, San Mateo, 1987
28 Proc. of the Third Int. Conf. on GA, Morgan Kauffman, San Mateo, 1989
29 Proc. of the Fourth Int. Conf. on GA, Morgan Kauffman, San Mateo, 1991

New words and phrases:

1. Genetic Algorithm 遗传算法
2. working *n*. 作用，操作，处理
3. survival of the fittest 适者生存
4. chromosome *n*. 染色体
5. broadly *adv*. 概括地,大致地,广阔地
6. calculus *n*. 计算法,微积分学
7. gradient *n*. 梯度
8. unimodal *a*. (曲线)单峰的
9. spectrum *n*. 范围,系统
10. probabilistic *a*. 概率的
11. panacea *n*. 万灵药
12. convex *n*. 凸(面)的;*n*. 凸状,凸面
13. trade-off *n*. 折衷(办法,方案),权衡
14. cardinal *a*. 主(要)的,基本(的);*n*. 基数
15. species *n*. 种类
16. underlying *a*. 基础的,根本的,潜在的
17. effect *vt*. 实现,达到
18. empirical *a*. 经验(上)的
19. viable *a*. 可行的
20. discretize *v*. 离散化
21. string *n*. (一)串[行,队]
22. crossover *n*. 交叉
23. mutation *n*. 变异
24. population *n*. 群体
25. fitness value 适应值
26. elite *n*. 精华
27. pair *v*. 配对
28. uniformly *ad*. 均匀地,一致地
29. local *a*. 局部的
30. schema *n*. 模式,大纲,图解、概要. pl. schemata
31. laminate *a*. 层状的;*n*. 分层,层压
32. lamina *n*. 薄层[片],层
33. composite *n*. & *a*. 复合(的),合成(的)
34. (down) to date 至今,迄今
35. stiffness *n*. 刚性[度],硬度,稳定性

36. simulated annealing 模拟退火

37. concatenate *vt*. 使连接[连续，衔接]起来；*a*. 连在一起的

38. premature *a*. 早熟的，过早的；*n*. 过早发生的事物

39. phenotype *n*. [生]表型，表现型，遗传实现型

40. genotype *n*. [生]遗传型

41. threshold *n*. 阈(值)，门限，范围

42. arsenal *n*. 兵工厂，武器库

43. infusion *n*. 渗入，引入，浸入

44. collocation *n*. 排列，布置，配置，搭配

45. sparing *a*. 不足的，少量的，缺乏的

46. operator *n*. 算子，算符，操纵基因

47. in conjunction with 和一起[共同，会合]

48. swap *v*. ；*n*. 交换，交流

49. vice versa *ad*. [拉丁语]反之亦然

50. roulette *n*. 轮盘赌

Notes:

1. Genetic algorithms are parameter search procedures based upon the mechanics of natural genetics. They combine a Darwinian survival-of-the-fittest with a random, yet structured information exchange among a population of artificial chromosomes.

译：遗传算法是一种基于自然遗传机理的参数搜索方法。它们将达尔文的适者生存原理与人工染色体的群体中的随机但结构化的信息交换相结合。

2. Techniques that are used today for general optimization can be broadly classified under either calculus-based or direct-search methods.

译：目前一般的优化方法可大致分为两类：基于积分的方法和直接搜索方法。

3. The calculus-based techniques work well on problems where ① the gradients (and in some cases the second derivatives) are well defined; ② the search space is unimodal; and ③ order of the search space is small. Thus, calculus-based methods lack robustness over the broad spectrum of functions that arise in engineering optimization.

译：基于积分的方法适于下列问题：① 梯度（有时包括二次梯度）有明确定义；② 搜索空间是单峰的；③ 搜索空间的阶次较小。因此基于积分的方法对处理工程优化中遇到的很多函数缺少鲁棒性。

4. When mutation is used sparingly (about one mutation per thousand bit transfers); with selection and crossover, it improves the global nature of the genetic algorithm search.

译：偶尔使用变异（大约每一千个位变换时有一次变异）时，结合选择和交叉，可改进遗传算法搜索的全局特性。

5. In a simple GA, the fitness value of a string is interpreted as the probability of that particular string receiving a certain fraction of the total population for crossover and mutation.

译：在简单遗传算法中，一个字符串的适应值可被解释为该字符串接受整个群体的一部分用于交叉变异的概率。

6. If the system parameters are known to have certain probability distribution, then in every generation parameters randomly drawn based on the known probability distribution can be used to simulate the system.

译：如果已知系统参数服从某种概率分布，则在每一代运算中，基于该已知概率分布随机得到的参数可用于仿真该系统。